WINSTON

AND THE

WINDSORS

WINSTON
AND THE
WINDSORS

How Churchill Shaped
a Royal Dynasty

ANDREW MORTON

HANOVER
SQUARE
PRESS

**HANOVER
SQUARE
PRESS™**

Recycling programs
for this product may
not exist in your area.

ISBN-13: 978-1-335-25099-5

Winston and the Windsors

Hanover Square Press
22 Adelaide St. West, 41st Floor
Toronto, Ontario M5H 4E3, Canada
HanoverSqPress.com

HarperCollins Publishers
Macken House, 39/40 Mayor Street Upper,
Dublin 1, D01 C9W8, Ireland
www.HarperCollins.com

Printed in U.S.A.

To the memory of my grandfather, Harry Sykes,
a sapper during the First World War.

CONTENTS

A Day to Remember

IT WAS A moment to savour on a day that no one who was there could ever forget. At three o'clock in the afternoon of 8 May 1945, Britain's indefatigable war leader, Winston Churchill, made the formal announcement that hostilities in Europe were now ended, and that Germany had agreed to an unconditional surrender, due at one minute past midnight.

By chance, the announcement took place on a Tuesday, the day King George VI and his Prime Minister held their regular lunchtime meeting at Buckingham Palace. It wasn't supposed to happen then – 7 May was supposed to be the date. The King had already recorded his victory address, but Russian leader Joseph Stalin and new American President Harry S. Truman wanted to delay the announcement by a day. It was an example, if any more were needed, that Britain was now firmly a junior partner in the war to defeat Nazi Germany.

Still, the hold-up meant that both men could congratulate one another face to face on the end of the European war, acknowledging this moment as one of thanksgiving and subdued elation. After all, there was still the war in Asia against Japan to resolve.

For the many thousands who stood outside the gates of Buckingham Palace and along the Mall, it was a time for exuberant celebration. No longer would Londoners have to sleep in rudimentary bomb shelters or fear the sudden death that rained from the sky in the form of terrifying self-propelled missiles colloquially known as doodlebugs. As the day of sunshine and blue skies wore on, the clamour for the royal family to appear on the famous balcony at Buckingham Palace grew louder. 'We want the King!' the red-white-and-blue crowd cried, and, 'We want Winnie!' In the popular imagination these two men represented a united nation under siege, fighting together for the same cause: victory in Europe. While Churchill's afternoon radio broadcast was short and factual, it marked the starting pistol for days of celebration – even though there were still queues for bread that reminded revellers of the long road ahead.

Nonetheless, the cheering in Parliament Square and Trafalgar Square could be heard in the Cabinet Room where Winston gave his succinct broadcast. He ended with the words 'Advance, Britannia! Long live the cause of freedom!' With his voice breaking with emotion, he then uttered the time-honoured phrase 'God save the King!'

Climbing into an open-topped limousine, he then made his slow, smiling way from 10 Downing Street to the Houses of Parliament where he delivered a slightly longer version of the same speech he had given over broadcast. After the short journey to St Margaret's Church to give thanks for the victory, he joined the chiefs of staff and the War Cabinet in the grounds of Buckingham Palace where the King thanked them for their tireless efforts in delivering victory. While the military men and politicians gathered in the 1844 Room to hear the King, that quintessential stick-in-the-mud, Alan 'Tommy' Lascelles, the King's private secretary, snatched Churchill's iconic homburg hat, which he had left in the Bow Room, and tried it on for size. He passed it along to his fellow courtiers, Group Captain Peter Townsend and Piers 'Joey' Legh, to put on a piece of history, such was the excitement of the day[1].

Then came the moment millions had been waiting for. The King in his naval uniform, along with the Queen and their daughters, Princess Elizabeth, in her khaki Auxiliary Territorial Service (ATS) uniform, and Princess Margaret, in a day dress, went out onto the balcony to acknowledge the wildly cheering, flag-waving multitude. It was to be the first of eight balcony appearances made by the King and his family, the Sovereign gesturing for his Prime Minister, the man who had represented the nation's bulldog, never-say-die spirit, to join the joyous quartet. After the slightest of hesitations, the great political showman stood amid the family he had got to know so well. Once outside, he flashed his famous 'V for Victory' salute to the ecstatic crowds.

Churchill was in the place he loved best: centre stage, the King and his family happy to let him soak up the adulation. When the crowd spontaneously broke into a chorus of 'For He's a Jolly Good Fellow', it wasn't certain if it was for the King or Winston.

What a difference just five years had made. On what was known as Peace Night, 30 September 1938, the inexperienced King George VI had invited his then Prime Minister, Neville Chamberlain, and Chamberlain's wife, Anne, to join him and Queen Elizabeth on the balcony at Buckingham Palace to celebrate the signing of the Munich Agreement with Nazi leader Adolf Hitler, in which the two leaders pledged not to go to war with one another again. Chamberlain was the first Prime Minister to be so honoured, a sign of the royal family's enthusiasm for his policy, constitutional impartiality be damned. When he arrived back at 10 Downing Street, intoxicated by the adulation of the crowds and the admiration of his King, Chamberlain stood at the same window from which Disraeli had announced peace after the Congress of Berlin in 1878, proclaiming 'peace for our time'.

It was nothing of the sort. Within a year, he was soberly declaring war on Germany after Hitler had breached the deal by invading Poland, leaving Chamberlain's policy of appeasement in tatters.

On the fateful night his predecessor stood on the balcony with the King and Queen, Churchill and his wife, Clementine, together with a few like-minded souls, seriously considered marching down to Downing Street and throwing bricks through the Prime Minister's windows, such was their bitter contempt for the betrayal of Czechoslovakia and other Eastern European nations.

Winston was then firmly in the wilderness: his warnings unheeded, his career going nowhere. Yet within a year of the Munich Agreement, he was reappointed as First Lord of the Admiralty and then made Prime Minister, leading the country when it stood alone against the Nazi hordes. In this tale of two balcony appearances, it seemed on that sunny day in May 1945 that Churchill would run the country for many years to come, working hand-in-glove with a Sovereign he had come to respect and admire. Few of the revellers on that day of undisguised delirium would have thought that within two months he would, once more, be out of favour and out of office, the watching world perplexed by this contrary turn of events.

Not that anything was straightforward about Mr Winston Leonard Spencer Churchill. Technically and legally his surname was Spencer-Churchill, but his father had dropped the hyphen, and Winston generally dropped the Spencer name. In a career that was to span six reigns, he managed to irritate, anger and frustrate every one of his sovereigns without ever losing sight of his devotion to the monarchy. As his long-suffering wife Clementine, or Clemmie, once said, Winston was 'the last believer in the Divine Right of Kings.'[2] And in a world populated by Roundheads, he was arguably the longest serving Cavalier. Even the day of his birth, on a stormy November night in 1874, was freighted with speculation and mystery.

CHAPTER ONE

Invitation to a Duel

THE LAST FULL week of November 1874 was unseasonably warm. Much of the recent snowfall melted, leaving in its place a quiet, gloomy mantle of fog. In many areas of Great Britain, transportation was next to impossible, as the dense haze severely limited visibility and snow-melt caused rivers and streams to burst their banks. Amid the general chaos, meteorologists were concerned by 'irregular' readings from their barometers. Despite these ominous signals, however, no one seemed prepared for the mayhem to come.[1]

When it arrived, the gale raged for three days without ceasing, the worst storm meteorologists had seen in many a year. The north was blanketed in snow while the south succumbed to floods. Grim tales of shipwrecks populated the press, which did its best to keep up with the growing lists of drowned sailors. For the whole of Sunday, 29 November 1874, the great storm was unrelenting.[2]

It was clearly a day for huddling around the fire with a hot tea and a good long book, not for venturing out into the driving wind and rain. Not everyone was so wise. Picking its way across the shooting fields of rural Oxfordshire was a horse-drawn carriage. Inside was the anxious and heavily pregnant Lady Randolph Spencer Churchill, who was pushed into labour – prematurely, as the story goes – by the combination of the low-pressure storm system and the violent shakes it had given to her buggy.[3] Lady Randolph, known as Jennie, had only married the controversial politician Lord Randolph, the younger son of the 7th Duke of Marlborough, some seven and a half months previously, following a whirlwind courtship. In spite of her condition and the foul weather, she had joined the guns on the 2,000-acre estate at Blenheim Palace, the family seat, for a weekend of shooting and dancing. It was the event of the season, the St Andrew's Ball.

Alerted to the emergency, palace staff hurriedly prepared a makeshift birthing room. The ground-floor room they chose was not, perhaps, ideal: for decades, it had been used variously as furniture storage, a servant's quarters and a cloakroom. However, it had the virtue of being close to the main door, so that Lady Randolph had the shortest possible distance to walk or be carried as she entered the 186-room palace. Servants carried a horsehair mattress down the grand staircase and made the young woman as comfortable as they could before the country doctor, who lived in nearby Woodstock, managed to make his way to Blenheim. He had still not arrived by around one-thirty in the morning on Monday, 30 November 1874, when – with the storm still raging outside and after a difficult eight-hour labour – Lady Randolph Churchill's first son made his hasty entrance into the world. The boy's first name came from his paternal grandfather, his middle from his mother's father: he was dubbed Winston Leonard Spencer Churchill, though it would be years before he would go by any such name. For now, the 'wonderfully pretty' baby with 'dark eyes and hair' was little Winnie.[4]

This, at least, is one version of the story. The other, supplied by Sir John 'Shane' Leslie – Winston's first cousin, whose mother was among the guests at Blenheim that weekend – was that Jennie's labour began while she was watching the merry dancers at the St Andrew's Ball, held in the Long Library on the palace's west wing. When the signals of imminent childbirth became undeniable, Jennie was hastened off to the nearest room, where Winston was born shortly after, before the servants could even manage to procure a bed.[5]

Sir Shane's story, though alluring in its romanticism, leaves the same unanswerable questions as the first. If there was such a large gathering at Blenheim Palace, why are there no attendance lists or signed pages of guest books, which adorned the entryway of every stately home in Britain?

If Winston's birthing room had currently been employed as a cloakroom, then surely such a place, stacked floor-to-ceiling with luxurious furs and tartans, would be the last place for an endeavour as messy as childbirth?

Which of the two stories is actually true, if either, is by now impossible to know. The curiosity that there should be so much uncertainty surrounding the origin story of such a high-status figure – since Winston, even before becoming the historical legend that he is today, was in the direct line of succession to the Duchy of Marlborough for the first twenty-two years of his life – has caused remark from numerous observers. The 10th Duke of Marlborough, another of Winston's cousins who, with his own birth, displaced Winston in the hereditary pecking order, once asked the great man himself for specifics concerning that late-November night at Blenheim. Churchill replied, 'Although present upon that occasion I have no clear recollection of the events leading up to it.'[6] By the time of this exchange, Winston had mastered the art of quip, which he deployed in order to divert the conversation from fact-finding and towards jocular repartee. Nor was it in Winston's interest to clarify the circumstances of his birth: it was much better for his legacy as a mythic figure of British history that his entry into the world should be occluded by a shroud of mystery.

What is not up for debate is that Winston was born small, with ruddy pink cheeks and wisps of dark hair that soon transformed into curly locks of strawberry blonde. His dramatic advent on that dark and stormy night gave a hint about the man he was later to become: impatient, vivacious, eager to get on and find opportunity in the midst of any number of storms, be they political or meteorological.

Winston's later influence in shaping and supporting the royal dynasty still lay in the distant and unknown future. No blazing bonfires or fired salvos greeted his arrival. His entrance into the world was announced only by the standard-issue line in the Births section of *The Times of London*: 'On the 30th Nov., at Blenheim Palace, the Lady Randolph Churchill, prematurely, of a son.'[7] Queen Victoria took no notice; on the night of Winnie's birth she was at Windsor Castle, listening intently as her youngest daughter, Princess Beatrice, read aloud about the life and death of Bishop Patteson, a Christian martyr in the South Sea Islands who was killed by Nakapu islanders mistaking him for a slave trader[8]. Victoria's silence on this watershed moment for the Churchill clan was matched by other members of the royal family. Not even Lord Randolph's close friend and fellow mischief-maker, the Prince of Wales, sent any congratulatory lines – at least, none that has survived.

Although Winnie's arrival attracted little notice, his palatial birthplace showcased the intertwining fortunes of the Churchills and the royal family for over 170 years. The Duchy of Marlborough had been created in 1702 for Winston's sixth-great-grandparents, Sarah and John Churchill, as a prize for the couple's faithful service to the British monarchy. Two years later, John led British forces to a legendary success in the Battle of Blenheim during the War of Spanish Succession. The pivotal battle, praised by the poet Robert Southey as 'the greatest victory which had ever done honour to British arms',[9] earned further gratitude from Queen Anne, who bestowed upon them the historic grounds of Woodstock and a sum of £240,000 (equivalent to £50 million today) to build a suitably grand residence. For centuries, the land had been used as a royal retreat: as far back as 1129, Henry I built 7 miles of wall on the grounds to create a wildlife enclosure – the first of its kind – where he kept lions, camels and England's first porcupine. Four centuries later, Queen Elizabeth I was imprisoned by her elder half-sister, Queen Mary, in Woodstock Manor. By the time the Churchills acquired the plot in 1704, the castle lay in stoney ruins, thanks mostly to the artillery barrage launched by the parliamentary forces against a royalist battalion that had stationed itself there during the Civil War.[10]

While Queen Anne appreciated John Churchill's military brilliance and political acuity, it was his wife, Sarah, who brought the couple into the innermost circle of royal life. She had been the Queen's friend since childhood, and in 1683, became one of the princess' ladies of the bedchamber. In adulthood, their friendship evolved into something that today would be uncontroversially labelled as romantic. Anne wrote long, intimate letters to Sarah, pleading with her to return to her side after any brief period of absence. 'I long to be with you again and tis impossible for you ever to believe how much I love you except you saw my heart,' Anne wrote. And later, 'If I writ whole volumes I could never express how well I love you nor how much I long to see you.'[11]

Shortly after taking the throne, Queen Anne conferred upon her old friend and her decorated veteran husband the newly minted and bespoke title, the Duke and Duchess of Marlborough. As a historian, Winston Churchill would later claim that the golden era of Queen Anne's early reign – marked by a 'vehement outpouring of books, poems, and pamphlets' and the flourishing of 'art and science' – was largely due to the influence of the 1st Duke of Marlborough, whom she allowed to act as 'not only her chief but her sole guide'.[12] The ability to guide and instruct a Sovereign was a privilege and status woven into the history of the Marlborough family from the very beginning – but so, too, was an air of suspicion around their influence. Others were more wary. Prime Minister Gladstone expressed a common view that 'There never was a Churchill from John of Marlborough down who had either morals or principles.' It was an opinion that was to stain Winston's career long after Gladstone had left the political stage.[13]

The ducal couple soon learned that what the royal hand giveth, it can also take away. Almost as soon as construction of Blenheim had begun, a rift appeared in Anne's relationship with Sarah, who had never quite reciprocated the Queen's intensity of passion. What began as a difference in temperament was aggravated by a political schism. The same personal qualities that had so endeared Sarah to the monarch – her fiery stubbornness, her willingness to make herself heard and stand her ground – were the same ones that made their falling out inevitable. In 1711 Queen Anne decided that she had had more than enough of Sarah Churchill. She dismissed the Marlboroughs from their royal posts and rescinded the funds that she had allotted for the construction of Blenheim. Ostracized from Court, and fleeing political persecution, the duke and duchess went into voluntary exile and lived in Antwerp until Anne's death in early August 1714, when they sailed back to Britain and resumed construction on the palace.

Once the Marlboroughs returned to Britain, Sarah led the charge to complete the palace, constrained by a budget that was much tighter than it had been at the outset. Despite her fervent efforts, the palace was still not finished by June 1722, when John Churchill died. The palace was finally completed eleven years later, when Sarah had John's body exhumed and relocated to the onsite memorial. Ever since, Blenheim Palace has been not only a palatial residence for the Marlborough family, but also a mausoleum for the early Churchills and a national monument commemorating the saviour of the nation, John Churchill.

By the time of Winston Churchill's birth in 1874, it was obvious that the glory days of Blenheim Palace lay in the distant past. The Marlborough family's fortunes had withered, forcing successive dukes to sell off the estate's possessions piece by piece, in a vain attempt to stave off a financial reckoning that would eventually call the dukedom itself into question. Everything about the setting of Winston's birth drove home the importance of being in good standing with the royal family – the grandeur of the estate, the sparse library whose prize volumes had all been auctioned off, and, perhaps most poignantly, the larger-than-life statue of Queen Anne, which stood at the head of the long, hollow library. The imposing statue bore an inscription that deftly avoided any reference to the bad blood between the Marlboroughs and the Queen in her final years: 'To The Memory of QUEEN ANN Under Whose Auspices JOHN DUKE OF MARLBOROUGH Conquered and to Whose Munificence He and His Posterity with Gratitude Owe the Possession of BLENHEIM.'

For a youngster with a romantic imagination, the dire financial state of the great house mattered little. Winnie was enchanted by the stirring military scenes depicted in the rich tapestries that lined the corridors;

each time he toddled down the hall, he would have been reminded that it was his ancestor, the 1st Duke of Marlborough, who had saved his country from the French. Even as a child, he could imagine himself in the first duke's shoes. When he and his cousins played a wild, rugby-like family game, called 'The French and the English', it was Winston who insisted on playing the general, a role he played well into adulthood.[14]

In fact, the royal family had played a leading role in creating the conditions for Winston Churchill's birth. In August of 1873, English royals and gentry descended upon the Isle of Wight to celebrate Cowes Week, the longest-running and most prestigious annual regatta in the United Kingdom. This year, the high-society attendees had gathered to celebrate not just the yacht racing but also the engagement between Queen Victoria's second son, Alfred, and the Grand Duchess Maria Alexandrovna, the daughter of Russian Czar Alexander II. Among the guests was Lord Randolph Churchill, a relatively recent addition to the inner social circle of Albert, Prince of Wales. This group, called the Marlborough Set, was widely known as a circle of boisterous comrades who enjoyed shooting, hunting, drinking and carousing with the most beautiful belles of the day. Queen Victoria watched their antics with a reproachful eye: 'They lead far too frivolous a life and are far too intimate with people – with a small set of not the best and wisest people who consider being fast the right thing.'[15]

Randolph, then twenty-four, was a curious-looking character. Short, slender, with the air of a dandy, he was cleanly shaven except for an over-full moustache crowding the lower half of his face, his frenetic manner giving an almost manic alertness to his large, round 'popeyes'. Randolph arrived at Cowes that August with his friend, Colonel Edgecumbe, hoping for a week of the usual high jinks.[16] What he hadn't bargained for was to meet his future bride, Jeanette Jerome, the middle daughter of wealthy American businessman Leonard Jerome, a shareholder in *The New York Times*, passionate yachtsman, and owner of a small opera house, with a reputation for seducing his singers. As every socially aspiring American family knew, money alone could not buy entry into the self-contained class that was the British aristocracy. Though American interlopers were typically given the cold shoulder, they found a champion in the Prince of Wales, Albert Edward. It was largely thanks to his influence that wealthy American upstarts were not only tolerated but celebrated – especially the attractive females among them. Since the prince's warm reception in New York during a visit in 1860, he maintained, as Jennie's biographer Anne Sebba has described, 'a lifelong enthusiasm for the refreshing vitality and openness of American women, as well as for the extravagant brashness of their self-made millionaire husbands and fathers.'[17]

As the sun began to sink westward on Tuesday, 12 August, swathing the Solent in a warm late-afternoon glow, the first guests ascended the gangway of HMS *Ariadne* for the ball, which was to cap off the week of celebration. It was only once the dancing began that Randolph Churchill spotted Jeanette Jerome from across the room. He was immediately smitten. The nineteen-year-old beauty, dressed in white tulle, was the very picture of a fashionable Victorian belle; the lines of her physique sloped softly down to her slim waist, while her delicate bare ankles always peeped out from under a skirt hemmed ever-so-slightly too short.[18] With a round jaw that added to the impression of absolute self-assurance, Jennie had the attitude of one who instinctively knew that she deserved a place at any table. Her face, as striking as it was, served merely as a frame for her dark, deep-set eyes, which many compared to those of a panther. As one friend noted of her later, 'Had Lady Randolph Churchill been like her face she would have governed the world.'[19]

From the moment their eyes met across the crowded dance floor, both Jennie and Randolph were convinced that they had found 'the one'. They began a whirlwind three-day romance, spending as much time together as they could steal away from Clara, Jennie's protective mother. On the third day, Randolph proposed, and Jennie accepted. The following day, Randolph had to return to Blenheim Palace. No sooner had he arrived home than he penned a stream of love letters and waited anxiously for a reply. When one finally came, it was not from Jennie but from her mother, who was far from encouraging. She wrote that although he had 'quite won her heart', she was unconvinced that she would ever see him again. 'We shall always think of you with the kindest remembrance,' she concluded.[20] Though this must have been crushing for the lovesick Randolph, Clara was merely following the strict social mores of the time: until Randolph managed to secure his own parents' blessing for the match, it was unthinkable that she would endorse his proposal or encourage the couple's continued affections.

Clara's doubts were well founded. Randolph's family were hostile to the match, their attitude fuelled by aristocratic snobbery. In spite of Jennie's many accomplishments in languages, classical piano and fashion, she was still the daughter of an American tradesman whom the duke dismissed as a 'vulgar kind of man'. Randolph's older brother, George, was especially unhelpful, mocking Randolph for his desire to marry so young and painting an unflattering picture of Randolph's beloved to their parents. He wrote that Randolph had gone 'mad, simply mad'.[21]

But Randolph was not to be deterred. In August, he returned to Cowes and introduced Jennie to the Prince of Wales as the woman he intended to marry. The prince, as Randolph later recalled, was enthusiastic, encouraging the match and telling Randolph that he was a lucky fellow indeed. With that approving comment from a senior member of the royal family, the Marlboroughs' hostility evaporated. A hand-written note from the Prince of Wales was the knockout blow. Some thirty-five years later, the prince – by then King Edward VII – would remark of Winston Churchill, 'If it had not been for me and the Queen [Alexandra], that young man would never have been in existence ... The Duke and

Duchess both objected to Randolph's marriage, and it was entirely owing to us that they gave way.'[22]

In April of the following year, Jennie and Randolph married at the British Embassy in Paris. Lord Knollys, private secretary to the Prince of Wales, stood as Randolph's best man. The prince himself sent Randolph a silver cigarette case from Moscow as a wedding gift, and with Princess Alexandra, sent Jennie a locket of pearls and necklaces.[23] The next time they met, Randolph wrote to his wife that Bertie – as the prince was known to friends – was 'very cordial and nice, asked much after you and said that … he was very glad that everything was so pleasantly settled at last.'[24]

For the next two years, the happy newlyweds were popular additions to high society, attending frequent dinner parties for the great and the good while, politically, Randolph was seen as the up-and-coming man, his much-admired oratorical skills bolstered by his coterie of friends at Court. All seemed to be going swimmingly. Until it wasn't.

In early 1876, the Prince of Wales embarked on a royal tour of India. Among his party was Lord Aylesford, known to friends as 'Sporting Joe'. But the pair's sporting was doomed to be cut short. Almost as soon as they arrived in India, Aylesford's wife, Edith, wrote to tell him that she had been carrying on an affair with George Spencer Churchill, Marquess of Blandford – that is, Randolph's older brother, uncle to the eighteen-month-old Winston and heir to the Dukedom of Marlborough. Edith wrote that the affair was serious – and made it clear that although she was willing 'to be your wife in front of the world', she would do 'no more'.[25]

Lord Aylesford shared this news with the Prince of Wales and then promptly departed from their camp in Nepal atop an elephant. The prince watched this unfolding saga with mixed feelings. He himself was alleged to have had, in times gone by, an improper association with

Lady Aylesford, to the point where he had sent her numerous potentially compromising letters. But he – unlike Lord Blandford – had the good sense to know the proper limits of an extramarital affair. In spite of the possibility that his name would be mentioned in the court proceedings of a divorce, pursued on the basis of infidelity, he advised Sporting Joe to file for a divorce.

Back at Blenheim, Lord Randolph Churchill was horrified. In the late 1800s, divorces were excruciating public scandals, particularly for members of the aristocracy. This was despite the fact that infidelity was a common infraction among the aristocracy of the time, thanks especially to the antics of the prince's Marlborough Set. In fact, allowing the lascivious Prince of Wales to make advances on one's wife was often as good as the cost of admission to the exclusive social group. As Bertie's biographer Jane Ridley has written, 'Corridor-creeping was the dangerous sport of house party entertainment.'[26] Nevertheless, the first and last word on any extramarital dalliance was simple and unforgiving: Do Not Divorce. Randolph knew that the Aylesford trial would bring the uncouth behaviour of George Spencer Churchill into the public spotlight, possibly forcing him into a divorce of his own. Not only would the reputation of the Marlborough dukedom be sullied, but Randolph's own political career would take an indirect hit as a result. He therefore tried his best to convince his brother to withdraw his petition for Edith's hand. But George was intransigent.[27]

Randolph then turned to more drastic measures. In a private meeting several days earlier, Edith had revealed to Randolph that she had kept all of the letters that Bertie had written to her in the course of their involvement. In a desperate attempt to avoid public humiliation, Lord Randolph, accompanied by Edith Aylesford herself, as well as Henry Sturt, 1st Baron Alington, journeyed to Marlborough House, the London home of the Prince and Princess of Wales, to confront Princess Alexandra, Bertie's wife and future Queen.

In a meeting that was as awkward as it was embarrassing, Lord

Randolph informed her that he had in his possession certain letters, highly compromising, written by her husband to Edith. As the princess absorbed this information in the presence of her husband's alleged former mistress, Randolph put a sharper point on the matter: if he released the letters to the British press – which, he said, he was perfectly prepared to do – then her husband 'would never sit on the throne of England'. Left unsaid was the fact that Alexandra would never become Queen. Randolph emphasized that his lawyer had confirmed that this was indeed possible. There was, he suggested, only one way out of the conundrum: Princess Alexandra had to convince her husband, as the leader of London Society, to forbid the divorce between Lord and Lady Aylesford.[28]

If Lord Randolph's opening gambit was utterly reckless and intemperate, his antics were matched by those of his friend, the Prince of Wales, who had remained behind in India. After he read the telegram recounting Randolph's blackmail and betrayal, the furious prince responded by challenging Randolph to a duel. His honour and that of his wife had been assailed, his dignity compromised and his position as the heir to the throne threatened. And all of it had been orchestrated by one of his closest friends. His fury knew no bounds.

Sensibly, Randolph declined the challenge, since he could never kill the heir to the British throne – both on account of his innate sense of patriotism, which rebelled against the notion, and because of the fact that he would rightly be found guilty of treason for endangering the succession of the British Crown. (This logic had apparently not prevented him from threatening it in a less violent manner.) Randolph wrote, 'No one knows better than HRH the P of Wales that a meeting between himself and Ld R. C. is definitely out of the question.' The patronizing tone only infuriated Bertie more.[29]

Meanwhile, the man at the centre of the scandal – George, Lord Blandford – had fled the country and was staying in the Hague, in the Netherlands, leaving his younger brother to take the social heat alone. In an astonishing misreading of the basic facts of the situation, George wrote to Randolph of his intention to 'kick [His Royal Highness] within an inch of his life for his conduct generally' and let Bertie take the whole matter up 'with the Police Courts'.[30] With Blandford out of the picture, the full wrath of the Prince of Wales descended on Winston Churchill's father. The future King made it clear that anyone who welcomed Randolph Churchill into their homes, or did business with him, would be axed from his social circle. None dared to disobey the will of the future King.

Inevitably, the news of the affair reached Queen Victoria. It merely reinforced her disapproval of her son's private life. It would be better, she felt, if the whole Marlborough clan left the country for a time. Her Prime Minister at the time, Benjamin Disraeli, suggested that she renew the offer of the Viceroyalty of Ireland to the 7th Duke of Marlborough, which he had previously refused. With circumstances changed so dramatically, it seemed sensible for him to accept the new reality. The duke could not fail to realize, Disraeli suggested, that 'the dignified withdrawal of the family from metropolitan and English life at the moment and for a time' was their only remaining option.[31] So Winston, just two years old, sailed with the rest of the Marlborough family to Dublin, where Randolph took on the unpaid post of private secretary to his father.

As for Winston, his first memory was of a ceremony at which his grandfather, the duke, unveiled a statue of an Anglo-Irish imperial war hero. From that moment onwards, two things were forever imprinted in his mind: a deep well of respect for the British monarchy, and the notion that those who served it well would duly earn a place in history.[32]

After an exile lasting four years, Randolph and Jennie returned to London in March 1880 to test the social and political waters. Stafford Northcote, the Conservative Party leader, had raised the issue with Disraeli, now out of office, asking whether Randolph had been 'forgiven yet in high quarters'. Disraeli replied that Randolph 'was all right so far as the Queen was concerned, but that the Prince of Wales had not yet made it up with him'. Disraeli went on to suggest a backdoor approach to reconciliation: 'Nothing will help Randolph into favour again so much as success in Parliament. The Prince is always taken by success.'[33]

It did not take long for Randolph to conform to this royal criterion. While the general election held that year delivered a walloping to the Conservative Party, who were turned out of government, one man stood out once the dust had settled: Randolph. Not only did he hold his contested seat, but he even increased his majority from the previous election. It was clear that he had the potential to lead his party back to the promised land.

Lord Randolph cemented his position as an up-and-coming figure of the Conservative Party by hosting, on Winston's sixth birthday, the inaugural banquet of the Woodstock Conservative Association at Blenheim Palace. It was attended by many party grandees, underlining Randolph's position as a force to be reckoned with, a star whose meteoric rise from near political and social oblivion attracted as many enemies as it did supporters. Though he was seen as a dynamic if controversial figure inside the upper echelons of the Tory Party, his short burst of political success failed to secure the forgiveness of the Prince of Wales. Their feud continued.

For her part, Jennie had mixed emotions about their return to London. On the one hand, she was overjoyed to be back in the bustling metropolis; on the other, she found herself with little to occupy her time, on account of both the family's dire financial straits and their continued social exclusion. In July, she wrote to her mother, 'London is very gay just now. I haven't been to many balls as I simply can't afford to get dresses and one can't always wear the same thing. Besides I am not bidden to the ones I want to go to and I do not care about the others.' That said, she ended her missive by saying that she was out 'every night' that week.[34]

It was not until 1882 that a casual encounter between the Prince and Princess of Wales and the Churchills opened an opportunity for reconciliation. This came in the form of a dinner at the home of Lord Salisbury, the Conservative Leader of the Opposition, followed by a ball hosted by Lady Cornelia Wimborne, Randolph's sister. Unfortunately, just before the double-barrelled event, Randolph succumbed to a bout of sickness that left him bedridden and close to death. Jennie attended on her own, though she was disappointed that there was little in the way of conversation with the prince's entourage. As she recorded in her diary that night: 'The Prince and Princess there. Not wildly amusing.'[35] It was a start, though: for the first time in six years, the Prince and Princess of Wales had deigned to breathe the same air as a member of the Churchill family.

There was another, not insignificant, effect of the gathering that ought to have cheered Jennie considerably. The Wales' decision to attend the Salisbury dinner party with the formerly disgraced Churchill couple sent out a clear signal to polite society: Lord and Lady Randolph were allowed back into the fold. This was all to the benefit of Randolph's political career, as he and Jennie began to host dinner parties with eminent politicians, artists, journalists and financiers of the day.

Just as Winston's parents clawed their way back into London's elite class, they decided to send their seven-year-old son to school at St George's, Ascot, one of the most fashionable and expensive boarding schools for little boys of privilege and primogeniture. Winston had a terrible time there, flogged frequently by his headmaster for various infractions. When he wasn't being beaten, he often lay prone in bed due to some ailment or other. From his infancy, Winston had always been a sickly child, but the regular beatings caused his health to deteriorate further. Nor did his infirmity do anything to help his academic performance. Instead of focusing on maths, a subject in which he particularly struggled, he constantly wrote plaintive letters to his parents, begging them to visit him. They were busy with their social and political lives, and rarely complied. Two years passed before they finally transferred him to Brunswick School, where his academic performance showed some signs of improvement, though he was never particularly strong in any subject besides history. His teachers were astounded by his remarkable memory, but when it came to applying himself to learn mathematics or the rules of Latin grammar, little Winnie was beyond help.[36]

In 1883, the death of Benjamin Disraeli, Earl of Beaconsfield, sent the country into a wave of mourning. Disraeli had been the Conservative Prime Minister for almost seven years, and was a close personal friend to Queen Victoria, who sent a wreath of primroses – thought to be his favourite flower – to his funeral service. Randolph, along with several other members of the Conservative Party, hoped to turn the tragedy to political advantage, and so formed both the Primrose League and the Fourth Party to spread conservative political values. It wasn't long before Randolph's leadership in the group started raising eyebrows in Buckingham Palace. On 10 July, Queen Victoria recorded in her diary that during her audience with Liberal Prime Minister William Gladstone, they 'spoke of the Duke of Marlborough's ... strange troublesome son Ld Randolph Churchill'.[37] Just as Bertie and Randolph began to tentatively resuscitate their friendship, Queen Victoria, who had encouraged the reconciliation, now performed a volte-face. She increasingly began to see Randolph as an untrustworthy, distasteful and potentially dangerous person for any member of the royal family to associate with.

Randolph's attitude first irritated the Queen when the Conservatives were returned to office in June of 1885, following Gladstone's resignation. The new Prime Minister, Lord Salisbury, asked Randolph to accept the position of Secretary of State for India. Randolph agreed, but only on the condition that Sir Stafford Northcote was removed from his current position as Leader of the House of Commons. This bold demand, coming from the man who had blackmailed her eldest son, sparked indignation in the Queen. She wrote to Salisbury, 'With due consideration to Lord R. Churchill, do not think he should be allowed to dictate entirely his own terms, especially as he has never held office before.' In spite of the Queen's resistance, Randolph held his ground and won, securing Northcote's removal from his post through a promotion to the House of Lords.[38]

The second of the Queen's irritations, and by far the more severe, related to her late, much beloved husband, Prince Albert. During his lifetime, he had made it clear that he wanted to see a member of the royal family presiding over a territory in India, the 'Jewel in the Crown' of the British Empire. To honour that wish, the Queen proposed her son, Prince Arthur, Duke of Connaught and Strathearn, to be Commander-in-Chief of the Bombay District, one of the most populous regions of India. As Secretary of State for India, Randolph would hear none of it. He insisted that such an appointment would inevitably drag the royal family into politics, not to mention accusations of nepotism, and he declared that if the appointment were made against his judgment, he would resign. During any discussions about this matter, he would fly into such a rage that on at least one occasion he was given a dose of calomel – a popular smelling salt at the time – to calm him down. Hoping to force the issue to a crisis, Randolph insisted on a vote in Cabinet, in which fourteen out of sixteen members voted with him to forbid the Queen's third and favourite son from taking up the imperial post. Victoria was 'a great deal annoyed'. But she would have her way eventually. When Randolph moved to another office a year later, she renewed the request, and the Duke of Connaught was promptly and quietly installed to the post. Prince Albert's wish was fulfilled at last – Randolph's apoplexy be damned.[39]

While Randolph was busy making his political mark, his wife was quickly becoming the talk of the drawing rooms of London's High Society. Jennie's beauty and arresting wardrobe earned the plaudits of gossip columns and courtiers alike. In the winter of 1885–86, she was twice invited to be presented to Queen Victoria, who made a point of personally bestowing upon Jennie the Insignia of the Order of the Crown of India during her first appearance. Her second appearance, in January, was more crowded. At an event called a Drawing Room, around two hundred young women were presented to the Queen in a ceremony that marked their formal entrance into High Society.

Jennie was hardly lost in the crowd. *Vanity Fair* magazine singled her out for special praise, describing her spectacular outfit as 'a startling and successful toilette. Diamonds flashed in her ears, on her throat and arms, and her dress glistened like a glass of golden wine held to the sunlight ... It was,' they concluded, 'the most remarkable in the room.' As much as Randolph's success in Parliament had earned the respect of his peers, it was Jennie's beauty and elegance which made their re-entry into the very centre of high society very nearly inevitable.[40]

A time of social triumph almost ended in medical tragedy. In early March 1886, Winston, then eleven, suffered his most serious bout of illness. Lonely, chilled and gloomy, he came down with a serious case of pneumonia, a feared and deadly disease at the time. Such was his parents' concern that they paid a top London doctor to temporarily move to Hove on the south coast, where Winston's school was located, to oversee his medical care. His health began gradually to improve. On 15 March, the Prince of Wales held a formal ceremony at St James' Palace, called a levée, during which members of the court were presented to him individually, wearing full uniforms, regalia, or court dress. When Moreton Frewen, husband to Jennie Churchill's older sister, Clara, was announced by the page, the prince stopped the whole line to ask after Winston. Frewen later told Jennie that the prince had 'seemed so glad to hear' that her son had improved.[41]

It was only two months after Winston's recovery that the formerly close relationship between the Prince of Wales and the Lord Randolph Churchills would finally be revived in earnest – a full ten years from the beginning of their feud over the Aylesford affair. The occasion, in mid-May 1886, was a dinner party hosted by the Churchills at their Hyde Park home. The prince was wary, feeling that it would be 'best to be on speaking terms though we can never be the same friends again'.[42] His reservations soon vanished. When he and his wife entered, Jennie respectfully dropped into a deep curtsy, though the princess quickly took hold of her by the elbow, pulled her up, and gushed about their former days of playing piano together: 'We haven't played Bach in a long time!' Their husbands' bad blood would no longer prove an obstacle to their friendship.[43]

During dinner, Jennie could not have played her part better: their dining room was decorated impeccably, the dinner was sumptuous, and the conversation flowed with intelligence and wit. The Prince and Princess of Wales were utterly charmed. At one point in the evening, when Winston and Jack were trotted out to say their hellos to the gathered company, the Prince of Wales gave them each a small gift.[44] It marked the final end of a royal feud that had gone on far too long. The Churchills were back in business.

For Lord Randolph, there might have been reason to lament that the Prince of Wales had enjoyed himself so much at their dinner party. So pleased was the prince, with the lovely hostess in particular, that in the summer months that followed, he and Jennie picked up a private relationship. They often met for lunch or tea – in the absence of Jennie's husband. While various biographers have come to differing conclusions about whether or not an illicit affair was underway, it was without question a secret friendship that raised eyebrows at Court. It was difficult to escape gossip when the notoriously libidinous prince and the woman with the panther eyes, who was later rumoured to have had over two hundred lovers, began to enjoy each other's private company.

At the same time, the Prince of Wales maintained his close friendship with Lord Randolph, and there is little to suggest that Randolph had any notion of his wife's rumoured infidelity with the heir to the throne. During the summer of 1886, his career prospects grew increasingly promising, and the prince was happy to have a friend whose political star was in the ascendant. Queen Victoria, however, remained sceptical. 'He is so mad and odd and has also bad health,' she wrote.[45] In spite of her misgivings, Lord Randolph became, at just thirty-six years old, Chancellor of the Exchequer (that is, minister of finance) and Leader of the House of Commons.

Randolph did well in his elevated office, conducting the business of the government with effectiveness and charm. One of his tasks as House Leader was to write a nightly report to Queen Victoria, to keep her informed of all the goings-on within the chamber, from which she was ritually forbidden to enter. Randolph's reports were so reliable in their regularity and accuracy that the Queen, uncharacteristically, relented in her judgment against him. Her private secretary wrote: 'Now that the session is just over the Queen wishes to write and thank Lord Randolph Churchill for his regular and full and interesting reports ... Lord Randolph has shown much skill and judgement in his leadership.'[46]

But as autumn turned to winter, and the following session of parliament began, the Queen's doubts returned. Lord Randolph, as Chancellor, was at loggerheads with the Prime Minister, Lord Salisbury, over the budgets for the army and navy. On 20 December 1886, Randolph met with Queen Victoria at Windsor Castle. After dinner, he quietly retired to his designated bedchamber and wrote out a letter of resignation on Windsor Castle stationery. If Salisbury refused to accede to his budget proposal, he would publish the letter the following day. Though Randolph likely intended this as an empty threat, the Prime Minister was only too happy to get rid the moustachioed thorn in his side. He promptly called Randolph's bluff and accepted the resignation.

During his stay at Windsor, Randolph had not mentioned a word of his strategy to Queen Victoria, nor to his wife or mother. Everyone was left to read about his resignation in *The Times*, which printed his letter in its entirety, including the 'Windsor Castle' stationery heading, lending the missive an air of royal sanction. The Queen was outraged that her official residence was associated with Randolph's political rebellion and told her son as much. But this time, it was Bertie who came to the defence of poor Randolph: 'You are, if you will allow me to say so, rather hard on Lord R. Churchill. I do not enter into the question whether he was right or wrong in resigning ... but he has at any rate the courage of his opinions.' He continued by trying to foment his mother's sympathy, never a very bountiful resource, writing, 'Lord Randolph is a poor man and a very ambitious one, but he gave up £5000 a year in ceasing to be Ch[ancellor] of the Exchequer ... Should his life be spared (and he has not a good life) he is bound to play sooner or later a prominent part.'[47]

The prince, however, was sadly mistaken in his forecast. This political gamble was to be Randolph's last. Never again would he hold any position in government. Instead, as his health continued to deteriorate, he became increasingly irritable and prone to fits of rage and mania. He did, at least, maintain his close relationship with the Prince of Wales – as did Jennie, in her own way. As a result, the young Winston, now twelve years old, was continually presented to the prince in settings that were as informal and familiar as was possible with such an eminent figure. At dinner parties, Jennie would parade him and his younger brother, Jack, in front of the prince, who sometimes brought the boys small but dazzling presents. At one of these meetings, in 1887, the Prince of Wales gave them each a tiepin made of gold and set with a diamond. Almost immediately, Winston lost his – but the prince promptly replaced it with another.[48]

The young Winston spent June of 1887 bombarding his mother with letters, begging her to let him leave school in order to attend Queen Victoria's Golden Jubilee, even threatening that his fragile health would suffer if he were denied the pleasure. Finally, Jennie and Randolph gave way, bringing both of their boys home for the festivities. Not only did Winston get to attend the Golden Jubilee celebrations – including the much-anticipated Buffalo Bill show – but a few weeks afterwards, the whole family was invited as guests of the Prince and Princess of Wales to Cowes, that dreamy yachting station on the Isle of Wight where the Churchill parents had fallen in love over a decade before. While there, the Churchills were brought on board the royal yacht, where Winston was first introduced to Bertie's two eldest sons: Prince Albert, the Duke of Clarence, and Prince George, the future King George V. When all were aboard, the royal yacht sailed past an entire battle fleet of twelve warships, their names evoking glorious moments of British history. Winston's presence on the royal yacht in a ringside seat to watch the passing parade was, quite literally, a dream come true: his earliest surviving letter, written at age seven, was about toy soldiers, flags and castles. His campaign to attend the jubilee festivities had been rewarded with great returns.[49]

A further sign of the renewed friendship between the Churchills and the royal couple came a few months later, over Christmas, when Winston's parents travelled to Moscow to visit the Czar and Czarina as emissaries of the Prince of Wales, carrying letters of goodwill from himself and his wife, the Czarina's sister. The vague impression that this was an official visit was allowed to go unchecked, with Randolph himself even intimating that the Prince of Wales had sponsored the journey, and the Churchills were happy to behave as ersatz royalty. Queen Victoria, Lord Salisbury and the Foreign Office were utterly scandalized. Lord Salisbury published an official statement, declaring that Randolph represented no one but himself, while the Queen begged her son to cease his 'most objectionable … and even dangerous correspondence' with such an indiscreet man.[50]

But the Prince of Wales would not allow his mother to drive a wedge between himself and the friend with whom he had so recently reconciled. Bertie remained close to Randolph for the better part of the next decade – the last years, as it happened, of Randolph's life. It could no longer be said that their friendship was down to Randolph's political success, as the politician had nothing to offer in terms of sway, aside from the odd public statement. In July of 1889, for instance, Randolph delivered a speech in which he argued that more money should be devoted to the Civil List – that is, the slice of the national tax revenue set aside for the Royal Family – for the sake of the children of the Prince of Wales. Naturally, the prince was pleased to hear his children's interests defended by such a vivacious and witty speaker. But those moments became increasingly elusive as Randolph's sickness affected his mental faculties.[51]

As the friendship between Randolph and the prince carried on through the late 1880s and early 1890s, so too did the alleged affair between Jennie and the prince, whom she and others nicknamed 'Tum-Tum' on account of his increasingly rotund belly. Soon after the prince praised Randolph's speech on the Civil List, Randolph returned home unexpectedly to find Bertie there – alone with his wife. At this time, for any aristocratic woman to be alone with a man to whom she was not married had the potential to cause an outright scandal. Lord Randolph flew into a fit of rage and demanded that the prince leave immediately.[52]

Whether Randolph ever suspected more profound impropriety between his friend and his wife is uncertain. There is, however, one telling clue into Randolph's feelings about the prince's extramarital activities. On 14 January 1892, Lord and Lady Randolph attended a party thrown in Bertie's honour. The prince, however, was unable to attend, because his eldest son – the twenty-eight-year-old Duke of Clarence, second in line to the throne – had been taken terribly ill with a fever. The duke, with both his parents at his bedside, died in the morning on the same day of the party, which went ahead without the guest of honour. Randolph recounted the evening in letters to Winston and to his own mother. To Winston: 'The party was broken up by the death of the poor Duke one of the saddest events I have ever known. Our party was naturally gloomy & dull.' To his mother, he showed perhaps a bit more of his hand: 'How very sad is this death of the poor Duke of Clarence. Perhaps this grief may bring [the prince and princess] together more and put a stop to importunate affairs.'[53]

Winston's academic performance at school, meanwhile, had steadily improved, with particular strengths in history and composition beginning to shine through. His memory was prodigious, on one occasion winning a school-wide competition and astounding the headmaster when he recited 1,200 lines of a Macaulay poem by heart.[54] He had been encouraged by his father to study hard for his entrance exams to Harrow School, which he passed by a small margin in 1888. Randolph also convinced him that, because he wasn't clever enough to go into politics, he should take the military path instead. It was for this reason that Winston chose a military course at Harrow, intending to go into the Royal Military Academy at

Sandhurst. It took him three attempts to pass the entrance exams, but finally, in September 1893, he matriculated at Sandhurst and began training for the cavalry.

Towards the end of 1894, leading up to Winston's graduation, Randolph's health took a serious turn for the worse. The prince was worried and asked his royal physician to speak to Randolph's doctor to find out what was wrong. His verdict was that he was suffering from 'general paralysis', the coy phrase used at the time to indicate late-stage syphilis. This diagnosis has been largely dismissed as a canard put about by Winston's political enemies some years later, though the interpretation that it was a malignant brain tumour, now widely accepted, would hardly have offered more consolation. The prince wrote to Jennie, 'I cannot describe how much I feel for you ... You have indeed had a fearful time of it, but you have done your duty by him most nobly.'[55]

On 24 January 1895, about a month after Winston graduated, Lord Randolph Churchill died, aged only forty-five. The first letter of condolence that Jennie received was from the prince, then staying at Sandringham: 'The sad news reached me this morning that all is over ... & I felt that for his and for your sakes it was best so ... There was a cloud in our friendship but I am glad to think that it has long been forgotten by both of us. Be assured that I shall always deeply regard him.' Before long, the prince changed the address of his letters, from 'Dear Lady Randolph' to 'Ma chère amie'. Over the next five years, Jennie would see much more of the Prince of Wales, having no lurking husband to create a scene.[56]

CHAPTER TWO

An Unheeded Warning

IN FEBRUARY 1895, shortly after his father's death, Winston received his commission from Queen Victoria as a second lieutenant. He was to spend the next five years as a cavalry officer, beginning with the 4th Queen's Own Hussars in an army garrison at Hounslow, a West London suburb. His world was one in which pomp and ceremony blended into bloody military conflict. Even before he was posted, Churchill found himself under fire when he and a fellow officer, Reginald Barnes, travelled to Cuba in November 1895 as observers with the Spanish Army who were trying to quell a rebellion of colonized Cuban people. Both young officers were decorated by the Spanish authorities with the Red Cross of Military Merit. It was Winston's first medal for gallantry, the award whetting his appetite for more.[1]

It is, though, harder to discern which he preferred: the thrill of active combat or his occasional encounters with royalty, particularly the Prince of Wales, and other dignitaries. In May 1895, he reported to Jennie that he had been invited to the prince's levée. Then there was the Queen's official birthday, the Trooping of the Colour, to look forward to: 'Of course it is here celebrated by much military display.'[2]

Two weeks later, Winston again wrote to Jennie to update her on the part he had played during the state visit of Shahzada Nasrullah Khan, the second son of Abdur Rahman Khan, the Emir of Afghanistan. He wrote, 'I was selected as the officer to attend on and to escort the Duke of Cambridge – so I had a rather tiring – though complimentary job – jogging along by his carriage & tittupping after him when he was on horseback. I went to luncheon at Government House and generally made myself sociable to the foreigners on the staff. The Prince was there and saw me ... Everyone of course asked after you ... it was a great honour to have been selected.'[3]

Later in the year, Winston was selected for another significant social event: he was invited to a weekend party in honour of the Prince of Wales at Deepdene, the country home of Lord William Beresford, who was married to Winston's aunt by a previous marriage. The evening did not begin well. From an early age, Winston had the reputation for poor time management, always arriving at the last minute for social engagements. On this occasion he missed his train, and though he caught the next one, it meant that he was late to dinner. Without him, the party consisted of only thirteen men. The Prince of Wales was a superstitious man, as Winston later wrote, and so 'refused point-blank to go in, and would not allow any rearrangement of two tables to be made. He had, as was his custom, been punctual to the minute at half-past eight. It was now twelve minutes to nine.' When Winston finally arrived, the party of fourteen proceeded to the table, but not before the prince chastised him severely: 'Don't they teach you to be punctual in your regiment, Winston?' He then 'looked acidly at Colonel Brabazon' – Churchill's commanding officer – 'who glowered. It was an awful moment!' But the evening was not yet lost. It was only about fifteen minutes later when 'the Prince, who was a naturally and genuinely kind-hearted man, put me at my ease again by some gracious chaffing remark'.[4]

Shortly afterwards, in the autumn of 1896, his regiment sailed to India, where they were stationed in the southern city of Bangalore. As a belated graduation present his Aunt Lilian bought him a racing pony and had it shipped to him in India. This was not to Jennie's liking – nor, indeed, to Bertie's. The Prince of Wales had spent some time in India and had witnessed firsthand the disreputable practices surrounding horse racing there. He worried that Winston could be headed for either financial or reputational fall, and Jennie, after hearing the prince's concerns, wrote to Winston to ask him to sell the pony: 'He begged me to tell you that you ought not to race only because it is not good business in India.'[5]

Winston, then twenty-one and desirous of glory in sport and battle, chose to ignore the pleadings of his mother and her rumoured royal lover who now adopted the position of a concerned yet solicitous uncle in Winston's life. He replied: 'You should tell His Royal Highness, if he says anything further about racing in India, that I intend to be just as much an example to the Indian turf as he is to the English as far as fair play goes.'[6] Winston went ahead with his pony racing, excelling also in polo where he became a member of the All-India polo championship team.

In September 1897 – Queen Victoria's Diamond Jubilee year – Winston obtained a post as a war correspondent with the Malakand Field Force, commanded by Sir Bindon Blood, on the North-West frontier of India, near the border with Afghanistan. His thirst for action was met in full measure, Winston coming under heavy fire on numerous occasions, once for thirteen hours without pause. During his two-month attachment, first as war correspondent then on the commanding officer's staff, his bravery and calm were noted by superior officers, and earned him a Mention in Despatches. Word of Winston's exploits reached the ears of the Prince of Wales, who told Jennie that he had heard good things about Winston's development.[7]

The prince's praise continued through that autumn, a period when his relationship with Jennie was at its most intense. In November, when Winston had returned to the garrison in Bangalore, Jennie wrote that he had again been the subject of Bertie's compliments about his character and activities in India. Winston wrote back, 'I am glad that the Prince has been kind about me.' At this juncture Winston had his hands full: he was 'working incessantly' on what would be his first published book, *The Story of the Malakand Field Force*.[8] As his army pay of around £120 a year (equivalent to about £13,000 today) didn't begin to cover his outgoings, the publisher's advance helped to keep the wolves from his door. He couldn't, after all, seek much help from his mother, whose extravagance was such that the Prince of Wales recommended his own financial adviser,

Sir Ernest Cassel, to help put her on the straight and narrow. Cassel soon hired Winston's younger brother, Jack, and over the years gave Winston financial advice. She wrote to Winston, 'The Prince means to be very kind to you both.'[9]

Every inch the pushy opportunist, Winston tried to take immediate advantage of his mother's cozy relationship with the future King. He wrote to Jennie asking if she would speak to the Princes of Wales to use his influence to secure him a promotion to the Tirah Field Force, under commanding general Sir William Lockhart. 'You must,' he implored, 'get the Prince to speak to him on my behalf.'[10] He later described his mother as the person 'who tapped the men and opened the doors' for him.[11] Though that particular request came to nothing, the publication in the spring of 1898 of his book on the Malakand field expedition brought him some notoriety for his willingness to criticize senior officers. Prime Minister Lord Salisbury was so intrigued by the book that he invited Churchill to see him to discuss its contents. The young whipper snapper, who was anxious for more military honours and action, used the interview to lobby for a position on General Kitchener's upcoming campaign to reconquer the Sudan from the Mahdists. Churchill also enlisted the not inconsiderable help of his mother, writing to her: 'Oh, how I wish I could work you up over Egypt! I know you could do it with all your influence—and all the people you know. It is a pushing age and we must shove with the best. After Tirah and Egypt—then I think I shall turn from war to peace and politics. That is— [if] I get through it all right.'[12] Kitchener, though, was suspicious of the ambitious young man who would, apparently, happily stab senior officers in the back with his quill. Yet thanks to the influence of society hostess Lady Jeune, Winston managed to get himself appointed by the War Office as a supernumerary lieutenant in the 21st Lancers. Kitchener was furious.

Though Winston was personally dismissive of his first book, calling it a 'slovenly work' and an 'eyesore', it marked a step change in the relationship between the young officer and the Prince of Wales. For the first time, the

Prince of Wales wrote directly to the young Churchill, sending him high praise for the literary merits of his first book. On 16 February 1998, Winston proudly told his mother that he had received in that day's post 'a long & charming letter from the Prince – which I am Tory enough to regard as a great honour and which I have duly acknowledged.'[13] Over the next few months, the Prince of Wales sent excerpts of Winston's writing around to his friends and quoted it in speeches.

The Prince's praise touched a deep nerve in the young Churchill's psyche. As he admitted later in his autobiography, *My Early Life*, 'I had never been praised before.'[14] Though he revered his mother and almost worshipped his father – both from afar – he had learned to expect nothing but chastisement from his parents. When he had finally passed the Sandhurst exam, for instance, he received a scathing letter from his father: 'I am certain that if you cannot prevent yourself from leading the idle useless unprofitable life you have had during your schooldays & later months, you will become a mere social wastrel one of the hundreds of the public school failures, and you will degenerate into a shabby unhappy & futile existence.'[15] By contrast, the Prince of Wales was a man of great warmth and joviality, one who was always prepared to offer a word of encouragement when he felt it would do some good. To Churchill's mind, the prince's generous remarks merely exemplified 'the extraordinary kindness and consideration for young people which the Prince of Wales always practised'.[16]

This contact over Winston's first book began an extended personal correspondence with the Prince of Wales, which touched on, among other topics, the officers' code, military censorship, and Winston's career prospects. The tone of their written communications was remarkably intimate – not at all what one would expect between a man who was expecting, at any point, to accede to the British throne on the one hand, and on the other, a penniless subaltern. That autumn, the prince warned him against starting too soon on a political career: he should 'certainly stick to the Army', the prince advised, before rushing to add MP to his name.[17] But after reading Winston's response to this letter – which does not survive – the King seems to have changed his mind, exhibiting the gentle firmness that is the trademark of a good father, something Winston had never before experienced: 'I can well understand that it must be very difficult for you to make up your mind what to do, but I cannot help feeling that Parliamentary & literary life is what would suit you best as the monotony of military life in an Indian station can have no attraction for you – though fortunately some officers do put up with it or else we should have no Army at all!' The prince invited Winston to come visit him: 'I hope you will come & see me & tell me all about the recent campaign & about your future plans.'[18] Their one major disagreement concerned publicity. The Prince of Wales often emphasized that junior officers should not write for newspapers or express strong opinions about how military operations were carried out. Churchill disagreed.

In September 1898, within weeks of wrangling his way into Kitchener's expedition to retake the Sudan, Winston found himself taking part in the last full cavalry charge by the British Army at Omdurman. It was a bloody affair as the British cavalry had been lured into a trap, and Churchill, who hacked and shot his way to safety, was fortunate to survive. 'It was I suppose the most dangerous two minutes I shall live to see,' he wrote later, as he relived his experiences in a letter to Colonel Ian Hamilton.[19]

The restless officer now tried a new avenue for success as a Member of Parliament. However, the people of Oldham, the Lancashire town where he threw his hat into the ring for election, were not sufficiently impressed by his exploits to vote in his favour. In the July 1899 by-election, he failed to emulate his father and take a seat in Parliament. But his time would soon come.

Within months he was back in action, this time as a war reporter, aged just twenty-four, describing the fighting between the British Army and a ragtag but very effective army of Boer farmers in South Africa. His part in the war did not last long. Just two weeks after his arrival, the armoured train he was travelling on to the front lines was ambushed and derailed.

His capture, in November 1899, made headlines, and Jennie wrote to the Prince of Wales of her concerns for his safety. The prince was sanguine that Winston would be well treated in military prison. His instincts were confirmed when he received a letter from the man himself.

During his incarceration Winston wrote only two letters, one to the Prince of Wales. His missive, written on thin, prison-grade paper, stated confidently, 'I venture to think that Your Royal Highness will be interested to receive a letter from me and from this address,' referring to the State Model School prison in Pretoria where he was held. While he pointed out that his letter would be censored, he wrote of his regret at being captured so early after his arrival, and praised the Boers for their 'courtesy, courage and humanity', emphasizing that since his capture, he had been treated well. He confessed that, 'It is something to be alive and well and when I saw so many soldiers and volunteers torn with such horrible injuries, I could not help feeling thankful that I had been preserved – even though as a prisoner.'[20]

Even as he penned these assurances, Winston was concocting an audacious scheme to regain his freedom. His great escape from the Boer prison camp, which made front-page news in London, was a sunny public distraction from the clouds of gloom that had accompanied the British forces, who suffered a series of setbacks in the field. When Winston reached safety, he wrote his mother a long account of his dramatic journey, which included hiding in mine shafts and open woodlands as well as hitching a ride on a goods train. She, in turn, copied out the letter and sent it to the Prince of Wales, who was grateful to receive the 'most interesting' story.[21]

At this time the future King had a more than usual concern for the family of his late friend Lord Randolph Churchill. Not only did he keenly follow the fortunes of Lord Randolph's son, but he was alarmed by Randolph's widow's romantic dalliance with George Cornwallis-West, who was – like Winston – only twenty-four years old. The prince, who was widely rumoured to have illegitimately fathered Jennie's new love interest, dismissed their affair as a 'flirtation'. Jennie was not, however, a woman who liked being told what to do. In 1900, when she discovered that the prince's favourite mistress, Alice Keppel, was expecting a child, Jennie promptly announced her intention to marry the man rumoured to be the bastard son of the Prince of Wales. In the meantime, on his return from South Africa, Winston signalled his decision to leave his military life behind and try his luck once more as a Member of Parliament in the colours of the Conservative Party. It is hard to divine which item of family news would have astonished the late Lord Randolph more: his wife's choice of companion, the youthful, impecunious George Cornwallis-West, or Winston's decision to seriously run for Parliament, a feat that his father thought was far out of his intellectual reach.

In what was known as the 'khaki election' of 1900, Winston enjoyed a fair wind, the Tories buoyed by recent successes in the Boer War. Always short of funds, in spite of the healthy payments he received for his freelance writing, Churchill gratefully accepted a financial contribution from his cousin, the 9th Duke of Marlborough, that helped ensure a successful campaign which saw him elected to the Oldham constituency on the second attempt.

Churchill had long understood that the pen was more lucrative than the sword and, in an era where MPs were unpaid, he chose to delay taking his seat in the House of Commons so that he could gather some attendance fees on a lecture tour of North America. By now, he enjoyed a reputation as a compelling public speaker, his talks drawing large and enthusiastic crowds. What he could not have known is that his choice to delay taking the oath of office meant that he would lose the chance to 'kiss hands' with the longest-serving monarch the United Kingdom had ever seen. On the last night of his tour, 22 January 1901, he was in Winnipeg, Manitoba when he heard that Queen Victoria, the grandmother of European royalty and the living symbol of the British Empire, had died.

Reflecting on the momentous news, Winston wrote his mother a long letter, filled with eager uncertainty at what kind of an era the new King would usher in:

A great and solemn event: but I am curious to know about the King. Will he sell his horses and scatter his Jews or will Reuben Sassoon be enshrined among the crown jewels and other regalia? Will he become desperately serious? Will he continue to be friendly to you? Will the Keppel be appointed 1st Lady of the Bedchamber? I contemplated sending a letter of condolence and congratulations mixed, but I am uncertain how to address it and also whether such procedure would be etiquette. You must tell me. I am most interested and feel rather vulgar about the matter. I should like to know an Emperor and a King. Edward the VIIth – gadzooks what a long way that seems to take one back! I am glad he has got his innings at last, and am most interested to watch how he plays it ...[22]

Though the matronly empress had passed, that didn't mean that the British Empire was teetering on the brink of disaster – at least, not in Winston's eyes. The night after the Queen's death, Winston attended a dinner party at the home of an American millionaire, James C. Young, in Minneapolis. When the conversation turned to the British Empire and its prospects for survival now that Victoria was gone, Young suggested that within ten years, the British Empire would find its position in the world 'substantially reduced by loss in Australia, or Canada, or India'. Winston, feeling flush after his successful tour and a patriot to his core, wagered £100 (the equivalent of £12,000 today) that the British empire and its social and constitutional apex, the monarchy, would not only survive, but thrive. They scrawled out the bet on a piece of paper, and the document was duly dated, signed and witnessed.[23] A few weeks later, in early February, Winston sailed home and, in a less raucous atmosphere, entered Parliament where he solemnly swore his fealty to the new Sovereign, King Edward VII. He was one of the first Edwardians.

Winston's entry into the political sphere added an extra dimension to his relationship with the King, who had a penchant for politics and an influence on the political landscape that far outpaced that of his successors. Churchill, for his pains, infuriated, annoyed and pleased his Sovereign in unequal measure, the energetic parliamentarian proving himself to be a frequent thorn in the King's side. He started as he meant to go on, committing his first-ever speech as an MP, known as a maiden speech, to memory as he held a packed House of Commons in his thrall for close to an hour. Many MPs had come to watch the performance of the scion of the late Lord Randolph Churchill and came away impressed, if slightly nervous. Like his father, Winston seemed to display a loyalty to the Conservative Party that was wayward and off-hand. The son of Blenheim had no qualms about attacking his front bench and core Tory beliefs, vociferously supporting free trade while many of his colleagues voted for protectionism. The new member for Oldham also wanted less money spent on defence and more on social welfare programs. He quickly earned himself a reputation as a man who would not be cowed by authority or toe the party line. To some he was bold, self-confident and principled, while to his more senior colleagues he was brash, impudent and arrogant. In a vain attempt to put him in his place in 1904, the front bench stood up and walked out of the chamber when Winston began to speak.

As he engaged in the verbal pyrotechnics that would one day make him famous, his mother enjoyed the simple country pleasures that come with a stay at Balmoral Castle, the Highland home of the King and his family. In early February of 1902, Jennie was one of the guests for a weekend shooting party, and spent several hours walking through the castle grounds discussing the latest society news with the King. It was a testament to Jennie's charm, discretion and social awareness that she managed to remain a close personal friend not only to him, but also to his wife, Queen Alexandra, and to his preferred mistress, Alice Keppel, known as 'La Favorita'.

Shortly after her stay at Balmoral, the King wrote to inform Jennie that he had arranged her tickets to attend his coronation in August. She, along with her sister Leonie, Alice Keppel and other lady friends of the King, were seated in a gallery box above the chancel of Westminster Abbey, the area described forevermore as 'the King's loose box'.[24]

Another one of Winston's relatives, his cousin by marriage Consuelo, the 9th Duchess of Marlborough and heiress to the Vanderbilt fortune, was one of the four women holding up the canopy that shrouded Queen Alexandra as she was anointed. Consuelo watched the Queen's face as a drop of holy oil ran down her nose and later wrote that she felt a lump in her throat and 'realised I was more British than I knew'.[25] It was the only coronation during Winston Churchill's lifetime that he did not attend, though he was thrilled to be invited to Balmoral weeks after the majestic event. It was a signal honour so soon after the coronation, the King inviting only those he knew and liked to share his Highland retreat. Certainly, it was not routine for a newly elected MP, just twenty-seven years old, to find himself entertained by the King. Edward's affection for his mother and his avuncular regard for Winston, whom he could see in his better moments as almost a surrogate son, played a substantial part in a friendship noted by friends and enemies alike.

Winston was not one to let such a weekend go to waste. While there, he wrote to his mother to assure her that he was having a splendid time: 'Dearest Mamma, I have been v[er]y kindly treated here by the king, who has really gone out of his way to be nice to me. It has been most pleasant & easy going & today the stalking was excellent, tho I missed my stags.' Winston was keen to ensure that Jennie would communicate his gratitude to her friend: 'You will see the King on Weds when he comes to Invercauld. Mind you gush to him about my having written to you saying how much etc. etc. I had enjoyed myself here.'[26]

Winston realized that his friendship with the King would accelerate his political career by enabling him to rub shoulders with powerbrokers both in and out of Parliament. The King's hospitality may have been part of the reason why Winston, as a junior MP, felt confident in cutting out the usual parliamentary middlemen and taking his concerns straight to the top. For instance, as he locked horns with his own party over their policy of protectionist trade tariffs, known as Imperial Preference, Churchill wrote an impassioned, unsolicited letter to Prime Minister Arthur Balfour, outlining his reasons for preferring free trade. His unbending attitude, combined with a growing sense of outrage at the poverty that touched the lives of so many in an island empire brimming with wealth and plenty, caused him to pull away from the Tory party, declaring himself a Unionist Free Trader. It had become a central enough issue that Churchill was even willing to contemplate a realignment of his party loyalty. In a letter he wrote in October 1903, he confessed, 'I am an English Liberal. I hate the Tory party, their men, their words and their methods. I feel no sort of sympathy with them.'[27]

Though the Crown was supposed to remain aloof to matters of politics, Winston's growing disillusionment with the Tory party, and his adamant support of free trade, coincided with an increasing distance between him and the King. Winston spent the autumn of 1903, a year after his previous visit to Balmoral, on various hunting trips with friends in Scotland, though this year he waited in vain for an invitation from the King. He wrote to his mother in September, 'I have put my name down at Balmoral – but I fear I am still in disgrace.'[28]

Indeed, he was, and would remain so. Royal eyebrows were very firmly raised when, on 31 May 1904, Winston's separation from the Conservatives became official as he dramatically crossed the floor of the Commons to join the Liberal Party, conveniently seating himself next to his friend and rising Liberal star, David Lloyd George. His free trade policy was not only opposed by many in the Tory party but also, it seems, inside the royal house. When his mother stayed at Sandringham to celebrate the King's sixty-third birthday, in November 1904, she made a point of saying that the Sovereign had not discussed any of Winston's polemical speeches, although the subtext was clear that the King was not a fan: 'Here I am in a hotbed of protectionists,' she reported.[29]

Winston was trying the King's patience. In February 1905, speaking as a Liberal MP, he made a speech criticizing some members of the aristocratic military elite – 'those gorgeous & gilded functionaries with brass hats and ornamental duties who multiply so luxuriously on the plains of Aldershot & Salisbury.' The King was heard to comment, 'What good words for a recent subaltern of Hussars!'[30]

And yet, as much as Winston's opinions irritated the King, he gave the young politician endless leeway, launching a one-man campaign to correct his missteps, whether political or personal. At the end of October 1905, shortly before his thirty-first birthday, Winston wrote to his mother that he had received an invitation for a private dinner with the King: 'His Majesty,' he wrote with an almost legible smirk, 'has been graciously pleased to signify his desire to meet me at dinner on Tuesday night and his determination to bring home to me the error of my ways.'[31]

As there was nothing in the Sovereign's job description suggesting that he guide and develop junior politicians, it owes more to family links and his own affection towards Winston that he would take on, so consistently, the role of personal tutor. He handled his late friend's son with fatherly indulgence, meting out an equal measure of patience and discipline. Later that winter, when Winston fell ill with a curious infection that affected his throat, heart and tongue, the King wrote to him to express his sympathy and wishes for a speedy recovery.[32] By the new year, Winston was sufficiently recovered to take an active part in the general election called by the Conservative Prime Minister, Arthur Balfour. The Tories fell to a landslide defeat, with Winston, who stood as a Liberal for the Manchester North West constituency, winning his seat easily.

He had only been a member of the Liberal Party for a matter of months, but such was his popularity that he was offered and accepted a junior ministerial position as Under Secretary of State for the Colonies. The post ensured he was in the thick of parliamentary debate as the session would be dominated by the twin questions of whether to grant responsible government to the defeated Boer republic as well as end Chinese slave labour in South African mines.

The King and his eldest son, George, the Prince of Wales, welcomed Winston's parliamentary progress with a high degree of caution. The prince wrote to his father, 'Winston Churchill, I see, is Under Secretary for the Colonies, Lord Elgin [Winston's superior] will have to look after him!'[33] During this time the King and his family kept a safe distance from Churchill, the King seeing him as more of a cad in office than opposition. One episode involving Lord Milner, the former high commissioner of South Africa, particularly rankled. Winston, now speaking on behalf of the government, dismissed a censure motion concerning Milner in relation to the question of Chinese slave labour. He argued that Milner wasn't worth censuring, because he was nothing more than a 'burnt out figure from the past'.[34] The King was only one of a number of public figures who were incensed by Churchill's condescending, off-handed manner towards the established and well-regarded public servant. The King wrote to Winston's cousin, Lady Londonderry, in a critical manner: 'The conduct of a certain relation of yours is simply scandalous.'[35]

The King's view reflected attitudes inside the government department. Sir Francis Hopwood, an established civil servant who was then serving as permanent secretary to the Board of Trade, wrote a scathing letter to Colonial Secretary Lord Elgin complaining that Churchill was 'tiresome to deal with' and feared that, like his father, he would cause trouble in any position he was given. Hopwood, who had frequent private dealings with the King and other members of the royal family, seemed to have caught the mood inside Buckingham Palace. He wrote, 'The restless energy, uncontrollable desire for notoriety and the lack of moral perception make him an anxiety indeed.'[36]

Churchill was, though, never shy about going straight to the King to ask for his advice and guidance. In the preamble to his visit to Germany to watch, at the Kaiser's invitation, a series of military manoeuvres, he wrote to the King requesting advice about what to wear. On 11 August 1906, Winston received a response from his private secretary, Francis Knollys, who was on board the royal yacht *Victoria & Albert* at Cannes in the south of France. 'I have shown your letter to the King and he desires me to say that he thinks you will be quite right to wear your Yeomanry at the German manoeuvres.'[37]

Alongside this suggestion, the King made sure to convey a more serious message to Winston in advance of the trip. Tensions between Britain and Germany had already begun to escalate and, knowing Winston's lack of discretion, the King asked his Prime Minister to pass along a word of caution. Churchill wrote to Jennie to tell her that in an 'amiable' letter, Campbell-Bannerman had mentioned that the King had asked him 'to warn me not to be too frank with "his nephew" at the manoeuvres. I confess I will have to avoid any P's & W's, so as to appear entirely candid & yet say nothing either platitudinous or indiscreet.'[38] It was clear that Winston, who was worried about every detail of his appearance and conduct, was keen to meet the King's expectations on his maiden foreign trip.

He was equally keen to earn the King's approval for his performance in the House of Commons. Just after parliament broke for recess in mid-August, he wrote a long letter to the King, recalling all the challenges he had faced:

> I hope I may venture to say that the session that is now over has been full of difficulties to me ... I have had to speak more than any other minister except Mr Birrell [at the Board of Education] & to answer something like 500 questions, besides a great number of supplementary questions put & answered on the spur of the moment. I have had no previous experience in this kind of work ... If therefore I have from time to time turned phrases awkwardly, or not judged quite the right time or tone, I feel certain that Your Majesty will have put the most favourable construction upon my words & will have credited me throughout with loyal & grave intentions.[39]

Winston then went on to list his successes in his position as Colonial Under Secretary in the face of such difficulties.

Winston's unctuous flattery had the desired effect. He received a response from the King's private secretary, which included a line by the royal hand (given here in italics): 'His Majesty is glad to see that you are becoming a *reliable* Minister and above all a serious politician, *which can only be obtained by putting country before Party.*'[40] But Winston seemed not to notice the admonition hidden within the King's praise. A few days later, on 26 August 1906, he wrote to his brother Jack, 'I have had an active and gracious correspondence with the King, & I think have put everything on a much better footing in that quarter. This is secret.'[41]

Though Winston was treated with suspicion inside and outside Buckingham Palace, it was his firm intervention in a thorny issue of protocol the following year that was to transform the royal family and its public rituals forever.

CHAPTER THREE

Diamond in the Rough

THE SUN WAS setting over Premier Two mine outside Pretoria as manager Frederick Wells made his final rounds before closing up for the night of 26 January 1905. He was about eighteen feet beneath the surface when a glimmer of light caught his eye. Wells took out his pocketknife and carefully dug the shiny object out of the rock. What eventually came into his possession after a few minutes of careful scratching was perhaps the most valuable single object ever to touch a human hand – a diamond weighing over 3,000 carats and of near perfect quality. When he took it to the mine office, legend has it that his colleagues dismissed the find as a piece of glass and threw it out of the office window. He retrieved it and quietly had the rock examined. It was confirmed as a unique and priceless stone. The following week, the Cullinan Diamond, named after the mine owner Thomas Major Cullinan, was put on display at the Standard Bank in Johannesburg where thousands stood in line for the chance to see this marvel, the largest diamond in the world.[1]

It soon became apparent that ownership of such a gem was something of a curse as it was too dangerous to keep and, because it was priceless, it was more or less unsellable. The *Transvaal Leader* caught the mood, observing that the stone was 'too large for personal adornment and so precious as to make its ownership a matter of anxiety and even danger'. It was soon shipped off to secure offices in London, locked in a state-of-the-art safe and monitored by armed guards. The elaborate security precautions, however, were for a decoy stone, while, somewhat audaciously, the real diamond was sent by regular three-shilling parcel post and arrived safely.[2]

So, what, then, was to be done with this unique acquisition? The same newspaper proposed one possible outcome. 'It seems to us,' they wrote, 'that if an individual cannot buy it an Empire might and better still the people of an Empire themselves. There is in the British Empire one man whom all men reverence and love. We are happy in being ruled by King Edward VII, a type of all that is best in British manhood, a wise statesman, just and sympathetic.' For the King, they proposed a special price of £500,000, the equivalent of about £50 million today – 'A great sum,' they admitted, 'but surely not too great for the vast population of the Empire to raise.'[3] Amid the discussion surrounding the diamond's fate, Winston Churchill gradually inserted himself.

The diamond was held captive for two years by the delicate political climate then prevailing in South Africa, particularly the Transvaal province where much of the fighting in the Boer War had taken place. Dominating the debate was whether the Transvaal should be a self-governing province or ruled directly from London. It was an issue that vexed the King, prompting frequent communication with Winston, whose position of Under-Secretary of State for the Colonies brought him to the centre of the debate. The King and his advisers worried that, with the Boers in the majority and the British settlers in the minority, those of Dutch-German descent would win the election and form a pro-independence government, which could very well lead to another armed conflict with the British Crown. The King was assured by Churchill that, to the contrary, granting self-government would usher in an influx of British settlers who would eventually constitute the ethnic majority. Though the King remained sceptical, he gave Winston a cautious approval to go ahead with his plans. Winston delivered a magisterial speech in support of the Transvaal Constitution, which was passed by a healthy majority in the Commons.[4]

The first election held in the Transvaal rendered the very outcome the King had feared – namely, a Boer majority government, with General Louis Botha, who had led the Boers against the British in the war – indeed, the very man who had captured Winston Churchill in 1899 – elected as Prime Minister. The decorated veteran tried to placate the

King by privately proposing to buy the Cullinan diamond and present it to the Sovereign on his sixty-sixth birthday as a token of the Transvaal's continued allegiance to and admiration of the Crown. Unsurprisingly, it was to prove a contentious issue, especially among the British settlers, who felt that London was allowing them to be treated as second-class citizens in the South African colonies.

As all this unfolded, Winston was hard at work organizing the 1907 Colonial Conference, which brought together the political leaders of Britain's far-flung empire. Churchill was careful to keep the King apprised of his plans and the agenda, his courtesy earning a heartfelt letter from the Sovereign on 6 April which reflected on their familial links and Winston's talents:

> I was very glad to have the opportunity of having several communications with you on various interesting subjects – It is quite true that we have known your parents for many years (even before their marriage) & you & your Brother since your childhood. Knowing the great abilities which you possess, I am watching your political career with great interest. My one wish is, that the great qualities you possess may be turned to good account & that your services to the State may be appreciated.[5]

Before the Colonial Conference began, the King backed his belief by inviting the young politician to join his Privy Council, a small group of senior advisers who are summoned to guide the Sovereign. It is a signal honour to be invited into this close cadre, one that is withheld from all but the most important and senior of politicians. On 6 May, King Edward wrote to Jennie, 'I shall be very glad to receive Winston as a "P.C." He works very hard and is very ambitious.' It marked perhaps the high-water mark of Churchill's relationship with the King.[6]

At the same time the King made it clear that he viewed Botha's proposal to gift him the Cullinan diamond with 'great disfavour' and Winston was informed via the King's private secretary that the matter should not be pursued further.[7] Of course, Winston pursued it nonetheless, laying the flattery thick onto Botha during his time in London for the Colonial Conference, and even making an obsequious speech at the conference where he singled out Botha and the Transvaal for particular praise.[8] The former soldier returned to South Africa with an enlivened sense of loyalty and fondness for the British Empire, thanks in no small part to Churchill's skilful flattery. Shortly after he arrived in Pretoria, Botha put forward a motion to gift the diamond to the King, despite the fact that, politically, he had not prepared the ground. Though the motion was carried, there was a substantial minority– mainly, as King Edward had feared, made up of English settlers – who voted against the proposal.[9]

The King was on the horns of a dilemma. If he accepted the diamond, he risked further alienating the British minority. If he turned it down, it would effectively mean rejecting a unique olive branch from the Boers, Britain's former foes. He sought the advice of his ministers, but they were hesitant and vainly tried to shift responsibility back upon the King's shoulders. Prime Minister Campbell-Bannerman wrote to the King saying that although the government 'did not really want to shirk the responsibility', they could not help thinking 'that the King himself was so good in matters of this sort that they might safely leave it in his hands.'[10]

Only two men were willing and able to take the matter into their own hands. One was the High Commissioner of South Africa, Lord Selborne, and the other was the thirty-two-year-old Under-Secretary of State for the Colonies, the indefatigable Churchill. Winston asked Selborne's opinion on the matter, to which Selborne replied that he had always 'been in favour of gift of Diamond to His Majesty.' Churchill then forwarded that message on to the King's private secretary, with an added note of his own where he criticized his colleagues in Cabinet for their lack of imagination:

> Believe me it is a genuine & disinterested expression of loyalty
> & comes from the heart of this strange & formidable people.

The Cabinet takes a v[er]y unimaginative view wh[ich] in my opinion does not do full justice either to the significance or to the importance of the event. The feeling of loyalty to the King & of gratitude for the liberties which have been restored to them in His Majesty's name, are the strongest links between this country & the Transvaal.

I write this to you privately; but pray do not hesitate to show the letter to the King if you think that course would be proper.[11]

Just four months prior, Knollys had written to Winston expressing the King's disdain for the idea. Now conditions were more favourable for Winston to press the matter more forcefully. He had his thumb on the scales towards acceptance and was pressing down hard, helped by a further letter from Selborne. Based on this advice, the King, a stickler for constitutional proprieties, reversed his earlier position. 'I agree with this letter and after High Commissioner's telegram feel bound to agree with his advice.'[12] On the King's sixty-sixth birthday, the diamond was presented to him at a ceremony at Sandringham in the presence, among others, of the Queens of Norway and Spain, the Duke of Westminster and Revelstoke, and Alice Keppel, accompanied by her husband. Surprisingly, no one from the Churchill family was in attendance: Winston was, at the time, touring the East African colonies but the absence of Jennie, who was by now a regular at such events, is harder to explain.

This episode reflects, with remarkable accuracy, Winston Churchill's relationship to the King at the time. Although Churchill was, in no small part, personally responsible for the most valuable single object ever acquired by the British throne, he was not included in the festivities or offered an honour as were several other participants in this intricate drama.

As for the diamond, it was cut and polished, with the largest two fragments, Cullinan I and II, set in the Sovereign's Sceptre and Imperial State Crown, respectively. Both these stones are still in the regalia today and dazzle visitors to the Tower of London where the Crown Jewels are displayed. The remaining numbered diamonds were kept by Asscher as payment for their work in cutting the stone. Cullinan VI and VIII were later bought privately by King Edward VII as a gift for Queen Alexandra, and the others were acquired by the South African government and given to Queen Mary in 1910, in memory of the Inauguration of the Union. They were bequeathed to Queen Elizabeth II in 1953.

Churchill did not come away from this affair totally empty-handed. For his part in unravelling this delicate issue, the Transvaal government presented him with a model replica of the raw stone as thanks. Churchill took great pride in the gift and often brought out the diamond to show it off to his friends. At one luncheon, when the topic of the diamond came up, Churchill bid one of his attendants to fetch the replica to show his guests. After some delay the model rock was finally presented on a silver tray to one guest, Winston's cousin, Lilian Grenfell, who thought it was some kind of 'not-very-well-strained white jelly' being brought out for dessert. As Winston's private secretary Eddie Marsh recorded, 'She eyed it with distaste, and said: "No thank you!"' No account exists of Winston ever showing it off again.[13]

Certainly, the watching public concluded that the King had taken Winston Churchill under his wing and mischievously suggested that Winston had allowed this proximity to the monarch to inflate his ego. On 9 October, a poem appeared in the *Glasgow Evening Times*. It mocked the perceived closeness between the uppity junior statesman and the Sovereign. The poem, written in Churchill's voice, is a toast. 'The King and I – we two, and no one else!' it began.

How happy the conjunction of such shining stars!
Not King and Campbell Bannerman, I pray you note;

Not King and Elgin, I beg you to observe;
But King and Mr. Churchill – that is all.
How right and fitting, splendid and appropriate!

It continued to poke fun at Churchill's arrogance and superior attitude, comical in such a young and, as yet, unaccomplished politician:

We two – the King and I – are all that count.
… we two stand out pre-eminent,
In isolation splendid, unapproachable.

Finally, the toast wraps up in a joyful request that the speaker's wine glass is refilled so that he may heartily toast 'The King and Churchill – Churchill and the King!'[14]

Poetic caricatures aside, there was no doubt in the King's mind that Churchill was earmarked for great things. As a man who cleaved to the status quo and shuddered at the thought of radical change, Edward VII felt a mixture of admiration and concern at the rapid progress up the greasy pole made by this scion of Blenheim. However, the King, if he was anything, was a stickler for proper constitutional form. When Asquith, who had taken over as Prime Minister following the death of Campbell-Bannerman, suggested Churchill for a Cabinet position, the King, in spite of his affection for Winston, objected to a promotion that had Winston, effectively a deputy minister, leapfrogging over more senior candidates. If Asquith wanted Churchill in the Cabinet, the King required that he first be given a real title to justify the seat. Although Asquith argued for Churchill, the King would not be persuaded. 'The King agreed and was quite warm in his praise of Winston, but thought he must wait till some real Cabinet Office fell vacant.'[15]

In early April, Asquith went to Biarritz, where the King was staying, to formally kiss the royal hand. He came prepared with a list of names for his Cabinet appointments, including Churchill who was nominated for the post of President of the Board of Trade. This time the King approved as it was a senior Cabinet post in its own right.

In those days, new Cabinet ministers had to win a by-election for their existing seat, which in Winston's case was Manchester North West. Much to the satisfied amusement of the Prince of Wales and other smirking inhabitants of Buckingham Palace, Churchill lost the seat. George, the Prince of Wales, noted in his diary, 'We were all very excited when we heard that Winston Churchill has been beaten.'[16] It was a sign that not everyone inside the palace gates shared the King's qualified admiration for the thrusting politician. Unfortunately for them, he soon found a safe seat in the Scottish city of Dundee, where he was elected with a sizeable majority. As a result, he became, at thirty-three years old, the youngest Member of Parliament since 1866.

Taken in sum, 1908 was a was a happy season for Winston. This was the same period that he met, courted and married Clementine Hozier. Their first real encounter was at a dinner party in March. Fate played its part. Clementine had only been invited at the very last minute, as a sudden cancellation had left the party with thirteen guests. The hostess, as superstitious as the King himself, refused to go to table with such an unlucky number. In desperation she called Clementine, who, tired from a long day of teaching, reluctantly accepted. She found herself seated next to Winston and thus began a six-month whirlwind courtship that led to an engagement, quickly followed by a Society wedding, with 1300 guests.[17]

King Edward VII was warm in his praise of Winston's choice. Almost as soon as Churchill had proposed in the romantic Temple of Diana in the matchless grounds of Blenheim Palace, Churchill sent an announcement to his Sovereign, who was then out of the country. The King replied by telegram: 'Many thanks for announcement [sic] to me your engagement to Miss Hozier & I offer you my best wishes for your happiness. Edward R.'[18] In the coming years, even when Churchill's behaviour was at its most infuriating, the King would always compliment Clementine, saying that 'he liked Mrs Churchill immensely'.[19] When Winston and Clementine married on 12 September, the King sent Winston a wedding gift of a gold-headed malacca cane, engraved with the Marlborough coat of arms. Thirty years later, the same cane style would remain an essential component of Winston's trademark look.[20]

Despite these happy domestic tidings, tension was growing between Churchill and the royal family, both personally and politically. Just before Asquith became Prime Minister, Winston was invited to Windsor to dine with George, the Prince of Wales. In the course of their chat about who would succeed Campbell-Bannerman, George got carried away. He unwisely voiced his opinion that, although he trusted Asquith, he was conscious of the fact that he was 'not quite a gentleman'. In this opinion, he felt he was backed up by his father, who had previously expressed his view that Asquith was 'deplorably common and very vulgar'. At the best of times, it was foolhardy and constitutionally inappropriate for a member of the royal family to discuss a Minister of the Crown in this manner, but it was particularly unwise in the company of Winston, who was after all a fellow Cabinet member. He promptly shared the prince's comments with Asquith himself, thus humiliating the Prince of Wales and stoking hostility between Prime Minister and Sovereign. Several years later, George, now King, reflected on the incident: 'I ought not to have said it, and it was a damned stupid thing to say; but Winston repeated it to Asquith, which was a monstrous thing to do, and made great mischief.'[21]

Also during the fateful year of 1908, Winston joined David Lloyd George, then Chancellor of the Exchequer, on the radical wing of the Liberal Party. The two allies were dubbed the 'Terrible Twins' by their Tory enemies. Friendlier folk saw them as a dynamic duo who successfully marshalled social reforms through Parliament: Labour Exchanges, national unemployment insurance and old-age pensions all came into law thanks to their energies.

At a time when the country was increasingly gripped by war fever over

Germany's military expenditure, Lloyd George and Churchill argued for greater spending on social welfare rather than matching Germany's ship-building program by commissioning more dreadnought battleships, which were then seen as a measure of national virility, much like nuclear weapons today. In this position, they alienated the King and Prime Minister, who were agreed that the nation had no choice but to match Germany's military spending.

It was, though, the 1909 People's Budget, introduced by Lloyd George as Chancellor of the Exchequer, which caused bitter controversy. The budget sought to introduce new taxes, particularly a land tax, on the wealthy in order to establish and fund social welfare programs and pay for increased defence spending. The Liberal government felt that they had been forced down this road by the behaviour of legislators in the House of Lords. Even though they had won the 1906 election with an overwhelming majority, every cherished piece of legislation approved in the Commons, such as education reform, had been eviscerated once sent to the largely Conservative second House of Parliament. A showdown was past due. This was, in Liberal eyes, peers against the people, a slogan that was used *ad nauseam* by Lloyd George, Asquith and Churchill as they campaigned for the radical budget, Winston becoming president of the Budget League. In a dramatic speech made in Edinburgh, he warned that if the Lords continued to reject the budget, the government would have no option but to create hundreds of new Liberal peers to vote through the stalled legislation. His bold claim earned a rebuke from both his Liberal Prime Minister and his nominally apolitical King. 'That way revolution lies,' warned Asquith. However, Churchill would soon be proven correct as mainstream Liberals, including Asquith himself, began to see the truth of Winston's prognosis.

Not so in Buckingham Palace, where the constitutional issues raised by Churchill stirred a hornet's nest of indignation. Lord Esher, a trusted adviser to Edward VII and later to George V, wrote an alarming report of the situation to the King's private secretary, Lord Knollys. His report stated that the Cabinet was currently considering 'whether, instead of attempting to alter by Statute the relations between the two Houses of Parliament, they shall advise the King to place permanently in the hands of the Prime Minister of the day H.M.'s prerogative to create Peers.' This, Esher argued, would amount to 'an abdication by the Sovereign of his prerogative not only on his own behalf but on that of his successors.' 'I cannot conceive a more monstrous proposal,' he concluded. Knollys agreed with Esher's assessment and took it one step further, arguing that King Edward VII should rather abdicate altogether than consent to such a severe restriction of the most significant prerogative that remained to the British Sovereign.[22] Following Winston's Edinburgh speech, Knollys wrote a tart note to the Prime Minister expressing royal disfavour. 'The King desires me to say,' he began, his irritation clearer with every stroke of his pen, 'it is painful to him to be continually obliged to complain of certain of your colleagues.'[23]

Winston remained firmly unchastened. His next speech, given in Leicester on 4 September, was even more inflammatory. 'The wealthy, so far from being self-reliant, are dependent on the constant attention and waiting of scores and sometimes even hundreds of persons who are employed in ministering to their wants,' was one of his more pungent observations.[24] This tirade, coming from a man who travelled with his own host of attendants, never cooked his own meals, never took a bus in his life and was, according to his sister-in-law Lady Gwendeline Bertie, at his happiest when a servant was pulling up his socks, left him open to the charge of hypocrisy.[25] For Winston to betray his party was one thing, but to betray his class, who numbered in their ranks many of his relatives, was quite another. Little wonder there were those in the shires who wanted to see him torn limb from limb by a pack of hunting hounds.[26]

In the same speech, Churchill infuriated the King when he suggested that the former Prime Minister Arthur Balfour, now Leader of the Opposition, had used his position to elevate newspaper proprietors into barons and so secured undue praise from their newspapers. This was taken as an insult to the King as it was on the monarch's authority, not the Prime Minister's, that the distribution of honours was decided. Lord Knollys wrote to the editor of *The Times* stating, 'In reply to your letter of yesterday's date I beg to inform you that, notwithstanding Mr. Winston Churchill's statement, the creation of peers remains a Royal prerogative.'[27]

Once again, Winston would not be cowed, observing to his wife that it was 'the most extraordinary thing': 'He & the King must really have gone mad. The Royal prerogative is always exercised on the advice of Ministers, & Ministers & not the Crown are responsible; & criticism of all debateable acts of policy should be directed to Ministers – not to the Crown. This looks to me like a rather remarkable Royal intervention, & shows the bitterness wh[ich] is felt in those circles. I shall take no notice of it. It will defeat itself.'[28]

The King also complained that Winston's speech at Leicester was 'full of false statements of Socialism in its most insidious form and of virulent abuse against one particular class,' and that it could 'only have the effect of stirring up "class" against "class".' He concluded with bitterness, 'It is hardly necessary, perhaps, to allude to its gross vulgarity.'[29] The King further expressed his derision when he wrote to his son and heir, George, that Churchill's 'initials are so well-named!' (W.C. being the initials for water closet or toilet.)

Vulgarity aside, the threat to create hundreds of peers if the House of Lords voted against the budget greatly disturbed the King, who firmly believed in the pursuit of consensus. In his view, the legitimacy of the House of Lords being so publicly undermined posed an existential threat, not only to the aristocracy, who constituted the venerable institution, but to the monarchy itself. In this opinion, though, he was swimming against the tide of ideas; it had barely been two decades since the 1885 publication of Karl Marx's second volume of *Das Kapital,* which contained theories of class warfare that would ultimately lead to the destruction of many European monarchies.

And yet, despite all of these squabbles, the King still had a soft spot for young Churchill. Less than two weeks after this latest exchange, on

26 September, King Edward spoke kindly, if back-handedly, of Winston, saying that he 'was even younger in spirit than he was in years' and that, in the course of his adult development, there was still a chance that he would 'change very much'.[30] What he most desired was that Churchill would mature into a less bellicose and impudent politician. He saw potential in the young man and was optimistic about his future – his present, however, was another story.

Churchill's controversial prediction turned out to be accurate. As he had forecast, the House of Lords rejected the budget after it had been approved by the House of Commons. An election was duly called. Asquith kicked it off in January 1910 with the full-throated radical call: Peers versus the People. The election became, by proxy, a referendum on the House of Lords and, by extension, the entire British aristocracy.

The campaign season gave Churchill an opportunity to make impassioned speeches on subjects far beyond his Cabinet brief, including women's suffrage, British foreign policy and the growing possibility of war in Europe. It was not long before he irritated the King once again, this time with his views on British foreign strategy. The monarch wrote to Conservative Charles Hardinge: 'It is a mercy that we have you as Under-Secretary at the Foreign Office, and that Lloyd George and Winston Churchill do not occupy that position! I cannot conceive how the Prime Minister allows them ever to make speeches on Foreign Affairs, concerning which they know nothing.'[31]

The constitutional wrangling between the two Houses of Parliament failed to ignite much enthusiasm in the wider world outside Westminster. The Liberals, who had been unpopular leading up to the election, lost their hefty majority and were reduced to relying on support from the fledgling Labour Party and the Irish nationalists to form a majority. Though the Liberals faded, Churchill's own star was firmly in the ascendant. In February 1910, Asquith promoted him to one of the great offices of state as the new Home Secretary. His new position, which brought him into regular contact with the King, reflected the up-and-down nature of this long-standing relationship. So, the King would have had good reason to be alarmed when he discovered that Winston, after quietly studying the constitutional case for an unelected upper chamber, sent a memorandum to his Cabinet colleagues arguing for the 'total abolition' of the House of Lords.[32]

Churchill's memorandum laid out a formulation of a totally new system of bicameral government, wherein the house which had formerly been the Lords would be democratized, and the hereditary principle entirely removed.[33] As the King sat at the apex of this ancient hierarchical structure, such a proposal threatened the future of the monarchy itself. It was inevitable that Churchill's recommendation was perceived as a direct threat to the King's claim to power.

At the same time, one of Churchill's duties as Home Secretary was to summarize the day's events inside Parliament in a regular missive to the King. Not knowing the correct form, he sensibly asked to see reports written by previous Home Secretaries. But the journalist in him adopted an entirely original tone, one that was at once intimate, jovial, gossipy and judgmental. The King clearly enjoyed these reports, as Lord Knollys encouraged Winston to include in them what amounted to the latest party gossip. The King 'does not wish to add to your labours,' Knollys wrote, but 'anything you can say in your letters about the state of the Party feeling & the general effect speeches have made, will always be interesting & therefore welcome.'[34]

Thus, there was always a thread of communication that relaxed the various tensions that arose in other arenas. A major blow to the King was the Veto Bill, which was placed before Parliament in March 1910. Amid the ongoing budget crisis, the Bill proposed to prevent the House of Lords from rejecting any monetary legislation that had been passed by the Commons. The King, who was on a rest cure in Biarritz, was furious with Winston and others for their support of the Bill, which he again viewed as an existential threat to the monarch's powers and prerogatives. Such was his pique that he ordered Knollys to prevent Churchill, Asquith and Lloyd George from following the ministerial custom of meeting the royal train when it arrived at Victoria Station, near Buckingham Palace, when the King returned to London in April. The rebellious ministers disregarded the request and, when the King's train pulled in at 5:45 in the morning, all three of them were on the platform, awaiting the grumpy Sovereign's arrival.[35]

Finally, on 28 April 1910, the House of Lords bowed to the mounting pressure and passed the Liberal budget. While the fight was lost, they knew that their reckoning was not yet over, as the Liberals had no intention of abandoning their social reform plans included in the Parliament Bill.

Those plans, however, had to take a backseat after the unexpected death of King Edward VII on 6 May 1910. As soon as she heard the news, Jennie sent Queen Alexandra her most heartfelt condolences, lamenting the 'terrible calamity which has befallen not only the Royal Family but the whole nation. Personally, I can never forget that for thirty five years the King showed me and mine the greatest kindness and I look back on many pleasant memories. He was a great King and a loveable man.'[36]

Throughout his reign, King Edward VII had been troubled by Winston's radical politics and his opportunist behaviour. At the same time, he admired his drive, his ideas, and his charm. It was clear to all that Winston was born for the great game of politics, and the King respected him for that. Not so others inside Buckingham Palace, who saw him as the 'Blenheim rat' who would step on anyone, use any underhand tactic, to climb the political greasy pole. They had their revenge when the King passed. As Home Secretary, Churchill had various ceremonial duties to perform and he was summoned to Buckingham Palace by courtiers upon the demise of the Crown, a legal term that denotes the transfer of the crown from the Sovereign to his or her heir. Rather than admit him into the royal apartments, however, the palace courtiers kept him waiting downstairs as the King breathed his last.[37]

Several days later, during the King's lying-in-state in Westminster Abbey, a similar scene played out. At half-past ten at night, Winston led his family – including his cousin, the Duke of Marlborough, and his mother Jennie – in a procession of four motorcars onto the Abbey grounds. He was refused entrance at the door and a heated argument with the Keeper of Westminster Hall ensued. The Home Secretary shouted at the Keeper, an official called Schomberg McDonnell, that if anyone had a right to pay his respects, it was him. Eventually, Winston had to accept defeat, and he departed with his entourage. The Keeper, who recorded the event in his diary, observed that it was 'an amazing instance of vulgarity and indecency, of which I should not have thought that even Churchill was capable.'[38]

McDonnell's antagonism towards a senior politician reflected the hostility Winston now faced from the royal family and their court. With the moderating influence of the late King now gone, his successors and allies made no secret of the fact that, in their eyes, the rapid death of the King was due to the unnecessary stress caused by the political upheavals engineered by Churchill, Lloyd George and Asquith. As far as they were concerned, his general ill health, constant cigar smoking, poor diet and louche lifestyle had nothing to do with the rapid decline of a man paunchy enough to earn the moniker Tum-Tum. When Queen Alexandra learned that her husband was dead, she turned to accusation in the extremity of her grief. She made no effort to conceal her fury: 'They have killed him!' she wailed. 'They have killed him!'[39]

CHAPTER FOUR

The King and his 'Concubine'

O N 9 MAY 1910, the accession of King George V was proclaimed from the balcony of St James Palace, where Winston Churchill stood among the uniformed Privy Counsellors in Friary Court below, looking up at the fresh-faced Sovereign he would serve for the next quarter of a century.[1]

It would be difficult to exaggerate the differences between the new monarch and his predecessor. Where Edward had been almost unfailingly warm and gregarious, prone to excess and indulgence, George was stern and serious, a remote disciplinarian to his five sons. He followed a strict daily routine. After he rose at eight, he went for a ride in Hyde Park before a plain breakfast with Queen Mary. Then he would retire to his study to deal with affairs of state, including the interminable squadrons of red boxes containing official papers to sign and review. After lunch, he held meetings with his ministers before visiting his mother, Queen Alexandra. On most afternoons, he walked about 3.5 miles around the gardens of Buckingham Palace before sitting down for a few quiet minutes with his fabled stamp collection. His regimented lifestyle of early to bed, early to rise meant that he hosted few dinner parties, soirees, dances, or shooting retreats. As a result, the well of gossip and general political shop talk was shallow indeed. His admirers thought of him as upright and dutiful, while his detractors, who included Churchill for a time, mocked him as a dullard.[2]

It is hardly surprising that a man with such self-restraint and temperance would be in constant tension with a man like Winston Churchill, who wore his indulgence like a fine fur. While the late King had watched

Winston develop from an indifferent student and foolhardy army officer to a dynamic politician, his son, only eight years older than Churchill, had inherited none of his countervailing brotherly affections. The new King found him untrustworthy, undisciplined and utterly self-interested. In his eyes, Churchill's behaviour during the constitutional crisis that was prompted by the 1909 budget and the subsequent Veto Bill had driven his father into an early grave.

If Churchill sensed the King's hostility he did not show it. In his eyes, he owed fealty to the monarch and was prepared to strain every sinew to ensure the stability and continuity of the Crown. It would not be long before Churchill was presented with an opportunity to do just that.

As with the Cullinan diamond affair, Churchill's decisive behaviour resolved a weighty dilemma for the King and, in so doing, maintained the righteous and honourable image of the monarchy in the public eye. Unfortunately for King George V, his dilemma was a far more sordid and personal one. For years, it had been rumoured that in 1891, when Prince George was Duke of York and a midshipman with the Mediterranean fleet in Malta, he had secretly married the daughter of an admiral. Before the 1892 death of his elder brother, the Duke of Clarence, George was not the presumptive heir, so he lived a life of relative privacy and may have felt that he was at liberty to choose his wife from outside of strictly royal ranks. But when his brother's death brought George into the line of succession, his marriage prospects became a matter of public debate – the daughter of a mere naval captain would not be eligible as a future Queen of England. So, the rumour went, Queen Victoria and Bertie, then Prince of Wales, convinced him to abandon his common wife in order to marry someone with more strategic advantage. As a result, George inherited not only his elder brother's position in the line of succession, but also his fiancée, Princess Mary of Teck. If it truly happened, this previous marriage would make his present marriage to Princess Mary of Teck, now Queen Mary, bigamous and therefore invalid, and it would likewise make his children, including two future sovereigns, illegitimate.

The story first appeared in the *Star* newspaper in 1893, and then socialist MP Keir Hardy mentioned the canard in the House of Commons a year later. Prince George, as he then was, and Mary – then his fiancée – initially laughed off what they considered to be an absurd and preposterous story, refusing to dignify it with any formal denial. 'I say, May,' Prince George told his betrothed, 'we can't get married after all. I hear I have got a wife and three children.'[3] When George acceded to the throne in 1910, he could no longer afford to treat the rumour with such flippancy, and the King's private secretary, Sir Arthur Bigge, issued an official denial. He ended his letter to *Reynolds's Newspaper* with a statement of the obvious: 'Moreover nothing in His Majesty's life could give the slightest ground for the conception of such a cruel and wicked lie.'[4]

However, radical republicans saw their opportunity to make mischief and strip some of the dignity away from the thick veneer of monarchy by repeating and embellishing the original story. Belgian-born journalist Edward Mylius penned a vitriolic article about the immorality of the monarchy for a revolutionary Paris-based magazine called the *Liberator*, which he published and distributed in November 1910. He picked a perfect time, as the pamphlet was sent out shortly before the general election, when antiestablishment sentiment over the Lords veto was at its height. The article, replete with contempt and derision for the King, drew attention to 'the spectacle of the immorality of monarchy in all its sickening, beastly monstrosity' and described the King's marriage as a 'sham and shameful', directly accusing the King of having 'committed the crime of bigamy ... with the aid and complicity of the prelates of the Anglican Church.' Mylius and his colleagues lit the blue touch paper by circulating the incendiary pamphlet to every member of the House of Commons and senior Anglican clerics.[5] Then they sat back to watch the fireworks.

BRITAIN SHAKEN WITH FEAR OF KINGLY EXPOSE

Monarchy Dare Not Let Publisher of Alleged Seditious Article Appear at a Trial.

GEORGE V URGES SECRECY

Real Story of Ruler's Marriage Might Cause Great Upheaval Is Apparent Belief of King.

The *San Francisco Examiner* made merry with reports of a libellous story accusing King George V of bigamy.

The explosion was not long in coming. Inside Buckingham Palace, courtiers wrestled with a dilemma that would be familiar to royal officials today. Ought they take action against the author and give him and his magazine the oxygen of worldwide publicity? Or should they ignore it and hope the story would be suffocated and die?

Courtiers and lawyers who argued for prosecution felt it was a golden opportunity to squash the damaging rumour once and for all by proving that it was a preposterous lie. Those against contended that the King might be called as a witness and that, if the whole article were read out in court, the monarchy would be brought into even more damaging ridicule. Worse, should Mylius be acquitted on account of a technicality, it would merely endorse the veracity of the rumour in the eyes of casual observers. Both the Attorney-General Sir Rufus Isaacs and Solicitor-General Sir John Simon hesitated with regard to prosecution.

Enter Home Secretary Winston Churchill. Even though this was primarily a Palace matter, Winston felt sufficiently alarmed at the prospect of the new King and Queen's reputation being maliciously traduced that he demanded action. He sent Prime Minister Asquith a long memorandum outlining with painstaking clarity the necessity of taking decisive action with a formal prosecution. In a covering letter he said he was 'strongly of the opinion that action should be taken & the King's good name cleared from such cruel & widely circulated aspersions'.[6] He wrote to King George on 18 December, arguing that despite the potential risks, it was crucial that they move forward with arrest and prosecution: 'The libel is only an obscure undercurrent circulating among the credulous and base,' he wrote. 'Still it is sufficiently widespread to be a source of vexation to Your Majesty.'[7] As Winston's son and biographer Randolph later wrote, Churchill saw in the fray 'an opportunity of cementing his relationship with the new King by performing signal services in what was largely a personal matter.'[8] Churchill's bold confidence in writing to the King and setting out the case for prosecution was enough to sway the Sovereign's sentiment. The King decided to follow the advice of his Home Secretary.

There was obvious irony in Churchill's involvement. For the past several months, his anti-aristocratic campaign tactics had been more or less aligned with Mylius' intention to undermine the monarchy, though nothing was further from his mind. Just a few weeks before the offending *Liberator* issue was distributed, Churchill himself published a campaign manifesto in which he claimed that 'the Tory Party regard themselves as the ruling caste, exercising by right a Divine superior authority over the whole nation'.[9] He later wrote to Asquith telling him that the Liberal government, back in power after a slim victory, should make it clear that they would not hesitate to create 500 new peers if necessary. Asquith went even further, warning the novice King that if he refused to create new peers to overturn the Tory majority he would 'immediately resign and at the next election should make the cry: "The King and the Peers against the people".'[10] King George complained that Asquith was putting a pistol to his head, but reluctantly agreed.

Although Churchill and Asquith were parliamentary allies, Churchill was enough of a monarchist to have shrunk back from threatening his Sovereign in the manner of the Prime Minister. As an army officer he had drunk too many toasts pledging allegiance to his monarch, be it Queen Victoria or Edward VII, to ever consider holding the institution to ransom. While Churchill robustly and sometimes cavalierly treated members of the royal family with undue familiarity, he nevertheless viewed the monarchy itself as a mystical entity that represented the spiritual heart of the nation. He had travelled to enough countries to see that the British system of constitutional monarchy was infinitely preferable to a regal despotism or dictatorship. His reverence for the monarchy helps explain why, even during the most radical period of his political career, he was so animated and decisive regarding the Mylius affair. Even as he raged against the aristocracy and its 'gilded functionaries', mocking the view that those born into power innately deserved to wield it, he was no less willing to stick his neck out to protect his Sovereign from defamation, using all of the powers available to him to ensure a conviction.

While Mylius waited in jail for his day in court, Winston ordered that his correspondence to fellow revolutionary Edward James be intercepted and forwarded on to Buckingham Palace. On New Year's Eve, the King's assistant private secretary, Arthur Bigge, wrote to Winston: 'The King is much obliged to you for keeping him *au courant* as to the progress of the *Liberator* affair – all you tell His Majesty confirms him in the opinion that the absolutely right thing has been done to go for these scoundrels.'[11]

When Mylius decided to represent himself in court, Bigge wrote to Churchill emphasising that the journalist should have no excuse for complaining that he did not have a fair trial. Winston agreed, knowing that the trial would attract worldwide interest: the proceedings must be seen as both unimpeachable and yet, quietly weighted, unambiguously, in favour of the Crown. To this end, he wrote to Lord Northcliffe, owner of the *Daily Mail* and the *Daily Mirror*, to ask him for help in shaping the press narrative of this 'most important' trial: 'The reception of the event by the Press will count for a good deal in this respect. I thought you would like to be informed so as to give any necessary instructions.'[12] In shaping the media's narrative, Churchill was functioning less as a traditional Home Secretary and more as a public relations official of Buckingham Palace.

The trial took place on 1 February 1911 in the court of the King's Bench, with eager spectators, including the famed fiction writer H. Rider Haggard, rapidly filling the gallery. Even Churchill, who decided to attend the proceedings, struggled for a seat. In the packed court room, the least imposing figure was Mylius himself. As the *Manchester Guardian* reporter described:

> You had to peer about in the grey, sad light to find him – a woebegone little person, dwarfed between two monumental warders, sitting at a table just below the jurymen … His face was ashen, as well it might be – a snub-nosed and undistinguished face; and as the case went on the wan sulkiness of its expression seemed to deepen until at last when the time came for him to make his speech it was only human to feel a twinge of pity.[13]

As had been feared by courtiers, Mylius did attempt to call King George as a witness, but the tactic was quickly and robustly deflected by the judge, who ruled that there was no precedent for the King, the fount of all justice, being obliged to testify on oath. But that was not the most threatening bullet dodged by the Crown. What Mylius did not know, and what any solicitor might have told him if he had hired legal counsel, was that in a case of criminal libel, he could have claimed that the rumour was already in public circulation, and that he was merely doing his duty as a journalist in reporting on those claims. Luckily for the King, for Churchill, and for the judge – who had every intention of ruling in the Crown's favour – Mylius failed to present this defence.

In any case the jury would have been unsympathetic to Mylius' case after hearing from the key witness for prosecution, Admiral Michael Culme-Seymour, the father of the woman King George was alleged to have married. He told the court that the so-called marriage between the then-prince and his daughter, who had died in 1895, would have been impossible, because the two had never even spoken to one another. With this compelling evidence, the jury took little time to find Mylius guilty, the judge sentencing him to the maximum of one year in jail. There were some stirrings of dissatisfaction about the way the case had unfolded, with the *Manchester Guardian* describing the widespread feeling that Mylius 'seemed to have crawled out of remote obscurity to be resolutely stamped upon, he and his libels, by the whole weight of law and authority, and then spurned back to the remoter obscurity of prison'.[14]

Though the royal family had initially been buoyed by Churchill's utter confidence in the verdict, it still came as a relief to quash the rumour for good. King George wrote in his diary: 'The whole story is a damnable lie and has been in existence now for over twenty years. I trust that this will settle it once and for all.' Within hours of the verdict, he wrote to Churchill in the warmest terms: 'I desire to express my most grateful thanks to you for your valuable assistance in your position as Home Secretary, in carrying out my wishes to prove to the world at large the baseness of this cruel & abominable libel.'[15] It was a note for Winston to cherish as the words 'thank you' did not trip readily off the royal tongue – or pen.

Though the King praised Churchill for his role in the Mylius affair, it does not seem that he considered offering him a personal honour in appreciation of his services, whereas two of the other chief participants in this aggravating affair, Isaac and Simon, were each appointed to the Royal Victorian Order, an award founded by the King's grandmother to reward personal services to the royal family.

In the end, Winston's advice, as with the Cullinan diamond issue eight years previously, had proved reliable, and his standing with the royal family correspondingly improved. To a large degree his proximity to the royal house was woven into his job description. As Home Secretary he enjoyed, on 16 May 1911, the ceremonial responsibility of carrying the texts of the speeches, one made by the King, the other by Lord Esher, at the unveiling of the long-anticipated monument to Queen Victoria, the structure at the end of the Mall now known colloquially as 'the wedding cake'. Of course, there were, too, the daily reports Churchill sent to the King in which he outlined the business of Parliament.

Like his father, King George mostly found these entertaining. For instance, when a heated debate over women's suffrage took place in the House of Commons on 12 July 1910, Churchill described it in colourful terms. The next day he received a response from Knollys: 'My dear Churchill, The King desires me to thank you for your House of Commons letter of yesterday & to say that your account of the debate amused him very much.'[16] Two weeks later, Knollys sent a similar message: 'H. M. directs me to take advantage of the opportunity to express his best thanks to you for the many interesting letters which you have written to him on the proceedings of the House of Commons during the session.'[17] In these early days, Churchill had reason to feel confident and competent in these communiqués.

With one sentence it all went wrong. Shortly after the Mylius trial, the King complained about the tone of one of Churchill's parliamentary reports. Until this point Churchill had received nothing but an occasional line of thanks or praise for these letters. As time passed, he grew increasingly comfortable weaving his own opinions into his accounts of parliamentary proceedings. But when he described the debate in the House over the provision of government support to the unemployed – referred to as 'wastrels' – Winston wrote to the King that it must not 'be forgotten that there are idlers and wastrels at both ends of the social scale'. This was a casual remark too far for the prudish Sovereign, who instructed Knollys to send a letter to the Prime Minister's private secretary, Vaughan Nash, expressing his dissatisfaction with the tone and sentiments of Winston's report. Asquith then showed Knollys' note to Churchill who was – as his son recalled decades later – 'much taken aback, mortified, indeed affronted at this rebuke'.[18]

On the face of the matter, nothing dramatic had happened. The King had been displeased with his minister's communication and had issued a formal complaint through the constitutionally appropriate channel. For Churchill, though, this was a deep personal insult, and it wounded him deeply. From childhood he had been used to enjoying familiarity and frankness with members of the royal family. He felt that if the King had voiced his complaint directly to him, that would have been the end of the matter. It was the icy formality of the King's complaint that stung, especially after his mature performance during the Mylius affair.

Winston expressed his pique in a series of letters to Knollys in which he complained that, as Home Secretary, his plate was already overflowing, so that these parliamentary reports were composed at the end of long, stressful days. If the King was unhappy about his way of writing, he suggested, then perhaps another, more junior minister could be nominated to take over the duty. His basic complaint, though, was the route the King took to express his disapproval. 'I was surprised and grieved to receive through the PM a formal notification of the King's displeasure,' he wrote to Knollys. He suggested that it would have been more appropriate that, if he had made a misstep in his letter, 'some friendly suggestion or guidance might be conveyed to him from some person like yourself near to the King. The slightest indication of HM wishes and feelings w[oul]d always be studied by me with the most prompt and earnest attention. But I felt and feel that the serious and exceptional step of a formal signif[icatio]n to the Home Sec through the PM of the King's displeasure was utterly undeserved on this occasion, and bore no proportion to any error unconsciously committed. It was this that led me to express the pain I felt.'[19]

Knollys and the King thought it prudent to try and put the matter to bed. 'My dear Churchill,' Knollys responded on the next day, 'I have shown your letter to the King, and he desires me to thank you for continuing your "House of Commons letters" which are always very interesting.' After sending this perfunctory reply, Knollys again wrote to Nash, 'I enclose you Churchill's reply. He means it to be conciliatory I imagine, but he is rather like 'A Bull in a China Shop' … he is quite wrong in what he intimates would have been the right way of finding fault with him.' There was little left for Churchill to do but to compose his nightly reports in a more neutral, measured tone.[20]

It was but a bump in the road, as there remained many perks when it came to Churchill's proximity, political and personal, to the King. As the nation prepared for the King's coronation on 22 June, there was concern in the Churchill household that Clementine, who was expecting their first child in May, would be unable to attend the ceremony. Winston asked Knollys if any special arrangements could be made to ease Clementine's journey. On 29 April, Knollys told him, 'I spoke to the King today about his giving Mrs Churchill a ticket for his Box in Westminster Abbey on the occasion of the Coronation. He said he should have much pleasure in giving her one, and you may like to know.' He concluded that the King had been 'very nice about it'.[21] The King arranged for a royal brougham to collect Clementine from their London home and convey her to and from Westminster Abbey. Jennie, hearing that her daughter-in-law had been provided with a box seat, at once asked to take up the newly vacant place next to Winston.[22]

This relatively minor gesture was somewhat of an olive branch following the snappy back-and-forth over the Home Secretary's faux pas in his nightly letter to the King. Indeed of all the government ministers, it was Churchill who took the leading role at the July 1911 investiture of the seventeen-year-old Prince David, Prince of Wales, at Caernarfon castle in northwest Wales. Though the ceremony itself was a ruse by the Chancellor of the Exchequer Lloyd George, a Welshman himself, to boost his own popularity in his native country, he encouraged Churchill to perform the front-of-house duties while he himself remained, for the most part, in the background.

On an exceptionally hot day Churchill, wearing the heavy dress of a Privy Counsellor, proclaimed the Prince's Letters Patent, or titles and style, from the castle battlements. If Churchill was hot, the Prince of Wales was most uncomfortable, wearing what he called a 'fantastic' and 'preposterous' rig of a purple velvet mantle and surcoat, trimmed with ermine. While he felt it would make him a laughing stock, the King and Queen insisted. The King wrote in his diary: 'The dear boy did it all remarkably well and looked so nice.'[23] (Though the Prince of Wales thought he would be ridiculed, he felt sufficiently positive about the event to take the gold coronet with him when he went into exile a quarter of a century later.[24])

For all the costumed flummery, Churchill saw beyond the wardrobes, describing the ceremony as 'beautiful and moving'. He marvelled at 'the little prince', writing to his wife that Edward had spoken 'as well as it was possible for anyone to do'.[25] He congratulated David for having a voice 'which carries well and is capable of being raised without losing expressiveness'.[26] Years later, he reflected on the occasion of the investiture as the moment when the prince began to honour him 'with his personal kindness and, I may even say, friendship ... In this Prince there was discerned qualities of courage, of simplicity, of sympathy, and, above all, of sincerity, qualities rare and precious.'[27]

The prince's comments about Churchill at this time were similarly appreciative – he looked up to the young, spirited, and accomplished politician, who had appointed himself as the prince's public speaking coach. 'He is a wonderful man and has a great power of work,' David wrote.[28]

After the investiture, Churchill and Lloyd George were invited to dine on the royal yacht and had a 'good & useful talk' with the King, who was concerned by the threat of imminent industrial action at the docks and on the railways. Sure enough, general strikes in vital industries later that autumn almost brought the country to a standstill. Tensions ran so high that the shelves of gun-maker shops in the ritzy Mayfair district of central London were emptied as well-heeled residents armed themselves with revolvers and shotguns 'just in case'. The King anxiously asked Churchill whether it would be possible to preserve order. 'The difficulty is,' Churchill replied, 'not to maintain order but to maintain order without loss of life.'[29]

During the crisis, Churchill contemplated whether to send armed forces into the fray, especially as accounts emerging from Liverpool suggested, as the King observed, that the situation was 'more like revolution than a strike'. Even facing quasi-revolution, the King was understandably hesitant to deploy the military against his own subjects, and in a telegram to Churchill on 16 August, he made it clear that troops should only be used as a last resort if the situation threatened to get out of control. In the event that they were in fact called on, the King conveyed his expectation that 'they should be given a free hand & the mob should be made to fear them'.[30] Four days later, however, the King viewed the situation with greater equanimity, impressed by Churchill's forceful handling of a volatile situation. He thanked Churchill for the 'very full accounts' he had written, adding that he felt 'convinced that prompt measures taken by you prevented loss of life in different parts of the country'.[31]

The following month, Churchill was invited to Balmoral for a ministerial visit – his first of George V's reign. He arrived shortly after the departure of the Chancellor of the Exchequer Lloyd George, who had alarmed – indeed, in Winston's word, 'electrified'– the King and Queen by discussing the probability of war with Germany. Lloyd George had apparently gone so far as to say that it would be a shame if war were not declared immediately. It was a rare occasion where Churchill was called upon to play the role of soother-in-chief, but, knowing as he did that the King and Queen had numerous German relations, he played down the prospect of an outbreak of hostilities. After he managed to allay the King's anxiety, Churchill was impressed by the casual, familiar air of his visit. 'The King talks much to me about affairs,' he wrote to Clementine. 'Everyone is most civil & friendly … There is very little formality & much comfort.'[32]

In late October 1911, when Churchill was moved from the Home Office and appointed First Lord of the Admiralty, he nursed the expectation that his new role would deepen his relationship with the sailor King who had served in the Royal Navy for fifteen years. The day Winston received his seals of office, he wrote an obsequious note to his Sovereign, saying that he hoped to avail himself of the King's vast expertise as he grappled with his new office of State. Inside the palace, opinions of Winston's new post were mixed. The Prince of Wales was optimistic, while Lord Esher, the King's longtime adviser, was less sanguine: 'I fear Winston as a First Lord of the Admiralty,' he wrote.[33]

In the event, the King's familiarity with naval affairs turned out to be more of a burden than a help to Winston. The King had his own opinions about how the navy ought to be governed, and these often contradicted Winston's own views. While the King, as a former naval officer, placed a high premium on the traditional way of governing the Royal Navy, the reformist Churchill could see little benefit in carrying on in the same old ways. In one of his more telling phrases, he remarked: 'Naval tradition? Naval tradition? Monstrous. Nothing but rum, sodomy, prayers, and the lash.'[34]

Their first row was not long in coming. Churchill had been in the job for only a little over a month when, in December 1911, he submitted for the King's approval his list of four names for newly commissioned battleships: *Africa*, *Liberty*, *Assiduous* and *Oliver Cromwell*. Winston was bewildered when the King rejected all of them but *Africa* and, in reply, suggested three others: *Delhi*, *Wellington* and *Marlborough*. Winston was flattered by the suggestion that his sixth-great-grandfather should be represented, and he accepted *Marlborough* immediately. As for *Wellington*, Churchill suggested that *Iron Duke* would be catchier, a revision the King accepted. Nevertheless, Churchill was dismayed that the King should have denied his initial suggestions.

The conflict over ship names had only just begun. That autumn, Winston submitted four more names: *King Richard the First*, *King Henry the Fifth*, *Queen Elizabeth* and – once again – *Oliver Cromwell*. Churchill felt justified in resubmitting the name of the English Civil War revolutionary following consultations with Prime Minister Asquith, who agreed with Churchill's letter to the King, praising 'the almost unequalled services which [Cromwell] rendered to the British Navy should find recognition in Your Majesty's Fleet'.[35] Of course, the King's reservations were not linked to Oliver Cromwell's significance to the history of the Royal Navy, but rather to the fact that he was the man who orchestrated the execution of King Charles I in 1649 and the subsequent, though temporary, abolition of the monarchy. To put it mildly, Oliver Cromwell is not remembered fondly by the British royal family. The King's private secretary, Sir Arthur Bigge, now Lord Stamfordham, responded to Winston's argument in alarmed haste. 'The King,' he wrote, 'feels sure there must be some mistake in the name of *Oliver Cromwell* being suggested.' When it had come up the previous year, the King 'personally explained' to Winston 'the reasons for his objection'. These had not changed.[36]

This time around, Winston showed himself less willing to back down to what he considered to be constitutional overreach from the Sailor King. He replied with several counterarguments, his frustration apparent through a thin veneer of high-flown rhetoric. 'His Majesty is the heir of all the glories of the nation,' Winston wrote, '& there is no chapter of English history from which he should feel himself divided. I am satisfied that the name would be extremely well received; & that it would mark in a way that little else could the permanent ascendency in this country of monarchical over republican ideas.'[37]

There was more back and forth until Prince Louis of Battenberg, the First Sea Lord, entered the fray, warning Churchill that, traditionally, the First Sea Lord accepts as final the Sovereign's decision on the naming of ships. After making one last begrudging appeal for *Oliver Cromwell*, Churchill threw in the towel. Later in his career, he would not allude to Cromwell's contribution to Britain's constitutional history in such glowing terms. He described him as a 'military dictator' and at best felt his reign of terror was a necessary evil in the nation's development. In his volume of *A History of English-Speaking Peoples*, he focused on Cromwell's cruelty rather than his naval innovations. 'If in a tremendous crisis Cromwell's sword had saved the cause of Parliament he must stand before history as a representative of dictatorship and military rule who, with all his qualities as a soldier and a statesman, is in lasting discord with the genius of the English race.'[38]

At this point in his political career, Winston took up an attitude of combative defiance towards the monarch, though he remained fundamentally stalwart in his loyalty to monarchy as an institution. He went into battle yet again the following year over the naming of ships after the King once more rejected two of Churchill's proposed names, *Pitt* and *Ark Royal*. This time, Churchill fired a constitutional broadside at the King's prerogative to overrule the First Lord of the Admiralty. After he delved into precedent and constitutional history, Churchill suggested that the King might prefer not to be 'troubled' by being consulted on ships' names in the future.[39]

The King's private secretary met Churchill's argument head-on, stating that Winston might have had a point if the topic 'involved questions of organisation, efficiency, or expenditure' of the navy – that is, anything that would come under the umbrella of efficient power. However, the naming of battleships was 'a matter of fancy, sentiment, and suitability', that is, precisely the realm over which the King was expected to exert his influence as a shaping force of British identity. 'The King assumes,' Stamfordham went on, 'that in submitting the names for his approval you expected to have His Majesty's views upon your selection.' In an effort to find a way out of the impasse, Stamfordham suggested a time-worn compromise: face-to-face conversation. 'Would it not avoid difficulties if in the future you were to ask to see the King and talk over such matters with his Majesty before sending in the formal submission? As you know, the King is only too glad to receive you at any time.'[40] With this gesture of goodwill, Churchill finally accepted defeat and changed the names of the two battleships in question.

In between these spats, other contentious issues came between the First Lord and the King. One of these involved the promotion of admirals. While Churchill took a meritocratic view, arguing that after a requisite period of service, these promotions should be granted based on qualification by conspicuous good service, the King held to the idea that promotions ought to be awarded by seniority alone. In this exchange, Churchill won the upper hand, much to the King's lasting chagrin. Two years later, when Lord Balfour wanted to publish the decision they had reached, the King wrote, 'These regulations were forced upon me by Churchill after many discussions. I disagree with them.'[41]

As tensions on continental Europe escalated, Churchill was often on board the Admiralty yacht, HMS *Enchantress*, cruising around the coasts of England and the Mediterranean to get a first-hand view of British readiness for possible conflict. In the spring of 1912, he felt that the growing German naval threat left Britain vulnerable to attack and proposed that the fleets harboured in the Mediterranean be brought home to bolster the naval presence in the English Channel. The King violently disagreed and was in despair when Churchill got his way. Both men wrote privately to express their frustration. Churchill wrote to Clementine, seething at the King's meddling in matters of military conduct, while George V wrote a letter of lamentation to his adviser, Lord Esher, expressing his concern not only that the decision would prove deeply unpopular among the British public, but that it would also highlight Britain's naval limitations to their enemies. Uncharacteristically falling prey to pessimistic catastrophizing, he felt that Churchill's policy would bring about a swift and total British defeat.[42]

There was also the question of the naval budget. When Churchill was serving as president of the Board of Trade, he and Lloyd George raged at the spending on battleships instead of progressive welfare reforms. Now from his eyrie at Admiralty House, he saw matters rather differently. He argued that the current estimates allotted to building new ships were nowhere near what was needed to bring the British Navy abreast of its German rival. While the King had never taken issue with naval expenditure, he disapproved of Churchill's method of increasing the budget, namely, by scaring the population half to death with dire warnings about Britain's unpreparedness for what lay ahead. He was also irritated to see Churchill following in the footsteps of his father, Lord Randolph, by threatening to resign if he did not get his way. The King found these tactics obnoxious and immature, but Churchill did manage to secure a substantial increase in funding.

In May 1912, Winston was joined aboard the HMS *Enchantress* by the King and his second-born son, Prince Albert, later King George VI, whom Churchill called in a letter to Clementine 'a little puppy kitten prince'. The King and his bashful, stuttering son made their way to the yacht via submarine, and Churchill joined them for a two-mile expedition below the water's surface. Afterwards, Churchill showed them around the fleet – he wrote, 'The ships looked magnificent. The air full of aeroplanes, the water black with Dreadnoughts.' That night, Churchill dined on board the royal yacht with the two royal men. For most, this would have been an honour; for Churchill it was cause for further complaint about the King's failure to understand the role of the modern navy. 'The King talked more stupidly about the Navy than I have ever heard him before,' he wrote to his wife. 'Really it is disheartening to hear the cheap & silly drivel with wh[ich] he lets himself be filled up.'[43] As Europe drifted inexorably into war, the First Lord of the Admiralty and his monarch moved further apart on naval matters.

On the surface, all remained superficially friendly, the two men agreeing to disagree. Churchill was, for instance, invited for another shooting weekend in Balmoral in September 1913. He wrote to Clementine, 'The King has been extremely cordial & intimate in his conversations with me, and I am glad to think that I reassured him a good deal about the general position. Altogether it has been most pleasant, & not at all dull or embarrassing.'[44] There was the added entertainment of the young Prince of Wales, then nineteen years old, who rather admired Churchill since they had bonded at the Investiture. They stayed up late one evening, Churchill showing the future King the correspondence and other papers he had received that weekend from the Admiralty. In the same letter to Clementine, he confided that the royal family were concerned about the prince's spartan routine, rising at six in the morning and barely eating all day. 'He requires to fall in love with a pretty cat, who will prevent him from getting too strenuous.'[45] It would be a quarter-century before a certain 'pretty little cat' would have the future King purring.

The following summer, in July, the Third Fleet assembled at Spithead for a routine naval review, to be attended by the King. Churchill called it 'incomparably the greatest assemblage of naval power ever witnessed in the history of the world'.[46] As the ships prepared to disperse and head back to their home ports, Prince Louis of Battenberg issued an order commanding that they instead maintain their position, and eventually make their way to the North Sea, in preparation for what seemed an increasingly inevitable outbreak of international conflict.

Long days passed in suspense, but Winston had one final idea up his sleeve to avert an all-out war. He suggested that a conference of kings, many of whom were related as descendants of Queen Victoria, might be a way of reducing tensions, finding a peaceful solution to territorial demands, and untangling the knot of diplomatic alliances. He felt that the only chance of circumventing a war might be in a gathering of the royal rulers of the sparring European powers – the Austro-Hungarian Emperor, the Russian Czar, the German Kaiser, the English King, and an assortment of princes – together with the President of the French Republic – to see if a compromise could be reached. He suggested as much to Asquith at a Cabinet meeting on 27 July 1914, but before his proposal could be seriously discussed, a telegram arrived from the British ambassador in Berlin to say that it would be impossible: the Austro-Hungarian Empire was already committed to declaring war on Serbia. Churchill's idealistic hopes for a 'conference of Sovereigns' to prevent the outbreak of war came to naught.[47]

While he ruminated on this strategy, Churchill was busily assuring the King that sending the fleet to their North Sea stations was only a 'preparatory & precautionary' measure: war was by no means a certainty. 'It is needless to emphasize,' he wrote to the King, 'that these measures in no way prejudge an intervention or take for granted that the peace of the great powers will not be preserved.'[48] The King's anxiety was only partially assuaged by Churchill's reassurances. 'Winston Churchill came to see me,' the King recorded in his diary three days after this note; 'the navy is all ready for war, but please God it will not come.'[49]

In private, Churchill's forecasts were less optimistic. On 28 July, just as he was reassuring the King, he wrote a very different note to Clementine:

> Everything tends towards catastrophe & collapse. I am interested, geared up & happy. Is it not horrible to be built like that? ... I wondered whether those stupid Kings & Emperors cd not assemble together & revivify kingship by saving the

nations from hell but we all drift on in a kind of dull cataleptic trance. As if it was somebody else's operation! … You know how willingly & proudly I wd risk – or give – if need be – my period of existence to keep this country great & famous & prosperous & free. But the problems are v[er]y difficult. One has to try to measure the indefinite & weigh the imponderable.[50]

Just three days later, on 1 August, Germany declared war on Russia. The First World War had begun.

CHAPTER FIVE

Act Fast, Dread Nought

THE COMING OF the war thrust Winston and the King together more frequently. For the most part, theirs was a tetchy, increasingly antagonistic relationship. The King, like many in his circle, found Churchill energetic but bumptious, careless of protocol, irreverent towards authority, and dismissive of the contributions of others. As far as Churchill was concerned, his sole focus was to prepare the fleet for battle in order to beat the Germans. Nothing else could come in the way of that primary war aim, not even when his colleague Lloyd George suggested that the King, army and navy chiefs, and senior politicians like Churchill take a pledge to abstain from drinking alcohol for the duration of the war. The King agreed, but Winston, who loved his brandy and champagne, would have none of it, ridiculing the proposal as 'absurd' and declaring that he was 'not going to be influenced by the king'.[1]

In public, Churchill's language was anything but temperate, much to the concern of the now teetotal King. On 22 September 1914, for example, Winston gave a rousing speech in Liverpool in which he asked for a million young men to volunteer for the war effort. While he urged his audience to put aside party differences in favour of national unity, he had nothing but ridicule and contempt for the German foe. He poured scorn on the German Navy for staying in port and pledged, to loud cheers, that 'if they do not come out and fight they will be dug out like rats in a hole'.[2]

Although Churchill's phrase was met with an outpouring of cheers and laughter, his jingoistic speech was ill-timed. That same day, news reached England that a German submarine had sunk three reservist Royal Navy cruisers, killing 1,459 British sailors. In the aftermath of the news, Lord Stamfordham was asked by the King to send a formal complaint, by no means the first, to the Prime Minister, objecting to Winston's bloodthirsty rhetoric. 'His Majesty,' Stamfordham wrote, 'did not quite like the tone of Winston Churchill's speech especially the reference to "Rats in a Hole"! ... Indeed seeing what alas! happened today when the rats came out of their own accord and to our cost, the threat was unfortunate and the King feels it was hardly dignified for a Cabinet minister.'[3]

Conflict between the King and his ministers, not just Winston, was as good as baked in, as there was a continual difference of opinion between the elected political leaders and the military top brass. This was particularly true for the head of the army and Secretary of State for War, Field Marshal Lord Kitchener. His stern moustachioed face stared out from recruitment posters, Kitchener's pointed finger and the slogan 'Wants You' calling all curious onlookers to action. It was the most iconic and enduring poster of the war. He was the public face of the conflict, his fame and influence overshadowing 'frock coat' politicians like Prime Minister Asquith, Lloyd George and even Churchill. Effectively his word was law, and it was a daring politician who took him on. Naturally Churchill was the one who led with his chin, often the sole voice in the War Council to question Kitchener, especially as he found Kitchener's views and strategies backward, overly rigid, and lacking in creativity.

His attitude rankled with the King, a Royal Navy veteran, who thought it reprehensible to question the wisdom and authority of men who had spent years, if not decades, honing their skills on the battlegrounds of Empire. The King trusted his top military brass implicitly, and felt it was almost treasonous to question their decisions and recommendations.

One of the few topics on which Churchill and the King were of one mind was in regard to the hostile treatment of Prince Louis of Battenberg, which ended in his resignation as First Sea Lord. With the country now at war, anti-German sentiment rose dramatically. Anyone with a Germanic name, accent or relation was automatically suspected of being a potential spy. It was not long before Prince Louis' German ancestry placed him squarely in the firing line. That he had served Britain's Royal Navy faithfully for close to half a century did not matter one jot. He was potentially the enemy within. In late October 1914, he decided to step down from his post, his decision coming as a blow to both the King and Churchill. 'I feel deeply for him,' the King wrote in his diary; 'there is no more loyal man in the Country.'[4] Churchill's own disappointment was both personal and professional. The First Sea Lord had proven himself to be an astute and dependable officer, and in acknowledging Battenberg's resignation, Churchill wrote, 'I cannot tell you how much I regret the termination of our work together ... No incident in my public life has caused me so much sorrow.'[5]

Prince Louis' resignation left Churchill with the responsibility of finding someone to take his place. The man he settled on was Admiral John 'Jacky' Fisher, who had previously served in the post from 1906 to 1910 and had been an unofficial adviser to Churchill for the previous three years. As with the naming of battleships, Fisher's appointment needed the King's stamp of approval. Churchill soon learned that this approval would not be forthcoming. In his diary, the King recorded, 'I did all I could to prevent it ... I think it is a great mistake.'[6] When it was suggested that the King feared that the stresses of the job might kill the 74-year-old Fisher, Winston responded, 'Sir, I cannot imagine a more glorious death.' He then went on to reject all of the King's alternative candidates. The King tried to break the stalemate by recruiting the Prime Minister to his side. He sent Lord Stamfordham to Downing Street to talk to Asquith, but it was no use: Asquith stated simply that there was no one else for the job. Stamfordham continued to press, saying that 'the appointment of Lord Fisher would place the

King in a very painful position as the Navy would think His Majesty should not have sanctioned it'. Asquith responded that to refuse Fisher's appointment would create an even more painful situation, as Winston had (again) threatened to resign if he didn't get his way.[7]

The following day, the King summoned Asquith to Buckingham Palace to discuss Fisher at greater length. According to Asquith's account of the meeting, King George gave him 'an exhaustive & really eloquent catalogue of the old man's crimes & defects, and thought that his appointment would be very badly received by the bulk of the Navy, & that he would be almost certain to get on badly with Winston. On the last point, I have some misgivings of my own, but Winston won't have anybody else.'[8] 'In the end,' the King wrote privately, 'I had to give in with great reluctance.'[9] Asquith ended his account with a sense of nervous foreboding: 'I hope his apprehensions won't turn out to be well founded.'[10]

For the first few months of Fisher's tenure, it seemed that the King had indeed been overly cautious. George V's biographer Kenneth Rose has noted that the pair worked 'in tandem round the clock' and 'generated an energy and enthusiasm that made the Admiralty hum with confidence. They planned daring operations and amassed the men and ships to sustain them.'[11] Rival historians have suggested otherwise, Andrew Roberts for example describing Fisher's conspiring, leaking and general troublemaking as creating a tense and unstable atmosphere at Admiralty House from the beginning. Nevertheless, at the end of 1914, Churchill was highly optimistic, recalling in *The World Crisis* that the widespread sentiment was one of 'absolute confidence in final victory'.[12]

It was in this spirit of confidence, or perhaps overconfidence, that Churchill began, in January 1915, to muse about the possibility of attacking and occupying Gallipoli. The Turkish peninsula lines the northern bank of the Dardanelles Strait, which connects the Sea of Marmara to the Mediterranean, and thereby Europe to Asia. Never wider than 4 miles, and sometimes as narrow as 1 mile across, the

Dardanelles Strait was a virtually impregnable vista of minefields, guns and enemy forts. For years the strategic significance of the strait had been recognized but so, too, had the considerable risks inherent to such an attack. As early as 1911 Churchill had observed that 'nobody should expose a modern fleet to such peril'.[13] By late 1914, however, the battle lines in Belgium and France had hardened into attritional trench warfare, and Churchill began to feel that the possible advantages of an operation in the Dardanelles might outweigh the costs it would entail in funds, ammunition, and lives. Churchill suggested the plan at a War Council meeting on 25 November, and although there were murmurings about the unlikelihood of the operation's success, Churchill's plan received the approval it needed to proceed. Fisher remained silent during this vital, top-secret meeting.

King George, too, recognized the potential benefits of the attack when Churchill first revealed it to him in February 1915. After one meeting, the King hand-wrote Churchill a letter from Buckingham Palace to promise his discretion and support: 'Your mind can be entirely at rest. I have not mentioned our conversation of this evening to a soul ... I was much interested by all you told me this evening & I only hope that our various schemes for overcoming the enemy may prove successful.'[14]

Though the War Council had not voiced their disapproval of the plan, that did not mean – as Churchill assumed it did – that they were fully on board. Kitchener had grown resentful over the number of men he was asked to divert from the Western Front, while Fisher was pessimistic about the operation's chances of success and knew that his reputation was on the line if it should fail. As soon as the Dardanelles operation got underway, cracks began to show in the Churchill-Fisher alliance. Fisher had never fully supported Churchill's extravagant ambition to take Constantinople, but as catastrophic losses in men, ships and munitions mounted, he increasingly distanced himself, gesturing more and more frequently towards resignation. Churchill still defended the strategy, as, surprisingly, did Lord Kitchener, but most other ministers were not so optimistic.[15]

After several abortive attempts to resign as First Sea Lord, Fisher finally stepped down on the morning of 15 May. Winston replied to Fisher's vitriolic letter of resignation with a forlorn note lamenting his betrayal: 'In order to bring you back to the Admiralty,' he wrote, 'I took my political life in my hands with the King & the Prime Minister— as you know well. You then promised to stand by me and see me through.' After two days of back-and-forth, it was clear that Fisher was intent on resigning. In a letter to Asquith on 19 May, Fisher dictated the conditions for his return: first and foremost, he wanted Churchill demoted, so that he could have full control over British Royal Navy. Asquith wrote to the King that Fisher's letter showed 'signs of mental aberration!'[16] The King's instincts had proved true. While Fisher was clear that he would not return to the government if he had to serve under Churchill, both Asquith and Lloyd George knew that if Fisher did step down, Churchill would be forced to do likewise, because he would never survive the political crisis that would inevitably follow such a resignation. Whether Fisher stayed or went, then, Churchill's political fate was sealed. Though he pleaded to remain in post, Churchill did not have the Cabinet's backing. This was doubly underlined when Asquith and others agreed to a national government to prosecute the war.

The King was relieved to see Winston go and expressed as much to Queen Mary: 'Personally I am glad the Prime Minister is going to have a National Government. Only by that means can we get rid of Churchill from Admiralty ... he is the real danger.'[17] To his diary, the King described Churchill as 'impossible' and expressed his hope that the Conservative and former Prime Minister Arthur Balfour would take his place as First Lord. For once the King's eldest son, the Prince of Wales, who found his father something of a fossil, shared his father's opinion. 'It is a great relief to know that Winston is leaving the Admiralty,' he told the King. 'One does feel that he launches the country on mad ventures which are fearfully expensive both as regards men and munitions and which don't attain their object.'[18] To his friends, the Prince of Wales was even more candid: 'Thank God both Winston and Fisher have gone.' Churchill, he thought, had become an 'intriguing swine' and was 'nothing short of a national danger'.[19] (The prince could hardly have anticipated that it was this 'national danger' who would later come within a hair's breadth of sacrificing his own career for the sake of the prince when he became King.)

On 21 May, after a week of frantically searching for a solution, Winston finally accepted the inevitable, writing to Asquith that he would 'accept any office—the lowest if you like—that you care to offer me'.[20] He was utterly humiliated, and worried that his political career had come to a premature and unsavoury end. Clementine later told Churchill's official biographer, Martin Gilbert, 'When he left the Admiralty he thought he was finished ... I thought he would die of grief.'[21] As part of an extensive government reshuffle, the Chancellor of the Exchequer, Richard Haldane, was removed from office but was rewarded with the Order of Merit for his service. Winston received no such signal of the King's or the Prime Minister's favour. Quite the contrary. As Asquith told his wife, 'Winston is far the most disliked man in my Cabinet by his colleagues ... Oh! He is intolerable!'[22] On 27 May, Winston went to Buckingham Palace for a meeting of the Privy Council and for a private audience with the King. While there, he was given the seal for the minor office of the Chancellor of the Duchy of Lancaster, a post responsible for managing the King's private estate, which only took a couple of days per week. He was effectively a minister without portfolio, able to join in discussions with the War Council by invitation only, not of right.[23]

After languishing for two months in his powerless post, Churchill was asked to go to the front in Gallipoli to get a first-hand appreciation of the situation on the ground. Though he knew it would be a perilous trip, Churchill preferred to meet his end in the heroic glow of active fighting, rather than as a disgraced and disgruntled politician. In fact, he seems to have anticipated the possibility with, if not eagerness, then at least a stoic resolve. Days before his planned departure, he penned a letter to Clementine in which he wrote a romantic final farewell: 'Do not grieve for me too much … If there is anywhere else I shall be on the look out for you. Meanwhile look forward, feel free, rejoice in life, cherish the children, guard my memory. God bless you. Good bye W.'[24]

The mood among the royal family was far less sentimental. When Winston wrote to the King to announce his departure for the Dardanelles, the royal response, penned by Lord Stamfordham, was coolly matter-of-fact. 'The King desires me to thank you for your letter of today,' it read. 'His Majesty is glad to hear of your mission to the Dardanelles and quite understands that you cannot ask for an audience before leaving tomorrow. His Majesty will look forward to seeing you on your return.'[25]

Just before Winston was due to leave for Turkey, however, the Cabinet revoked his commission, thinking that Winston was too invested in maintaining the battle when a more objective observer might counsel retreat. With this last chance at glory so suddenly snatched away, Churchill despaired at the prospect of sitting on the sidelines, a mere spectator of the action that he had no power to influence. He spent the next weeks and months begging for a 'front seat', and asked to serve as an officer commanding a corps at the front. Kitchener found this request embarrassing, believing that senior officers would be offended to have such a controversial politician parachuted into their ranks. It was a common view, ironically one shared by the Prince of Wales, who was himself prevented from serving on the front line, this time by the King who feared it would be too dangerous for the heir. Instead, the prince was confined to army headquarters in France and, on the one occasion he visited the front line, he was nearly killed. As he wrote to royal adviser Lord Esher, he was entirely opposed to political leaders 'interfering' with military operational affairs – then, with a wink and nudge, noting that Winston had visited the French HQ the previous Friday night.[26]

When Asquith announced his newly reconfigured War Council, which again excluded him, Churchill asked the Prime Minister to submit his resignation to the King: 'I am an officer, and I place myself unreservedly at the disposal of the military authorities, observing that my regiment is in France.'[27] Four days later, on 15 November 1915, Winston rose in the House of Commons to deliver a masterful resignation speech, then went home, donned his old yeomanry uniform from the Queen's Own Oxfordshire Hussars, and travelled to France.[28] Less than a week after his arrival, Kitchener ordered the complete evacuation of the Gallipoli Peninsula. 'My scorn for Kitchener is intense,' Winston wrote home to Clementine.[29]

After a brief stint in regular service at the front line, Churchill was given the rank of lieutenant-colonel and command of the 6th Battalion of the Royal Scots Fusiliers.[30] He spent the next five months in the trenches, sharing the hardships of his men and on many occasions witnessing the utterly arbitrary line between life and death. While his decision to serve at the front attracted the obloquy of his enemies in London, he left a positive impression with those who served under him. One of his officers, Andrew Dewar Gibb, later wrote that 'No more popular officer ever commanded. He left behind men who will always be his loyal partisans and admirers.'[31]

While his friends urged him to return to London and resume his political career, Winston for once listened to counsel towards patience. He felt that to return early, abandoning his regiment, would only give ammunition to his detractors. A natural break appeared after his force was combined with another unit following heavy losses in battle. As a result, a more senior officer took over the restructured regiment, leaving Churchill surplus to requirements and free to resume his political career without abandoning his post. As expected, his return still met with criticism. Alan 'Tommy' Lascelles, who would later become assistant private secretary to Edward VIII and private secretary to George VI and Queen Elizabeth II, held nothing back. Lascelles had himself served in the Bedfordshire Yeomanry and was awarded a military cross for his bravery, and he scathingly commented, 'It is only the harlequin-politician who can lay aside the King's uniform the moment it becomes unpleasantly stiff with trench-mud.'[32]

Try as he might, Winston could not shake off the stench of failure and misjudgement following the disastrous Dardanelles campaign. Inevitably the man in the street blamed him for the humiliating defeat. Churchill urged a public inquiry that would make all the facts of the case known, so that he would have the opportunity to clear his name. Eventually he got his wish, and Asquith appointed a commission to investigate the failure of the campaign.

The commission had only been in session for a month when the battle of the Somme was launched, the War Council intending it to be a forceful push on the Western Front to reclaim German-held territory. From the beginning, casualties were staggering. During the first three weeks of the attack, more lives were lost than during the entire eighteen-month Gallipoli campaign.[33] Winston, still operating under the toxic cloud of the Dardanelles, was now even more eager to redeem his reputation by way of comparison to the current bloodbath. From the start he had been violently critical of the Somme campaign, arguing that the War Council's approach to the offensive was both wasteful and strategically foolish. His open hostility to the campaign was seen by his many enemies to be wholly motivated by self-interest. In a scathing critique, the conservative magazine, *The Spectator*, described 'his influence on our political life [as] almost wholly bad because it is wholly dissociated from any motive except that of personal advancement'.[34]

In the autumn of 1916, just as the Dardanelles Commission was preparing its report, Churchill presented a Cabinet memorandum criticizing the military strategy behind the Somme. His negative analysis provoked a furious response from the 'brass hats' and King George V himself. In spite of the industrial scale of the losses, no one was more convinced of the wisdom of the Somme operation than the King. When he went to visit the French headquarters in August 1916, he was glad to find General Haig 'in capital spirits & pleased & satisfied with what our troops are doing'. After their meeting, Haig recorded in his diary that the King spoke 'a great deal' about Churchill's Cabinet memorandum. In the King's eyes, any attempt to besmirch the noble mission of winning back territory on the western front was dishonourable. He viewed Churchill's intervention as an unthinkable disgrace. Haig, too, was infuriated by Winston's criticism, writing to the King, 'Winston's head is gone from his taking drugs.'[35] The King was not likely to have read this comment with incredulity.

In these turbulent and savage times, it came as no surprise when, in December 1916, Asquith's beleaguered government was toppled in a long-anticipated political coup consisting of both Liberal and Tory Cabinet members. Coup leader David Lloyd George formed the new government, the Welsh wizard now reigning supreme at Number 10 Downing Street. If Winston had expected his erstwhile friend to give him a seat in the new government, he was sorely disappointed. Suspicion, mistrust, and personal dislike of Winston Churchill were as intense as they were widespread. Several other ministers under consideration for Cabinet positions – Austen Chamberlain, Walter Long, Lord Robert Cecil and Lord Curzon – declared that they would refuse to join Lloyd George's government if it was to include Winston.[36] Lloyd George had little choice but to comply. When the government's composition was finally announced, Churchill was pointedly left out. Years later, he called this the 'toughest moment of his life'.[37]

Within a matter of weeks, Churchill's fortunes turned around when the Dardanelles report was published in February 1917. It was Asquith who was severely condemned, and Churchill exonerated. The commission could find no grounds to indict Churchill, concluding that his plan was right and that the subsequent delays and poor organization were not his fault.

Nonetheless, the dismal news from the front, along with shortages and rationing at home and a total absence of a resolution of the conflict on the horizon, made for a febrile domestic atmosphere. In the summer of 1917 this discontent manifested itself in a resurgence of anti-German sentiment. Shopkeepers and tradesmen with Germanic names were vilified or physically attacked. Even owners of dachshunds – the sausage dogs originally bred in Germany – were targeted by mocking anti-German propaganda campaigns. For the first time the King and his family came in for abuse, the assault led by the most popular and prolific novelist of the age, H.G. Wells. He published a sharply critical essay about what he called Britain's 'Germanic monarchy', where he argued that the British institution had always been fundamentally German in spirit and custom, and that the monarchy, if it were to survive, must undergo the most profound modification. The change that Wells had in mind was 'for the British monarchy to sever itself definitely from the German dynastic system, with which it is so fatally entangled by marriage and descent, and to make its intention of becoming henceforth more and more British in blood as well as spirit, unmistakably plain'.[38]

Another work by Wells, a novel called *Mr Britling Sees It Through*, had been published in late 1916 and quickly soared to bestseller status, becoming the most popular novel of the First World War.[39] George V was no avid reader, but he had come across a particularly blistering line in the text: 'Too long had British life been corrupted by the fictions of loyalty to an uninspiring and alien Court.' According to one apocryphal story, a Minister came into the King's office to find him throwing his copy of the book on the floor in a sailor's rage. 'That's mean,' he shouted. 'That's not fair ... I know I'm uninspiring but I'm everlastingly damned if I'm alien.'[40]

Wells' comments threw down the gauntlet to the King: prove your Englishness or prepare for a republican revolution. The King, though incensed, took Wells' strictures seriously – the writer was, after all, one of the most influential minds in Britain. But his allegations puzzled the King. While he conceded that the royal family had retained their

German titles, and that there was a long history of British royalty marrying members of German royal houses, he still felt the criticism was unfair. After all, he was the first King for 200 years to speak English without a German accent while his wife, Queen Mary, was the first consort for 400 years to have English as her first language.

But when it came to the most obvious marker of cultural heritage – that is, a surname – the King was at a loss. What was the formal name of his royal house, after all? When he formally learned that it was likely to be Germanic, he 'started and grew pale', quickly asking Stamfordham to investigate. The Royal College of Heralds finally revealed that it was, in fact, the very Teutonic-sounding 'Saxe-Coburg and Gotha', the result of Queen Victoria's marriage to Albert, a German prince.[41]

Prudence suggested that a more English sounding surname would be more appropriate at such a delirious point of the war. The King did not wish to be another bushel added to the harvest of European dynasties currently taking place. And so ensued a deadly serious parlour game, in which the King reviewed several suggestions ranging from 'York' to 'Plantagenet', from 'Lancaster' to 'Tudor-Stewart'. Finally, Stamfordham suggested that he revive the very English-sounding name used by Edward III: Windsor. It was immediately recognized as the correct choice and announced as the new official name for the ruling family by royal proclamation on 17 July 1917. Lord Rosebery wrote to Stamfordham in congratulation: 'Do you realize that you have christened a dynasty? ... It is really something to be historically proud of. I admire and envy you.'[42]

On the occasion of such a symbolically significant event as changing the name of the ruling dynasty – a completely unprecedented act in the long history of British monarchy – one might expect the newspapers to

BY THE KING.

A PROCLAMATION

Declaring that the Name of Windsor is to be borne by His Royal House and Family and relinquishing the use of all German Titles and Dignities.

GEORGE R.I.

WHEREAS WE, having taken into consideration the Name and Title of Our Royal House and Family, have determined that henceforth Our House and Family shall be styled and known as the House and Family of Windsor:

AND WHEREAS We have further determined for Ourselves and for and on behalf of Our descendants and all other the descendants of Our Grandmother Queen Victoria of blessed and glorious memory to relinquish and discontinue the use of all German Titles and Dignities:

AND WHEREAS We have declared these Our determinations in Our Privy Council:

NOW, THEREFORE, We, out of Our Royal Will and Authority, do hereby declare and announce that as from the date of this Our Royal Proclamation Our House and Family shall be styled and known as the House and Family of Windsor, and that all the descendants in the male line of Our said Grandmother Queen Victoria who are subjects of these Realms, other than female descendants who may marry or may have married, shall bear the said Name of Windsor:

And do hereby further declare and announce that We for Ourselves and for and on behalf of Our descendants and all other the descendants of Our said Grandmother Queen Victoria who are subjects of these Realms, relinquish and enjoin the discontinuance of the use of the Degrees, Styles, Dignities, Titles and Honours of Dukes and Duchesses of Saxony and Princes and Princesses of Saxe-Coburg and Gotha, and all other German Degrees, Styles, Dignities, Titles, Honours and Appellations to Us or to them heretofore belonging or appertaining.

Given at Our Court at Buckingham Palace, this Seventeenth day of July, in the year of our Lord One thousand nine hundred and seventeen, and in the Eighth year of Our Reign.

GOD SAVE THE KING.

LONDON: Printed by EYRE AND SPOTTISWOODE, Limited, Printers to the King's most Excellent Majesty.

In 1917, in the face of mounting wartime criticism,
King George V changed the royal family's German surname to
the more English-sounding name of Windsor.

be full of pronouncements, poetic elegies, editorials and criticisms. Not a bit of it. The new House of Windsor was completely overshadowed by a controversial scion of the Marlborough dynasty. Winston was back, appointed as the Minister for Munitions by Lloyd George in a move that infuriated as much as it delighted. He took up the post on the very same day that the royal name change was made official.

All publicity centred on Winston who, not for the first time, had eclipsed the royal family in seizing the spotlight. Reaction to Winston's appointment was swift and unrelenting. The *Morning Post* jibed, 'Although we have not yet invented an unsinkable ship, we have discovered the unsinkable politician.'[43] The editor of the same paper, H. A. Gwynne, wrote to Lord Esher to invoke the Latin aphorism *Deus vult perdere, prius dementat*: those whom the gods would destroy, they first make mad. Having never witnessed such furore as he saw in the aftermath of Churchill's re-admission to Cabinet, Gwynne saw in Lloyd George's strange decision a sure portent of political self-destruction.[44] Meanwhile, Tory politician, decorated admiral and lifelong Churchill enemy Lord Beresford complained in *The Times* that Winston was 'unfitted for his present or any other position in the Government', pinpointing his failures, his want of foresight and ignorance of the elementary principles of warfare.[45] The Earl of Derby, serving as Secretary of War, wrote to Bonar Law privately, threatening to resign.[46] One hundred Conservative MPs signed a motion in the House of Commons condemning the move.[47]

Nor was the response more welcoming within palace walls. When the Prince of Wales was told about Churchill's appointment, he rolled his eyes: 'I suppose,' he wrote, 'he has silently wormed his way in again.' He added, in a more conciliatory tone, 'Perhaps it is safer to give him a job than to have him hanging around unemployed.'[48]

Two days after the announcement of Winston's appointment, he attended a privy council at Buckingham Palace where he kissed hands and once again took the Oath of Office. While there is no record of their conversation, it is not hard to imagine Churchill waxing lyrical to the King at the choice of the ancient name of Windsor, and the King, through pursed lips, congratulating the new minister on his return to government.

Despite the initial scepticism of Churchill's capacities, his time at the Ministry of Munitions was hugely successful and indeed critical to Britain's ability to continue waging the war. It was his drive and imagination that converted the tank from an idea into a reality, the massed ranks of this metal monster first appearing at the battle of Cambrai in 1917. The following April, a month after the German Ludendorff offensive began on the Western Front, Churchill was able to write to the King that 'every gun that has been lost in this great battle had been replaced' by his industrious and energetic work at the ministry.[49] Moreover, he was taken completely back into the confidence of Prime Minister Lloyd George, regularly serving as his emissary at meetings with French allies. When the war finally drew to its close on the eleventh hour of the eleventh day of the eleventh month of 1918, Winston was back at the heart of government.

After the war, Churchill was moved from the Ministry of Munitions to the combined Ministry of War and Air. As a sign of things to come, the King made no objection to the Prime Minister putting forward his name.[50] As soon as Churchill took up the job, he made a noticeable difference, specifically on post-war demobilization. Until Churchill arrived, the government policy was to demob servicemen whose work was most essential to the economy. They, though, had also been the last to be called up. This infuriated those who had served longest, and riots broke out in Glasgow and Belfast. Winston agreed with their case, accepting that they deserved an earlier release. He signed off on a new demobilization policy which recognized both length of service and the number of wounds sustained in determining release order. Once the new system went into action, the riots promptly ended, and servicemen were released from their posts at a rate of fifty thousand per day.[51]

Despite Churchill's success in this new post, the King still clashed with his sometime political adversary. One encounter concerned the wartime achievements of David Lloyd George, who returned from Paris in June 1919 after negotiating the Treaty of Versailles, formally concluding the war. Even though the draconian provisions humiliated the Germans and sowed the seeds for the rise of Hitler, the treaty terms were well received in Britain. The King was sufficiently impressed by Lloyd George's leadership during and after the war to award him the Order of Merit. The honour, first introduced by King Edward VII in 1902, was seen as the pinnacle of Britain's honours system, described by one observer as 'quite possibly, the most prestigious honour one can receive on planet Earth'.[52]

Several months after Lloyd George was presented the Order of Merit, Churchill took it upon himself to request that the King also award his political friend the Distinguished Service Order, a military medal usually presented to those who have experienced combat and served under fire. Churchill felt that there was not a single politician who had sacrificed more in the pursuit of victory than David Lloyd George. George V responded in the negative, pointing out that the Prime Minister had no greater claim to recognition than the rest of his Cabinet. But Churchill begged to differ, having seen Lloyd George in action close-up during the war. He wrote: 'There is no doubt that the purely military work done by Mr Lloyd George stands on an entirely different plane to that done by other Cabinet ministers.'[53] The King, as the fount of all honours, was always prickly about matters of precedence, protocol and royal prerogative. He would not be drawn in and resented Churchill's pesky persistence. In his eyes, the honours train had left the station, and Churchill was merely standing alone, waving from the platform. As with the naming of battleships, the King was always prepared to take on those who tried to step on his 'patch' – and Winston was the most frequent and brazen of trespassers.

Shortly after the Lloyd George honours affair, both Churchill and the Prime Minister found themselves in another storm over protocol. In the spring of 1920, they agreed that they wanted to appoint General Nevil Macready as the commander of military forces stationed in Ireland. Macready indicated that he would accept the position, and the appointment was prepared for the King's approval. Before he had a chance to give or withhold his assent, however, the *Daily Express* leaked the news – much to the King's annoyance. While Churchill expressed himself as shocked as the King, Lord Stamfordham pointed out that he had not followed the correct protocol, which dictated that they must secure the King's consent before offering the position. Stamfordham argued, 'If the reverse method be adopted, then should the King refuse approval it is known that, though the authorities favour the appointment, the Sovereign has declined to acquiesce in it.'[54] In the King's eyes, proper form and constitutional etiquette mattered.

At this time Ireland was much on the minds of the King, Lloyd George and Churchill. Though the guns were silenced over mainland Europe, a bloody conflict consumed lives and limbs in Ireland where the nationalist party, Sinn Fein, and its military arm, the Irish Republican Army (IRA), had refused to recognize the British Parliament and their offer of limited devolution. Instead, they wanted a full republic, completely independent of the British Empire, and took up arms to oust the army and end British rule once and for all. From 1919 to 1921, an Anglo-Irish war raged, with little quarter given on either side.

In May 1920 Churchill, now at the War Office, was largely responsible for the recruitment of the Black and Tans, a paramilitary group tasked with crushing Irish militants by any means necessary. They fought terrorism with terror, earning a notorious international reputation that evokes a shudder of fear and anger among the descendants of those who lived through their depredations. Villages and towns like Cork were burned and civilians slaughtered in revenge killings. Even today, visitors to Ireland are counselled not to order a 'Black and Tan' ale.

A deadly cycle of assassinations and reprisals began, the most notorious being the killing in cold blood of fourteen British agents all across Dublin in November 1920. On that same afternoon, in what became known as Bloody Sunday, a raid on the Croke Park Gaelic football club left fourteen spectators dead and dozens injured after British forces, mainly the Black and Tans, fired indiscriminately into the crowd. The following year, the IRA hatched a plot to shoot Churchill as he drove through Hyde Park on his way to Whitehall in central London. The assassination attempt failed at the last minute, but no one was taking any chances. Lloyd George, who, along with Churchill and the Prince of Wales, was on the IRA hit-list, took to wearing a bullet-proof vest. The Prince of Wales took the deadly intent of the IRA enemy in his stride, writing to his mistress Freda Dudley Ward, 'Winston is first on the list to be murdered ... and your poor little parpee' – that is, himself – 'is the second!!'[55]

After failing to crush the IRA there was a general, if reluctant on Churchill's part, realization among politicians of all colours that the Irish question could only be resolved by conciliation and compromise. The King's position was typical. Initially he had been hawkish about snuffing out revolutionary nationalism, but when he saw the violence perpetrated against his own subjects, he changed his tune. He wrote to Lloyd George, 'Are you going to shoot all the people in Ireland? ... I cannot have my people killed in this manner.'[56]

A meeting at Downing Street between Lloyd George and Sinn Fein president Eamon De Valera was inconsequential, but it set the ball rolling. Churchill, now Colonial Secretary, was one of what he called the 'second rank' negotiators during the labyrinthine talks. The King delivered an emollient speech at the Northern Ireland Parliament in Belfast in June 1921. The trip was not without physical risks, and at the last minute Queen Mary, concerned that the King might be assassinated by a lone gunman, decided to be by his side. In his opening remarks, the King asked everyone 'to pause, to stretch out the hand of forbearance and conciliation, to forgive and to forget, and to join in making for the land which they love a new era of peace, contentment, and goodwill'.[57]

Although the King's appeal mostly fell on deaf ears among the nationalists in the audience, Churchill thought it perfect, writing to the King the following day:

> I cannot resist expressing to Your Majesty the profound thankfulness with wh[ich] I welcome Your Majesty's safe return from a duty in Ireland of such great importance to the whole Empire. I am sure that the results of the visit of Your Majesty accompanied by the Queen will help materially to facilitate the reunion of the two islands. Certainly every loyal subject must feel a special debt of gratitude to Your Majesty for the unswerving sense of public devotion wh[ich] led to the undertaking of so momentous a journey.[58]

The first Cabinet meeting outside London took place in September 1921 in the Scottish town of Inverness, where the Irish question was top of the agenda. Inverness was chosen as it was near to where the King was shooting and close to the Northern Ireland ferry, so that messages could be sent to the Sinn Fein negotiators. While there was little common cause, some deft linguistics kept the peace process alive before a full peace conference the following month in London. Following intense negotiations, a peace agreement was brokered, and the Anglo-Irish treaty signed in December 1921, a welcome Christmas present for the war-weary of both sides. Churchill was optimistic that the settlement would hold, telling the Prince of Wales, 'I am full of hope and confidence about Ireland. I believe we are going to reap a rich reward all over the world and at home.'[59]

Though initially his typical aggressive self, Churchill won high praise for his judicious and sober manner when Parliament debated the Irish Free State Bill. In March 1922, Conservative Party leader Sir Austen Chamberlain sent several reports to the King in which he was fulsome in his praise of his Liberal opponent. 'He has shown parliamentary talent of the highest order and greatly strengthened his parliamentary position.' In a later speech, which was both brief yet convincing, Churchill, according to Chamberlain, again 'succeeded in maintaining the high reputation he has won as a resolute yet conciliatory debater. The House listened with marked and almost breathless attention to Mr Churchill's comments.'[60] Lord Knollys, private secretary to both Edward VII and George V, went so far as to suggest, 'This exercise of judgment brings him nearer to the leadership of the country than any one would have supposed possible.'[61] Churchill's mature political skills even won over IRA quartermaster Michael Collins, who told him through an intermediary, 'We could never have done anything without him.'[62]

Immediately after the Irish Free State Bill became law on 31 March, Lord Stamfordham wrote to Churchill to express the King's congratulations 'upon the successful conclusion of a difficult and responsible task thanks to the skill, patience and tact which you have displayed in handling it and for which you have earned universal gratitude'.[63] This was much more than a standard 'herogram'. It seemed to mark a sea change in attitude by both men towards one another. After surviving a war that had taken so many colleagues and friends, they were thankful that they were still standing once the storm had passed. During his wartime reign, George V had witnessed the toppling of eight kings, five emperors and four imperial dynasties and felt the chill winds of disapproval from his own subjects. He realized that anarchy and revolution were just one misstep away. The slaughter of his cousin, Czar Nicholas II of Russia, and his family by Bolshevik rebels in July 1918 had rattled the King's 'confidence in the innate decency of mankind'.[64]

While disagreement and controversy were the price to be paid for associating with Churchill, he was, in spite of it all, considered to be part of the family, ultimately 'one of us'. It didn't hurt that Churchill's disposition towards the British Monarchy had undergone a transformation for the better. As historian David Cannadine has described, Churchill 'no longer regarded the British Sovereign as the ignorant, blimpish reactionary of his Liberal days, but as the embodiment of decency, duty and tradition … The solution of the Irish problem seems to have had a great deal to do with this.'[65] The unpromising political soil of Ireland had proven fertile ground both for Churchill's political career and a late flowering in his relationship with the House of Windsor.

A sense of Churchill's changing priorities was caught by young diplomat Alfred Duff Cooper, who attended a dinner party at Wimborne House, the principal London home of Winston's aunt Cornelia. 'Winston was splendidly reactionary,' Cooper noted in his diary, amused by the political veteran's declaration that he was a firm monarchist. 'Not only did he swear that his one object in politics was now to fight Labour. He also declared that he was a monarchist, that he hoped to see all the deposed European monarchs back on their thrones – including Prussian Hohenzollerns.'[66]

It was a far cry from the days when he adopted a casual disregard for the British monarch and dismissed European monarchies out of hand.

CHAPTER SIX

Silver and Gold

Like father, like son. While the Prince of Wales disagreed with his father about many issues, including matters of dress, there was one important point on which they almost always saw eye to eye. In their view, and that of their wider court, Winston Churchill was an 'interfering politician' who should have kept his nose out of military matters. The prince and his coterie had revelled in Churchill's ousting from the Admiralty over the Dardanelles fiasco and applauded his abrupt exclusion from other high office.

However, as the war drew to a close, the future King Edward VIII, like his father, slowly came to appreciate Winston's abilities as a politician, a wartime strategist and, most importantly, as an outstanding orator. For his part, Churchill had watched as the prince, twenty years his junior, grew from a naïve and self-doubting teenager into an international icon who added new zest and life to the doughy House of Windsor. Every girl wanted to be able to brag that she had danced with the Prince of Wales. As the prince sowed his wild oats, Churchill saw it as his duty, largely self-appointed, to guide and tutor the prince in the art of oratory.

One of their first joint outings took place in July 1919 when Churchill, then Secretary of State for Air and War, accompanied the prince to a review of troops in London's Hyde Park. Edward delivered a homecoming speech, drafted by Churchill, which focused on the historical significance of the military partnership between the various English-speaking nations.[1] The success of this speech cemented Churchill in his position as the prince's public speaking coach. As the Prince of Wales, who was initially an uncertain public speaker, later recalled, 'The more appearances I had to make the more I came to respect a really first-class speech as one of the highest of human accomplishments. No one that I knew seemed to possess that rare or envied gift, the art of speaking well, in so high a degree as Mr. Winston Churchill.'[2]

One of Churchill's main lessons for the budding royal orator was to be clear and direct in delivering his message: 'If you have an important point to make,' Churchill told him, 'don't try to be subtle or clever. Use a pile driver. Hit the point once. Then come back and hit it again. Then hit it a third time – a tremendous whack.'[3] Winston went on to advise that it would always be preferable to memorize his speeches, but that if he had to read it from the page, 'I should do so quite openly, reading it very slowly and deliberately and not making the least attempt to conceal your notes.' As far as the notes themselves were concerned, Winston imparted some ingenious advice as to how to prop them up on the dinner table. He counselled: 'Take a tumbler and put a finger bowl on top of it, then put a plate on top of the finger bowl and put the notes on top of the plate; but one has to be very careful not to knock it all over, as once happened to me ...'[4]

Under Churchill's guiding hand, the prince, who had a light, soft voice with a hint of a lisp, became increasingly confident on the public stage and in time came to enjoy the applause of great crowds. Several years later Churchill recommended a speech therapist, Cortland MacMahon, who was based at St Bart's hospital in central London, to help him further project his voice. [5] As well as Winston, he also treated the prince's mistress, Freda Dudley Ward. While the Prince of Wales eventually became a proficient public speaker, what he didn't relish was his life on the road as the face of imperial Britain. Prime Minister Lloyd George saw how the people responded to the prince's relaxed, unpretentious manner, and he hoped to spread the royal stardust around the globe. At the end of the war in 1918, the prince was asked to tour the colonies and dominions to thank the people for their support and sacrifice during the Great War. During the 1920s, he visited some forty-five countries and travelled an estimated 150,000 miles by train and ship. Treated like some exotic animal that had escaped from a zoo, the prince was pinched, pummelled, punched, squeezed, grabbed and shaken by near hysterical crowds. When he returned from an arduous trip to Australia and New Zealand in 1920, he understandably balked at the request to set sail immediately for a goodwill tour of India.

He wanted a rest from what he called 'princing' and to be reunited with his current love interest, Freda Dudley Ward, the half-American wife of a Member of Parliament and the Vice Chamberlain of the Royal Household. Even to the casual observer, the prince's adoration for Freda was plain to see. Churchill, who typically refrained from passing judgment on the emotional entanglements of others, was moved to write to Clementine about his experience with the couple on a train to Nottingham: 'It was quite pathetic to see the Prince and Freda. His love is so obvious and undisguisable.'[6] He could, though, appreciate the attraction, finding the diminutive socialite enchanting: 'a delightful little porcelain shepherdess'.[7]

When Churchill was in London, he would often see the pair together at their favourite nightclub, The Embassy. While for Winston the late-night venue made for a relaxing end to a long day's work, for the prince it was a welcome escape from the dull formality of life at Buckingham Palace with its onerous rhythms and routines. From time to time, Churchill met with the prince and Freda socially. On 9 February 1921, Winston was invited to a party in the Prince of Wales' honour at the home of portrait artist Sir John Lavery and his wife, Hazel, a woman so beautiful that her likeness appeared on the first Irish banknotes. Never an accomplished dancer, Churchill rather put his foot in it. He explained to Clementine afterwards, 'Unhappily in dancing I trod with my heel upon the P. of W. toe & made him yelp. But he bore it v[er]y well – & no malice.'[8]

Within a matter of weeks, Churchill lost the woman who had never accepted no longer being the most beautiful woman in the room: his mother, Jennie, who died on 29 June 1921, aged just 67. In the eyes of

Churchill, who suffered numerous bereavements that year, including his two-year old daughter, Marigold, his mother's passing represented the end of the glorious Edwardian era. As Churchill himself noted, 'The old brilliant world in which she moved, and in wh[ich] you met her is a long way off now, & we do not see its like today. I feel a v[er]y great sense of deprivation.'9

Change was indeed in the air. When the Prince of Wales eventually left for India in October 1921, he would return to a country on the brink of major social and political upheaval. While the prince was away, Winston followed his young friend's progress with interest. After receiving the prince's Christmas card, he responded with a long, somewhat obsequious letter where he suggested that the prince note down his political and cultural observations during the tour, telling him that he 'would get a truer impression than anyone else'. Winston went on to express his dissatisfaction with the British policy towards India – which would grow significantly more intense over the next two decades – and lamented that the prince 'must have had sombre moments in feeling that the gracious gifts you brought and offered were in some cases spurned. It has worried me to think we should have committed you to such experiences … I feel we have been asking a very great deal of Your Royal Highness.' He closed by praising the prince's vigour and willingness to represent the empire. 'Thank God,' he wrote, 'we have you to help and someday guide our country in all its problems.'

Aside from these political questions and observations, Winston discussed sporting issues, namely their joint interest in polo. 'I expect, Sir, you will become so good at polo that you will pass far above the class of our humble games: and sail about in tournaments with the champions.'10

Once the prince returned from his travels in 1922, Churchill eagerly organized a dinner in his honour. As the long-suffering hostess, Clementine refused to be fazed when Winston wrote that the guest list had expanded to around eighteen. 'Don't be alarmed,' he consoled.11 Clementine, however, had another reason for concern. Their seven-year-old daughter,

Sarah, had caught measles and, as the prince had never had the disease, the dinner was postponed.

At the time, the proximity of the future King to this disease, which was suspected of causing sterility in males, reignited the debate in court circles about when the prince was going to take a suitable wife and continue the Windsor line. That he showed no inclination to do so, choosing instead married women as his public companions, caused a ripple in the palace.

The tectonic plates were indeed shifting but not in the way the palace wanted or appreciated. After the fall of the Lloyd George government in 1922 over its potential conflict with Turkey, the election saw the rise of the Labour and Conservative parties and the long-term collapse in support for the Liberals. Though few realized it at the time, the Liberal party was undergoing, in the words of author George Dangerfield, a 'strange death'.

Churchill himself felt that loss in full measure during the 1922 election, during which he lost his Dundee seat in humiliating fashion to Edwin Scrymgeour from the Scottish Prohibition Party. Churchill had an excuse for coming fourth in the ballot: he was incapacitated by appendicitis, an ailment in those days that often proved fatal. It took Winston so long to recuperate from his appendectomy that he only spent three days campaigning in the Scottish city.

The King watched Churchill's progress with interest – and a degree of partiality that underscored their long friendship. In a sympathetic, quite jocular letter, Stamfordham, writing on behalf of the King, said, 'His Majesty is very sorry about the Dundee Election ... but of course realises how heavily handicapped you were after your severe operation. But the Scotch Electorate is rather an incomprehensible body!'[12] Further he expressed his regret that Winston was confined to bed and unable to be present at Buckingham Palace to hand over his Seal of Office and take his leave of the King.

Overall, the election returned a clear Conservative majority of 344 MPs, followed by 142 Labour and 115 Liberal seats, which were in turn split between Asquith's Liberal Party and David Lloyd George's National Liberals. Feeling sorry for himself, Winston lamented that he was 'without an office, without a seat, without a party, and without an appendix'.[13]

Churchill's downfall was a blessing in disguise. He and Clementine journeyed to the south of France where he was able to recuperate properly, indulging in his painting hobby and finding time to write *The World Crisis*, his five-volume memoir of the First World War. As was to become tradition, he sent one of the first published copies to the Prince of Wales, who thanked him for the tome, adding, 'I'm so glad you've had a lot of polo & are fit enough again to enjoy it ... I hope we'll get lots of games together.'[14] As for Churchill, his best days of polo were behind him, but he refused to retire. They played together in 1924 when Winston was nearing fifty. Their fellow player Patrick Thompson described Winston's style as akin to 'heavy cavalry getting into position for the assault'.[15]

The Churchills were back in England in time for the wedding of the year in April 1923 at Westminster Abbey, when the Prince of Wales' younger brother, the Duke of York, married the diminutive Elizabeth Bowes-Lyon, the youngest daughter of the Earl of Strathmore. No one, on the day of the wedding, could have guessed the impact that Winston – described by the *Yorkshire Post* as looking 'chubby and sleek' after his days in the sun – was to have on the bride and groom's lives in the years to come. Of course, the duke knew all about Churchill and, as a congenital stammerer, was quietly envious of his fluent public speaking in spite of his slight lisp. When the duke was a student, he had seen Churchill perform in debate at the Cambridge Union and was suitably impressed.

The newlyweds met Churchill again the following summer when they were guests of honour at the Mayfair mansion home of philanthropist Maggie Greville. Seventy years later, Elizabeth described Winston during that evening as 'extraordinary'. As they chatted over dinner, he convinced her that she and the duke should travel to East Africa. As course followed course, he whetted her appetite for Africa by recounting his own adventures seventeen years before. 'It's got a great future, that country,' he told her. Even though the dancing lasted until two in the morning, to the tunes of the fashionable Savoy Havana Band, Churchill remembered to follow up on his plan for the young couple the following day and used his influence to kickstart the official approval process. Less than a month later, the King agreed to the plan, and the Yorks spent three months on safari in Kenya, Uganda and the Sudan, the couple shooting a wide variety of big game. Elizabeth later said that she had 'always been grateful' to Winston for this intervention, because without it, 'I don't think we would have thought of going.'[16]

While Winston maintained his status as a political 'big beast', he was out of office for nearly two years, during which time the Labour Party under Ramsay MacDonald formed their first-ever government. Even when the Labour government lost their majority in the November 1924 election, Churchill had little hope of regaining a position of significance as Conservative leader Stanley Baldwin, not one of his admirers, had been invited by the King to form a government. As Baldwin considered names for his Cabinet, he received a letter from Austen Chamberlain that argued Churchill needed a seat: 'If you leave him out,' his argument went, 'he will be leading a Tory rump in six months' time.'[17] Baldwin heeded the advice and invited Churchill, who was for once lost for words, to become Chancellor of the Exchequer.

It was an unexpected promotion, but also something of a poisoned chalice. Since the war, the British economy had floundered. Productivity and wages were both down, while the threat of industrial action cast a further pall over an ominous economic landscape. Internationally, matters were no better as Britain, France, the United States and Germany haggled over the size of the war reparations to be paid by the losing nation.

Churchill, delighted to be back in harness and, importantly, receiving a salary, took on these burdens with gusto. After all, as a small boy he had said, 'My father is Chancellor of the Exchequer and that's what I'm going to be too.'[18] Once again, he rubbed shoulders with his destiny. When parliament broke for Easter recess in April 1925, Winston stayed at his desk. 'In these days of national holiday making,' the *Democrat* magazine reported, 'there is one Minister who is keeping his nose to the grindstone. Winston Churchill will be hard at it whilst others play.'[19] By the time his colleagues returned from their holidays he had hammered his first Budget into shape, giving the King a confidential early look at his proposals in a fifteen-page, hand-written letter. Then the Cabinet approved his measures, whose centrepiece was a return to the gold standard, essentially emphasizing the importance of a uniform standard of value in trade.

Though the return to the gold standard was subsequently deemed economic folly, at the time the Cabinet and the Crown alike were enthusiastically in favour of the move. The King had read Churchill's letter with 'deep interest' and 'much approval', and listened carefully when Prime Minister Baldwin relayed a personal summary of Churchill's two-and-a-half-hour budget speech to the House of Commons on 28 April 1925. Baldwin observed, 'The general impression was that Mr Churchill rose magnificently to the occasion. His speech … was one of the most striking Budget speeches of recent years.'[20] Just as Churchill's father, Lord Randolph, had won his way back into Bertie's good graces by way of political success, so Winston renewed the respect and trust of the King thanks to his expansive rhetorical feats.

But if Winston's rhetoric put bread on his own table, it hardly did the same for the British working classes. Britain's return to the gold standard had made goods, including coal, too expensive, and the nation's mine owners decided that they had to cut their labourers' wages to retain their markets. The plight of the miners, who threatened strike action, was matched by the ugly mood among the workforce as a whole, and in early May 1926 the ruling trades union body, the Trades Union Congress, voted for a general strike. Unsurprisingly, Churchill was in the thick of the action, proving himself to be one of the more aggressive members of the Cabinet. He established an emergency publication, called the *British Gazette*, whose ostensible aim was to cover the news of the day from the government's perspective. It soon became an anti-striker sheet, inflaming feelings on both sides.

The General Strike saw, in the King's attitude, a pattern that was by now familiar: at the outset, he was inclined to favour repressing the strike by any means necessary. Several days in, when he saw the scale of the protest, he changed his mind, feeling that the most important thing was to protect the safety and interests of all concerned and to bring the strike to a peaceful conclusion as soon as possible. So he was alarmed when, in the 8 May issue of the *Gazette*, it was announced that should the King's armed forces be called in to quell the strike, they would receive the full support of His Majesty's Government. As ever, the King felt Churchill had gone beyond his remit, and he instructed Stamfordham to write a note of rebuke. He felt it was neither helpful nor constitutionally appropriate for Churchill to speculate about what the King's troops would or would not do to secure peace among his own people. 'His Majesty cannot help thinking that this is an unfortunate announcement and already it has received a good deal of adverse criticism.'[21] The Prince of Wales was less scrupulous, even lending Churchill his personal limousine and chauffeur to transport the *Gazette* for distribution in Wales.[22] The General Strike, which was over in a matter of days and, to general relief, without bloodshed, even became the cause in the House of Commons for a degree of levity. At the end of one particularly fierce debate, Churchill's final reply built up to a menacing pitch: 'I have no wish to make threats,' he said. 'But this I must say; make your minds perfectly clear that if ever you let loose upon us again a general strike, we will loose upon you – another *"British Gazette"*.' Prime Minister Baldwin, along with the rest of the House, found the line and delivery hilarious.[23]

The British Gazette

Published by His Majesty's Stationery Office.

No. 1.   LONDON, WEDNESDAY, MAY 5, 1926.   ONE PENNY.

FIRST DAY OF GREAT STRIKE

Not So Complete as Hoped by its Promoters

PREMIER'S AUDIENCE OF THE KING

Miners and the General Council Meet at House of Commons

FOOD SUPPLIES

No Hoarding: A Fair Share for Everybody

MILK DISTRIBUTION

Control of Supplies in the Metropolis

LAW COURTS AT WORK

Judge on the Duty of the Public

LONDONERS' TREK TO WORK.

G.P.O. SERVICES

Restrictions on Telegrams and Telephones

THE KING RECEIVES THE PREMIER.

HOLD-UP OF THE NATION

Government and the Challenge

NO FLINCHING

The Constitution or a Soviet

COMMUNIST LEADER ARRESTED

Mr. Saklatvala, M.P., Charged at Bow Street

SEQUEL TO MAY DAY SPEECH

THE CHOICE

SPECIAL CONSTABLES

Appeal to Capable Citizens in London to Enrol

RESERVE OF OFFICERS

PROSPERITY AT STAKE

THE "BRITISH GAZETTE" AND ITS OBJECTS

Reply to Strike Makers' Plan to Paralyse Public Opinion

REAL MEANING OF THE STRIKE

Conflict Between Trade Union Leaders and Parliament

GOVERNMENT'S VIEW

NO ADVANCE ON JULY.

NO SECTIONAL DICTATION.

DANGER OF RUMOURS.

By the time Churchill announced his third budget as chancellor, in April 1927, his status as a parliamentary celebrity was firmly established. Hopeful spectators queued outside the House of Commons for hours to get a seat to watch his performance, while his public-speaking pupil, the Prince of Wales, took a seat in the Peers' Gallery shortly before his tutor entered. After Churchill's presentation of the budget, Baldwin wrote to the King that the chancellor had 'a power of attraction which nobody in the House of Commons can excel'.[24] 'A masterpiece of ingenuity' Baldwin called the speech.[25]

Churchill was now back in the heart of the British establishment and was accordingly invited to join the King and his court at Balmoral that summer. He was even allowed to turn one room into an artist's studio so that he could paint the Highland landscape from his bedroom window. He wrote to Clementine, 'I took particular care to leave no spots on the Victorian tartans.' He continued, 'I enjoyed myself very much ... It is not often that the paths of duty and enjoyment fall so naturally together. I had a particularly pleasant luncheon with the King when we went out deer driving, and a very good talk about all sorts of things.' The product of his stay was also financially fruitful: he ended up auctioning off the painting he made there for £120 (about $8,500 or £6,400 today). He wrote jokingly of his success to Stamfordham, 'If I could be sure of equally skilful auctioneering, I really might endeavour to reduce our national liabilities by turning out a few pictures.'[26]

It was not quite the same happy, sylvan scene the following year. During his stay in September 1928, Churchill couldn't help but notice the diminished vigour of his host, who had never fully recovered from a bronchial attack in 1925. The King also remained troubled by an old injury he sustained by falling from his horse during a military parade in 1915. Now, the sixty-three-year-old monarch could barely participate in the hunt. 'He no longer stalks but goes out on the hill where the deer are "moved about for him",' Winston wrote to Clementine.[27] Even so, Churchill rejoiced to be on the right side of royal affections. He wrote,

'The King is really v[er]y kind to me & gives me every day the best of his sport.' The two discussed any number of political issues, sharing a negative view about the 'Yankees', a perspective Winston would eventually reverse.[28]

Just two months later, Churchill – along with the rest of the Empire – was alarmed at the news that the King was severely ill with a chest infection. Such was the concern that the Prince of Wales, who was in East Africa on safari, was ordered to return home at full speed. As the King slowly recuperated, his spirits were always raised when the cheerful figure of Princess Elizabeth, the daughter of the Duke and Duchess of York, entered his sick room. Churchill could understand why, having met the self-possessed two-year-old previously at Balmoral. Though she was, at that point, third in line to the throne, there was no thought that she would ever become Queen, since it was still taken for granted that the Prince of Wales would marry and have issue. And yet, even as a toddler, Elizabeth's demeanour and comportment led observers to comment on how well-suited she seemed to be for a life of royal service. Winston was utterly enchanted, describing her as 'a character' with 'an air of authority & reflectiveness astonishing in an infant'. He was so impressed that he referred to her not as 'Princess Elizabeth' but – whether out of wit or prophecy – 'Queen Elizabeth'.[29]

Just as the princess was being viewed as the next Queen, so Churchill was being tipped for the job he had always coveted: Prime Minister. His parliamentary performances, which attracted both the Prince of Wales and the Duke of Gloucester to the Peers' Box, earned plaudits all round. Baldwin told the King that Churchill himself was 'a master in the art of oratory and of tantalising the imagination'.[30] After one three-and-a-half-hour speech, Churchill received a letter from his friend and cousin Freddie Guest who wrote, 'It seems to me that you have taken a sure step towards your future premiership.'[31]

Within months, though, the fickle finger of fate moved on, and Churchill found himself once again out of office and cast into the political wilderness when the Labour Party formed its second minority government in 1929. It would take him a few years to realize that, in fact, he and his Conservative Party had dodged a bullet of overseeing the great economic crash of that year and the many hardships and hard choices of the depression era, as the early 1930s were dominated by high unemployment, particularly in the north and west, non-existent growth, and governments around the world groping for an adequate response – and excuses for the calamity that affected all.

Where Churchill alienated many of those who saw leadership potential was in his relentless opposition to the Simon Commission on India, whose report was published in 1930. He furiously opposed its recommendations to give a degree of autonomy to the fledgling nation and refused to cast away what he called 'that most truly bright and precious jewel in the crown of the King'.[32] As a result, he resigned from the Conservative shadow Cabinet in protest at its support for the Labour Party's India policy. For much of the 1930s, he cut an isolated but potentially powerful figure.

Within two weeks of losing office, Churchill launched himself into writing the biography of his sixth-great-grandfather, John Churchill, the First Duke of Marlborough. After just two years of work, he had finished the research and writing of the biography. The King and members of his family were, as was his custom, among the first to receive complimentary copies. Churchill's laudatory inscription to George V could not have been couched in terms more courtly. Not only did he extol the first duke's association with Queen Anne, but he sang the praises of the Sovereign himself: 'This is the story of how a wise Princess and Queen gave her trust and friendship to an invincible commander, and thereby raised the power and fame of England to a height never before known, and never since lost; and is submitted in loyal duty to a Sovereign under whom our country has come through perils even more grievous with no less honour.'[33]

Winston's association with the royal court, however fawning and ingratiating, did not pay his many bills. So, in December 1932, he did what he had always done when he was strapped for cash: he travelled to America where he planned to embark on a lucrative lecture tour. The trip very nearly ended in irreparable disaster. One evening, as he stepped out of a taxi, he glanced to the right to check for oncoming traffic and stepped into the road. But he had looked the wrong way, forgetting that traffic in New York would be coming from the opposite direction, and his portly frame was flung in the air after being hit by an off-duty taxi. For several minutes he lay unconscious in the road before he was sufficiently revived to be taken to the nearby Lenox Hill Hospital on the Upper East Side. As he waited for treatment, he was given a dubious welcome by the admitting receptionist. She had no idea who he was, and there was no way of telling if he had sufficient funds to pay for hospital care. Battered, bewildered, bleeding and dazed, Churchill managed to play his trump card. 'I am a British statesman and friend of the King,' he announced, and was promptly taken to a private room.[34]

The hospital was soon to find out that Mr Churchill wasn't bluffing. When news of Winston's accident broke in London, the King immediately asked one of his officials to make an international telephone call, then something of an expensive novelty, to Churchill's hospital to check on his condition. The King wasn't alone in wanting to know about Churchill's health; from his hospital bed, Winston had to worry about all sorts of tactics by unscrupulous members of the press who wanted an inside scoop. Fortunately, Churchill's bodyguard, Detective Inspector Walter Thompson, had accompanied Winston on his travels and was able to keep the journalists at bay. On one occasion, an enterprising female reporter, dressed as a nurse, almost obtained access to Winston's hospital room but was spotted and stopped by the sharp-eyed detective.[35] One benefit from the accident was that he requested and was given a doctor's note allowing him unlimited supplies of alcohol in Prohibition America.

While he was recuperating, Winston also heard from a figure of the past: Edward Mylius, the man who had been jailed for a year following his trial for libel against King George V. Now living in New York, Mylius wrote to thank Winston for extending two kindnesses before and during the trial, namely making sure he had access to legal volumes and granting his appeal for the remission of a week of his sentence. 'And now, after this long period of time,' Mylius continued, 'I am writing this, not so much to thank you, but to prove to you – not that you need any proof – because your heart is bigger than mine – that a kind and unusual act springing from bigness of heart and soul is never forgotten. But I do thank you too, and am glad you are in this country, which is quickly warming up to you.'[36]

Mylius' heartfelt note was not the only gesture of kindness Churchill received in the aftermath of his near-fatal accident. In Britain, around 140 people joined together and pitched in for the cost of a new car – a luxurious £2,000 Daimler limousine – for Winston upon his return. Among the donors, who included press baron Lord Beaverbrook, Bob Boothby MP and the Duke of Westminster, was his friend, the Prince of Wales. Ironically, Churchill made a small fortune churning out articles describing his accident in vivid detail. And after recovering in the Bahamas, he was even able to resume his lucrative lecture tour.

It was not long after his accident before Churchill was back in the fray. On his return home, he roundly condemned the headline-making debate held at the Oxford Union on 9 February 1933, where attendees voted in favour of the pacifist motion that 'this house will under no circumstances fight for its King and country'. It was seen by many as an insult both to the King and the war dead, and understood as giving succour to Britain's enemies. In a trenchant speech made just ten days after Adolf Hitler had become chancellor of Germany, Churchill criticized the vote as an 'abject, squalid, shameless avowal ... It is a very disquieting and disgusting symptom.' Hitler, who was, according to American columnist Joseph Alsop, deeply impressed by the sentiment of the resolution and what it said about Britain's youth, regularly cited the debate when discussing Britain's resolve with his generals.[37]

In spite of Churchill's indignation, the resolution reflected a significant current in the national mood. The British public had voted in their many millions to support the League of Nations' 'Peace ballot'. There was little appetite in the country for another bloodbath on the fields of Flanders, and no more willingness to take on the role of the world's policemen. Not for the first time, and not for the last, Winston was swimming against the tide.

In February and March of 1934, Churchill rose in the House of Commons to alert Parliament to the fact that Hitler would soon amass a powerful Air Force capable of threatening British territory. He confessed that he 'dreaded the day when the means of threatening the heart of the British Empire should pass into the hands of the present rulers of Germany'. His pronouncements fell on deaf ears. As Prime Minister MacDonald wrote to the King, Churchill received scarce support after his speech, coming 'only from a very small group of Members'.[38] He could have added that Churchill had made dire warnings before that had fallen wide of the mark, crying wolf a few times too often. Others felt differently about the rise of the Nazi party. During what historian John Wheeler-Bennett described as the 'respectable years' of the National Socialist regime, the King, the Prince of Wales and several senior politicians believed that Hitler would ultimately adhere to certain immutable principles of peace and respect concerning the sovereignty of other nations. The prince, in particular, was seen by contemporaries as pro-Nazi, a middle-aged man who flirted with the idea of becoming a dictator king.[39] The King took a more nuanced approach. While both father and son vociferously wished to avoid another war, the King made it clear to German diplomats and other Nazi visitors that he found the pace of German rearmament, not to mention what he called the 'Jew baiting', highly concerning.[40]

Both men believed Churchill was dangerously wrong-headed in his analysis of the international scene. Churchill thought otherwise, conclusions supported by credible information. What ministers found alarming about his public and private forecasts was that they were based on accurate inside knowledge that he should not have been able to access. It was increasingly clear that disaffected scientists, civil servants, military personnel and others were visiting his Kent home of Chartwell and quietly briefing Churchill about Britain's readiness for war and Germany's future plans. He came to be seen as such a threat by the establishment that his private phone conversations were tapped in order to identify his well-placed sources.[41]

In spite of his headline-making 'scoops', Churchill was slowly sliding down the pecking order of social influence, his star wattage not what it once was, and dimming further by the week. In the winter of 1934, at a dinner party in honour of the Prince of Wales and his new paramour, Wallis Simpson, organized by Society hostess Sybil Colefax, it was the American journalist H. R. Knickerbocker who was the main attraction. He had interviewed Stalin's mother and won the Pulitzer Prize for his articles on Russia's Five-Year Plan. During his time in Berlin, he had reported in detail on the ruthless Nazi government's sponsored harassment and murder of the Jews and was kicked out of the country for his pains. The stage was set for the American journalist and the veteran politician to make common purpose. It didn't turn out that way as Wallis, who was seated next to Winston, later recalled:

> The conversation turned to Russia and the European political scene. Sitting beside me, slumped back in his chair, the old statesman finally took exception to some of the visitor's opinions. When he could stand no more, like a battleship going into action, he turned on Knickerbocker to crumple him under extemporaneous salvos of logic and irony that would have done Winston proud on the floor of the House. A little later, as if regretting the expenditure of such powerful ammunition, he

After a hesitant start, the Queen enjoyed a convivial relationship with her first Prime Minister. He saw it as his central role to guide and nurture the young Queen in her constitutional duties, although their Tuesday night meetings often meandered into discussions of horse racing, which they both loved. Here they are with a young Prince Charles, later King Charles, and his sister Princess Anne.

'At Blenheim I took two very important decisions: to be born and to marry,' observed Sir Winston Churchill. Blenheim Palace was a gift of Queen Anne to the first Duke of Marlborough. It is the only non-royal and non-ecclesiastical palace in Britain.

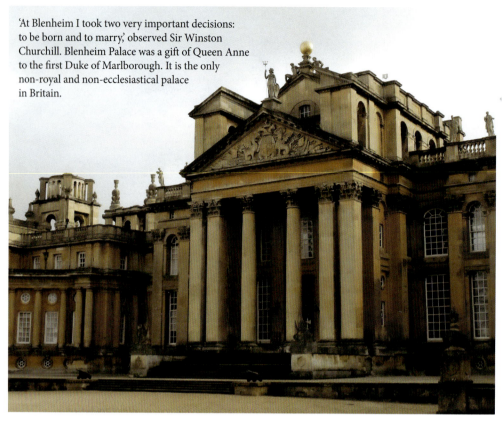

Winston's father Lord Randolph Churchill enjoyed a rumbustious relationship with the royal family, for a time the boon companion of the Prince of Wales, later Edward VII, before being challenged to a duel by the future King after a spectacular fall out.

Lady Randolph Churchill, the former American socialite Jennie Jerome, enjoyed a whirlwind courtship after meeting her future husband on board the royal yacht, *Victoria and Albert*, in 1873. King Edward VII boasted that Winston only came into the world thanks to his matchmaking.

Churchill liked to say he served six Sovereigns. Here is Queen Victoria with the future Edward VIII, flanked by (*right*) her son the future Edward VII and her grandson the future George V.

Though Winston loved history, which he studied at Harrow School, he was an indifferent scholar, much to the annoyance of his father, who thought his son would amount to nothing.

Aged twenty-one and looking very pleased with himself, Winston in the full-dress uniform of the 4th Hussars. When he was attached to the 21st Lancers in Sudan in 1898, he took part in the British Army's last cavalry charge in the battle of Omdurman.

In 1899, during the Boer War, Winston became an international celebrity after escaping from a South African prisoner-of-war camp. Before the grinning war correspondent left Durban, he sent his royal mentor Edward VII a letter detailing his audacious exploits.

When the German Kaiser Wilhelm II invited Winston to a review of military manoeuvres at Breslau in September 1906, Edward VII warned him to guard his tongue lest he give away sensitive military information to his host.

A couple of swells: Winston with Welsh firebrand and political mentor Lloyd George. The two young politicians introduced radical social measures that concerned and angered, among others, Edward VII.

When the young politician was offered a Cabinet post as President of the Board of Trade in 1908, he had to undergo a by-election in his Manchester constituency, which he lost. He found another seat in Dundee and took both his place in Cabinet and the hand in marriage of Clementine Hozier. As a wedding gift, the King gave him a gold-mounted walking stick engraved with the Marlborough arms.

Winston and the newly minted Mrs Churchill inspect an exhibit at the Hendon Air Pageant in 1910. He was an enthusiastic advocate of this new, if precarious, mode of transport. Winston learned to fly himself and set up the Royal Naval Flying Corps.

King Edward VII and his eldest son, the Prince of Wales, later King George V, had very different relations with Churchill. While Edward VII treated him like an errant son, George V was much less forgiving.

Winston, then Home Secretary, and his cousin, the Duke of Marlborough, about to depart for Buckingham Palace upon the death of King Edward VII.

As First Lord of the Admiralty, Churchill travelled around the coast inspecting Britain's Navy. Often, he joined King George V on the royal yacht to brief him on progress. It was not all plain sailing, the bumptious politician privately accusing the King of talking ill-informed nonsense.

During World War One, King George V frequently inspected troops stationed in northern France. On this occasion he was accompanied by the Prince of Wales. Both royals were privately delighted when Winston was removed from any post of substance after the cancellation of the disastrous Dardanelles campaign, of which he was the driving force.

Winston deep in conversation with the Prince of Wales outside the House of Commons, after a luncheon in June 1919 honouring American aviators. Once the war ended the two men became much closer.

In a speech written by Winston, the Prince of Wales addresses American troops in Hyde Park in 1919. The Prince admired Churchill's linguistic ability and strived to emulate his delivery.

Winston, his son Randolph and daughter Sarah, watching Trooping the Colour in 1920 as George V, on horseback, also observes the passing parade. After the war, the King's relationship with Churchill was much improved.

After two years out of the House of Commons, Winston returned to power in 1924, when he was made Chancellor of the Exchequer, a position he had aspired to as a small boy. George V came to admire his diligence and for the most part agreed with his policies.

The Duke of York, later King George VI, leaving his London home, 145 Piccadilly, in January 1936 to swear allegiance to the new King, Edward VIII, a role he assumed after the death of their father George V. The duke was horrified, as were the rest of the royal family, when Edward VIII promised to abdicate unless he could marry the twice-divorced American Wallis Simpson.

Edward VIII delivering his famous abdication broadcast from Windsor Castle, which was written in part by Churchill. The veteran politician suffered a mauling in the House of Commons when he argued that the King be given more time to consider his options. He also alienated the royal family, who felt the behaviour of the now Duke of Windsor was beyond the pale.

After their wedding in a French chateau in June 1937, the Duke and Duchess of Windsor accepted an invitation to visit Nazi Germany and meet with German leader Adolf Hitler. Their honeymoon visit created controversy in Britain and America, where another trip was cancelled after widespread protests.

growled to me, 'You know, Mrs. Simpson, I don't get a chance to do this sort of thing very often since my break with the Tory leadership. As a matter of fact, this is the first time Clemmy and I have been invited out this year.'[42]

In large part thanks to intimate social gatherings like this dinner party, Churchill rather warmed to Mrs Simpson. Like many within the prince's circle, Churchill at first considered Wallis to be a positive influence. She cut down the prince's drinking – allowing him to pour his first drink at seven o'clock sharp and not a minute earlier – and unlike his previous lover, Lady Thelma Furness, who thought that punctuality was for 'little people', Wallis impressed upon him the necessity for turning up to engagements and meetings on time. It was basic good manners. She was less successful in helping him to gain weight, the prince at times verging on the anorexic in his eating habits. Not for a moment did Churchill – or, for that matter, Wallis herself – contemplate that the prince might wish to marry the twice-wedded lady from Baltimore. Winston saw her as little more than a pleasant diversion for the prince before the main event: marriage to a suitable young English woman, preferably the daughter of a titled family with a stately home lurking in the background. Wallis, though, did one better than her dinner table companion. While both she and Churchill were monitored by MI5, it was only Wallis who was under the additional scrutiny of Scotland Yard surveillance.

He may have been out of favour politically, but as the King's silver jubilee approached, Winston found himself in a key position to shape the image of the royal family in the eyes of the nation and the Empire, present and future alike.

In 1934, Winston was introduced to the Hungarian filmmaker

Alexander Korda by his son Randolph. It was a creative match made in heaven. They both relished new challenges, were prepared to take risks and had an eye for the daring, innovative, exploratory. Korda was fresh off the success of his Oscar winning film, *The Private Life of Henry VIII*, which starred Charles Laughton, and he was eager to snag another royal drama, this time focusing on the reign of George V to coincide with the Silver Jubilee in May 1935. It was an ambitious project, the first time a history of a contemporary reign had been explored through the international medium of cinematography.

Korda asked Churchill to write the screenplay, which would focus on the major events of King George's time on the throne, from the People's Budget and the suffragette movement to the First World War and beyond. Winston dropped everything and got to work, his enthusiasm encouraged by the subject matter and the hefty £10,000 fee (about £600,000 today). Rather like *The Crown* television series of our time, the Korda film, provisionally entitled *The Reign of King George V*, was intended to introduce a young audience to events in the life of the nation that they were not fully aware of. Churchill told Korda that the film would 'bring home to a vast audience the basic truths about many questions of public importance'.[43]

The royal family's public image was a touchy subject, especially after the war, when so many monarchies lay broken on the side of the road of history. When a play exploring the relationship between King George III and the woman rumoured to have been his mistress, Hannah Lightfoot, was proposed for the stage, the playwright received an unambiguous thumbs down from the palace. 'In these days when some Thrones have disappeared, others are shaking and the wave of democracy appears to be rising it seems to His Majesty undesirable that the story should be given on the stage,' wrote the Lord Chancellor, Lord Cromer. Another play about George V's grandmother, Queen Victoria, was also given short shrift. 'The King will not hear of this play being produced,' wrote his private secretary, Lord Stamfordham.[44]

With Churchill at the helm, Buckingham Palace could be assured that the depiction of the royal family on the big screen would be respectful. It was about, in Churchill's phrase, 'England building'.[45] And that included defining the House of Windsor's role in the life of the nation.

The opening scenes, penned by Churchill in furious writing mode, show a fanfare of trumpets sounding out news of the accession followed by the coronation itself. Winston was most particular that every scene was authentic down to the last buttonhole. George V, a stickler for correct protocol and uniform, would have approved. This demand, though, added to the projected filming time and cost. Unlike *The Crown* or playwright Peter Morgan's Oscar-winning film, *The Queen*, there was no attempt in Churchill's screenplay to explore the interior or private life of the monarch, or of anyone in his family. What emerged instead was a broad, sweeping history of England during the King's reign with only a handful of scenes actually portraying the King himself, like, for instance, the King and Queen on the balcony at Buckingham Palace or at a baseball game in honour of the American troops. Left on the figurative cutting-room floor were Churchill's many, often contentious, interactions with the Sovereign.[46]

The film remains one of the tantalizing 'what ifs' of Churchill's story, because sadly, it was never made. Time constraints, government red tape and runaway costs ensured that the venture was stillborn. Instead, Churchill converted some of his ideas for the film into a seven-part essay series for the *London Evening Standard*. As someone who kept a statuette of Napoleon on his desk in appreciation of the triumphs of a supreme man of action, Winston was the polar opposite in instinct and character to King George V, who lived his days in 'well-considered inaction', to use Bagehot's phrase, with an infinite capacity for being bored where time-worn precedent was a royal virtue.[47] In Churchill's mind, though it may have been a virtue, it was not a particularly exciting one. What emerges from his profile of the King is that while Churchill appreciated the King's routine stoicism, there was little warmth or genuine affection for the man. He respected, rather than admired, the King.

By comparison, his description of George V's father, King Edward VII, was much more generous and affectionate. In his *Evening Standard* profile, he describes Edward VII as a good and attractive King who had a 'warm heart and much worldly wisdom'. He praised the 'sparkling quality' of a man who was 'greatly loved for himself by a host of friends … he moved in an atmosphere of gaiety and kindliness'.[48]

Compared to these high praises, the language Churchill used for George V was stiff and distant. He described the King as having a 'manly, straightforward nature'; as being 'by no means ill equipped' to deal with the problems of his time, which were many and varied. During his various trials and tribulations, he demonstrated a 'scrupulous self-restraint' and 'quiet courage'. In conclusion, he calls George V 'one of the best and truest Sovereigns who have occupied their ancient throne'. He was a king who had 'done his duty'.[49] It was a toddler, indeed, who summed up George V the best: Princess Elizabeth, known as Lilibet among the family, called him simply 'Grandpa England'.[50]

Where Churchill's essay did wax lyrical was in his description of the robust response of the Crown to the political tribulations of the early part of the century, particularly the period leading up to the First World War. 'Without the monarchy and without the skilful conduct and scrupulous personal self-restraint of a constitutional king, British political society might well have sunk into chaos at the very moment when an awful trial was approaching.' In Churchill's eyes, the monarch was 'more indispensable than ever to the civilisation of Britain and the cohesion of its Empire'.[51]

When the King died at Sandringham eight months later, on 20 January 1936, Churchill was in Morocco, preparing to leave Marrakesh for Tangier. He was tracked down by Sir Emsley Carr, the editor of the Sunday newspaper the *News of the World*. His newspaper needed a tribute by the following Sunday, 26 January. Churchill immediately changed his plans and began writing a profile of the late King, which had similar contours and sentiments to his previous newspaper work. Winston dictated the article to his personal secretary, Violet Pearman, as they travelled on the train, and the completed profile was in Carr's hands just four days after the King's death.[52] It was his last salute to a man with whom he had clashed swords, whom he had learned to respect if not revere, a sailor King who had reliably done his duty to his country, his kingdom and his empire for seventy years.

CHAPTER SEVEN

Three Minutes to Oblivion

WHEN IT CAME to dealings with royalty, Winston Churchill adhered to the counsel of Benjamin Disraeli, Queen Victoria's favourite Prime Minister: 'Everyone likes flattery; and when you come to Royalty you should lay it on with a trowel.'[1] No matter how thorny his relationships with Edward VII and George V had occasionally been, he cleaved to the Uriah Heep school of ingratiation. Indeed, some of his responses to royal complaints were so obsequious as to seem slyly mocking in their over-the-top tone and content.

Even though the new King, Edward VIII, was the younger man who owed much to Churchill's guidance and experience, it was the veteran politician who swore fealty and faithful service to the new incumbent on the throne, first in the loyal address he gave on behalf of the House of Commons on 27 January 1936, and second in a private letter he wrote to the King on 2 February. Though from this distance it reads like an extract from the script of the historic TV drama *Game of Thrones*, the sentiments, gracious and grandiloquent, deeply moved the new King.

I could not let these memorable days pass away without venturing to write how deeply I have felt for Your Majesty in the sorrow of a father's death, and in the ordeal of mounting a Throne.

I have many memories of the Prince of Wales since the Investiture at Caernarvon Castle twenty-five years ago, which are joyous and gay in my mind, and also above all I have the sense of a friendship with which I was honoured.

Now I address myself to the King; and offer dutifully yet in no formal sense my faithful service and my heartfelt wishes that a reign which has been so nobly begun may be blessed with peace and true glory; and that in the long swing of events Your Majesty's name will shine in history as the bravest and best beloved of all the sovereigns who have worn the island Crown.[2]

The new King felt he could rely on Churchill for his loyalty and generous spirit in the battles that lay ahead. Indeed, Churchill was one of the first politicians to be invited to dine with him after his accession to the throne. For his part, once the constitutional details regarding the new reign were completed, Winston returned to the pressing concerns of Japan annexing Chinese territories and the breakneck pace of German rearmament, a stick with which he continually beat the national government throughout the 1930s. With European tensions mounting following Germany's invasion of the demilitarized zone of the Rhineland in March 1936, the focus should have been on weightier matters than the King's girlfriend. But that was far from the case. London society was gripped by the King's infatuation with Mrs Wallis Simpson.

In Churchill's eyes, the King's current enchantment was, like all of his prior ones, a passing phase. When her name was uttered in dinner table conversation, his considered view was that in time Mrs Simpson would be dropped like all the others and that the King would move on to another grand passion. Like most practical men of the world, Churchill felt the prince ought to marry a suitable bride and take as many mistresses as he liked, just as his grandfather, King Edward VII, had done. It was an arrangement that, conducted with discretion and diplomacy, would be perfectly acceptable for all the parties concerned. He was confident he knew his man and felt comfortable psychoanalyzing the prince's love life during a conversation with novelist Mrs Belloc Lowndes: 'Women play only a transient part in his life. He falls constantly in and out of love. His present attachment will follow the course of all the others.'[3] Even so, Churchill was sensitive enough to notice that when Edward was with Wallis, all the nervous tics that had come to define his social presence – fiddling with his cufflinks and tie, shifting his weight from one foot to another, darting his eyes around the room – dropped away completely, and he became calm and whole. She was, he concluded, as necessary to his life as the air he breathed.[4]

At the same time, the very idea of giving up the throne of the greatest empire the world had ever seen for the sake of a middle-aged, twice-divorced American, with whom he claimed to enjoy a strictly platonic relationship, was utterly preposterous, indeed scarcely believable. It was, perhaps, the one single issue on which Churchill, Prime Minister Baldwin, President Roosevelt, and the German and Italian dictators Hitler and Mussolini could all agree: at various times, every one of these leaders expressed incredulity at the course Edward VIII eventually decided to take.[5]

As the months ticked by and Mrs Simpson remained on the scene, the public sightings of her in the King's company became more frequent. In March, the King dined at the Simpsons' apartment in Bryanston Court; in April, they both attended a house party at Himley Hall, the home of the Earl of Dudley; and on 28 May, Wallis and Ernest Simpson appeared in the Court Circular for the first time after dining at York House with the King, Prime Minister Baldwin and his wife, the Mountbattens and the Duff Coopers, as well as the American aviator Charles Lindbergh and his poet wife, Anne. Queen Mary read the romantic runes with concern. She told her friend Mabell Airlie, 'He gives Mrs. Simpson the most beautiful jewels ... I am so afraid that he may ask me to receive her.'[6]

Nor were dinner parties the end of it. In June, Wallis appeared by Edward's side as his guest at the Royal Ascot races, having been delivered to the storied racecourse in a private carriage. The rumour mill began to churn with speculation that the Simpsons were to divorce.

The King's lawyer and longtime adviser, Walter Monckton, was concerned by this spurious gossip – the notion of the King actually marrying Mrs Simpson was still considered completely outside the realm of possibility – and the potential damage to the Sovereign and the monarchy should this 'friendship' become more publicly conspicuous. He sought out Churchill's opinion on the best way to deal with an issue that needed careful handling. After Monckton gave his briefing, which had the King's own approval, he found Winston extraordinarily sympathetic, ready to help, and plainly anxious. He was dead-set against divorce proceedings for the Simpsons, believing it to be a most dangerous course. Churchill recorded of their meeting that, 'If any judgement was given in court against Mr Simpson it would be open to any Minister of Religion to say from the pulpit that an innocent man had allowed himself to be divorced on account of the King's intimacies with his wife. I urged most strongly that every effort should be made to prevent such a suit.'[7] The continued public presence of Mr Simpson was clearly a safeguard.

Like Monckton, Winston believed that the King's friendship should be kept as discreet as possible, and for that reason Wallis ought not to go to Balmoral as a guest that summer. Instead, he felt she should stay with friends in the vicinity. Churchill recorded: 'I deprecated strongly Mrs. Simpson going to such a highly official place upon which the eyes of Scotland were concentrated and which was already sacred to the memories of Queen Victoria and John Brown.'[8]

Two days after this discussion with Monckton, on 10 July, Winston and Clementine were invited by the King to dinner at York House, where Edward intended to introduce Wallis – sans husband – to his inner social circle, including Chief Whip David Margesson and Sir Samuel Hoare with their respective wives, together with the Duke and Duchess of York.

Winston, perhaps trying to break the ice, brought up the story of Mrs Fitzherbert, who had secretly married the heir to the throne, later King George IV, in 1785. Horrified, the Duchess of York tried politely to shut him down by saying, 'That was a very long time ago!' They eventually moved on to lighter topics.[9]

At the dinner, Churchill briefly mentioned to the King that he had spoken to Monckton and given him his view. Later, the King summoned Monckton to be fully briefed. He was dismayed to learn that Churchill was opposed to her plan to petition for divorce, trotting out the familiar argument that Wallis shouldn't be tied to an unhappy marriage simply because she was a friend of the King. Nor did he accept the advice to leave Wallis off the guest list for Balmoral: if Winston's intention was to suggest that the King should keep their relationship secret, that was a non-starter. In the King's eyes, he had nothing to be ashamed of in his friendship with Wallis.

He decided instead that he would refrain from asking Churchill for his advice in the future, knowing that he was unlikely to get the responses he wanted. He could hardly ignore Churchill altogether, though, since he still relied on his old speaking tutor's oratorical guidance. Within a couple of weeks, he was at Blenheim Palace at the unveiling of the Vimy Ridge Memorial. Before he addressed the crowd, he asked Churchill to look over the draft of his speech.[10]

That summer, the King hired the steam yacht *Nahlin* for a cruise along the Dalmatian coast. Wallis, once again unaccompanied, was one of the small group of guests. They stopped at various ports, followed, like seagulls behind a fishing boat, by a motley assortment of international media who made hay with the alleged royal romance. Noticeable by their absence were the British media, whose proprietors had made a gentleman's agreement to give the King privacy during his holiday – and beyond.

The King did, though, make himself a hostage to fortune by rejecting Churchill's common-sense advice to leave Wallis off the guest list for the traditional house party at Balmoral. Though she initially tried to cry off, the King was insistent that she join him up north. When she arrived at Aberdeen train station the King was photographed in goggles, kilt and tam-o'-shanter standing by his open-topped tourer, waiting to pick her up. In order to be there at her arrival, he had cancelled a long-standing invitation to open a local hospital, asking the Duke and Duchess of York to take his place. Local dignitaries were not amused, and their displeasure was made known within the corridors of power down south. Once again, Wallis' name appeared in the Court Circular as a guest at Balmoral. Inside the castle walls, it did not escape notice that Edward had given Wallis the best guest bedroom and had installed himself, not in the usual bedchamber of the reigning monarch, but in the small room that adjoined her suite.[11]

While the sleeping arrangements at Balmoral raised eyebrows, Wallis' arrival on 27 October at a law court in the town of Ipswich, where her divorce petition was heard, really had tongues wagging. At least, everywhere in the globe apart from Great Britain, where the King had successfully argued with press barons, notably Lords Beaverbrook and Harmsworth, that it was unfair to publicize Mrs Simpson's private life simply because she was a friend of the King.

The King was, as it turned out, clearly being disingenuous, since it was only three weeks later, on 16 November, that he met with Prime Minister Stanley Baldwin to officially declare his intention to marry Wallis Simpson and if necessary renounce the throne. That same evening he gave the news to Queen Mary. Baldwin thought this would be impossible, given the Church's views on divorce. Nonetheless, he agreed to put the matter to Cabinet who, after some discussion, convened a deputation of senior politicians, led by Lord Salisbury, to talk through the matter at greater length. Churchill was invited to join the group but demurred. His decision was strategic. Though he had not been personally consulted by the King on this issue since July, he felt certain that that would soon change, and he wanted to be seen as independent. Churchill planned to tell the King that, just as his fellow countrymen 'had made every sacrifice in the War', so the King 'must now be willing to make every sacrifice for his Country'.[12] This was almost word for word Queen Mary's horrified response when her eldest son had broached the news during dinner at Marlborough House, the Queen's London home.

As London Society gossiped wildly about the King's scandal, Churchill, as was his hallmark, was busy thinking outside the box. He came up with a plan also suggested by Esmond Harmsworth, son of Lord

Rothermere, that he felt could square the romantic circle – namely, a morganatic marriage. While this was a step change from his previous policy of playing a long game in the hope that the romance would fizzle out in time, he never thought for a moment of the 'dreadful possibility' of a Queen Wallis.[13] Popular among European royalty, a morganatic arrangement would have allowed their marriage, but without Wallis taking the equivalent title to the King's – that is, Queen or Queen Consort. Instead, she would take a lesser title, such as Duchess of Lancaster or Cornwall. It would require a special Act of Parliament, but in Churchill's eyes this was not an insurmountable obstacle. After all, even Queen Mary's grandparents had married under such an arrangement. While the King was in Wales visiting impoverished mining communities on 18–19 November, Winston arranged a lunch at Claridge's hotel between Wallis and press baron Esmond Harmsworth, where he explained the morganatic option.[14]

Wallis did not know what to make of the proposal, but she promised to raise the subject with the King when he returned to Fort Belvedere. Winston wrote to Clemmie, 'Max [Beaverbrook] rang me up to say that he had seen the gent [that is, the King] and told him the Cornwall plan was my idea. The gent was definitely for it. It now turns on what the Cabinet will say. I don't see any other way through.'[15] Baldwin's support though was essential if this plan was to be a runner. It was not forthcoming.

On 24 November, Baldwin started to think about damage control, should the King prove unwilling to comply with the government's advice. So, he summoned the three parliamentarians who could possibly lead an alternative government if the current Baldwin administration stepped aside: Clement Attlee, Sir Archibald Sinclair and Winston Churchill. He informed them that, if the King refused to abandon his determination to marry Wallis – morganatically or otherwise – he and his government would resign. Attlee and Sinclair immediately assured Baldwin that they would support this line of action and promised to refrain from forming their own governments in the event of an impasse. Churchill gave a more ambiguous response, declaring that 'he would certainly support the government'. His colleagues were unconvinced. His popularity and support of the King made him the object of widespread suspicion. Many inside and outside Parliament were concerned that he would lead a 'King's Party'. Diarist and politician Henry 'Chips' Channon noted, 'Winston Churchill, the old time-server, will summon a party meeting, create a new party and rule the country!'[16] The novelist Virginia Woolf was gripped by the same thought. She wrote, 'The different interests are queuing up behind Baldwin, or Churchill.'[17] There was never anything so formal as a King's Party, either before or during the royal crisis, but that did not prevent rampant speculation among London Society. A vexed former Prime Minister Ramsay MacDonald wrote, 'The danger is that a new Govt might get hold of the Executive and act as dictators. A person like Churchill might well put his hand to that job!'[18]

In the meantime, Baldwin and his Cabinet agreed to consult the Prime Ministers of the Dominions for their views on the morganatic marriage proposal. Channon wrote, 'It is the great week, and who will emerge triumphant? Love or the middle classes? Passion or the Empire?'[19] The response was mainly in the negative, giving Baldwin latitude to say that plan would not be supported either at home or abroad.

For his part, Churchill felt that the scandal was in the process of effecting an unjustifiable, perhaps even a sacrilegious shift in the balance in power in the constitution between the monarch and his government. What Churchill feared most was that if Baldwin successfully convinced Edward VIII to abdicate, it would establish a constitutional precedent for politicians to choose their kings, and the hereditary principle would be permanently tarnished. He said as much to the King himself, stating that, 'Whatever else might happen, the hereditary principle must not be left to the mercy of politicians trimming their doctrines "to the varying hour".'[20] A king was a king, Churchill felt, regardless of whether the politicians of the day liked or admired him.

In a conversation with Duff Cooper, Churchill worked himself up over what he considered to be the widespread betrayal of the King. Cooper recorded the questions that Churchill had peppered him with: 'What crime had the King committed? Had we not sworn allegiance to him? Were we not bound by that oath?'[21]

Though Winston argued the King's case from noble motives, there were many who thought they detected a strain of personal ambition in his response to the crisis. He and Baldwin were estranged both politically and individually. While Baldwin admired Churchill's qualities as a speaker and phrase maker, he thought his judgment on the major issues of the day fundamentally unsound, and deliberately kept him out of Cabinet, failing to recognize until it was too late that Churchill's concerns over German aggression were legitimate. Years later, when the former King reflected on the abdication, he was convinced that Churchill and his newspaper magnate crony Lord Beaverbrook were 'united in a common purpose to unhorse Baldwin'.[22] (Similarly, when Winston's son, Randolph, asked Beaverbrook why he and Churchill had played such a prominent part in the abdication, he replied simply, 'To bugger Baldwin.')[23]

All this jockeying for power and position was taking place with the British public blithely unaware of what was going on with their new King. At the time, the BBC and the daily newspapers adhered to a voluntary vow of silence. The story only came spilling out after the Bishop of Bradford, Dr Alfred Blunt, inadvertently sparked the crisis with a few remarks mentioning the King's 'need for grace' in a sermon about the forthcoming coronation. 'The storm has burst,' wrote Channon on 2 December, after several newspapers including the London *Evening Standard* coyly alluded to the matter.[24]

That day, while the Cabinet was in session discussing the issue, Churchill had lunch with Sir Walter Citrine, the leader of the Trade Union Congress. Citrine later recalled that Winston 'was very concerned about what might happen' and 'stressed that the King was deeply in love with her and would not give her up'. Towards the end of lunch, Churchill 'very quietly' remarked, 'I will defend him. I think it is my duty.'[25] He exhibited the same loyalty to both the man and the Crown as he had as Home Secretary when he intervened in the Mylius libel case at the beginning of George V's reign.

The following day, 3 December, front-page stories about the King and his cutie – Churchill and Beaverbrook's nickname for Mrs Simpson – were published in most London newspapers. Even *The Times*, known as the paper of record, made an oblique reference to 'a marriage incompatible with the throne'.[26] In the House of Commons, Churchill rose to speak, asking Baldwin, 'Would my right hon. friend give us an assurance that no irrevocable step will be taken before a formal statement has been made to Parliament?' There was, he argued, no need to rush. Winston's question seemed sensible and reasonable and was accompanied by cheering from both sides of the house. Baldwin gave a non-committal response.[27]

Afterwards, Winston drove to Stornoway House, Max Beaverbrook's London residence, where Max was waiting with the King's two legal advisers, George Allen and Walter Monckton. In their hands was a document that threatened to escalate the crisis. The King had written a speech, outlining his predicament, that he hoped to broadcast on the radio so that the public could hear him argue his case at first hand.[28]

Before taking such a momentous step, Edward felt that he needed to bring in the big guns – as Churchill had previously anticipated. The King later recalled he decided to consult his 'old friend Winston Churchill, whose reverence for the monarchy and knowledge of British constitutional conduct was unequalled. He had been in and out of my life so long that I was confident he would not desert me in my hour of trial'.[29] Moreover, the King wanted to know whether Winston might support his leaving the country for a time to put some distance between himself and the crisis. It would give the public time to decide if they wanted him to resume his reign, with Wallis as his consort.

Somewhat surprisingly, given that it was the first time Winston had been formally consulted by the King since July, he staunchly opposed both of the King's wishes. He and Beaverbrook were in agreement that for Edward to give his broadcast over the heads of his ministers would be a grave constitutional overreach, since by convention, he could only speak the words of his ministers. When Monckton returned to see the King at Buckingham Palace, he told him that Churchill considered the broadcast would be 'a tactical blunder of the first magnitude'.[30] Edward later softened the rhetoric in his memoir, *A King's Story*: 'While Mr. Churchill and Max Beaverbrook were both ardently in favour of my carrying the fight to Mr. Baldwin, they doubted that the broadcast as devised was quite the right way to do so.'[31]

On the question of the King travelling abroad, Churchill and Beaverbrook were even more uncompromising. Edward recalled, 'They deplored the idea of my leaving the country even for a day. Mr. Churchill particularly maintained that the immediate effect of my departure would be to leave Mr. Baldwin in undisputed command of the situation; on that account alone he advised that my plan, if carried out, would almost certainly prove to be a major mistake.'[32]

The King later saw Baldwin at Buckingham Palace to discuss his idea of giving a broadcast. Inevitably, the Prime Minister's response was unenthusiastic, as it was when he agreed to the King's request that he formally see Churchill for advice. Baldwin immediately regretted his decision to allow the rogue monarch to consult with his political arch-nemesis. 'I have made my first blunder,' he wrote.[33]

Meanwhile, by the evening of 4 December, the lady in question had vanished. After kissing the King goodbye at Fort Belvedere, she headed for the Channel ferry and was driven pell-mell to the south of France in a vain attempt to escape the physical and mental assaults upon her body and mind. A brick had been thrown through the window of her rented home in Regent's Park – Churchill thought by one of Beaverbrook's men – to encourage her to leave. While she travelled to a villa owned by her friends, Herman and Katherine Rogers, Baldwin was giving the last rites to Churchill's plan of a morganatic marriage. He told the House of Commons that there was no precedent for a morganatic marriage of the reigning Sovereign, only for lesser members of the royal family. 'The lady whom he marries,' Baldwin argued, 'by the fact of her marriage to the King, necessarily becomes Queen.' He then touched on the most sensitive part of the problem, that any children of the marriage would be in the direct line of succession to the throne. When he declared that the government was not prepared to introduce legislation to deal with such a case, the chamber broke into cheers so loud that Baldwin was prevented from speaking for several minutes. The morganatic option, upon which Churchill had expended so much political capital, was officially dead in the water.[34]

Afterwards Winston motored to Fort Belvedere for dinner with the King. During his drive to the Fort, Churchill resolved that, since it was the first time he had been directly consulted in several months, he must be discreet with his counsel and only stick to one piece of advice. That counsel would be that the King should bide his time, asking for a delay rather than committing to any course of action. He would further suggest inviting two palace doctors, Lord Dawson and Sir Thomas Horder, to the Fort, in order to examine him with a view to stating that the strain of the past weeks had taken such a serious toll on the King's health as to make him unfit to make any rash decisions or public comments on the matter. The King thought the scheme amusing, but he did not agree with playing for time if, in his heart, his decision was already made.

Practical matters aside, during dinner the King was deeply touched and felt a swelling of pride and patriotism when Churchill spoke about the monarchy. 'It lived, it grew, it became suffused with light,' he recalled. By contrast, Baldwin's monarchy was a 'dry and lifeless thing, sheltered and remote'.[35]

Churchill expressed disgust with Baldwin and his Cabinet, who were forcing their Sovereign into an ultimatum, one which threatened the very hereditary principle on which their constitutional monarchy was based. Churchill told the King that he 'should retire to Windsor Castle and close the gates'. It was past midnight by the time Winston took his leave; his last words to Edward were, 'Sir, it is a time for reflection. You must allow time for the battalions to mass.'[36] Though the King was moved by the veteran politician's royalist rhetoric, his lovesick mind was made up. If he couldn't marry Wallis and keep the throne, he was prepared to tell the Prime Minister that he intended to abdicate.

The following day, 5 December, Winston sent a letter to Baldwin rehashing the need for more time and emphasizing the King's inner turmoil. He argued that 'it would be most cruel and wrong to extort a decision from him in his present state.'[37] Baldwin was not convinced, nor were the majority of the Cabinet. Nonetheless Churchill must have received enough positive feedback to send an almost manically optimistic letter to the King: 'News from all fronts! No pistol to be held at the King's head. No doubt that this request for time will be granted. Therefore, no final decision or Bill till after Christmas – probably February or March … Good advances on all parts giving prospects of gaining good positions and assembling large forces behind them.'[38]

But it was already too late. The King had not been able to bring himself to tell his political champion that he had withdrawn from the lists and had already sent Monckton to Whitehall to officially inform Stanley Baldwin of his intention to abdicate.[39] When Beaverbrook heard the news, he tried to tell Winston, 'our cock won't fight', but Churchill refused to believe what he called the 'miserable news'.[40] Returning to Fort Belvedere for lunch, Churchill spent the whole meeting on the brink of tears as he spoke at length about 'the twisting, crooked tricks of Government'.[41] As much as Churchill's company and support encouraged the King, it did not reverse what had quickly become a firm resolve to abandon the throne.

While the Prime Minister had not allowed Edward VIII to speak directly to the nation, there was nothing to stop his knight errant from proclaiming the King's case to an eager public. On Sunday morning, Winston published an article voicing his concerns and complaints about the government's handling of the crisis. He pointed out the practical point that, whatever happened, legally there was no possibility that the King would be able to marry Wallis before her divorce was finalized, which would take at least six months and, he wrote, 'may for various reasons ... never be accomplished at all.' He continued, 'That on such a hypothetical and suppositious basis the supreme sacrifice of abdication and potential exile of the Sovereign should be demanded, finds no support whatever in the British constitution.'[42] It was an appeal to reason and the sense of fair play that is at the heart of the British character. While Churchill's article gained support from the man and woman in the street, the political class remained suspicious of his motives, seeing him as trying to establish himself as the leader of a King's Party. In this febrile atmosphere, Churchill's secret meeting at Chartwell, his country home, that fateful Sunday with his loyal political ally Bob Boothby and the leader of the Liberal Party, Archie Sinclair, had hackles bristling. They drafted a statement, hoping the King might sign it, which promised that he would never, as long as he was King, contract a marriage against the will of his ministers. As Chips Channon explained, 'It would give him a way out for in the future, should his position become intolerable, he could still abdicate, or, as might easily happen, his future ministers might eventually allow the marriage.' It was effectively a new version of Churchill's strategy of playing for time. Again, it was too late. As they drafted their statement, the Cabinet was drafting the Bill of Abdication.[43]

On Monday, 7 December, Churchill spoke at the Anglo-French luncheon club where there was some embarrassment, according to Lady Milner, when he proposed a loyal toast to the King's health. He ventured to speak at greater length about the King's predicament, but he was prevented from doing so by the club chairman. This should have been a clue about the change in mood towards the King. He arrived at the House of Commons as Prime Minister Baldwin was telling MPs that while no final decision had been reached, it was up to the King to make up his mind whether to stay or go. After he finished, Churchill was on his feet asking once again for a delay. Whereas the previous week he had been listened to respectfully, this time he had misjudged the mood of the House.

MPs erupted with a cold fury, shouting him down as he tried to be heard above the din. Realizing it was a losing battle, he bellowed one last question at Baldwin: 'You won't be satisfied until you've broken him, will you?' before stalking out of the chamber only minutes after he had entered.[44] It was a turning moment for the King's supporters, their champion leaving the field of battle unhorsed, his lance broken. 'I think he is done for,' wrote author Blanche Dugdale in her diary. 'In three minutes his hopes of return to power and influence are shattered.'[45] Diarist Harold Nicolson measured it at five minutes.[46]

Even his closest friends and supporters accused him of self-seeking and scheming against the Prime Minister.[47] Boothby wrote a scalding note savaging his colleague. 'This afternoon you have delivered a blow to the King, both in the House and in the country, far harder than Baldwin ever conceived of. You have reduced the number of potential supporters to the minimum possible.'[48] The backlash against Churchill even overshadowed Wallis' statement, which she made from the south of France, renouncing any intention to marry the King. For the last few days, she had been reduced to shouting down a poor international telephone line telling the King, 'Do not abdicate. Do nothing reckless. Listen to your friends.'[49] Her words went unheeded, the Prime Minister spending hours at Fort Belvedere discussing the terms and language of the Abdication Bill which was to be presented before the House of Commons the following day.

On Thursday, 10 December, barely a week after the crisis became public, Edward's three brothers, the Dukes of York, Gloucester and Kent, arrived at Fort Belvedere to bear witness to perhaps the most important royal document since the Magna Carta. By signing it – placing the initials 'R. I.' behind his name for the last time – Edward officially declared his 'irrevocable determination to renounce the throne for Myself and for My descendants'. A packed House of Commons heard the speaker read the Bill, his voice breaking at the words 'renounce the throne'.[50]

Baldwin then gave his speech, in which he praised the King's constitutional and upright behaviour through the duration of the crisis. As Winston listened to the proceedings, he sat doubled over in the depths of grief.[51] He then rose to give his own speech in which he extolled the virtues of King Edward VIII, soon to be the Duke of Windsor: 'I venture to say that no Sovereign has ever conformed more strictly or more faithfully to the letter and spirit of the Constitution than his present Majesty. In fact, he has voluntarily made sacrifices for the peace and strength of his realm which go far beyond the bounds required by the law and the Constitution.'

He also made a point of trying to explain his own position during the crisis. 'It was essential,' he said, 'that there should be no room for assertions after the event that the King had been hurried in his decision. I believe that if this decision had been taken last week it could not have been declared that it was an unhurried decision, so far as the King himself was concerned.' Speaking as a friend, he continued, 'I should have been ashamed, if, in my independent and unofficial position, I had not cast about for every lawful means, even the most forlorn, to keep him on the Throne of his fathers, to which he had only just succeeded amid the hopes and prayers of all.'[52]

Winston had recovered his dignity in the three days since his humiliation in the House of Commons, and now a captivated chamber listened to his speech with sympathy and understanding. When he spoke of King Edward's 'discerned qualities of courage, of simplicity, of sympathy, and, above all, of sincerity rare and precious, which might have made his reign glorious in the annals of this ancient Monarchy,' he was greeted with supportive cries of 'Hear, hear!' To cheers, he went on to 'assert that his personality will not go down uncherished to future ages that it will be particularly remembered in the homes of his poorer subjects and that they will ever wish from the bottom of their hearts for his private peace and happiness and for the happiness of those who are dear to him'.[53]

As the consummate public speaker, in full possession of his powers, he concluded his speech by looking forward rather than back, weaving German rearmament into the future of the Crown. 'Danger gathers on our path,' he told the House. 'We cannot afford – we have no right – to look back. We must look forward.' The dangers presented by a rapidly rearming Germany, he suggested, must be met by a unified Britain under the leadership of its new Sovereign. 'The stronger the advocate of monarchical principle a man may be, the more zealously must he now endeavour to fortify the Throne and to give to his Majesty's successor that strength which can only come from the love of a united nation and Empire.'[54]

Meanwhile, at Fort Belvedere, the future of King George VI and the Duke of Windsor, two brothers now taking different paths in life, was being determined. Money was the central topic. In a letter to George VI, dated 21 February 1937, the ex-King admitted he had previously told him that he was 'very badly off'.[55] He was being, at the very least, fluid with the truth. At that time, he had a fortune of approximately £1.1 million (£66 million today), which on its own would have given him an extremely comfortable life. He told, according to his official biographer, Philip Ziegler, a 'foolish lie', stating that he had only £5,000 a year. When he spoke to Churchill about his finances, he gave the distinct impression that he was so poor he could not survive without being subsidized by the government or the new King. Later, when George VI and Churchill learned the full extent of Edward's duplicity about the substantial amount he had in savings, made from the Duchy of Cornwall estate when he was Prince of Wales, they both realized they had been double-crossed.[56]

One of the ironies of this tawdry affair is that Edward VIII had rejected Churchill's suggestion that he play the long game, go through with the coronation and then marry Wallis, since he did not want to mislead the British people. But he had no misgivings about lying to Churchill and his younger brother, the man who would soon be his anointed Sovereign.

As Philip Ziegler has observed, Edward's lies 'alienated the two men on whose good will he was to rely most heavily: his brother and Winston

Churchill ... [It was] the worst mistake of his life. He was to suffer the consequences until the day he died.'[57] This would never be more true than during the upcoming war. The exposure of his trickery was inevitable, and it would permanently alter the dynamic between the King, ex-King and Churchill.

On 11 December, the day of the abdication, Churchill had lunch with the Duke of Windsor at Fort Belvedere. Edward wanted to say goodbye to his old friend and to let him run the rule over the farewell speech he was due to broadcast later that day. Winston made only two changes, inserting the phrases 'bred in the constitutional tradition by my Father' and 'one matchless blessing, enjoyed by so many of you and not bestowed on me, a happy home with his wife and children'. During that lunch, the King ceased to be King.

While they sat at the table, at exactly one fifty-two that afternoon, His Majesty's Declaration of Abdication Act was passed by the House of Lords with the resoundingly medieval words, '*Le Roy le veult*'. King Edward VIII was no more. Winston was struck at just how matter-of-fact it all was: one minute he was sitting across the table from his Sovereign, and the next he was not. No bells rang, no bagpipes wailed, no trumpets sounded, there was no formal ritual exchange of the royal sceptre or crown.

Edward later recalled that when he walked Churchill out of the Fort, the aged politician stood in the doorway, his hat in one hand, his trademark walking stick in the other. With tears in his eyes, Churchill began to tap out a beat on the floor, and recited the words of a poem by Andrew Marvell, on the occasion of the beheading of King Charles I: 'He nothing common did or mean, Upon that memorable scene.' He turned towards his car, and by the time he got inside, the tears had already begun to roll down his cheeks. His chauffeur drove him to Chartwell in silence.[58]

That evening, he listened to the duke's broadcast, made from Windsor Castle. Tears were never far away as he heard the ex-King pledge his allegiance to his younger brother and confess to his audience that he had 'found it impossible to carry the heavy burden of responsibility and to discharge my duty as King as I would wish to do, without the help and support of the woman I love'. Wallis listened to his words as she lay on a sofa in the villa where she was staying, her head covered by a blanket.[59]

As for the man who was now Duke of Windsor, his bags were packed, and a naval destroyer, HMS *Fury*, was waiting to take him to France where he would disembark and board a train to Austria where he intended to wait out the next six months in a private castle before being reunited with his cutie. Before he left, he found time to pencil a small note of gratitude to Winston: 'Thank you again for all great help and understanding. Au Revoir. Edward.'[60]

When the trembling Duke of York accepted his dreaded destiny, there was little in the way of courtly hyperbole from Churchill. It would doubtless not have escaped the new King's notice that Churchill, that great monarchist, showed scant enthusiasm for the advent of his reign. Where were the ringing romantic phrases that had greeted his elder brother? *His* name, according to Churchill, had been destined to shine in history as the bravest and best beloved of all the sovereigns – what of that? His inexperienced, self-effacing younger brother was an also-ran in the hyperbole stakes. It took Winston until April to formally pledge his allegiance: 'I have served your Majesty's grandfather, father and brother for very many years, and I earnestly hope that your Majesty's reign will be blessed by Providence and will add new strength and lustre to our ancient Monarchy.'[61]

Though the new King and Queen regarded Churchill with suspicion – like so many of the court and political class – the King had to recognize that Churchill had, at the expense of his own hard-won reputation, strived to keep his brother on the throne, a campaign that the Duke of York desperately hoped would succeed. Shy, stammering and prone to what his staff called 'gnashes' of temper, he felt utterly adrift as the tide forced him in the direction he feared – to occupy the throne as King George VI. If Churchill had prevailed and the morganatic marriage solution had been accepted as the elegant way of untying the constitutional knot, the Duke of York would have been spared his doom. He would have continued in his family life, perfectly happy to live in his elder brother's shadow.

There is a further irony in this constitutional conundrum. If Churchill had been successful and Edward VIII, who was enthusiastically pro-Nazi and pro-appeasement, had remained on the throne, his own position against German rearmament would have been further weakened. Or at the very least, rearmament may well have been further and fatally delayed.

There was, too, the added possibility of Baldwin resigning, as he threatened to do, and Churchill leading a King's Party to keep Edward on the throne, his position endorsed by the will of the people. Certainly, as historian Susan Williams has argued, the British people wanted Edward, who had as Prince of Wales won the hearts of the public, to remain as Sovereign. Backed by the people and with Churchill as Prime Minister, Britain at the very least would have prepared for war more effectively and more quickly. Another of the many 'what ifs' of this storied slice of royal history.

CHAPTER EIGHT

Into the Wilderness

FOR A WEEK, the English public had held its collective breath as the abdication drama played out. Then, like an ocean liner that had once dominated the horizon, the newly launched ex-King sailed on and out of sight. When George VI presided over his first accession council, on which Winston served, he declared that his first act as King would be to grant his predecessor a full royal dukedom: the former Edward VIII would henceforth be styled His Royal Highness the Duke of Windsor.

Now the focus turned to the new head of state, King George VI. He had a hard act to follow. His older brother, who had travelled the world on behalf of Britain and the monarchy, was hugely popular and charismatic, by far the brightest star in the royal sky. His easy charm and disarming manner had endeared him to the watching millions who followed his travels on the cinema newsreels. George VI, on the other hand, was shy, stammering and unused to the public spotlight. His delightful daughters, Princesses Elizabeth and Margaret, and his captivating Scottish wife, Elizabeth Bowes-Lyon, were his secret weapons. They personified his image as a reliable, devoted family man, ready to do his duty – unlike you-know-who.

The Duke of Windsor's passage into exile would give the new King time and opportunity to establish himself on the throne and in the hearts of the people who were now his subjects. Everyone, including the duke, was agreed on that strategy. What had not been agreed was whether, when and how the ex-King and his soon-to-be bride, Mrs Simpson, would eventually return. It was one of the vexatious questions that Churchill grappled with in the years following the abdication. He saw it as his role to lay the groundwork for the duke's eventual homecoming, while using his experience and influence to help shape and support the new reign. As he wrote to a friend, 'The more firmly the new King is established, the more easy it will be for the old one to come back to his house.'[1]

Churchill was seen as the new duke's unofficial representative as he continued to fight on his behalf. Two days after the accession council, on 14 December 1936, Churchill met with senior Conservative MP Samuel Hoare to discuss their plans to protect the ex-King from unnecessary disgrace, through either unfavourable publicity or penury. When Winston wrote to the duke the following day to inform him of developments, he had both good news and bad to convey. On the one hand, he assured the duke that Hoare was a reliable ally. On the other, Winston insisted that the duke would have to adhere to the stipulation of Neville Chamberlain, then serving as Chancellor of the Exchequer, that the ex-King continue to live 'absolutely separate until everything is settled and the new Civil List is voted'.[2] The Civil List, a Bill which apportions the amount of public funding set aside for the maintenance of the royal family, was submitted to Parliament by the Sovereign at the beginning of every reign, until it was replaced by the Sovereign Grant in 2011. In the case of the 1937 Civil List, all eyes were on the question of whether taxpayer money would be funnelled towards a man who had abandoned his duty and fled the scene.

At his Austrian retreat, Schloss Enzesfeld, a castle near Vienna owned by the Rothschilds, the duke was on tenterhooks as he waited for his affairs to be settled in London. He had little to occupy his time and took to calling his younger brother at Buckingham Palace several times a day, acting like an unwanted back-seat driver, advising and correcting him until the King finally snapped and told the palace switchboard not to put through calls from his brother.[3] The duke's former equerry, Piers Legh, visited him during this time and found him 'playing the jazz drums very loud and long to a gramophone record'. This seemed to console him slightly, as did the copious amounts of brandy which he drank as he waited impatiently to be reunited with Wallis. His sleep was erratic, his waking hours spent playing golf or poker, skiing or shopping in Vienna. To kill time, he spent days organizing the castle's wine collection. When there were sufficient numbers of guests, he would amuse them with his celebrated imitation of Winston Churchill trying to persuade him not to abdicate: 'Sir, we must fight ...'[4]

In this miasmic atmosphere, the duke saw dangers in the shadows, feeling that those he had left behind in London were hatching plots to discredit him. A flurry of negative press left the duke with the impression that the whole of society was against him. He expressed these fears to his mother, Queen Mary, stating that he could not avoid drawing the conclusion that 'having got me "down" certain forces wish to keep me there'.[5] His suspicions seemed to be confirmed when the King commanded his youngest brother, the Duke of Kent, to postpone a visit in January to accompany his elder brother on a skiing holiday. In fact, George VI was only trying to help his outcast brother; his rationale was that, with the abdication so fresh in the public memory, a highly publicized royal visit could only stir up resentment towards the former King. But the duke felt that it was a gratuitous personal humiliation to be denied the visit.[6]

Among the duke's real critics in London, the most prominent was Cosmo Lang, the Archbishop of Canterbury, who attacked him for his refusal to put aside his 'craving for private happiness' at the expense of royal duty, preferring instead to mix with 'vulgar society'. The archbishop was quickly upbraided by those who felt his remarks lacked Christian charity, and Churchill reassured the beleaguered duke that Lang's comments did not represent mainstream opinion. As he wrote, 'Even those who were very hostile to your standpoint turned round and salved their feelings by censuring the Archbishop.'[7]

Still the hits kept on coming. The duke caught wind of plans for the removal of Wallis' security detail, up to then funded by the British taxpayer. They were only scrapped when the duke's boon companion, Fruity Metcalfe, argued that this would drive the duke 'mad quicker than anything else', and that it might provoke him to leave his seclusion in Austria to join her in France.[8]

As the weeks ticked by, the duke's official status gradually diminished, as he was informed that he was no longer a Knight Companion of the Order of the Garter (the highest rank of chivalry in the land), or a privy counsellor, or an Admiral of the Fleet, or an aide-de-camp to the new King. Much to his chagrin, the positions he held as honorary colonel-in-chief of a small army of regiments, including his favourite, the Welsh Guards, were also taken away. His bespoke royal dukedom, of only a few weeks' vintage, was the only title that remained to him.

Inevitably, he blamed his brother, the King, whom both the duke and his future bride referred to dismissively as 'that stuttering idiot'. The new King, on his side, had grievances of his own. By February 1937, his advisers had discovered the duke's duplicity with regard to his finances. The current calculations for the duke's allowance were based on his pre-abdication plea that he would be 'very badly off' and would need funding from either the government or the new King. Before the abdication, King George VI had agreed a figure of £25,000 a year (£1.5 million today) from the public purse to keep him in the style of an ex-King. Now that it was revealed that Edward VIII already had around £1.1 million in savings (£64 million today), the King's advisers told him that the previous agreement ought to be considered null and void.[9]

The year 1937 was a precarious time for the monarchy, what with a new, untested King, an increasingly disaffected elder brother and a Labour Party whose leader, Clement Attlee, considered the monarchy and the current conception of kingship to be out of date. Negotiations with regard to the Civil List, which the King submitted in March, needed delicate handling. Churchill, sensing the danger to the institution, quietly pointed out to the Chancellor, Neville Chamberlain, that any dispute between the two brothers would be 'a disaster of the first order to the monarchy'.[10] For his part, George VI was extremely anxious to avoid any controversy that might overshadow the upcoming coronation.

At the first Civil List committee meeting Churchill, working in tandem with Lloyd George, was keen to keep mention of 'awkward topics' with regard to discussion of the royal finances to a minimum. Here he performed a signal service not only for the new King but the Duke of Windsor. Given the fact that the duke had not been truthful about his financial position to Churchill as well as the King, the veteran politician could be excused for questioning his loyalty to the former Sovereign. However, in his eyes the monarchy could not be tarnished, whatever the behaviour of individual office holders. It was incumbent upon the committee to negotiate a settlement that maintained, in his cherished phrase, 'the honour and dignity of the Crown'.[11] He put forward an acceptable solution whereby the King would honour the original agreement and fund his brother with £25,000 annually, tax free. For his part, the duke would not request any financial provision from the Civil List. This agreement was negotiated verbally and through back channels so that the Civil List was able to be passed by Parliament without any mention being made of provision for the Duke of Windsor, who was able to live in grand style in a rented villa in the south of France. A measure of how adroitly Churchill had handled negotiations regarding the funding of the Civil List was the fact that private financial wrangling between the brothers dragged on until February 1938 with negotiations becoming so rancorous that at one point the duke threatened to prevent Balmoral being used as a summer holiday home by members of the family.

Not everyone agreed with the perspective of Churchill's overriding partiality towards the monarchy. Chamberlain, who supported the King, wrote to his sisters telling them that Churchill and Lloyd George had acted like 'pirates' who had made themselves 'champions of the Duke versus the King'. George VI didn't see it that way. He wrote an appreciative letter to Churchill thanking for his work in settling the Civil List in a very, well, civil manner: 'I know how devoted you have been, & still are, to my dear brother, & I feel touched beyond words by your sympathy & understanding in the very difficult problems that have arisen since he left us in December.'[12]

Churchill's devotion to the ex-King did not prevent George VI and his aides from seeking him out to test the murky political waters. Nor was his advice predictable. While he argued that the duke's payment should not be contingent – as some Cabinet ministers argued – 'upon the Duke not returning to England without the King's permission', he felt it was 'altogether a personal and brotherly affair'.[13] It was, he believed, no business of the government to interfere in the private matters of the royal family. But that belief did not stop him from voicing his own view, namely that although the duke would be under no explicit requirement to remain abroad, it would nevertheless be better if he did so for a considerable amount of time. Winston hastened to reassure the new Sovereign that he 'would urge [the duke] most strongly to allow several years to pass before taking up his residence in England. Time is a healer of many things.'[14]

The other matter that had palace courtiers, lawyers and ministers wringing their hands was what to call Wallis Simpson when she eventually married the ex-King. Would she take the title Her Royal Highness the Duchess of Windsor, equivalent to her husband's? It was a decision that ultimately would cause a bitter rupture between the duke and his family.

Sharp legal minds argued that the rank of Royal Highness was established as Edward's inalienable birthright by Letters Patent issued by King George V in 1917. It was customary for a wife to adopt the rank and titles of her husband upon marrying. Therefore, whether the King and his family liked it or not, Wallis would become a Royal Highness like her husband – as should any of their descendants.[15]

The King was unconvinced. In his eyes the abdication boiled down to the fact that the British people had rejected Wallis as a possible Queen, meaning that, by extension, she was unfit for any form of official incorporation into the royal family. He was backed in this position by his family and naturally the royal court. They believed that Wallis' third marriage would likely go the way of her previous two and if, after divorcing Wallis, the duke decided to remarry again, and again – how many rogue, despoiled Royal Highnesses might they be forced to recognize? Taking that road would cause untold damage to the status of the monarchy.

At the end of April, just weeks before the coronation, Clive Wigram, the King's private secretary, reached out to Churchill to gauge his opinion. In his response, Churchill wrote that he did 'not think that any Government will be found in England which would advise the Crown to take such a step', that is, to grant Wallis royal status. 'On the contrary,' he continued, 'I am sure that they would advise insistently against it.' Winston placed his thumb firmly on the King's side of the scale, even suggesting that the duke would be well advised to match Wallis' non-royal status by renouncing his own: 'Ranking only as a Duke. Such a course would undoubtedly give much greater freedom in many ways.' In particular, Churchill warned that if the duke were to insist on the royal title for Wallis, it 'would certainly be an obstacle to the duke's wishes in other respects' – namely, the Civil List provisions.[16]

Even though the law appeared to be on the duke's side, the King's men argued successfully that the duke's HRH title was derived as a gift from the King, which he could confer or withhold at his pleasure. He had given the HRH title to the duke as his brother, as a son of King George V, and as a gesture of recognition of his former status. None of these rationales extended to Wallis.

Although Churchill intervened on the King's side with regard to Wallis' title, he continued to defend the ex-King's reputation and interests in London. In April, distinguished royal writer Geoffrey Dennis, an Oxford-educated official in the League of Nations secretariat, published a book called *Coronation Commentary*, which was a scathing attack on the ex-King, his 'shop soiled' wife and their circle of 'contemptible' friends who included the 'unstable and ambitious' Churchill. He in turn was described as the 'first fruit of a famous first "snob dollar" marriage', suggesting that his parents' union was one of financial necessity rather than love. Churchill was incensed by what he considered a 'very offensive, wounding and insulting libel', as he wrote to his great friend Eddie Marsh on 30 April.[17] Unlike the Mylius affair, where the offending text appeared in a small circulation magazine, this was the Book Society of England's pick of the month, with a first circulation of a healthy 10,000 copies and the backing of a reputable publisher, William Heinemann. Winston urged prosecution. 'These people require a lesson,' he wrote to the duke, 'and the only thing they appreciate is being made to pay.' The duke, who was angered by the assertion that Wallis was his mistress before they married, took Churchill's advice and contacted his legal team at Allen and Overy to take action against the author and publisher. They promptly caved and withdrew the offending biography. While there were those in the royal family and among their courtiers who would have privately agreed with every word in the coruscating tome, it was feared that the legal action, so close to the coronation, would cast a shadow over the time-honoured display of purposeful grandeur and proud nationhood.[18]

The coronation of King George VI took place on 12 May 1937. Seated next to his wife in Westminster Abbey, Winston Churchill had tears in his eyes as he breathlessly watched the anointment of the new King and his consort, Queen Elizabeth, in the solemn, historic ceremony. Amid the ancient theatrics, Winston turned to Clemmie and confessed, 'You were right; I see now that the other one wouldn't have done.'[19] It was the first time Churchill acknowledged that he had backed the wrong horse in the abdication. Meanwhile, the Duke of Windsor listened to the coronation broadcast at the Château Candé in France as he knitted a blue sweater for Wallis. He later wrote to Winston to ask how the ceremony had gone and was told that it was 'a brilliant success'.[20]

The duke had earlier invited Churchill to join him in France, but Churchill politely declined, citing current events in politics. The Prime Minister, Stanley Baldwin, had announced his decision to step down after the coronation, and Churchill, still nursing ambitions of his own, thought the leadership overhaul might bring him back into government under the new man, Neville Chamberlain. He wrote to the duke, 'I do not think it would be wise for me to leave the country till after Whitsuntide.

The Government will all be in process of reconstruction, and although I am not very keen upon office, I should like to help in defence.'[21]

Not that the atmosphere at Château Candé was especially jolly. At the end of May, just days before Edward and Wallis' wedding, King George VI officially issued his decree that upon their marriage, Wallis would become the Duchess of Windsor but would not be styled 'Her Royal Highness'. The duke and duchess felt this to be a gratuitous and personal insult, a bitter blow that was to last a lifetime. Until the announcement, the duke had assumed, as he had written to the King, that 'Wallis's royal title comes automatically with marriage in our case'. The favour he felt himself to be asking his younger brother was not the granting of the title itself, but 'having it announced' so that they might be spared 'the last and only remaining embarrassment'.[22]

Edward was wrong in thinking this would be the last indignity. On 3 June, when the Duke of Windsor married the woman for whom he had abandoned the riches and responsibilities of the throne, not a single member of the royal family was in attendance, in spite of assurances by his cousin, Lord Louis Mountbatten, that they would make an appearance. Even the duke's staunchest defender, Winston Churchill, stayed away. In his stead, Winston sent his son, Randolph, who appeared in a quasi-official capacity as a journalist.[23] Randolph came bearing a gift from his father, accompanied by a carefully worded note wishing 'Your Royal Highness and your bride many days of mellow sunlight in the land you love'.[24] The so-called royal romance of the century petered out into a wedding populated by French functionaries and a handful of friends.

Burning with resentment, the duke was intent on showing his new bride the glamourous appeal of a royal honeymoon tour. Somewhat foolishly, given his growing reputation as an apologist for Hitler's Germany, he accepted an invitation to study labour and housing conditions in the shiny new Nazi nation. It was to be followed by a similar visit to the United States. Beaverbrook and Churchill both expressed hesitation and tried to dissuade him from making the trip, but the plans, initiated by their pro-Nazi industrialist host, Charles Bedaux, were already in motion.[25] When they arrived in Berlin to brass bands, top brass and cheering crowds, it was like they had stepped into a parallel timeline, one in which the disgraces and humiliations of the previous months had never happened. Wallis was treated as royalty, with those chosen to meet her referring to her as 'Your Royal Highness' and dropping into a full deferential curtsey. As for the British officials at the embassy in Berlin, they made themselves scarce. Not so Chancellor Adolf Hitler, who made time in his diary to meet the couple. They even exchanged brief Nazi salutes, a gesture that would come to haunt the duke.

For his part, Churchill never expressed remonstrance, whatever his public position. In October, even after scenes of the Duke of Windsor giving a Nazi salute played in London theatres, Winston wrote encouragingly to the duke: 'I am told that when scenes of [your tour] were produced in the news reels in the cinemas here your Royal Highness' pictures were always loudly cheered.' He continued, 'I was rather afraid beforehand that your tour in Germany would offend the great numbers of anti-Nazis in this country, many of whom are your friends and admirers, but I must admit that it does not seem to have had that effect, and I am so glad it all passed off with so much distinction and success.'[26]

The second part of the Windsors' honeymoon tour, to the United States, presented different and ultimately more decisive challenges. These began with a dispute over which ocean liner they would take to cross New York – either the French *Normandie* or the German *Bremen*. Winston, wary of the publicity that would inevitably follow in the wake of the duke's decision, strongly advised that choosing the German ship, for no practical reason, would needlessly offend millions of people on both sides of 'the pond', particularly Jews and other minorities persecuted by the Nazi regime. His advice, as so often, fell on deaf ears, the duke and the duchess making plans to set sail on board the *Bremen* in late October.[27] But the trip never came off. Thousands of American trade unionists demonstrated about the presence of Bedaux as the leader of their entourage. He and his revolutionary time and motion methods were loathed by workers. As a result, in early November the Windsors, fearing violent opposition, cancelled the tour. In spite of their behaviour, the Windsors remained friendly with Winston who visited them in their villa in the south of France in January 1938. It was the first time he had seen his former King since their teary-eyed parting during the abdication crisis. Winston wrote to Clementine, 'The Ws are very pathetic, but also very happy. She made an excellent impression on me, and it looks as if it would be a most happy marriage.'[28]

It was two outsiders reunited, the duke from his family, Churchill from the bulk of fellow politicians who steadfastly adhered to the government's policy of appeasement. The only significant ally Churchill had in criticizing Prime Minister Neville Chamberlain's approach was Foreign Secretary Anthony Eden, who resigned in February 1938 citing his 'strong political convictions' that the Prime Minister had been too lenient towards European dictators. He was replaced by the pro-appeasement aristocrat, Viscount Halifax. The hope was that Hitler would prove himself to be a reasonable man who would respect reasonable national boundaries. They were wrong.

That summer, the King and Queen were invited to a military review in France. Though the King did not intend to invite Winston, he was held in such high regard by the French that they sent a special invitation for him and Clementine. Winston could hardly contain his excitement as he watched 50,000 troops march past. Later, Lord Halifax recalled Churchill's disposition. 'Even now,' he wrote, 'I can recapture the strength of emotion with which Churchill, who was looking on, spoke of the French Army as the bulwark of European freedom.'[29] Another observer, the Dowager Duchess of Rutland, recalled Churchill's enthusiasm: 'Winston was like a school boy he was so delighted.'[30]

Two months after this reassuring show of French military might, Prime Minister Neville Chamberlain flew to Germany to sign the Munich agreement with Hitler and the leaders of France and Italy. The agreement, which guaranteed that Hitler, after taking control of the Sudetenland in current-day Czechia, would cease his expansionist pursuits, was understood by France and England to be a barrier against another war.

When Chamberlain returned to London, King George was elated, telling his mother that the signing of the deal marked 'a great day. The Prime Minister was delighted with the result of his mission, as we all are, & he had a great ovation when he came here.'[31] The King was so thrilled that he discarded the notion of regal impartiality and took the unprecedented step of inviting Chamberlain to the balcony of Buckingham Palace where they waved to the cheering crowds. This was even before the agreement, which was opposed by both opposition parties, had been debated in Parliament. Nonetheless, it was hailed by a jubilant Chamberlain as a document bringing 'Peace in our time'. Politician and diarist Chips Channon recorded, 'The whole world rejoices whilst a few malcontents jeer.'[32] The Duke of Windsor was among those who rejoiced. He, like everyone else, saw Chamberlain's intervention as a stroke of negotiating genius. Only one feature of the news failed to make sense – Churchill's opposition. He told Walter Monckton, 'I really cannot understand our old friend Winston Churchill's attitude, which is hardly worthy of the brilliant and experienced politician that he is.'[33]

In fact, Churchill could not have taken a firmer position against the Munich agreement. He, along with Lord Robert Cecil, 1st Viscount Cecil of Chelwood, entertained the idea of hurling a brick through Chamberlain's window in protest. Instead, he settled on the tried and tested, giving a masterful speech in the House of Commons, denouncing the pact as nothing less than 'the abandonment and ruin of Czechoslovakia'. In the most vivid terms, he described it as a humiliation, which would be 'only the beginning of the reckoning' that was to come. 'This is only the first sip,' he warned his audience, 'the first foretaste of a bitter cup which will be proffered to us year by year unless, by a supreme recovery of moral health and martial vigour, we arise again and take our stand for freedom as in the olden time.'[34]

In January 1939, he travelled to Cannes for a relaxing painting holiday, dining frequently with the Duke and Duchess of Windsor. One night, press baron Lord Rothermere was the only other guest, Churchill anticipating that the duke would want to discuss his plans for returning to England. He considered it a lost cause, writing to Clementine about the royal family's attitude: 'They do not want him to come, but they have no power to stop him.'[35] This position was to change sooner than everyone, including Churchill, realized.

The following day, 19 January, Clementine noted in her response that the whispers about the inevitability of war had grown to a noisy chorus. 'O Winston,' she wrote, 'are we drifting into war? without the wit to avoid it or the will to prepare for it?'[36] That night, the Windsors came to dine with Churchill. After dinner, with cigars lit and brandies in hand, the conversation turned towards the European scene. The duke had read Churchill's recent article on Spain, in which Churchill had called for an alliance with Soviet Russia, a position with which the duke strongly disagreed. One of the guests was freckle-faced American novelist Vincent Sheean, who watched the back and forth between political master and apprentice. He later noted it in his diary:

> Churchill frowned with intentness at the floor in front of him, mincing no words, reminding HRH of the British constitution on occasion – 'When our kings are in conflict with our constitution, we change our kings,' he said – and declaring flatly that the nation stood in the gravest danger of its long history. The kilted Duke in his Stuart tartan sat on the edge of the sofa, eagerly interrupting whenever he could, contesting every point, but receiving – in terms of the utmost politeness so far as the words went – an object lesson in political wisdom and public spirit. The rest of us sat fixed in silence; there was something dramatically final, irrevocable about this dispute.[37]

This episode was but a harbinger of clashes to come. The duke felt strongly that the preservation of peace ought to be the highest priority, even going so far as to give a radio broadcast from Verdun, the scene of the longest and bloodiest battle of the First World War, in May 1939. Even though his speech chimed with the British government's policy, the broadcast was censored in the duke's home country as it was seen as an attempt to upstage the King and Queen as they sailed to America for a goodwill visit to the White House and beyond. It did, however, play in the United States, and to great effect: the Duke of Windsor was established in the American mind as a spokesperson for peace, much to the satisfaction of the isolationists across the ocean. Try as he might, though, he could not take centre stage from the King and Queen, who shortly afterwards made a wildly successful tour of North America, one of the highlights being photographs of the new King gamely eating a hot dog. When they returned, the whole of London burst into a frenzy of adulation and thanksgiving. *The Times* reported, 'Never have a Sovereign and his Consort received a more enthusiastic popular welcome.' In a short but emotional speech, the King made a case for the modern-day relevance of monarchy, stating that it 'exists today as a potent force for promoting peace and good will among mankind'.[38]

Even though Churchill was moved to tears by the King's speech, it was clear he remained on the sidelines, banging his solitary drum for rearmament. He was attacked abroad by Hitler who dubbed him an 'apostle of war'[39] and at home where he only narrowly avoided deselection by executives at his local constituency.

George VI and the Prime Minister of Canada, William Lyon Mackenzie King, were equally sceptical, even after Hitler drove a coach and horses through the Munich agreement by invading the rump of Czechoslovakia in March 1939. The King told Mackenzie King that he would never wish to appoint Churchill to any office unless it was absolutely necessary in war time. Mackenzie recorded his agreement with this sentiment, writing in his diary, 'I must say that I was glad to hear him say that because I think

Churchill is one of the most dangerous men I have ever known.[40] There were a growing number who disagreed. A giant poster appeared in the Strand in central London with the words: 'What Price Churchill?' while numerous newspapers, particularly the influential *Daily Telegraph*, owned by Lord Camrose, lobbied for his return to Cabinet. Chamberlain refused to be moved. He even dismissed Churchill's suggestion that parliament reassemble on 21 August, rather than the government's preferred date of 3 October, since the Germans were massing troops on the Polish border and invasion looked imminent. Few believed him. Instead, Chamberlain went salmon fishing in Scotland as Russia and Germany were putting the final touches to a non-aggression pact that effectively gave Germany the green light to invade Poland, which it duly did on 1 September 1939.

Even though the invasion triggered a diplomatic tripwire that meant Britain and France would be obliged by treaty to declare war on Germany, Chamberlain hesitated. Instead, he gave Hitler a final opportunity to withdraw his troops without penalty. Hitler ignored his offer and continued to pour his military into yet another soon-to-be-subjugated nation. At eleven-fifteen on Sunday, 3 September, Chamberlain, his appeasement policy in ruins, made a radio broadcast in which he declared that Britain was once again at war with Germany.

It was at only at this point that Chamberlain finally relented and invited Churchill to join his government to take up his previous – and favourite – post, First Lord of the Admiralty. During Churchill's first official audience with King George VI, when he received the seals of the office, the King found him 'very pleased to be back in harness again'. He noted in his diary that Churchill 'wanted more destroyers. Liked the Board of the Admiralty.' But the King remained sceptical of the new First Lord, their relationship remaining rather tentative because of Churchill's involvement with his brother during the abdication crisis. For the first months, he found Churchill 'difficult to talk to', in part due to his use of florid language – referring to the King as 'our noble lord' for example – that even George VI found rather Victorian.[41] Gradually, their relationship warmed, in part due to the King endeavouring to understand the mind of the veteran politician: 'In time I shall get the right technique I hope.'[42]

Within days of his appointment, Churchill received a letter from the Duke of Windsor who was still in the south of France. Uncertain about what the start of war would mean for his safety, Edward requested a naval ship to transport himself and his party from Cherbourg, France, to Portsmouth, in the south of England.

Churchill ordered Mountbatten, the duke's second cousin and friend, who was then in command of the Naval destroyer HMS *Kelly*, to escort the Windsors across the English Channel. As Churchill was too busy to meet the Windsors at the quayside, he asked his son, Randolph, to accompany them on the crossing. When Randolph nervously asked his father what he ought to wear, Winston advised him, 'You should wear uniform, and look your best.' So, on the morning of 12 September, he donned his cavalry kit, boarded the *Kelly*, and set sail – the only problem being, he hadn't the faintest idea how to wear a cavalry uniform. His sword, spurs and uniform were certainly not shipshape and Bristol fashion. When the duke, a stickler for proper dress, saw this cartoon character he burst into laughter. He cried, 'Randolph, your spurs are not only inside out, but upside down! Haven't you ever been on a horse?'[43]

Blushing from his sartorial gaffe, Randolph handed over a message from his father: 'Welcome home! Your Royal Highness knows how much I have looked forward to this day. I know you will forgive me for not coming to meet you, but I cannot leave my post.' Then, ominously, he added, 'We are plunged in a long and grievous struggle. But all will come out right if we all work together to the end.'[44]

The royal party set sail at dusk, and as HMS *Kelly* nosed into port, she landed in almost total darkness, for fear of German air strikes. Not only had Churchill organized a guard of honour, consisting of 'a hundred men with tin hats & gas masks', but also a red carpet to be laid on all the gangways. As they docked, a Royal Marine band played 'God Save the King'.[45]

Winston had already arranged for the Commander-in-Chief at Portsmouth to invite the couple to stay the night at his navy home. The couple, who were naturally nervous about their welcome home, were deeply appreciative of Winston's willingness to pull out all the stops to ensure their safety, comfort, and recognition.

As for their blood relations, after three years of silence, nothing. Not a message, a royal personage or even a chauffeur-driven car to greet them. In spite of the scaled-down pomp of their arrival, they soon realized that as far as the royal family were concerned, they were personae non gratae.

They had hoped that their return would be recognized by a brief audience with the King and Queen and a dignified mention in the Court Circular. To their minds, it would restore a degree of nobility that they had lost in the wake of the abdication. Both the Queen and Queen Mary were adamant. Under no circumstances would they grant 'that woman' an audience.

King George, on the other hand, did at last consent to a meeting at Buckingham Palace with his elder brother on 14 September. While the Queen and other royals made themselves scarce, the duke sat with the King and asked him for a job that would help the war effort. The stumbling block was that there were no precedents, particularly in the British military, for utilizing the talents of an ex-King. The King offered him a choice between a civil defence post in Wales, or a staff liaison position in France. The duke chose Wales, and there the matter rested.

The following day, the Duke of Windsor met with Winston Churchill who, upon their first greeting on British soil in three years, merely followed up on the same message he had sent along with Randolph. He looked the duke in the eye and asked suggestively, 'I know sir that you and I have not always seen eye to eye on foreign policy but we are all in this together, aren't we?' When Edward responded, 'Of course. That is why I am here,' Churchill's face lit up. He said hastily, 'And we all want you back.'[46]

Churchill was so pleased to have the duke back on British soil that he controversially showed him around the navy's secret room, where the various positions of British and hostile fleets were presented on wall-mounted maps. This irritated numerous officers who felt that the duke, following his visit to Germany, was not to be trusted. The Earl of Crawford was incensed at Churchill's lack of caution, writing that the duke was

> too irresponsible a chatterbox to be entrusted with confidential information which will all be passed on to Wally at the dinner table. That is where the danger lies – namely that after nearly three years of complete obscurity, the temptation to show that he knew, that he is again at the centre of information will prove irresistible and that he will blab and babble out state secrets without realizing the danger.[47]

Any thoughts that he was back in the heart of British governance were disabused later that day. As the duke was making the rounds to his political connections, he learned that the King had had a change of heart. He rescinded the offer for the post in Wales, leaving only the less desirable liaison position in France. It seemed that the royal family wanted the Windsors at arm's length and out of the country. Notably, the First Lord of the Admiralty chose not to inject himself into this family matter. In his new position, Winston could quite literally have shipped the duke and his wife off to one of myriad navy bases – Malta for example – so that they could serve and stay out of the way. Instead, he left the brotherly dispute to the brothers themselves.

As a result, the Windsors found themselves in Paris, where it wasn't long before awkward questions of precedent and position caused trouble for the duke. During a trip to the British General Headquarters in mid-October, he accepted salutes from active-duty British servicemen. This in itself would not have been an issue, since he technically held the rank of a major-general. In this case, it was a *royal* salute, and, as he was accompanied by two officers more senior than himself – one of whom was the Commander-in-Chief – it was they, and not he, who were the rightful recipients of a salute.[48] Whitehall came to the swift conclusion that the Duke of Windsor's presence was interfering with the proper chain of command, and so it was decided that the duke be kept away from any area where active British military personnel were present. When he eventually discovered the directive, he was livid, complaining that he had been treated in an 'underhand way', in a 'back-door intrigue'. He demanded to see his brother and, on 12 November, he asked Monckton to make the necessary arrangements. Finally he wrote to Winston, seeking his advice not as a friend or 'minister of the crown', he admitted, 'but more as a father'. Winston's response was stern and to the point. He told the duke that since he had 'voluntarily resigned the finest Throne in the world ... it would be natural to treat all minor questions of ceremony and precedence as entirely beneath your interest and your dignity: otherwise one merely gives opportunity for slights from those who are unfriendly.'[49]

The duke having been swatted away, Winston turned his attention once more to the navy, whose first major wartime confrontation was about to get underway. The Battle of the River Plate took place on 13 December, when the *Graf Spee*, a heavy German cruiser, engaged a Royal Navy squadron, composed of HMS *Ajax*, *Exeter* and *Achilles*. The British ships sustained only moderate damage, while the *Graf Spee* suffered a crippling blow to her fuel system and was forced to dock at the Montevideo harbour. The Uruguayan authorities, who were neutral in the conflict, told the German captain that he could only stay for seventy-two hours and then he would have to leave. As this was not enough time to repair the damaged ship, the German captain ordered the *Graf Spee* to be scuttled in the harbour. Three days later he committed suicide.

It was a glorious victory for the Royal Navy, coming as it did after a period of losses, particularly the sinking, by an enemy submarine, of the HMS *Ark Royal* with the loss of 833 men. Another sunny point was the dramatic rescue of 299 British prisoners aboard the HMS *Cossack*, stationed off the coast of Norway, in mid-February 1939. Winston, whose reputation and character were always under attack, rejoiced at the naval successes and the 'wave of enthusiasm' that the two triumphs aroused among the British public. 'Both these events strengthened my hand and the prestige of the Admiralty,' he wrote. '"The Navy's here!" was passed from lip to lip.'[50]

The King, who had served in the Battle of Jutland during the First World War, was delighted with this navy-inspired rescue mission and sent Winston a personal letter of congratulations. Winston replied at once to express his gratitude, saying it was a very great 'encouragement and gratification' to receive the King's 'most gracious & kindly message of approval ... By none is Your Majesty's compliment more treasured than by the v[er]y old servant of Your Royal House and of your father & y[ou]r grandfather.'[51]

A showman by instinct, Winston recognized that the enthusiasm inspired by these victorious missions was invaluable and thought that a parade through central London, with the King and Queen acknowledging the returning ships' crewmembers and the kinfolk of lost sailors, would be hugely popular and help bolster the patriotic fighting spirit. So it proved. On 22 February, watched by a 'grateful and dramatic crowd, thirsting for something to celebrate', the crews of HMS *Ajax* and *Exeter* – the *Achilles* being needed for active service on another mission – marched from Waterloo Station to Horse Guards Parade, where Churchill presented the ships' captains to the King who decorated them with military honours.[52] The procession then marched to the Guildhall, where Churchill gave a speech honouring the 'joyous, memorable, and unique occasion'.[53] Meanwhile the King and Queen stayed behind and met with relatives of men who had lost their lives in the battle. It was the first occasion where the monarch and his consort offered their personal sympathy to bereaved subjects of the Second World War – but it was to be far from the last.

During what became known as the 'Phoney War', when neither side made moves against one another on land, it was naval actions that inevitably commanded the most attention. Churchill was in his element. The most ambitious of his schemes was to cut the Nazis off from their supplies of iron ore sent by neutral Sweden via the Norwegian port of Narvik, which was also neutral. As early as December 1939, he had extolled the virtues of the plan, which involved troop landings and a fleet of Royal Navy ships. When that was turned down by the Cabinet, he pleaded that at least magnetic mines be used around Narvik and other ports. The King was one of those who likened his adventurous tactics to those of the doomed Dardanelles campaign and confessed his fears to Prime Minister Chamberlain, who agreed. Eventually the Supreme War Council, set up to coordinate French and British military plans, agreed to landing a force at Narvik that would seize the iron ore fields and go on to join Finnish troops in their war with Russia. Evidently, the King also changed his mind, sending Winston an encouraging letter: 'I would like to congratulate you on the splendid way in which, under your direction, the Navy is countering the German move against Scandinavia.' He invited Churchill to Buckingham Palace at his earliest convenience, before finishing with a personal touch, begging Winston 'to take care of yourself & get as much rest as you possibly can in these critical days'.[54]

Three days later, Winston responded at length, clearly moved by the King's words. 'I am most deeply grateful to Your Majesty for the v[er]y kind & gracious letter,' he began. 'Since I received Your Majesty's letter we have had a good success wh[ich] I hastened to report to Sir Alexander Hardinge, & I trust that I shall have something more & better to say about Narvik before long … We are aiming at Trondheim which w[oul]d be an even greater prize than Narvik. It will be an operation of much difficulty & risk; but we must not fail to profit by success & speed.'[55]

In fact, the British Navy *did* fail to profit by success and speed, the eight-week campaign ending in failure, with the Germans invading Norway and Denmark, the British retreating in disarray, many ships (including an aircraft carrier) either sunk or disabled. The only consolation was that Germany had lost a substantial portion of their much smaller navy.

Under normal circumstances, Churchill's head would have been on the chopping block. It was his idea, his navy, his failure. However, when the House of Commons came to debate the disastrous Narvik campaign on 8 May, it was Chamberlain who was on trial for the nation's lack of preparation and its utterly failed appeasement policy. Several MPs called for Chamberlain's resignation, including Clement Attlee, the leader of the Labour Party, who argued that 'to win the war, we want different people at the helm from those who have led us into it.' Attlee's colleague Arthur Greenwood picked up the refrain: 'Wars are not won on masterly evacuations … more foresight and energy, and stronger and more ruthless will to victory, are required in the supreme direction of our war effort.' But it was Leo Amery, a Conservative minister without portfolio, who landed the heaviest punch, quoting from Oliver Cromwell's famous speech dismissing the Rump Parliament in 1653: 'You have sat too long here for any good you have been doing. Depart, I say, and let us have done with you. In the name of God, go.'[56]

Following the fiery debate in the House of Commons, a routine vote on whether to adjourn the session became, in effect, a crucial vote of confidence on Chamberlain's leadership. Although the vote was won with a majority of eighty-one for Chamberlain, this was a far slimmer margin than he would have needed to continue on as premier, and his attempt to form a national government was thwarted when Attlee told him that he and his party would refuse to participate if he remained Prime Minister.

The King himself had expressed some dissatisfaction in Chamberlain's government, encouraging his Prime Minister to get some 'new blood' into Cabinet. Although he may have still nursed some suspicion of Winston Churchill, he had, in the early months of the war, come to appreciate the man's stunning work ethic, energy and charisma, coming to find him 'amusing'.[57] Most importantly, he had the warrior spirit and the ability to inspire.

However, it was not Churchill but Lord Halifax that the King preferred to lead the nation at this critical time. Halifax was a sturdy, aquiline, blue-blooded aristocrat whose wife was a lady-in-waiting to the Queen. He was 'one of us' down to his plus fours, an arch appeaser whose natural inclination was towards compromise and conciliation. Long after Hitler's duplicity was apparent to all, he secretly endeavoured to work out a diplomatic peace with the German tyrant. Unlike Churchill, the aristocrat dubbed 'the Holy Fox' was no orator, nor did his behaviour inspire or uplift the common man. He had none of the fighting spirit, nor did he know much about modern military warfare. Looking inside himself, Halifax realized he did not have the stomach for the battles that lay ahead; he objected to the King's suggestion that he take up the premiership, citing as an excuse his membership in the House of Lords, which would require him to 'be a shadow or a ghost in the Commons, where all the real work took place'. The King was reluctant to take this as a firm no, and considered it might be possible to place Halifax's peerage in abeyance during the wartime administration. In essence, the King was putting his thumb on the scales to give Halifax room for manoeuvre. At this critical moment in the nation's journey, the King was playing kingmaker. All Halifax had to do was say 'Yes' and the crown was his. But Halifax was intransigent.[58]

Though the King was reluctant to admit it, there was only one man for the job, the only politician admired by the country and blessed with the 'fire and determination', in the King's words, to lead this beleaguered island nation.[59]

It could only be Churchill. At last, he had earned his date with destiny.

CHAPTER NINE

Brothers at War

IT WAS PROBABLY one of the most important meetings of their lives: King George VI confronting his new Prime Minister, Winston Churchill. Their encounter was as important, if not more so, as the first meeting between George VI, then the Duke of York, and Elizabeth Bowes-Lyon at an RAF ball, or Winston's first encounter with Clementine Hozier at a London dinner party. Both of these meetings were followed by proper courtships that ended in solid, supportive marriages that endured and weathered. But when Churchill was announced and entered the King's sitting room at six o'clock on the evening of 10 May 1940, both men knew that this was a shotgun marriage that had to work. Not just for themselves but for the nation and for the survival of the Empire. The King had seen his previous Prime Minister, Neville Chamberlain, some minutes before. Chamberlain had tendered his resignation and formally advised the King to send for Churchill. It was an emotional parting, the Queen later writing to the outgoing Prime Minister to express her sadness and admiration. 'I can never tell you in words how much we owe you. During these last desperate & unhappy years, you have been a great support & comfort to us both, and we felt so safe with the knowledge that your wisdom and high purpose were there at our hand ... You did all you could to stave off such agony and you were right.'[1]

Understandably, King George VI was wary of the man who now stood before him, with his bowed neck, bow tie, frock coat, black shoes shined, ready to accept the seals of office denoting his newly elevated position. Churchill's friendship with the King's elder brother and his fatal meddling in the abdication were still raw as far as the King and his family were concerned. Just hours before, the King and Queen had hoped that Chamberlain's replacement would be the aquiline aristocrat Lord Halifax. Unlike Winston he was, as they saw it, steady, trusted and reliable, not prone to rash judgements.

So, the two men circled one another, Churchill all bustle and brilliance, his King cautious, stuttering and correct, realizing that he had to accept the inevitable. Unspoken was the sense that each man had to be willing to let bygones be bygones for the sake of the nation's survival.

Though born with a silver spoon apiece, they were utterly different in temperament and outlook. Churchill, in another life, might have been an American tycoon: pushy, shameless, ambitious and altogether un-British in the sense that he grabbed hungrily at life's glittering prizes, rather than waiting for them to fall into his lap. His King was from different stock entirely: bashful, reticent, happy to live in the shadows but willing, when push came to shove, to take up the spotlight when duty demanded it. Hence the fact that Halifax, the quintessential unassuming amateur who never used his shoulders to push others to the side, was initially more to his personal taste.

Both the King and Churchill were well aware that they had a constitutional duty that transcended their political and personal differences. The new King had the right – indeed the duty – to counsel, encourage, and warn his government, and was entitled to express his opinions on government policy to Winston. Both acknowledged that their conversations were utterly confidential, a courtesy automatically accepted by every Sovereign and their numerous first ministers.

The King asked Churchill to be seated and then, after looking hard at his official visitor, asked him, 'I suppose you don't know why I have sent for you?' Adopting the King's mood of awkward levity, Winston replied, 'Sir, I simply couldn't imagine why.' The King laughed and said, 'I want you to form a government.'[2] Other accounts vary, but this version is quintessentially British: cracking jokes while with their backs against the wall.

Their working relationship, which was to become one of the most important of the Second World War, got off to an inauspicious start. In mid-May, within a week of taking office, Winston failed to appear for his first audience with the King, where he was meant to brief him on the week's events. He had a solid alibi: he had made an emergency trip to Paris to meet with French Prime Minister Paul Reynaud, who had woken the British PM with a panicked phone call. 'We are beaten,' Reynaud confessed, 'We have lost the battle.' Churchill promised to visit him in person, assuring him that all was not lost.[3]

During his whistle-stop trip – the first of five to France – Winston asked the French Army general, Maurice Gamelin, 'Where is the strategic reserve?' But Gamelin merely shrugged his shoulders: 'None,' he said. Dumbfounded, Churchill began to realize that the British Expeditionary Force (BEF), stationed in northern France, was trapped, their backs against a wall. The King was totally unaware of this dire development and would remain so for nearly a week.[4]

Cancelling meetings with the King at short notice or keeping him and the Queen waiting became something of an unwelcome routine. Little wonder the King confided in his diary: 'I cannot yet think of Winston as PM.'[5] His early dissatisfaction with his first minister spilled out to a wider circle, the King confiding his concerns to Lord Halifax, the same man he had preferred for the position. He complained that Winston was not willing to give him as much time, or information, as he would like, and of the 'difficulty of making contact with Winston' in general.[6]

Their first direct clash came as Churchill was choosing the ministers he wanted to serve in his government. He asked his friend and ally the Canadian press baron Lord Beaverbrook to take on the vital role of Minister of Aircraft Production, and also submitted the name of his close colleague Brendan Bracken, who had supported him throughout the 1930s when he was a lone voice for rearmament, as a Privy Counsellor. Though Bracken, if initiated as PC, would not have been in the government, the elevated status would give him increased access to government information, which he would not have had in his usual capacity as an MP.

The King balked. In his first letter to Winston as his Prime Minister, he expressed reluctance to approve Beaverbrook, arguing that the Canadians' dislike of him was an indication of his unsuitability, and asked him to reconsider. The King's tone was placatory. 'I hope you will understand why I am doing this as I want to be a help to you in the very important and onerous office which you have just accepted at my hands.'[7] Churchill, by now a veteran of similar conflicts with George VI's father, George V, shot back a reply stating that he should be able to appoint whomsoever he wanted for such a critical position at such a critical time. Beaverbrook was duly appointed.

The King was even firmer with Bracken and received from Winston a much more truculent reply. Winston began his response in a tone of bafflement: 'I should have thought that in the terrible circumstances which press upon us, and the burden of disaster and responsibility which has been cast upon me after my warnings have been so long rejected I might be helped as much as possible.' Then, in an oblique swing at the King, his court and his support for appeasement, Churchill stated that Bracken had 'sometimes been almost my sole supporter in the years when I have been striving to get this country properly defended ... He has suffered as I have done every form of official hostility. Had he joined the ranks of the time-servers and careerists who were assuring the public that our Air Force was larger than that of Germany, I have no doubt he would long ago have attained high Office.'[8] Churchill again got his way, and Brendan Bracken was promptly admitted as a member of the Privy Council. 'The last thing that His Majesty wants to do,' private secretary Sir Alec Hardinge soothed, 'is to create difficulties for you when you are bearing such an overwhelming burden of responsibility and anxiety – indeed his sympathy for you is beyond measure.'[9]

Tea and sympathy were all the King could offer in those dark days of May 1940, when the survival of Britain and the Empire hung by a thread. The King listened in horrified silence each week as his Prime Minister rattled through the roll call of military disasters that continued to befall the island race. In view of the imminent collapse of France, the first priority was to rescue the thousands of British soldiers marooned on the French coast. On 20 May, Churchill ordered the Admiralty to 'assemble a large number of small vessels in readiness to proceed to ports and inlets on the French coast'.[10] At their next audience, Churchill told the King that communication with France had broken down so completely that it was impossible to know just how dire the situation was. He still held out some faint hope that a counter-offensive by the French may take place. That was quickly exposed as a pipe dream and every effort was now made to save the remnants of the BEF at Calais and Dunkirk, leaving all their heavy weaponry and fuel supplies behind.

Two days after their meeting, the King received an alarming report from the Chief of the Air Staff, Sir Cyril Newall, and summoned Churchill to another audience at the palace. When the Prime Minister arrived at ten-thirty at night the King asked him, in suitable royal language, not to sugar-coat the situation, but to give it to him straight. Churchill duly obliged and outlined the harsh facts. If the French counteroffensive came to nothing, the BEF would have to retreat to England. The King's diary entry of that night shows that he understood the full severity of the military situation: 'This operation would mean the loss of all guns, tanks, ammunition, & all stores in France … The very thought of having to order this movement is appalling, as the loss of life will probably be immense.'[11]

The bad news didn't stop there. Churchill told the King that, if the operation went badly, the Germans would likely make a parachute assault on the British capital in a matter of weeks. He promised that he and his administration would go down fighting. Churchill was under no illusions about how he would fare amid a Nazi invasion. He gave himself three months before he faced his end.[12] 'Our intention is,' he told the King, 'whatever happens, to fight on to the end in this Island. Members of the present Administration would likely go down during this process should it result adversely, but in no conceivable circumstances will we consent to surrender.'[13] This moment gave the King his first close-up glimpse of his first minister's mettle and resolve – and his first clear sign that Churchill expected no less from his Sovereign. During their audience, the subject of whether to send the King's daughters, Princesses Elizabeth and Margaret, to Canada was raised. Churchill felt strongly that their departure would seriously damage public morale, and that this consideration must supersede that of the family's safety: the whole family, he argued, should remain in situ. He even ordered senior officers not even to plan for the contingency of evacuating of the royal family.[14]

In these turbulent days, the King was determined to save what he could of the country's priceless heritage. He and his trusted librarian, Owen Morshead, broke down the nation's symbolic history, the Crown Jewels, and stuffed the fabulous diamonds, rubies, pearls and insignia in hat boxes, hiding them away in the basement of Windsor Castle. Safely stored, the nation's heritage might have a chance of going with the royal family should German parachutists threaten Windsor Castle.

The terrible prospects facing Britain affected the King's Empire Day speech, which he made the day after his daunting conversation with Churchill. As if the existential threat to his kingdom were not enough, he still had his pesky stammer to deal with. 'The decisive struggle is now upon us,' he articulated carefully to his millions of listeners. He told them that it was not just a battle for victory, but a fight for survival. What the enemy wanted was nothing short of the 'overthrow, complete and final, of this Empire and everything for which it stands, and after that the conquest of the world'.[15]

Two days later, on 26 May, the evacuation mission, known by the codename Operation Dynamo, was scheduled to commence. Even the core rescue mission had to be scaled back. Instead of evacuating both Calais and Dunkirk, only the latter was selected, leaving the troops trapped in Calais to fight to the finish.

Churchill convened three War Cabinet meetings that day to debate the dismal prospects. With France down and as good as out, Belgium on the cusp of surrendering, and little immediate prospect of the United States joining the conflict, Britain was very, very alone in Europe, reliant on the Empire for assistance. The Foreign Secretary Lord Halifax argued that it was now time for Britain to re-open negotiations for peace. He threatened to resign if he was not permitted at the very least to gain some idea of Germany's proposed peace terms. Churchill was firm, stating that negotiations with the Germans at this particular juncture – with absolutely no bargaining power on Britain's side – would be to transform the embattled country into a 'slave state'. The only way out was through.[16] As he told Halifax and his other Cabinet colleagues, 'Nations which went down fighting rose again but those which tamely surrendered were finished.'[17]

The outlook was indeed bleak. There were no signs whatsoever of any movement of British troops in the French port of Calais. The outnumbered and outgunned battalions had followed instructions and gone down fighting. When surrounded, the Calais garrison surrendered and three thousand or so British troops were taken prisoner. With the surrender of the Belgians imminent and concern growing over the potential success of Operation Dynamo at Dunkirk, the Cabinet meeting of 27 May was critically intense – and intensely critical. A contingent among the Cabinet began to think of forming a new government, led by Halifax, which would try and hash out a negotiated peace with Hitler.[18]

This talk evaporated as a military miracle unfolded at Dunkirk. For the next few days, the prayers of the British were answered by a volunteer armada of vessels, ranging from fishing boats, motorboats, barges, dinghies, and yachts, which crossed the choppy English Channel to rescue grateful soldiers from the deadly beaches of Dunkirk. As Churchill watched his countrymen rise to the challenge, he felt there 'was a white glow, overpowering, sublime, which ran through our island from end to end'.[19]

Operation Dynamo far exceeded all expectations. The King, who had anxiously kept a daily tally of the number of troops rescued, was thrilled to be told that, on 4 June, when the mission was declared complete, the final count was 338,226 soldiers, including around 140,000 non-British troops from France, Belgium and the Netherlands.

Winston gave a speech that day in the House of Commons that was to become one of his most famous, where his sublime oratory transformed his name from a noun into an adjective, establishing the word 'Churchillian' in common parlance. He confessed that, when he had disclosed the plans for the rescue operation to the House of Commons, he feared that it would be his 'hard lot' to announce the greatest military disaster in history. The whole of the British Army 'seemed about to perish upon the field or to be led into an ignominious and starving captivity'. He then regaled the assembly with a full account of the rescue operation, and the miraculous efforts to fend off the Nazi onslaught. A 'miracle of deliverance, achieved by valour, by perseverance, by perfect discipline, by faultless service, by resource, by skill, by unconquerable fidelity, is manifest to us all'.

Though the mission was a success, he told the Commons that 'what has happened in France and Belgium is a colossal military disaster'. 'We must,' he went on, 'expect another blow to be struck almost immediately at us or at France. We are told that Herr Hitler has a plan for invading the British Isles.' Though the prospects were dire, he concluded on a note of high optimism, with closing lines that have endured down the generations:

> Even though large tracts of Europe and many old and famous States have fallen or may fall into the grip of the Gestapo and all the odious apparatus of Nazi rule, we shall not flag or fail. We shall go on to the end, we shall fight in France, we shall fight on the seas and oceans, we shall fight with growing confidence and growing strength in the air, we shall defend our Island, whatever the cost may be, we shall fight on the beaches, we shall fight on the landing grounds, we shall fight in the fields and in the streets, we shall fight in the hills; we shall never

surrender, and even if, which I do not for a moment believe, this Island or a large part of it were subjugated and starving, then our Empire beyond the seas, armed and guarded by the British Fleet, would carry on the struggle, until, in God's good time, the New World, with all its power and might, steps forth to the rescue and the liberation of the old.[20]

Many MPs were moved to tears by his oration and the King, who later heard it on the radio, was so captivated by the speech that he jotted down the salient phrases in his diary. Not only was the speech a special moment in British history, but it brought a closeness and respect between the King and his Prime Minister. That evening, Winston sent a letter to the King to thank him for approving Brendan Bracken's entry into the Privy Council. Its last line was a sombre expression of hope and perseverance: 'Better days will come – though not yet.'[21]

As the British clung on to survival by their fingernails, the fall of France presented many unforeseen issues, not least of all, what to do with the Duke and Duchess of Windsor. Whether the King or the Prime Minister liked it or not, the duke's influence on the popular imagination, even at the level of media mischief-making, remained profound. No sooner had the duke sent a hasty telegram to Churchill on 21 June, announcing that he and Wallis were leaving Paris for Madrid, which was neutral though controlled by Spain's Fascist leader General Franco, than they were contacted by journalists from Spain, Italy and elsewhere asking for confirmation of his role in negotiating an Anglo-German peace. In this parallel media universe, it was stated with certainty that British troops in France had mutinied and had demanded the ex-King's restoration to the throne.[22] To his credit, the duke entertained none of these stories, but it was clear that one sentence or even a word out of place, especially as the duke was known to be an arch appeaser, could make for damaging headlines around the world.

At this critical juncture in the war, the need to maintain a positive image of Britain's prospects was vital. After the retreat from Dunkirk and the fall of France, the most pressing need was to supply the British Army with basic equipment, namely guns and ammunition, much of which had been left behind in the general retreat. For this, they were crucially reliant on arms shipments from the United States. The continued supply of munitions depended on maintaining the impression that Britain was neither doomed nor downhearted; that the underdog nation, beleaguered but determined, needed urgent assistance to continue the struggle. Churchill understood that no nation, however friendly, would consent to donate weaponry, or sell it at a steep discount, to a lost cause. Both the King and Churchill maintained an active correspondence with the American President, Franklin D. Roosevelt, to reassure him on the one hand of the 'magnificent' fighting spirit in Britain, while requesting, on the other, fifty destroyer ships, however obsolete, as well as other basic munitions.[23] This was the bare minimum of Britain's requests. Churchill knew that Britain could not win the war without America joining in, too. All British diplomacy was geared towards this aim. No deviation was permitted.

The duke clearly hadn't read the memo. In private conversations and at dinner parties he talked openly about the need for peace talks, for an accommodation with Hitler, given the fact that Britain was probably within days of crushing defeat.[24] By ending the conflict sooner he argued that it would save an unnecessary loss of life. He was, though, considered a loose cannon, and his defeatist talk threatened to undercut British foreign policy.

As the Windsors inched their way to Spain, the British ambassador Samuel Hoare, himself a leading appeaser, wrote to Churchill from Madrid to warn him that the German embassy was issuing every kind of rumour and innuendo about the Windsors to the Spanish and other media. They printed speculative stories claiming that if the Duke of Windsor set foot in England, Churchill would have him arrested.[25] Given the duke's track record and the growing antipathy between the royal brothers, even Hoare was uncertain as to whether these stories were to be taken at face value. It wasn't just the media but diplomatic circles that baited the feeding frenzy of speculation surrounding the ducal couple. One particularly juicy tale came from the lips of Marcus Cheke, a junior secretary at the embassy. He had heard that the duke, encouraged by his French and Spanish contacts, had spoken of a revolution in Britain, followed by his brother's abdication and his own re-accession to the throne. After this palace coup, the duke would lead the British to form a coalition with France, Spain and Portugal, leaving Germany at liberty to march into Russia.[26]

With these rumours so widespread and the Windsors effectively free agents, it was important that they were brought into safe harbour as quickly as possible. The War Cabinet met to discuss the topic and decided after some debate to recall the duke and duchess to England as soon as possible. The only trouble was that this decision went very much against the will of the King and his family, especially the royal women. As Hardinge wrote to Churchill, the King did not think it would be possible for 'an ex-King to perform any useful service in this country'.[27] In the eyes of the British royals, the right place for Edward was anywhere but *here*.

Churchill once again found himself in the role of reluctant referee amid an increasingly rancorous family feud at a time of acute national peril. Unlike the abdication, where he threw his weight behind Edward VIII, on this occasion he had to navigate a solution that worked for the institution of monarchy, the monarch himself and the nation at large. There would be tears before bedtime before this matter was resolved.

Churchill could not allow the maverick royal to roam freely through a hostile Europe; the stakes were too high and the mood too fraught. Apart from anything else, there was their personal safety to consider. The monarchs of Holland and Norway had only just escaped capture by the skin of their teeth, and Churchill couldn't risk putting the duke and duchess under similar threat. He sent the duke an urgent telegram, which awaited his arrival in Madrid: 'We should like your Royal Highness to come home as soon as possible. Arrangements will be made through Ambassador, Madrid, with whom you should communicate.'[28] Subsequent telegrams ordered him to head to Lisbon, Portugal, where two flying boats were waiting to pick them up and bring them home. Given the paucity of military aircraft following the fall of France, it was a sign of just how important it was to bring the couple back to British shores that not just one, but two flying boats were assigned to the task.

As the Windsors considered their position from the splendour of their suite in the Ritz Hotel in Madrid, the duke began to vacillate. He realized that the British needed him more than he needed them, concluding that Churchill's invitation to return to England was only that – an invitation – which he was at liberty to accept or decline, depending on what would best serve his own self-interests. As Wallis later recalled, the duke 'started to send Winston some cables because he wanted more or less to know what were the plans for us on arrival in England. They mightn't have suited the Duke.'[29] In these telegrams, sent just a day before their scheduled departure, the duke laid out two conditions for his return; first, he wanted to know what kind of job was on offer, and secondly he demanded that he and Wallis be met by the King and Queen upon their return in some official capacity. He wrote to Churchill, 'My visits to England since the war have proved my presence there is an embarrassment to all concerned, myself included, and I cannot see how any post offered me there, even at this time, can alter this situation. I therefore suggest that as I am anxious to continue to serve the Empire, some useful employment, with more official backing than I have hitherto received, be found for me elsewhere.'[30]

The King and Queen were already horrified at the prospect of the Windsors' return and refused to countenance any of the conditions that the duke tried to impose. When they met with Churchill, they told him in no uncertain terms that they were strongly opposed to the duke taking up permanent residence in Britain. For the King, it was a matter of strategy. He did not want his big brother shadowing his reign, second-guessing his decisions and generally causing trouble. As for a possible audience with Wallis, the Queen was adamant: 'We could not meet "her".'[31] Churchill also had some skin in the game, since an alliance between Lord Halifax and the ex-King, both leading proponents of a negotiated settlement with Hitler, might have stirred up unwanted and unnecessary political opposition to his 'no surrender' policies.

Amid this royal impasse, the duke now saw no need to rush back to England unless there was a job waiting for him. With the precious seaplanes still waiting in Lisbon harbour, ambassador Hoare emphasized to Churchill that it would take a job to prise the Windsors away from the continent. He wrote, 'I feel that you will never have peace and perhaps I shall never get him away from here unless you can find something for him. I do feel strongly that this is the moment to get them both back to England and to clear up the situation. If the chance is lost, there will be a prince over the water who will be a nuisance and possibly an embarrassment.'[32] And, he could have added, a hostage. Wheels were now in motion in the Nazi high command to lure the duke and duchess of Windsor into their orbit. As the Nazis focused on baiting the trap for the royal couple, relations between the Prime Minister and the Windsors rapidly deteriorated. In a 'personal' telegram to the Prime Minister, the duke wrote, 'Regret that in view of your reply to my last message I cannot agree to returning until everything has been considered and I know the result. In the light of past experience my wife and myself must not risk finding ourselves once more regarded by the British public as in a different status to other members of my family.'[33]

While he had drawn his line in the sand, the duke was mistaken in thinking that Churchill's initial telegram had been an invitation. It was a command, as he made clear in a trenchant draft telegram: 'Your Royal Highness has taken active military rank and refusal to obey direct orders of competent military authority would create a serious situation. I hope it will not be necessary for such orders to be sent. Already there is a great deal of doubt as to the circumstances in which Your Royal Highness left Paris. I most strongly urge immediate compliance with wishes of the Government.'[34]

Churchill then submitted the draft for review by the King who promptly conveyed his enthusiasm for the tough tone Churchill had taken. He felt that the message's thinly veiled threat of military discipline would have 'a very salutary effect'.[35] As Jock Colville wrote, 'The King approves and says he will hear of no conditions, about the Duchess or otherwise.'[36] Upon further reflection, Churchill decided to delete the sentence about the 'great deal of doubt' about the circumstances of the Windsors' departure from Paris. He was already threatening the ex-King with a court martial. That would do for the time being.[37]

Before Churchill had a chance to send that message, however, he received a further update from Hoare, who reiterated that the duke would only comply with instructions if the King and Queen agreed to an audience with the ducal couple, with the meeting appearing in the daily Court Circular. Without this agreement, he proposed to remain on the European mainland, the couple even discussing whether to return to their rented villa in occupied southern France.[38]

By now, Churchill had had enough. On 1 July, he finally sent his carefully worded telegram. However, by the time it arrived at the British embassy in Madrid the Windsors were on their way to Lisbon. When the duke finally opened the top-secret communication he was taken completely off guard by its tone and content. After all, here was a man whom he considered to be one of his closest friends and most faithful supporters, threatening him with court martial. Once he had gathered his wits, he decided to dig his heels in. Wallis later recalled the duke's response: 'Much as he admired Winston and anxious as he was to be back in England, he was not to be persuaded.'[39] He told the British ambassador to send the sea planes back empty and then wrote a furious response to

Winston where he threatened to resign all of his military ranks.[40] Wisely, he decided against sending the hot-headed resignation letter. Instead, he sent word to London that they would return by plane – but he had missed his moment.

Max Beaverbrook was, by now, well accustomed to staying up into the wee small hours with Winston at Number 10, discussing urgent war matters over cigars and brandy. On 3 July, Winston had been forced to make what he called a 'hateful decision', namely the destruction of French warships near Oran, part of the fourth largest navy in the world. Now that France had fallen to the Nazis, Churchill suspected that its fleet must likewise become Germany's. It had to be destroyed, however painful that order was. He finally gave the go-ahead for Operation Catapult, resulting in the deaths of 1,300 French sailors. At the end of this disastrous and interminable day, he had to try and resolve the future of the Duke and Duchess of Windsor.[41]

As Beaverbrook and Churchill discussed their options, the Prime Minister called in his private secretary, Jock Colville, who was barely awake, to take down a message to the duke. Colville later described how the Prime Minister composed such missives: 'Before dictating a sentence he always muttered it wheezingly under his breath and he seemed to gain intellectual stimulus from pushing in with his stomach the chairs standing round the Cabinet table!' Winston took his time, because this telegram was a delicate one. He was proposing that the Duke of Windsor take up the governorship of the Bahamas, one of the smallest, most far-flung and most strategically insignificant of all the British colonies. 'I think it is a very good suggestion of mine, Max,' Churchill gloated. He asked Beaverbrook if he thought the duke would accept.

Beaverbrook answered, 'Sure he will. And he'll find it a great relief.'

'Not half as much as his brother will,' Winston said.[42]

They were both dead wrong. The suggestion pleased no one: not the King, not the Queen, nor any of the major royals – Queen Mary was especially baffled – not the Colonial Office, not the British Embassy in Washington, nor, of course, the Windsors themselves, who suspected that they were being banished to a tropical Elba, the island where Napoleon was exiled. They were quite right.

The King was vexed, not only by the appointment itself but by Churchill's handling of the matter. In short, he felt that his nose was put out of joint and that the Prime Minister had ridden roughshod over his own suggestions. Before the Bahamas came into the frame, the King had suggested that his brother take a position in Egypt under General Wavell. Churchill, who knew that North Africa was likely to become a zone of Allied conflict, was unconvinced and wrote a flat 'No' on the memo suggesting the plan.[43]

The King also faced pressure from the Queen and his mother, Queen Mary, who thought it impossible to believe that sending the Windsors to the Bahamas was even being contemplated. 'A great mistake to my mind on account of her,' Queen Mary wrote. As for the Queen, she was concerned that the ladies of the Bahamas would refuse to accept a woman of Wallis' moral standing. 'The Duchess is looked upon as the lowest of the low,' she remarked scornfully.[44] Instead, she suggested that the Windsors be sent to the Bahamas as visitors, as opposed to having any specific duties. The King asked Churchill to consult with Lord Lloyd, the Secretary for the Colonies, to explore alternative options. Rather than complying with the King's request, Winston – under the influence of Beaverbrook, late-night fatigue and top-shelf brandy – made the offer to the duke directly and sent it off to Lisbon. The King grumbled that it was 'most annoying as the matter has not been thought out'. After further discussions with his Prime Minister, however, the King conceded that 'this arrangement may be the best one in the end'.

The Duke of Windsor was even more taken aback than his younger brother when he received Churchill's telegram. The message was spare and to the point, offering him the post of Governor and Commander-in-Chief of the Bahamas. It ended with a personal note: 'Personally I feel sure it is the best option in the grievous situation in which we all stand. At any rate I have done my best.'[45] According to the Windsors' biographer, Michael Bloch, the duke stared at the cable in astonishment for a few minutes, unable to know what to make of it. It was, he realized from all his foreign travel, a 'third-class governorship'. Very reluctantly, he accepted the offer, later complaining bitterly to Churchill about his 'dictator methods'.[46] It was an exchange that marked a sea change in their relationship, with Churchill no longer seeing the duke through the rose-tinted spectacles of a romantic royalist, and the ex-King realizing that Winston was no longer at his beck and call. Nonetheless, with the duke's acceptance secured, Lord Lloyd, the Colonial Secretary, drafted a telegram to the Prime Ministers of the Dominions as if written by Churchill. It read:

> The activities of the Duke of Windsor on the Continent in recent months have been causing HM and myself grave uneasiness as his inclinations are well known to be pro-Nazi and he may become a centre of intrigue. We regard it as a real danger that he should move freely on the Continent. Even if he were willing to return to this country his presence here would be most embarrassing both to HM and to the Government.
>
> In all the circumstances it has been felt necessary to try to tie him down in some appointment which might appeal to him and his wife and I have decided with HM's approval to offer him the Governorship of the Bahamas. Despite the obvious objections to this solution we feel that it is the least of possible evils.[47]

Though the draft reflected current thinking about the duke and duchess, Churchill felt that it was too baldly critical of the Windsors. The telegram was substantially modified as Winston tried to avoid washing dirty royal linen in public. In his version, it was all the fault of the Nazi enemy. In a press release, published the following week, the appointment was painted as merely a natural extension of his military work in France. It was, for media consumption, a variation on: 'Move along, nothing to see here.' When the appointment was announced publicly on 10 July, the German high command moved into top gear. Foreign Minister Joachim Ribbentrop, who was rumoured to have had an affair with Wallis, tasked the German ambassador to Spain with wooing or compelling – either avenue would be acceptable – the Windsors to stay longer on the continent. At best, they should be encouraged to travel to Germany; at worst, to return to Franco's Spain, where Germany had much more influence than in the politically secluded suburbs of Lisbon. Ribbentrop sent his top spy, Walter Schellenberg, to their Portuguese villa to mastermind the project, codenamed Operation Willi. What with mysterious letters of warning, windows being broken in the night, rumours of explosives on board the ship scheduled to sail to the Bahamas, and worrying conversations with trusted Spanish friends, the Windsors were in an agitated state, seeing danger everywhere.[48]

After they accepted Churchill's offer, the duke made a further series of demands: that a soldier be released from active duty so that he could sail with him to the Bahamas as a personal valet; that the duchess' maid be given time to travel to Paris, to retrieve their precious linens from their rented apartment; and finally, that they be granted an opportunity to stop over in New York before heading on to the new post – according to their story, Wallis needed to see a medical specialist, but more likely they wanted to do some luxury shopping on Fifth Avenue. The King called them 'preposterous propositions', telling the Prime Minister that the duke 'has got to obey orders now. From telegrams I have read [he] has forgotten that we are at war & that the authorities here are busy with great problems.'[49] To Churchill, one of these demands was particularly unpalatable: under no circumstances would he allow the Windsors to travel to New York on the way to the Bahamas. As Lord Lothian, the British ambassador to the United States, warned Churchill, 'If he visits New York there will inevitably be a great deal of publicity, much of which will be of an icy character and which will have a most unfortunate effect at this present juncture.' Moreover, the duke's opinions would, either by ill luck or design, be dragged into the presidential elections due to take place in November, an involvement that must be avoided at all costs. The British were not alone in hoping to prevent the New York layover. By coincidence, the Windsors entertained Herbert Pell, the American minister to Portugal, during their stay in Lisbon. Without knowing what was under discussion in London, Pell independently came to the same conclusion as Churchill and Lothian. The American minister was so disturbed by their attitude that he sent an urgent wire to the State Department in Washington, stating that 'their presence in the United States might be disturbing and confusing' as the duke spoke of remaining abroad with or without Churchill's approval and of the duke's desire 'apparently to make propaganda for peace'.[50] The danger posed by the Windsors was demonstrated by an article in *The New York Times* which asserted confidently that the duke had urged the King to form a peace Cabinet around Chamberlain, Halifax and Lloyd George with a view to ending the war.[51] These diplomatic developments emphasized the need to install the Windsors in the Bahamas as soon as possible.

Intercepted diplomatic telegrams about the duke and duchess that were sent to Berlin alerted Downing Street to Operation Willi and the potential dangers facing the royal couple. The duke's request to postpone his departure from Lisbon set alarm bells ringing. Churchill summoned the duke's lawyer, Walter Monckton, and asked him to fly to Lisbon and convince the duke to sail as planned. His verbal messages of warning were accompanied by a letter from Churchill.

When Monckton arrived, he found the duke agitated and distraught, fearing for his life and totally uncertain as to whether he was being spied on by the Germans or by the British. The German strategy of intimidation had worked exactly as intended. Monckton, a friendly face and a trusted confidante, had arrived not a moment too soon.

The duke carefully read the letter from Churchill, which began in a friendly, fulsome vein, expressing satisfaction that he had been able to secure the couple a 'suitable sphere of activity and public service during this terrible time when the whole world is lapped in danger and confusion'. He felt certain that the couple would 'lend a distinction and dignity to the Governorship which … may well have other results favourable to British interests'.[52] After promising that they could travel to the United States after the election, he went to the heart of the business in hand:

> Many sharp and unfriendly ears will be pricked up to catch any suggestion that your Royal Highness takes a view about the war, or about the Germans, or about Hitlerism, which is different from that adopted by the British nation and Parliament. Many malicious tongues will carry tales in every direction … In particular, there is danger of use being made of anything you say in the United States to do injury, and to suggest divergence between you and the British Government. I am so anxious that mischief should not be made which might mar the success which I feel sure will attend your mission. We are all passing through times of immense stress and dire peril, and every step has to be watched with care.[53]

The increasingly flabbergasted duke read and reread the letter. Then Monckton chimed in and explained that the ducal couple were at the centre of a Nazi plot to kidnap them. 'But how could we possibly be of any use to [the Germans]? asked the duke incredulously'[54] As his every casual utterance made headlines, this was rather disingenuous. Indeed, even as the Windsors absorbed Winston's dramatic letter, Ribbentrop was in the process of composing a direct address to the ex-King where he repeated the German position: that they only desired peace with

Britain, that Churchill was the main impediment, and that the duke and duchess could play a central role in establishing an armistice for the good of mankind. It was a seductive prospect to a vain man who felt he had been jilted by his family, his friends and the powers that be. In a rare moment of good judgment, he turned down the offer, much as he desired peace in Europe. He told Oswald von Hoyningen-Huene, the German ambassador to Portugal who had delivered the message, that he had no option but to follow his government's orders, as 'disobedience would disclose his intentions prematurely'. Essentially, if circumstances changed, he would reconsider his position.[55]

Schellenberg was still working hard to unsettle the Windsors and delay their departure when the agitated and alarmed duke made a final demand of Churchill – that a Scotland Yard detective accompany them on board ship. The Prime Minister agreed immediately, knowing the genuine threat they faced. With options running out, Hitler ordered the immediate abduction of the ducal couple.[56] It was too late. Such was the growing concern for their safety that Churchill asked the Admiralty if a cruiser could be spared to convoy the passenger liner across the Atlantic. He was informed that every navy ship was on station in anticipation of an expected Nazi invasion.[57]

Finally, on 1 August, the ducal party boarded the American Export Lines vessel and sailed into the distance. They may have soon been out of sight, but they were by no means out of mind.

CHAPTER TEN

Their Finest Hour

Britain: August–December 1940

FIELD MARSHAL HERMANN Göring, Luftwaffe supremo, promised
Hitler that the Brits would crumble within a week once the might of
his German squadrons was pitted against the Royal Air Force. But when
the Germans launched their fearsome aerial attack on *Adlertag*, or Eagle
Day, 13 August 1940, Göring could have had no idea that he was trigger-
ing the law of unintended consequences.

After days of dog fights where the British fly boys came out on top,
it was clear that Göring had overpromised and under-delivered. 'Never
in the field of human conflict was so much owed by so many to so few,'
was Churchill's immortal phrase commending the bravery of the young
RAF pilots.[1] But because Hitler required complete dominance over
British airspace before he could properly launch his much-anticipated
seaborne invasion of England, codenamed Operation Sea Lion, the Nazi
high command adopted a new tactic. The invasion was delayed, and in
its stead came the nighttime bombing of London. Not only did this
answer Churchill's infuriating decision to bomb Berlin, but it limited
Luftwaffe casualties.

What became known as the Blitz began on 7 September. Londoners
suffered fifty-seven draining, deadly nights of continuous attack. During
the night, people sheltered where they could, the Underground network
doubling as a giant bomb shelter; when daytime broke, the remaining
population – a smaller number each day – kept calm and carried on.

Although everyday Brits did their best to maintain normality, the

Blitz brought about one relatively minor change at the highest level of leadership that would have an outsized impact on the course of the war. Instead of continuing to schedule their meetings in the early evening, George VI and Winston moved their weekly audiences into the daylight hours. There was no guarantee against raids at lunchtime, but a midday audience was far less likely to be interrupted or cancelled due to air raid sirens, as the British air defence system was much more effective at hitting German bombers when the sun was up.

As Churchill later wrote, his Tuesday luncheons with the King at Buckingham Palace became a 'regular institution' of their wartime relationship. They were, he thought, 'a very agreeable method of transacting State business, and sometimes the Queen was present. On several occasions we all had to take our plates and glasses in our hands and go down to the shelter, which was making progress, to finish our meal.' It eventually dawned on them that servants may listen in to their confidential conversations. They heeded the wartime slogan, 'loose lips sink ships', and dispensed with the attendants, preferring to take turns serving each other from a sideboard.[2]

In this relatively relaxed setting, there were no more complaints about Winston keeping the King waiting. It was not long before the King was on first-name terms with Winston. This was a first in itself as he was never so familiar with the three other Prime Ministers of his reign. He always called them, both in public and private, Baldwin, Chamberlain and Attlee.[3]

More than anything, the Tuesday luncheons gave them an opportunity for their best selves to come to the fore. The King now got to see Winston on top form, before the burdens of the day had a chance to take their toll. Seated together, tete-a-tete, the two men talked over every matter relating to the war, no matter how sensitive or secret. The King was relieved, too, to find that his Prime Minister 'does tell me what is in his mind'.[4] After just five of these meetings, the King wrote to his mother, 'I am getting to know Winston better, & I feel that we are beginning to understand each other ... His silly attitude over [the Duke of Windsor] in 1936 is quite over.' He finished the letter with a ringing endorsement: 'Winston is definitely the right man at the helm at the moment.'[5]

From his side, Churchill appreciated the King's attention to detail and the great care he showed in keeping abreast of the war's latest developments. He was at times taken aback at the 'extraordinary diligence with which the King read all the telegrams and public documents submitted to him'. Although he well understood that the 'Sovereign has a right to be made acquainted with everything for which his Ministers are responsible, and has an unlimited right of giving counsel to his Government', he frequently found himself playing off the back foot, the King having 'mastered papers which I had not yet dealt with'.[6] He later said, in tribute to the King, 'the care and thoroughness with which he mastered the immense daily flow of State papers made a deep mark on my mind'.[7]

Alongside his improving friendship with the King, Churchill's relationship with Queen Elizabeth flourished as well. From time to time, she ate with the men, listening carefully to their conversation and occasionally making relevant comment. This was unprecedented: never had a royal consort been accepted into the formal briefing of the Prime Minister. But these were no ordinary times.[8]

Though the doings of the Duke of Windsor remained a sore point between Churchill and the King's consort, the Queen had offered an olive branch to Winston when he was made First Lord of the Admiralty for the second time. During a dinner with other members of the War Cabinet, she handed him a note containing a few salient lines from the Romantic poet William Wordsworth that spoke to her, which she had copied out for him. The excerpt ended:

For by superior energies; more strict
Affiance in each other; faith more firm
In their unhallowed principles; the bad

Have fairly earned a victory o'er the weak,
The vacillating, inconsistent good.

At the head of the page, Elizabeth wrote, 'I suppose written when Europe was terrified of Napoleon?' This was not only a thoughtful gift, but a gesture of intimacy and shared understanding that Churchill cherished deeply. He had the scrap of paper framed and kept it among his most prized possessions for the rest of his days.[9]

This literary offering also taught Churchill something important about Elizabeth: that she shared his appreciation for the beauty of the English language. Nine months later, once he was Prime Minister, Churchill put this knowledge to use, giving her a copy of Fowler's *Modern English Usage* as a Christmas present, telling the Queen that he himself had made use of Fowler. 'He liberated me from many errors & doubts,' he wrote. In her thank-you letter, she called the volume 'entrancing ... very amusing and extremely instructive'. Their companionship was, by then, secure.[10]

They were both instinctively aware of how important image was in projecting a person, a family, an institution and a nation. It was arguably Winston's greatest service to the royal family in that he was pivotal in shaping the portrayal of the House of Windsor as tribunes of loyalty, decency and quiet courage: a family at peace within a nation at war.

Like her husband's great-grandmother, Queen Victoria, Elizabeth understood that nothing could unite the British public quite like a matriarch. She portrayed herself as the caring homemaker, the model of feminine strength. While she appreciated the tenacity that women demonstrated in filling men's jobs during the war, she worried that this would lead them to abandon their commitments to their homes and families once peace was declared. She stood firm in her conviction that the proper role of a woman was as a supportive wife, a diligent homemaker and a loving mother. She wanted the British public to think of her as the epitome of dutiful womanhood.

In fact, Churchill's earliest contribution to the Queen's public image took place at his very first lunchtime audience, on 10 September 1940. The day before, a delayed-detonation bomb had lain for hours in the courtyard at Buckingham Palace before it finally exploded, blowing out banks of windows and plasterwork. Before Churchill arrived for his audience, the King's assistant private secretary, Alan 'Tommy' Lascelles, arranged for forty journalists and photographers to wait in the palace courtyard, ready to capture the moment when the King and Queen, together with their Prime Minister, emerged to inspect the wreckage. The media event projected an image that signified solidarity, collective vulnerability, and yet, strength in the face of everything that Hitler could throw at them. Their message was clear: if the King, Queen and Prime Minister could carry on through the destruction of all they held dearest, then so too could the nation. The King wore his naval uniform, signifying his solidarity with the military; a cheerful Churchill wore his trademark three-piece suit with bowtie and homburg hat; and the Queen was dressed in a simple, shin-length dress with matching hat, similar attire to that worn by millions of her subjects. No couture dresses à la Mrs Simpson wanted here. The Queen was neither the hero nor the celebrity, but simply a dutiful, sensible, modest wife and mother – but one who knew, nevertheless, that a picture was worth a thousand words, and made sure to look at the camera rather than the damage! The King and Queen liked one of the shots so much that they chose it for their Christmas card.[11] Just to add icing on top of this public relations triumph, the Queen was later quoted as stating, 'I'm glad we've bombed. It makes me feel I can look the East End [the poorest part of London] in the face.' Solidarity within adversity was the message that came across loud and clear.[12]

Three days later, Buckingham Palace was bombed again, the King and Queen narrowly escaping injury. The Queen was being a supportive wife and helping the King get an eyelash out of his eye. At the very moment of this small act of marital affection, a solitary German aircraft emerged from a cloudbank, flew straight down the Mall towards the palace, and dropped five bombs, two hitting the palace quadrangle about thirty yards from where the King had been sitting.

Churchill, who was chairing a War Cabinet meeting when the attack took place, did not learn how near of a miss it had been until after the war, when he was writing his memoirs. The King decided that it would be wrong to trouble his first minister with such a morale-sapping prospect as the death of a Sovereign in the midst of war. Churchill paused the Cabinet meeting to read out the harrowing news from the palace. As Churchill told his colleagues, this close call for the King and Queen underlined the reality that the Germans 'meant business'.[13]

Churchill immediately saw a potential for useful propaganda in the incident. Not only did it present the King and Queen as suffering like, and indeed with their subjects; it demonstrated to the rest of the world, and particularly to America, that Britain's resolve in the face of German barbarism was stalwart and unshakeable.

In a speech to the House, Churchill mocked the German aim to crush the British fighting spirit by targeting the monarch and his consort. He suggested that all Hitler had achieved was to further unite British subjects behind their Sovereign in their common cause: defeating the Nazi regime and restoring peace and sanity across the world. Churchill understood as well as Hitler, if not better, that while this war would be fought with soldiers it would be won with symbolism, with effective communication and rhetoric resolute enough to rally the masses behind a clear message. The lives of the royal family now fitted into that narrative of a plucky island race fighting an evil enemy alone.

It was not just Churchill's and the King's voices the nation now heard on radio broadcasts. Soon after war was declared, the voice of young Princess Elizabeth joined the chorus as she gave a short but charming broadcast to the children of the Empire, focusing especially on evacuees or those whose parents had gone off to war. Her sister, Princess Margaret, also made a brief cameo. The Queen, who, much like the King, detested public speaking, knew that her turn would soon come. Her particular message would be addressed to the women of the Empire, especially mothers.

She laboured for days writing the draft, fretting about the construction of her broadcast. Initially, she asked her friend and the author of *Winnie the Pooh*, A. A. Milne, for help, but his contribution did not meet her requirements. 'She found it extremely difficult to find words to express her feelings towards the people of Britain in these days,' recalled Roosevelt's trusted envoy, Harry Hopkins. 'She thought their actions were magnificent and that victory in the long run was sure, but that the one thing that counted was the morale and determination of the great mass of the British people.'[14] She was well aware that the wrong word here, or an imprecise phrase there, could have a dire impact on morale. Inevitably she turned to Winston, the greatest and most inspiring speech writer Britain had produced in centuries, to help her rise to the challenge.

If the Queen struggled with the pressure to say the right thing to her own people, she suffered grievously at the idea of speaking to the Americans, whose support in the war was Britain's best – indeed, only – hope of victory, in her second broadcast. After amending the first draft, she sent it to Winston for the master's touch. 'I fear it is not very polished,' she apologized – 'a good deal of my own.'[15] The final text had Churchill's fingerprints all over it: the Queen talking of the hardship weathered by the British people, which 'has only steeled our hearts and strengthened our resolution', of the 'bright eyes and smiling faces' that she saw throughout the country. 'For though our road is stony and hard, it is straight, and we know that we fight in a great Cause.' The broadcast included an appeal to Americans to consider the fight their own as well as Britain's: 'However great the cost and however long the struggle, justice and freedom, human dignity and kindness shall not perish from the earth.'[16] The Queen's broadcast earned her at least one notable admirer: the American President, Franklin D. Roosevelt. FDR cabled to ask the King to convey his congratulations to the consort for delivering an address that was 'perfect in every way' and that would 'do a great amount of good'.[17]

The wartime portraits of the Queen and her daughters taken by royal photographer Cecil Beaton in 1942 further fixed the image of a happy but resolute family at the head of the nation, the pictures of the heir, Princess Elizabeth, impressing on the popular imagination the continuity of the Crown. For the Queen, her carefully crafted image of a steel fist in a velvet glove was so potent that Hitler referred to her as 'the most dangerous woman in Europe'. Though the palace had a reputation of utter silence when dealing with the media, it was noticeable that her sayings and doings soon made their way into the popular prints. The Queen was propaganda gold. In preparation for the expected Nazi invasion, she was said to be taking shooting lessons in the grounds of Buckingham Palace so that she could kill as many Germans as possible before she, too, was killed or captured. When it was suggested that her daughters sail to Canada out of danger, she was resolute. 'The children will not go without me. I won't leave the King. And he will never leave.'[18] She and Churchill were singing from the same hymn sheet, the Queen's image of indomitable strength one that endured long after the war was over.

In the first months of his premiership, Churchill had not only ingratiated himself with the King but had arrived at a convivial and understanding partnership with the Queen. They both instinctively appreciated the impact of image on the popular imagination, the Queen proving herself adept, with Winston's help, at shaping the public's impression of the royal family as well as their love and respect for the institution of the monarchy.

This was graphically borne out on the evening of Neville Chamberlain's funeral on 14 November, when between 450 and 500 Nazi bombers flew over London, headed for Coventry, where the city endured hours of unimaginable horror as the city centre was turned into an inferno. When the all-clear came at around six fifteen in the morning, the first rays of sun illuminated the raid's gruesome toll: streets littered with charred remains and still-smouldering debris. As soon as the King heard of the attack, he decided to visit the ruined city to show solidarity with its shell-shocked population.

He arrived the following morning, greeted by the city's mayor and other stunned dignitaries who showed him the devastation. 'I was horrified,' the King later wrote, describing the Coventry residents as 'quite dazed after what they had been through ... The shock to them was very great.' As he himself had suffered a near miss just weeks before, the King empathized completely. The people of Coventry felt it, too. 'England was behind us,' said one resident about the King's visit. 'We no longer felt that we were alone.'[19] With their quiet dignity and simple manner, the King and his consort were now widely accepted, by most, as the nation's consolers-in-chief. As George VI's biographer Sarah Bradford has observed:

> It was the shared experience of the Blitz in London in September 1940 which more than anything forged a bond between the King and his people. Just as his father after twenty-five years on the throne discovered his own popularity on his Jubilee drives through the East End of London, so just over five years later George VI on his visits to that same East End, now reduced to rubble, found real and immediate contact with his subjects in a way which royalty do not normally experience.[20]

Not everyone was impressed by the King's diffident demeanour, particularly when set against his showman Prime Minister with his trademark V for Victory salute. They felt, in a world of rapid change, that the monarchy was irrelevant to their needs and distant from their concerns. What was undeniable was that both men were under tremendous strain as they tried to lift the spirits of the nation amid a deluge of bad news.

The King's own spirits were briefly lifted a few weeks later when, in December 1940, Churchill called to deliver news of the fall of the Egyptian town of Sidi Barrani. Part of Operation Compass, the first British desert offensive in the war ended in triumph: 'My humble congratulations to you, Sir, on a great British victory – a great Imperial victory,' Churchill told the King over the phone. Jock Colville, Churchill's secretary, reflected wistfully, 'It is the first time since war began that we have really been able to make use of the word victory.'[21]

There was little time to savour the taste of success before Churchill received more bad news; Lord Lothian, the British Ambassador to the United States, had suddenly died. It was a critical post at a time when Britain was in need of support and supplies from America. There was wild talk that Winston would appoint the Duke of Windsor as Lothian's successor. When Roosevelt got to hear of it his response was blunt: 'There isn't a chance.'[22]

In fact, Churchill chose Lord Halifax, then serving as Foreign Secretary. He was furious at what he considered a demotion. On Christmas Eve, Halifax paid a visit to Windsor Castle, where the royal family were spending the holiday. Though the King was understanding and sympathetic, it was clear that he backed Churchill to the hilt in his policies and choice of personnel. If Halifax was looking for a royal shoulder to cry on, he had come to the wrong castle. The King argued that the post of Ambassador to America, at this critical juncture, was much more important than the role of Foreign Secretary, stuck in London. What a difference six months had made. In May of that year, George VI and his consort had backed Halifax for Prime Minister. Now they were wholly in Churchill's corner, recognizing that he had the 'right stuff' for the battles ahead. The languid aristocrat, realizing that his cause was lost, packed his bags and sailed for Washington.[23]

The Churchill family, like millions of others, gathered around the radio at Chequers to listen as the King reviewed a difficult year in his Christmas broadcast. The King had recruited Winston – 'a past master of this art', as he called him – to help with the composition of his most anticipated speech of the year. 'In the last great war,' he said, pronouncing every syllable with deliberate precision lest his stutter sabotage his sentiment, 'the flower of our youth was destroyed, and the rest of the people saw but little of the battle. This time we are all in the front lines and in danger together.' He spoke about the newfound unity among the British people and urged them to carry this spirit of togetherness with them through the war and beyond, when reconstruction would ask further sacrifices of them all. 'The future will be hard,' he concluded, 'but our feet are planted on the path of victory, and with the help of God we shall make our way to justice and to peace.'[24]

The King was more pessimistic in the privacy of his diaries, summarizing the closing year as a 'series of disasters'. The bright spot was the elevation of Winston who, he noted, 'stopped the political rot ... morale of the people splendid.' His fighting spirit had shown the world that Hitler was not going to have everything his own way in the coming year. In a note that he sent from Sandringham, the royal family's winter retreat, he was full of praise for Winston. 'I have so much admired all you have done during the last seven months as my Prime Minister, & I have so enjoyed our talks together during our weekly luncheons. I hope they will continue on my return as I do look forward to them so much.'[25]

In his response, Churchill was equally effusive. Not only was he able to inform the King of another victory in North Africa – Australian forces had taken the port city of Bardia in Libya – but also to sprinkle a little stardust on the King and Queen: 'Your Majesties are more beloved by all classes and conditions than any of the princes of the past.'[26]

Bahamas: August–December 1940

Churchill had, in some ways, made himself a hostage to fortune after his late-night decision, fuelled by brandy and fatigue, to send the Duke of Windsor to the Bahamas as governor. In the sober light of morning, it might not have seemed such a grand idea to send a believer in peace at any price to America's backyard, at a time when British foreign policy was laser-focused on bringing America into the war, or at least securing desperately needed munitions and ships that would enable Britain to continue the fight alone.

Not only was the duke a card-carrying appeaser who believed that heavy bombing would bring Britain to the negotiating table, but his line manager, that is to say Lord Lothian, the British ambassador to Washington, was likewise well known for favouring peace talks with Hitler. Roosevelt had little time for the Windsors, whose attitude of 'complete despair' in the face of German aggression angered him. Their arrival in Nassau, the capital of the Bahamas, far from bolstering Churchill's foreign policy, encouraged the isolationists and pro-Nazis in America's heartland. The British ex-King was their royal poster boy, a talisman for their cause, which involved Britain's defeat and business as usual with the Nazi regime.

Among his Bahamian social circle were Axel Wenner-Gren, a millionaire businessman and friend of Hermann Göring; the chairman of General Motors, pro-Nazi and anti-Semitic Alfred P Sloan; General Motors executive James Mooney, a right-wing zealot eager to see the fall of Britain; and, of course, Charles Bedaux, who had loaned the couple his French chateau for their wedding and organized their infamous visit to Germany. There were many more who welcomed the Duke and Duchess of Windsor to the Bahamas in the hope that the British Empire would soon be brought to its knees. Though the duke had been sent to a geographical backwater, he was a global character and catnip for the media, especially the American press, eager to encourage controversy between the royal brothers and prise open the divide between Britain and America, the Old World versus the New Order.

The Windsors had only been on the islands for a matter of weeks when a mischief-making German radio show pinpointed the propaganda downside of the duke's proximity to the American President. It stated:

According to reports from the United States of America President Roosevelt will try to bring about peace negotiations between Great Britain and the Axis Powers ... The Duke of Windsor may also play a part in this attempt ... The Government sent him to the Bahamas to get him out of the way, but he accepted the appointment so that he could be within easy access of the United States of America. He will shortly leave the Bahamas for the United States of America in order to talk with the President.[27]

The Foreign Office sent this extract of the broadcast to Lothian in Washington, as a warning about the 'risks attending even discussion of a meeting between President and Duke of Windsor'.[28] In this tense atmosphere, every communication counted.[29]

As for the ducal couple themselves, they were crestfallen when they arrived at the island capital. The climate was draining, and their new home, Government House, had long fallen into a state of decay – 'primitive' Wallis called it – while their treatment was as if engineered to infuriate. A standing Foreign Office instruction was that the islanders should bow and curtsey to the governor, but not to his wife. She was 'Your Grace' while he was 'Your Royal Highness'. They might be 3,000 miles from central London, but Buckingham Palace rules still applied. After a few months in exile the duke wrote but did not send a long letter to Winston detailing his many complaints.[30]

Churchill, having sent the duke to the Bahamas, now did everything in his power to prevent him visiting New York or travelling to Washington to meet with the President. For several months the excuse was that the presidential elections in November 1940 proved to be a stumbling block.

Almost from the moment they landed at Nassau, the ducal couple were looking to get out of Dodge. Within a week of taking up his post, on 21 August, the duke was writing to the Foreign Office asking to be given permission to visit his ranch in Alberta, in western Canada. The request was unceremoniously turned down. When that didn't work, he lobbied the Colonial Office for funds to renovate Government House in a style more to their liking. With London burning and a Nazi invasion expected imminently, Churchill made it clear that this was no time for genteel indulgence. 'Comment is needless,' he scrawled on a memo detailing their request. Or as the Queen commented acerbically, no time to focus on their 'pink sheets' when the majority of Londoners were 'spending nights in little tin shelters and then going to work in the morning'.[31]

Churchill did request that a comment from him be transmitted to the duke through Walter Monckton. He telegrammed that the Prime Minister was 'very grieved to hear you were entertaining such an idea' while the long-suffering people of Britain were being asked to tolerate such extremities of loss. He hoped the duke 'would be willing to put up with the discomfort and remain at your post until weather conditions made things less unpleasant'.[32]

Complicating matters was an invitation from Roosevelt for the duke to join him for lunch on a yacht he was taking on a tour of the Caribbean after the election. He pointed out that it was a tradition for governors to visit Miami and Palm Beach during the winter months. In the meantime, Churchill sent the President a letter emphasizing the dire straits Britain found herself in. 'You will, however, allow me to impress upon you the extreme urgency of accelerating the delivery of the programme of aircraft and other munitions ... The World Cause is in your hands.'[33] It was a plea that eventually led to the Lend-Lease Act.

In early December, the ducal couple sailed to Miami on board the yacht, *Southern Cross*, owned by Axel Wenner-Gren, or in the words of the *Daily Mirror*, 'Goering's Pal'. It was the Foreign Office's worst nightmare, especially as the duke defended his business friend as an investor and large-scale employer in the islands. His Nazi links seemed to count for little in the duke's eyes. While Wallis recovered from a tooth extraction, the duke, having been put off time and again by officials in Whitehall, accepted an invitation to join the newly re-elected President on his yacht while they viewed potential sites for future American naval bases on several of the British islands.[34]

Several days later, Churchill heard more about the trip, particularly about the duke's meeting with President Roosevelt, from the US special envoy, Harry Hopkins. Churchill was relieved to find that the duke had behaved with some tact, much to everyone's surprise. As expected, the duke was pessimistic about Britain's chances of winning the war, but he also – as Jock Colville recorded from the conversation – 'spoke very charmingly of the King (a fact which touched Winston)'.[35] As the President recalled, the nearest they came to discussing the war was when he praised the courage and fighting spirit of the British people. He did so deliberately to stave off any potential ducal diatribe against the war.[36]

There was, though, a sizeable downside to their meeting. While the President had been impressed by the duke, he was not so keen on his entourage, which was described as 'very bad'. Moreover, HRH's recent yachting trip with a 'violently pro-Nazi Swede [Axel Wenner-Gren] did not create a good impression'.[37] Whether Wenner-Gren was in fact 'violently pro-Nazi' was almost beside the point; what mattered was that both Roosevelt and Churchill had concerns about him – as did head of the FBI, J. Edgar Hoover, and Britain's spy chief. It was clear that the duke was making himself a hostage to fortune by his continued association with a suspected Fifth Columnist.

After listening to Hopkins' briefing, Churchill may have had cause to regret the appointment of the Duke of Windsor as governor. But this was only an appetizer for the revelations to come.

CHAPTER ELEVEN

Royal Defeatist at Large

WINSTON'S ONLY SON, Randolph Churchill, was a controversial figure. Few had anything positive to say about him. By most accounts, Randolph was 'objectionable, self-assertive, whining, extravagant, unpopular and, by and large, insufferable'; a man who could, according to his sister Mary, pick an argument with a chair. He was a drunk, a womanizer, a reckless gambler and a constant worry to his father, who forgave his wayward son time and time and time again.[1]

So, it was a vivid indication of his anger that when Winston learned of the latest indiscretion of his surrogate son, the Duke of Windsor, he was less able to forgive and forget. The incident concerned threatened to permanently mar their relationship, especially since, before the duke had set sail for the Bahamas, he had been warned by both Churchill and Monckton that the defeatist doctrines he had articulated in the salons of Paris, Madrid and Lisbon would not be acceptable in his new official position.

The duke had ignored Winston's strictures and secretly spoken at length to Fulton Oursler, editor of the New York-based *Liberty* magazine, about Britain's pitiful prospects in the war. The interview took place in December 1940, shortly after his lunch with Roosevelt, but was not published until three months later, in March, around the time that George VI had broken with all precedent to greet the new American ambassador John Gilbert Winant. The King, rather than meeting the envoy at Buckingham Palace, travelled to Windsor railway station where he impressed on the new arrival the relative informality and friendliness of the occasion. 'I am glad to welcome you here,' the King told him.[2]

Heartily endorsed by Churchill, the meeting was meant to underscore Britain's developing special relationship with the United Stated as well as impress upon the new ambassador the country's desperate need for American assistance. With Britain's survival hanging by a thread, thanks to the success of the German U-boat campaign, which had sunk thousands of tons of British shipping, it was important to ensure that Winant was on the side of Britain, unlike his predecessor Joseph P. Kennedy who thought 'England was gone' and supported 'appeasement one thousand per cent'.[3]

At the very moment when the King and the Prime Minister were working in tandem to convince Americans that Britain could win the war, but only with their help, the Duke of Windsor fired a most unwelcome broadside that could have torpedoed the growing mood of friendship and cooperation. If he was trying to scupper Allied relations, he could not have picked a more propitious moment to venture into print. Understandably, both Churchill and the King were furious, all the more so as further details of the duke's unpatriotic behaviour came to light.

The first inkling of the duke's treachery was contained in a brief telegram from the British Press Service in New York summarizing an article, entitled 'The Duke of Windsor talks of War and Peace'. The ex-King, according to the telegram, had expressed doubt as to whether 'England could hold out, even with American aid' and had voiced his 'opinion that Hitler might be persuaded to moderate his policies ... provided a powerful neutral mediator could exact guarantees "from both sides"'.[4] It later emerged that during his three-hour conversation with Oursler, he had secretly implored the journalist to speak with his friend, President Roosevelt, and convince him to take on that mediating role. If Roosevelt would offer his services as an international referee, the duke promised to immediately issue a public statement supporting this dramatic diplomatic step.[5] Needless to say, the duke's defeatist attitude was wildly at odds with official British foreign policy, his incendiary comments made without any consultation with Churchill or Halifax. Even though he was yet unaware of all the details, Halifax sent Churchill an emphatic telegram: 'It is essential that he should be stopped giving any more interviews of this sort.'[6] There was talk for a time of sending a press attaché to Nassau to keep an eye on the loose-lipped duke but no one was prepared to step up to the plate.

While Halifax, Churchill and the King absorbed the duke's latest indiscretion, he sent a telegram stating that he planned to tour the Bahamian islands on a borrowed yacht – widely thought to be Wenner-Gren's *Southern Cross* – and ending the journey with a two-week visit to America to give the duchess a chance to see her family in Baltimore. The tone of the duke's telegram suggested that permission was a formality. He could not have been more wrong. Halifax wrote to Churchill saying that the use of the *Southern Cross* would 'create the worst impression both on the Administration and on public opinion'. Halifax also feared that the duke would actively seek out isolationist leaders during his visit to the States.[7]

In a stiff telegram, Winston slammed the door on the duke's plans:

After much consideration and inquiry, I have reached conclusion that Your Royal Highness' proposed visit to the United States would not be in the public interest nor indeed in your own at the present time ... It would be impossible however for His Majesty's Government to approve the use of Mr. Wenner-Gren's yacht for such a purpose. This gentleman is, according to the reports I have received, regarded as a pro-German international financier, with strong leanings towards appeasement, and suspected of being in communication with the enemy. Your Royal Highness may not perhaps realise the tensity of feeling in the United States about people of this kind and the offence which is given to the Administration when any countenance is given to them.[8]

The duke later pointed out that the boat was in fact owned by Alfred Sloan, the chairman of General Motors who was, on closer examination, an active member of a pro-Nazi, antisemitic group called *Sentinels of the Republic*. Hardly a step up from the millionaire Swede.

Winston went on to scold the duke for the *Liberty* article, which he averred would 'certainly be interpreted as defeatist and pro-Nazi, and by implication approving of the isolationist aim to keep America out of the war'. He ended with an appeal to the duke's better angels: 'I could wish indeed that your Royal Highness would seek advice before making public statements of this kind. I should always be ready to help as I used to in the past.'[9]

Stung by Churchill's verbose rebuke, the duke fired back an angry telegram two days later claiming that his words had been twisted by Oursler. That was soon exposed as a lie when Oursler confirmed to Halifax that the duke had read and approved the article before the magazine went to press.[10]

The duke went on to complain:

> My first six months here have been spent doing the utmost to strengthen Anglo-American relations and I think I have had some success with the prominent businessmen and others. Now you say it would not be in the public interest or indeed in my own to visit America. Personally I do not share this view and your refusal of leave to go there in April is extremely inconvenient. However it is a small consideration for if as your message infers [*sic*] I am more of a detriment than of assistance to these vital Anglo-American relations then I would prefer to resign.[11]

After forwarding a copy of the duke's message to the palace – he always kept the King abreast of correspondence with and about his brother – Churchill sent the duke a brisk admonishing response. 'Your Royal Highness' appointment as Governor of the Bahamas is self-contained and is not specially concerned with Anglo-American relations ... H.M.G. do not think that a visit to the United States would be helpful at the present time and we have been so advised by very competent people on the spot.' This time, Churchill backed up his argument with evidence, sending along a passage of the offending article, one 'which has not been repudiated by Your Royal Highness [and] gives the impression and can indeed only bear the meaning of contemplating a negotiated peace with Hitler. That is not the policy of H.M.G.; nor is it that of the Government and vast majority of the people of the United States, where there is a very fierce and passionate feeling rising.' He continued: 'Later on when the atmosphere is less electric … I think an agreeable visit for you both might well be arranged. Meanwhile in this sad time of sacrifice and suffering it is not I think much to ask that deference should be shown to the advice and wishes of H.M.G. and of Your Royal Highness' friends, among whom I have always tried to bear my part.'[12] The King's private secretary thought Churchill's response 'admirable'.[13]

In the back-and-forth of telegrams, the duke's underlying grievances came to the surface. He told Churchill that he had seen a recent profile of the Queen in *Time* magazine, where she was quoted as referring to Wallis as 'that woman', a remark that he, not without reason, strongly resented. He knew how careful the British Royal Family was with their public statements, and questioned how this remark could have possibly passed the media censor. Then, he used the affront as grounds to return to his lifelong hobbyhorse, the denial of an HRH handle for the duchess. The duke concluded his letter bitterly: 'I have both valued and enjoyed your friendship in the past but … I find it difficult to believe that you are still the friend you used to be.'[14] It was an exchange that marked the low point in their long relationship. In the end, the duke did not resign; he did, however, defy Churchill's orders and visit Palm Beach on the way back from his tour of the western Bahamian islands. During his brief stay, he was watched by a team of FBI detectives.

The duke was not the only European royal giving Winston a headache. The first reports back to Washington from the new American ambassador to the Court of St James' painted a dire picture of the continent's prospects in the war. In May 1940, Churchill had expected stout resistance in Central Europe to stem the German advance and was badly let down by the surrender of the Belgian forces by King Leopold III. Without Belgian support, Churchill was left scrambling to save his army from the beaches of Dunkirk and Calais. Now another royal, Prince Paul of Yugoslavia, had bent the knee to Hitler and Mussolini. In March 1941, he signed a peace treaty with the Germans and Italians after vainly trying to remain neutral. Hitler, contemptuous of Paul's attempt at independence, soon invaded Yugoslavia, deposing Paul in the process. This was a personal trauma for George VI, who had been best man at Prince Paul's wedding to Princess Olga of Greece, the sister of Duchess Marina of Kent. Churchill, for his part, had never liked or trusted the Oxford-educated Paul. He was studious, cultured and weak, certainly not endowed with the cunning required in Balkan politics. It seemed to Winston that Paul had been feeble to the point of criminality. When Marina petitioned Churchill to allow the deposed couple to take refuge in England, Churchill immediately responded, 'Of course, Prince Paul could not possibly come here.' Instead, the couple were sent to Kenya and held in the equivalent of an open prison, the prince's reputation never recovering, even after the war.[15]

In other cases, Churchill had done his best to bring deposed or defeated European heads of state to England, where they formed 'free Allied governments' for use by the British propaganda machine. By keeping the governments active, even while their countries were occupied, Churchill hoped to instil a sense of defiance against the Nazis in the hearts of all the conquered peoples across the continent.[16] His unwillingness to provide refuge to Paul and Olga was an exception to this policy: he had too much disdain for their surrender, whatever sympathies the King and his sister-in-law, the Duchess of Kent, may have felt.

While the abject surrender of Yugoslavia set off a domino effect, with other small European nations falling under the heel of the Axis powers, Churchill was able to give the King one piece of good news. The signing of the Base Lease Agreement on 27 March 1941 allowed the United States to build military bases on a number of British territories, including the Bahamas, in exchange for fifty outmoded destroyers and other naval vessels. Churchill sent a cheerful, if slightly circumspect, notice to his royal governor: 'I wish to express to you my strong conviction that these bases are important pillars to the bridge connecting the two great English-speaking democracies.' As the duke had expressed his wish to strengthen the relationship between his homeland and America, this, Churchill suggested, was his chance to do just that: 'You have cause to be proud that it has fallen to your lot to make this important contribution to a better world.'[17]

Another modest consolation was a kind letter Churchill received from Princess Elizabeth, the heir apparent. Churchill had sent her some roses for her fifteenth birthday, on 21 April, and a few days later, she sent him a note of thanks, adding a thoughtful line of well-wishes: 'I am afraid you have been having a very worrying time lately, but I am sure things will begin to look up again soon.'[18]

While there was no sign of the war taking a turn for the better, as Elizabeth hoped, there was a moment of comic relief on the evening of 10 May, the one-year anniversary of Churchill's assumption of the premiership. Winston celebrated the milestone by treating himself to a Marx Brothers film to take his mind off pressing matters of state. Even in the darkened cinema, he found himself unable to escape his responsibilities when a pushy secretary refused to be dismissed. He carried an urgent message from the Duke of Hamilton. Rudolf Hess, Hitler's second-in-command, had flown himself into Scotland, parachuting safely to the ground after his plane ran out of fuel, in order to meet Hamilton, who he wrongly thought was the leader of a pro-peace, anti-Churchill political faction. In fact, the duke was the King's Lord Steward and, on that very night, was commanding the RAF squadron to shoot Hess' plane out of the air. 'Hess in Scotland!' wrote Churchill later. 'I thought this was fantastic.'[19]

According to Hess' testimony, he was on a lone-wolf mission to secure peace on behalf of 'all humanity'. He told his captors that when he had contacted the Duke of Windsor the previous year, he didn't receive an encouraging response. Instead, Hess felt he had to take drastic measures. His main goal was to convince the pro-peace faction in Britain to remove Churchill from power, install a new government that would be willing to negotiate with the Nazis, and thus bring the war to a prompt end, allowing Britain to maintain its empire intact while Germany did as it pleased in Europe. Hess claimed that Hitler 'did not want to defeat England and wished to stop the fighting'.[20]

When Churchill and the King next met for lunch, this episode lightened the mood from the otherwise depressing catalogue of damage and disarray brought about by fresh German attacks. Winston told the King that Hess 'would do us good'. The Nazi leadership, including Hitler, had neither known nor approved of Hess' plan. Embarrassed after the fact, they launched a propaganda campaign to discredit his defection by calling his sanity into question. But this approach, for a government that was ruthlessly exterminating the mentally disabled in concentration camps, raised an uncomfortable question: if Hess was insane, why was he in such a position of high authority? However which way the Nazis sliced it, this was a humiliating incident for German leadership.

When Churchill and the King discussed the significance of the episode, it was clear that, according to Hess, Hitler was prepared to end hostilities with England, ceasing all bombing and leaving the British Empire intact, on the simple condition that he was allowed to do as he pleased within the European continent. But there was one catch: Hitler would never agree to negotiate with Winston Churchill, whom he loathed. The King, once a vocal and earnest supporter of 'peace for our time', now found the entire premise absurd. 'Winston was sure I did not want him to resign!! Just when things looked brighter for us,' he confided in his diary.[21]

There was, however, a twisted logic to Hess' mission. At the time, Hitler was secretly amassing troops on his eastern border in preparation for an invasion of Soviet Russia. A respite from hostilities towards Britain would release men and machinery for Operation Barbarossa, the code name for the impending offensive to the east. On 22 June, the Nazis broke their non-aggression pact by launching the largest land offensive in military history. Until that point, both Churchill and the King had been staunchly anti-Soviet. That said, in 1938–9 Churchill had advocated an alliance with Russia as a counterbalance to Nazi Germany. Nonetheless Churchill hated the philosophy underlying communism, while the King had more personal reasons – they had murdered his cousins, the Romanovs, in 1918. But now, Churchill sensed in the invasion of the Soviet Union an unmissable opportunity to change the tide of the war. In his broadcast the next day, he offered Britain's help and support to the Russians. In spite of their differences, he told his listeners, they now shared a unified 'aim and one single, irrevocable purpose. We are resolved to destroy Hitler and every Vestige of the Nazi regime.'[22] With his historian's hat on, Winston realized immediately that Hitler had made a major tactical blunder. Like Napoleon, he was now fighting a major war on two fronts. There could only be one outcome – military defeat.

The King, meanwhile, could not help but marvel at Churchill's ability to put aside his private feelings about the Russians in the service of a larger objective. 'When Winston has made up his mind about somebody and something,' the King noted, 'nothing will change his opinion. Personal feelings are as nothing to him, though he has a very sentimental side to his nature. He looks to one goal and one goal only: winning this war. No half measures.' To Winston's thinking, the matter was simple and clear-cut. As he famously declared, 'If Hitler invaded Hell I would at least make a favourable reference to the Devil in the House of Commons.'[23]

The violent entrance of the Soviet Union into the conflict renewed Churchill's enthusiasm for bringing America on board. He began to press the King to allow him to make a visit to President Roosevelt. A month later, on 25 July 1941, the King finally approved of the plan. The British Prime Minister would meet the American President off the coast of Newfoundland in August. 'I am very glad that you are at last to have the opportunity of making his acquaintance,' the King wrote to Winston, 'and, as I told you before, I am sure that there is much to be gained by a meeting between you.' He went on to say that it was an auspicious time for Winston to leave, but even still, he could not help but express some concern: 'I confess that I shall breathe a sigh of relief when you are safely home again!'[24]

When Winston finally did meet Roosevelt, he did so with a note of introduction from the King: 'This is just a line to bring you my best wishes, and to say how glad I am that you have an opportunity at last of getting to know my Prime Minister. I am sure you will agree that he is a very remarkable man.'[25]

Over the years, Roosevelt had heard much about Churchill; his popular lecture tours, his daring escape from a military prison during the Boer War, his role as First Lord of the Admiralty in both the First and Second World Wars and, perhaps most importantly, his opposition to appeasement. In the corridors of Washington, he was also seen as something of a loose cannon, prone to impetuous decisions and emotional outbursts. His drinking habits were of particular interest. Indeed, when diplomat Wendell Wilkie returned home from a trip to London earlier that year, Roosevelt's first question to him was, 'Is he a drunk?'[26]

Now, onboard the USS *Augusta* in Placentia Bay, Roosevelt got his chance to run the rule over the British Prime Minister for himself. By all accounts, the meeting was a roaring success. On 11 August, FDR reported to the King, 'I have had three delightful and useful days with Mr Churchill ... It has been a privilege to come to know Mr Churchill in this way and I am very confident that our minds travel together, and that our talks are bearing practical fruit for both nations.'[27] Three days later, Winston sent the King an even more encouraging message: 'I have established with the President most cordial personal relations and trust Your Majesty will feel that results justify mission.'[28]

Churchill made it back to London in time for their Tuesday lunch date on 19 August, delivering another personal letter from Roosevelt to the British Sovereign. During the meal, Churchill relayed the unfortunate news that Roosevelt 'at the moment ... would not declare war'. In the President's eyes, the political conditions were still not ripe for direct engagement. However, Churchill told the King that he had secured from Roosevelt a promise that America 'would wage war with us, against Germany'.[29]

It was a measure of the respect and admiration the King felt towards his Prime Minister that within weeks of his return, on 11 September, he offered Winston Churchill one of the higher honours in his purview, that of Lord Warden of the Cinque Ports, a ceremonial office dating back to the twelfth century. As Jock Colville recorded, 'The P.M. is much attracted by the historic splendour of the appointment, which was held by Pitt, Wellington and Palmerston.'[30] Churchill wrote to the King eleven days later accepting the appointment, with his sincere thanks. 'I should certainly regard it as an extraordinary compliment, far beyond my deserts, to be included in the long line of Prime Ministers and eminent men who have across the centuries filled that office.' His only qualm concerned the costs of maintaining the house and grounds of Walmer Castle which the title demanded. This was, though, hardly a reason to refuse the King's largesse, so Churchill closed his letter with sentiments which reflected their relationship, thanking the King 'for this renewed mark of the confidence and kindness which has been so great a help and encouragement to me in the fateful months during which I have been First Minister of the Crown. It is this that makes Your Majesty's spontaneous intention so agreeable to me.'[31]

Now it was the Duke of Windsor's turn to make himself agreeable to the Prime Minister after his histrionics earlier in the year, when he had threatened to resign his post as governor and then travelled to the United States without government approval. Inevitably, the duke's flattery again centred on a request to leave the islands for a visit to North America, this time to his ranch in Winnipeg, Canada. As ever, it caused a flurry of ruffled feathers and much concerned clucking at the Foreign Office hen coop. Churchill, after consulting with the Foreign Office, the Colonial Office, and of course Buckingham Palace, came to the sober conclusion that it would be unfair to keep the ex-King on the islands when every previous governor had enjoyed considerable latitude of movement. On 15 July he wrote, 'I see no reason why the Duke of Windsor should not towards the end of September visit Canada and the United States if he so desires. Such a request would not be denied to any Governor of Nassau.'[32]

So, the duke was at last permitted to travel to Canada via the United States in September, the same month in which the King showed his appreciation for his Prime Minister by conferring the title of Lord Warden of the Cinque Ports. The duke showed his respect too towards Churchill, now established comfortably as his ersatz father figure, in a series of telegrams that were at once complaining and ultimately affectionate. Though the words 'apology' and 'member of the royal family' are rarely on nodding terms, the duke's letter made a stab at contrition – but with a sting in the tail.

After opening with a bashful apology for disturbing Winston at a time when 'the momentous task you have undertaken leaves you but little spare time for other thoughts,' the duke recalled a letter he received from the King, in July 1940. This was proof, in the duke's mind, 'that my banishment to these islands was as good a war time expedient for a hopeless and insoluble situation as could be found'. He recognized that he would never again be accepted as part of what he called 'Official England', but felt that this should not prevent him from pulling his weight in his position of governor. He took the opportunity once again to question the failure to confer an HRH handle on the duchess and felt that Churchill could have done more. 'I had hoped that since you became Prime Minister and are all powerful, you would by now have advised my brother to grant the Duchess her "Royal rank" and so put an end to a situation in which I am quite sure you would not allow your own wife to be placed. Titles count for less and less nowadays, and I am sure you do not think for a moment that I want the "H.R.H." for the Duchess for snobbish reasons: I would not hesitate to drop mine for that matter if occasion arose.' Of course, this was recognized for the empty gesture that it was.

Eventually, the duke broached the sensitive subject of his and the duchess' upcoming trip to the mainland, a matter which had, in his words, contributed to a 'lively exchange' some three months prior.

> No good purpose can be served by going over old ground, and suffice it to say that I have refuted any implications you made at that time by remaining at my post and not resigning, for I think you know me well enough to realise that so long as I hold an official position, I play the game of the Government that appointed me ... I want to assure you once more that I have no idea of making any utterances, public or private, that are not in line with your policy. Indeed, I have no desire whatsoever to make any speeches outside the Bahamas or to discuss politics, for in these days it is far too dangerous a topic with people's emotions keyed to such a high pitch.

The duke closed with a tug on Churchill's heart strings. 'Amongst the few high spots to which we are treated in Nassau are your radio addresses ... We hope that you and Mrs. Churchill are standing up to the great strain; you certainly both give that impression from the British news reels, and the welcomes we see you receiving are most inspiring.'[33]

The visit, towards the end of September, was carefully choreographed to allow the Windsors to keep a low profile; the only negative comment in the press was a scornful criticism of the amount of luggage in their entourage. On 25 September, the duke had lunch with FDR, and showed himself to be fully – finally – toeing the party line. Halifax wrote to Churchill about the success of the meeting: 'Prime Minister may like to know that the President spoke well to me yesterday on the Windsors after seeing them here. He reported the duke as being very robust on war and victory and his attitude generally showed a great improvement on the impression the President had formed when he met him a year ago in the Bahamas.'[34]

Not everyone was so impressed. During question time in the House of Commons, an MP named Alexander Sloan asked Winston if he was aware of the 'bitter comment' being made in American newspapers regarding the Windsors' 'ostentatious display of jewellery and finery' during their visit. He argued that their trip was doing more harm than good, and that they should therefore be recalled. The duke considered making a public statement to refute Sloane's accusations, but Churchill, admitting his regret, cautioned the duke from lending undue importance to the incident: 'I would strongly advise leaving the matter alone.'[35]

The duke, for once, was pacified, writing to Churchill in early December to thank him for his guidance. 'The Duchess and I send you our belated but none the less sincere good wishes for your birthday.'[36] Winston had, on 30 November, turned 67 years old.

The cementing of the British–American relationship was complete when only a few days later, on 7 December, the Japanese launched a surprise attack on the American base at Pearl Harbor, damaging or sinking twenty naval craft including eight battleships and killing 2,400 military personnel and civilians. Though finally Churchill could rejoice at America's inclusion in the war, the sense of triumph was short-lived. Just three days later, two British battleships, HMS *Repulse* and HMS *Prince of Wales* (ironically named after the pacifist duke), were sunk by Japanese bombers 50 miles off the coast of Malaya. It was the greatest single loss of life in the Royal Navy in a day, totalling 1,459 officers and men.

The tragedy delayed Churchill's plans to fly to America to see Roosevelt, his decision coming as a relief to the King who was, along with the rest of the country, deeply saddened by the loss of so many British seamen. He wrote to Winston saying that the news 'came as a great shock to the Queen & I ... For all of us it is a national disaster ... I thought I was getting immune to hearing bad news, but this has affected me deeply as I am sure it has you … I understand you are not undertaking your journey just now, for which I am very thankful.'[37]

His trip would not be delayed for long. Just two weeks later, the Prime Minister and a small entourage, including a personal doctor, made the perilous journey to Washington D.C. Not only did he spend Christmas at the White House, but he made a barnstorming speech to congress that had even the former isolationists on their feet. His address, like the King's Christmas broadcast, was aired around the world, the British tag-team working in harness. The King sent a 'Private and Personal' message of Christmas greetings to Winston and his delegation, as well as the President and First Lady. 'You, and the vital work in which you are all engaged, are much in my thoughts, and I pray that the success of your conversations may bring us nearer to happiness in the New Year.'[38]

A thousand miles south, in Nassau, all talk about peace settlements and secret missions had ended. The duke loathed the Japanese with a passion he had never felt for the Germans. He was devastated not just by Pearl Harbor but also by the sinking of a navy ship named after him. He was now fully committed to the war effort, as too was his wife, who served breakfasts in the military canteen on the island.

Meanwhile, Churchill summoned his doctor, Charles Wilson, later Lord Moran, after suffering chest pain and tingling down his left arm after he pulled open a stiff bedroom window – classic symptoms of a heart attack. When Lord Moran checked the Prime Minister in his hotel room he diagnosed that, yes, he had had a heart attack. He realized that his next decision had the potential to change the direction of the war.

CHAPTER TWELVE

Affairs of the Heart

IT WAS A very unwelcome Christmas present. Churchill's doctor knew
that the standard treatment for a heart attack was six weeks' bedrest, but
he realized just as well that Winston would never tolerate such an order.
Wilson pondered what to tell the war leader, worrying that if Churchill
knew the true nature of his condition, he might become so overburdened
with concern for his own health that it would affect his work. Instead,
Wilson made a decision to keep silent, even from the great man himself,
and simply told him to rest as much as he could.[1] This would not be
much: Churchill was committed to a hectic schedule, mainly a train
journey to Ottawa, the Canadian capital, to meet with Prime Minister
Mackenzie King before returning to Washington to renew his mission
of good fellowship with the President. From now on, though, the British
Prime Minister's failing health would be a factor in any future military
and political considerations.

Churchill finally arrived back in Britain, a week later than planned,
after making the precarious flight across the Atlantic. The time spent with
the Americans had buoyed his spirits, the Prime Minister telling the King
at their first luncheon on 19 January 1942 that he was 'confident now of
ultimate victory' with America having joined the war. The two countries,
Winston said with his characteristic wry smile, 'were now "married" after
many months of "walking out"'.[2] Their honeymoon period, however, was
virtually non-existent, with Britain suffering a series of military calamities
that threatened to torpedo the mood of optimism. The sinking of the two
battleships off the eastern coast of the Malaya peninsula in December
was only the beginning: at the start of the year, the Philippines and Hong

Kong surrendered to the Japanese while it looked like India, Ceylon (now Sri Lanka), Burma (now Myanmar) and Australia could soon follow. It would be some months before the tide began to turn in Britain's favour, during which time Churchill was subjected to a vote of confidence in late January. Though he won the vote decisively, it was clear that Parliament, and the British public more broadly, were growing impatient with the continuous deluge of bad news.

As if to highlight Britain's military incompetence, on 12 February 1942 three German warships made their way to the safety of their home port after sailing through a British blockade in the English Channel in broad daylight. Just to rub it in, they also evaded RAF bombers tasked with hunting them down. When Singapore fell three days later, Winston called it 'the worst disaster and greatest capitulation in British history'. The King wrote to Queen Mary, 'I am very depressed over the loss of Singapore and the fact that we were not able to prevent the 3 German ships from getting through the Channel ... We are going through a bad phase at the moment, and it will take all our energies to stop adverse comment and criticism from the Press and others.'[3]

Churchill was deeply affected by the unrelenting tide of bad news, his trademark twinkle replaced by a scowl and a grunt. The media continued to question his leadership, now joined by increasing numbers of MPs from Churchill's own party. The *Daily Mail* ran a scathing editorial, with the headline: 'It is a fact that we can lose the war. It is a fact that today we are losing it.'[4] Churchill's high-flying rhetoric was one thing; competence, prudence and strategic acuity were another. Had they been backing the wrong horse for the past two years?

Though Churchill, for the time being, maintained his characteristic self-confidence, the storm of negative media began to make his job difficult. In his audience with the King on 17 February, he compared the situation to 'hunting the tiger with angry wasps about him'.[5] The King, for his part, caught the mood of pessimism and took the widespread criticism seriously. He secretly asked his private secretary, Sir Alec Hardinge, to sound out members of the War Cabinet as to their level of commitment to Churchill – was there someone else that might be better suited to the role at this phase of the war? After testing the water, Hardinge reported to the King, 'Winston is the right, and indeed the only person to lead the country through the war.' No other option was available.[6]

Hardinge's report left the King with the conviction that, while the House of Commons wanted Churchill to lead them, they resented the way that he went about it, treating them in an offhand manner and insisting that he have his way, without any interference from his colleagues. This was a recipe for conflict and criticism since, as the King observed with pride, 'Nobody will stand for that sort of treatment in this country.'[7]

A sign of Churchill's uncharacteristically sour mood was shown after the King declared a national day of prayer for Palm Sunday, on 29 March. 'If we can't bloody well fight, we'd better pray,' Churchill said morosely. But the nation's prayers did little to stem the flow of bad news. Unable to catch a break on the battlefield, Churchill worried that he would be subject to an avoidable humiliation by the Nazis. In particular, he feared that much embarrassment might be made over the Duke and Duchess of Windsor: just as the Rudolf Hess fiasco had made an international laughing stock out of the German leader, so the possible kidnapping of the Windsors by a platoon of Germans would place him in an impossible position. As the only defence of Government House was a couple of light machine guns, it was essential that the ducal couple were protected. Churchill personally ordered the deployment of two hundred Cameron Highlanders to Nassau and proposed the placing of an electric fence around Government House based on the principle: 'The right rule is, one may always take a chance but not offer "a sitter".'[8]

The duke himself had another solution – move. He wrote to Churchill on 18 April arguing that he would be able to serve his country much better in an appointment either in the United States or Canada. This time around, his language was soothing and emollient, supporting the Prime Minister in his recent political trials. He wrote, 'I have personally

resented the recent political attacks to which you have been subjected …
It may sound fulsome, but I know of no one who could take your place as
our Leader or inspire the British people to the tasks and sacrifices which
still lie before them.'[9] His pleading fell on deaf ears – at least as far as
Colonial Secretary, Lord Cranborne, was concerned. To his mind, the
North American mainland was the 'worst possible place for' the unruly
and self-interested duke.[10]

Churchill nevertheless discussed the situation carefully with the King,
who was sympathetic to the challenges it presented but unyielding in his
attitude towards his brother. He wrote in his diary, 'Where can he go and
what job can he do? He cannot come here anyhow, W and I are certain
of this, the Dominions don't want him, there is nothing he can do in
America, and he wants a temperate climate to live in.'[11] Winston told
the King that the one hopeful possibility, the governorship of Southern
Rhodesia (now Zimbabwe) was effectively vetoed by South African leader
General Jan Smuts, who thought he was the totally the wrong character
in a country where anti-monarchist sentiment was on the rise. Plus, aside
from being a royal, the duke lacked the qualities that such a role would
require. As Smuts wrote in his response to Churchill, 'This duty requires
close attention and judgment. Would this be forthcoming?'[12] Everyone
recognized this for the rhetorical question that it was.

There was one consolation – the duke was, somewhat grudgingly,
given permission to travel to the United States where, for the first time,
he would meet the President in an official capacity at the White House
for substantive conversations about the growing economic relationship
between America and the Bahamas. On 27 May, Roosevelt telegrammed
to Churchill, 'I am having your Nassau friends to lunch next Monday.'[13]

Churchill was only a few weeks behind them, flying to Washington to
meet with Roosevelt in mid-June. In those early days of plane travel over
such distances, the risks were high, the North Atlantic already having
claimed the lives of several civilian and military personnel. Churchill
took his own precautions. On 16 June, he wrote to the King advising him

that his preferred successor as Prime Minister in the event of his untimely death was Foreign Secretary Anthony Eden who, he described, 'will be found capable of conducting Your Majesty's Affairs with the resolution, experience and capacity which these grievous times require.'[14]

In the end, Churchill's flight to Washington went off without a hitch, but the visit itself proved far less smooth. On 21 June, as he sat in the Oval Office with Roosevelt, Harry Hopkins and his own chief military assistant, Pug Ismay, an official delivered a message to the President, who then passed it to Churchill 'without a word'.[15] The news was shocking: German forces had succeeded in capturing the Libyan port city of Tobruk, where 35,000 British soldiers surrendered to a much smaller Nazi force. Churchill later called it 'one of the heaviest blows I can recall during the war'. 'Defeat is one thing; disgrace is another,' he told Roosevelt, whose response signalled the strength of the bond that had developed between the two men and the nations they led: 'What can we do to help?'[16]

Returning from the US, Churchill was greeted by what was arguably the largest political crisis he would face during the entire duration of the war. The House of Commons was up in arms: the defeat at Tobruk had been a bridge too far, and several MPs were calling for another vote of confidence, this time casting doubt on 'the central direction of the war'.[17] The King was very much on Churchill's side, telling his mother that the parliamentary debate was unedifying and threatened to cause 'such a lot of harm abroad'. He added that it was those currently sitting in the House of Commons who were 'really to blame' for the nation's state of unpreparedness.[18]

There was more bad news – this time for Soviet leader Joseph Stalin, who had petitioned his allies to open a second front in Europe as soon as possible to take pressure off the Eastern front. Soviet troops and civilians, Stalin felt, had borne the full brunt of Nazi aggression for long enough. But instead of Stalin's desired approach, America and Britain favoured a land invasion of North Africa, codenamed Operation Torch, which would give them control of the Mediterranean and allow them to enter

Europe through its 'soft underbelly'. Churchill volunteered to fly to Moscow to look Stalin in the eye, explain the Allied plan, and stand up to his understandable fury.

Just before leaving England, he received a heartfelt letter from the King, who was racked with anxiety over his Prime Minister's mission. 'I shall follow your journey with the greatest interest & shall be more than delighted when you are safely home again,' he wrote on 1 August. 'As I have told you before, your Welfare means a great deal not only to the United Nations, but to me personally.' He signed of as 'Your very sincere and grateful friend.'[19] It was the first time the 'f-word' had appeared in their correspondence.

After ten days in North Africa, Churchill made his way to Moscow to meet with Stalin, the man he would later refer to as 'the Bear'. Once he delivered the bad news, he received another touching message from his Sovereign: 'Your task was a very disagreeable one, but I congratulate you heartily on the skill with which you have accomplished it.' Once again, King George closed on a personal note: 'I hope that you are not too tired, and that you will be able to take things more easily now.'[20] When Churchill was safely back in London – 'not at all tired' after 'a wonderful journey back'[21] – he received the King's invitation to join the royal family for a few days of late-summer relaxation at Balmoral: 'A little scotch air would do you good.'[22]

A day after this warm exchange, however, all plans for a reunion were put on hold when news broke of the death of the King's youngest brother, Prince George, Duke of Kent, in a freak flying accident. He was only thirty-nine years old. Churchill wrote letters of condolence lamenting the death of the 'gallant and much-loved' duke to various members of the royal family. It was also his sad duty to write the letter of sympathy extended to the King on behalf of the Cabinet and the entire House of Commons.[23]

Churchill reserved his most effusive condolences for the deceased duke's widow, Marina, the Duchess of Kent, who was left to raise three children on her own. There was one glimmer of light in this gloomy scenario. Churchill, after an assertive intervention from the King, finally agreed that Marina's sister Princess Olga – the same one who had been exiled with her husband Prince Paul to Kenya – could come to Britain to help her widowed sister.[24]

For the rest of the royal family, Kent's death exposed the divide between them. While Queen Mary received a 'perfectly charming, sympathetic letter' from her eldest son, he took the gloves off when he wrote to the King, accusing his younger brother of having prevented him from seeing the Duke of Kent the previous year when he was visiting the United States. It was, he argued, the King's attitude towards him and the duchess, a position of hostility adopted by the whole family, that had stopped him from seeing the Duke of Kent when he had the chance. Neither the duke nor his wife wrote a note to the grieving widow, Princess Marina, as they knew that she and Queen Elizabeth were the most vocal members of the royal family in objecting to Wallis receiving an HRH handle.[25] Even in the wake of a death in the family, no olive branch was proffered by either side in this interminable war of the Windsors.

Nor would peace come easy in the gruesome battle for Stalingrad, which was in full bloody flood in the late autumn of 1942 when the Allies opened a second front in North Africa. Though the move was greeted with expected derision from Stalin, it was a decisive but inevitably risky throw of the dice by the Allies. Everyone was on tenterhooks, especially Churchill. The American First Lady, Eleanor Roosevelt, chose this critical moment to visit the King and Queen at Buckingham Palace. She, unlike her husband, was not impressed by the King's first minister, finding Churchill repugnant and suspecting him of misogyny and drunkenness to boot. Nonetheless, the King and Queen hosted a dinner at Buckingham

Palace for the First Lady on 23 October, inviting Lord Woolton, General Smuts, Lord Mountbatten, and Winston and Clementine Churchill. Winston was described by the King's assistant private secretary, Tommy Lascelles, as acting 'like a cat on hot bricks' as he waited for a phone call with news from the second battle of El Alamein, launched earlier that day. He couldn't even relax when the party settled down to watch the latest Noël Coward film, *In Which We Serve*. Events in Libya consumed his thoughts.

Eventually, Churchill gave up the waiting game and placed a call via the palace switchboard to 10 Downing Street. By the time he put down the receiver, his demeanour had dramatically changed. As he walked along the red carpeted corridor to rejoin the party, his booming, tuneless voice preceded him.

'Roll out the barrel! We'll have a barrel of fun!' he sang. 'Roll out the barrel! We've got those blues on the run!'

At long last, the Allies had made headway. Operation Torch had set North Africa aflame with the famed Afrika Korps in retreat. Codebreakers at Bletchley Park had intercepted two telegrams intended for Hitler, from German Field Marshal Rommel, known as the Desert Fox, which gave 'a very depressing account' of the battlefront. Rommel told the Fuhrer that he did not know how he could hold out. On 3 November, Winston deposited these telegrams into a red dispatch box and toted them to Buckingham Palace for his regular Tuesday luncheon, this time with the Queen present. He was late, which was by now unusual, and his tardiness irritated the King. When Churchill finally sauntered in, however, the frustration dissipated immediately: 'I bring you victory,' he declared. The Queen later recalled, 'We looked at each other ... and we thought, "Is he going mad?" ... We had not heard that word since the war began.'[26]

After the success of the battle of El Alamein, the King wrote in his diary, 'A victory at last, how good it is for the nerves.' He was lavish in his praise for the Prime Minister, telling him in a handwritten letter dated 5 November, 'I was overjoyed when I received the news and so was everybody else ... When I look back and think of all the many arduous hours of work you have put in, and the many miles you have travelled, to bring this battle to such a successful conclusion you have every right to rejoice; while the rest of our people will one day be very thankful to you for what you have done. I cannot say more.'[27]

While Churchill responded with effusive acknowledgment of the King's aid, his letter gave a sense not only of his regard for the King as a person, but for the institution of monarchy as a bastion of British identity. 'No Minister in modern times has received more help and comfort from the King, and this has brought us all thus far with broadening hopes and now I feel to brightening skies. It is needless to assure Your Majesty of my devotion to Yourself and Family and to our ancient and cherished Monarchy – the true bulwark of British freedom against tyrannies of every kind; but I trust I may have the pleasure of feeling a sense of personal friendship which is very keen and lively in my heart and has grown strong in these hard times of war.'[28]

To mark the occasion, Churchill ordered that all the church bells in England be rung for the first time since the Blitz. He was counselled to hold back until operations to secure the Suez Canal had been successful – otherwise he was tempting fate. He was not a characteristically superstitious man, but on this occasion, he conceded, agreeing to wait until after the British commander Field Marshal Montgomery sent a telegram to the King on 13 November proclaiming the complete success of Torch and a resounding Allied victory. The following Sunday, church bells rang out all over the country, and listeners to the BBC broadcast across the globe heard the jubilant peals. The bells presaged something more, a shift in the tide of war in the Allies' favour. The BBC announcer asked his far-flung audiences, 'Did you hear them in occupied Europe? Did you hear them in Germany?'[29]

Churchill famously cautioned: 'Now this is not the end. It is not even the beginning of the end. But it is, perhaps, the end of the beginning.'[30]

In the midst of these celebrations, however, Churchill's mind was once again cast towards the Bahamas. The Duke of Windsor had sent yet another letter, friendly but pleading, pressing his case for an HRH title for Wallis. 'I naturally still regard the King's last minute 'wedding present' to me in May 1937 as a gross injustice,' the duke complained. For once Churchill, who always tried to find common ground between the warring brothers, resisted any attempt to meddle in a family affair. He deposited the duke's letter in a red box and sent it directly to Buckingham Palace, without comment, for the King's attention.[31]

On 8 December, the King responded with a carefully considered memorandum. In diplomatic language, he wrote, 'I have read the letter from my brother with great care, and after much thought I feel I cannot alter a decision which I made with considerable reluctance at the time of the marriage ... When he abdicated, he renounced all the rights and privileges of succession for himself and his children – including the title 'Royal Highness' in respect of himself and his wife. There is therefore no question of the title being 'restored' to the duchess – because she never had it.' He was critical too of his brother's timing, stating that 'to bring the matter up again at this moment would be a tragedy'.[32]

Alongside his official response, the King appended a hand-written note for Winston's eyes only. 'I must tell you quite honestly', he confessed, 'that I do not trust the Duchess's loyalty.'[33] He was not alone in thinking that Wallis was a Fifth columnist or worse. The State Department in Washington actively monitored her mail for much of the war. 'I begin to think I'm Mata Hari!' said the duchess, sardonically referring to the infamous female spy of the First World War.[34]

When Churchill finally replied to the duke, there was no mention of the suspicion swirling around Wallis' character. His carefully worded refusal, which took two weeks to compose, was tactful but firm. He wrote,

> I laid Your Royal Highness's wish before the King. His Majesty is willing to let the question remain in abeyance, but not to take any action in the sense you desire. It would be impossible to

move the War Cabinet in that direction, and I should deprecate even bringing the matter before them.

I am very sorry not to have more agreeable news but I hope Your Royal Highness will not attach undue importance to this point after the immense renunciations you have made.

He marked the message 'top secret' and, for once, deliberately kept it from the King.[35]

The Prime Minister was still enjoying the fruits of victory when he travelled to Casablanca in Morocco in January 1943 to discuss the future direction of the war with Roosevelt. They agreed to send extra supplies to Russia to tie up German forces on the Eastern front, launch an invasion of Sicily and the Italian mainland to ease Italy out of the war (Churchill's preference), and amass forces in England for an invasion of northern France (Roosevelt's). Besides military strategy, what also emerged from the conference was the convivial relationship between the Allied leaders. On 26 January, as the conference wound down, Churchill and FDR sent salutations to the King. The American President, who toasted his health, was effusive. 'I wish much that you could have been with us during the past ten days – a truly unique meeting in its thoroughness and in the true spirit of comradeship ... As for Mr. Churchill and myself, I need not tell you that we make a perfectly matched team in harness and out – and incidentally we had lots of fun together as we always do. Our studies and our unanimous agreements must and will bear good fruit.'[36] Within a matter of days there was more good news. On 2 February 1943, the German Army which had besieged Stalingrad surrendered.

There was one dark spot in this brightening horizon which caused the King grave concern, namely the diminishing health of his Prime Minister. No sooner had he returned from Casablanca than he succumbed to pneumonia. At one Cabinet meeting, he turned up with a shawl over his shoulders for warmth before accepting the inevitable, taking to his bed on 12 February. The King, though sympathetic, realized that he could not function effectively without the sage presence of his Prime Minister who had become such a close and trusted adviser, friend, and confidante. He wanted reassurance about the political and military situation in north Africa and realized that only Churchill could provide it. He wrote, somewhat plaintively: 'I cannot discuss these vital matters with anyone but yourself.'[37] From his sickbed, Churchill dictated a seven-page letter to address the King's concerns, mostly defending the performance of the American troops. Not yet placated, the King drove to Chequers, where the premier was convalescing, to discuss the matter over lunch. When the King was about to leave, Winston insisted on standing and showing him the door, contrary to his nurses' firm advice to remain in bed.[38]

Despite Winston's valiant efforts at feigning robust health, the King remained concerned, telling Queen Mary that he looked drastically diminished. The King pleaded with Winston not to overwork himself and to get some much-needed rest.[39] It surprised no one when Churchill didn't listen, though it was another month before he finally felt well enough to go out and about. Winston enjoyed his first luncheon with the King on 23 March, just a few days after broadcasting a speech about the nation's post-war recovery.

Final victory in northern Africa was achieved by mid-May 1943, the King marking the triumph by sending Churchill an ebullient letter of congratulations. He was so proud of this achievement that he agreed to the newspaper publication of both his original missive and Churchill's response. He wrote: 'I wish to tell you how profoundly I appreciate the fact that [the campaign's] initial conception and successful prosecution are largely due to your vision and to your unflinching determination in the face of early difficulties.'[40] In reply Churchill wrote in part: 'No

Minister of the Crown has ever received more kindness and confidence from his Sovereign.'[41]

The following day, the King's newly appointed private secretary, Tommy Lascelles, encouraged *The Times* to publish a fawning editorial, entitled 'King and Minister', on the unique relationship between the Sovereign and his first minister. 'Nothing in British institutions,' the piece argued, 'does more to preserve the balance and temperate humanity of politics than the constitutional practice that makes the heads of the Government His Majesty's "Ministers".' It continued, 'While the ministers have ultimate responsibility, it is the Sovereign's part to be fully informed upon all their activities, and they will not look in vain to him for counsel and suggestion.'[42] This was not an abstract ideal but a working daily connection, the beating heart of the modern constitutional monarchy. The editorial continued:

In his moving references to the aid and comfort he has received in dark times, Mr. Churchill pays public tribute to the discharge of a duty that only the Sovereign can perform, and that only the few can see him performing ... Ministers come and go, but the King remains, always at the centre of public affairs, always participating vigilantly in the work of government from a standpoint detached from any consideration but the welfare of his peoples as a whole. He is the continuous element in the constitution, one of the main safeguards of its democratic character, and the repository of a knowledge of affairs that before long comes to transcend that of any individual statesman ... a powerful reminder that King George VI is doing a work as indispensable for English governance as any of his predecessors, just as he has set his peoples from the first day of the war an unfailing example of courage, confidence, and devoted energy.[43]

This ringing endorsement of the unseen but vital work of the monarch was also a vote of confidence in the man himself. When George VI ascended the throne in the wake of the abdication calamity, many Britons, even devoted monarchists, had serious doubts about the shy, stuttering prince who had always clung to the shadows. They had been proven wrong as George VI grew steadily into the cloak of a monarch.

And yet, all this veneration of proper constitutional monarchism tended to paper over the cracks in the relationship between Sovereign and first minister. Time and again, Churchill rode roughshod over proper constitutional procedure. The boundary between the job of Sovereign and Prime Minister, was, with Churchill at the helm, often blurred. Royal biographer Philip Ziegler recalled that when he was a small boy, it was Churchill rather than the royal family who was the crucial figure in the minds of the public. George VI 'undoubtedly inspired respect and affection', Ziegler wrote, 'but he was not the kind of glamorous rallying point, which was Winston Churchill.' Others who lived through the war were less black and white in their judgment. While the Archdeacon of York, the Venerable George Austin, accepted Churchill as a great war leader and hero, it was always the monarchy, for him, who 'were the nation, encapsulated in the person of the Monarch and his wife'.[44] The fact that this was even a question up for public debate was, however, a sensitive spot for the King and Queen. One of their close friends, Maggie Greville, seemed to make no bones about the fact that the royal couple felt that 'Winston quite unconsciously has put them in the background. Who will tell him?'[45]

Aside from the vague issue of national iconography, there were more concrete matters of constitutional propriety. It took all of Lascelles' years of palace diplomacy to avert confrontations between the two most senior British statesmen. On one occasion, Churchill sent an official message of congratulations to the Viceroy of India after a victory they enjoyed with their 4th Division. It was couched in terms, noted Lascelles, 'of a royal message', and when the King read it in the following day's newspaper, he 'was not unnaturally rather aggrieved'. But both Lascelles and the King realized that Winston, at this point, could hardly be scolded. Instead, Lascelles asked John Martin, Churchill's private secretary, to convey to his boss that 'there ought to be some general ruling arrived at as to when the King, and when the PM, should send such messages,' and 'that the PM should broach the subject at the weekly luncheon'.[46]

On another occasion in early August 1943, Lascelles described how he had seen a telegram from Winston to Roosevelt where he knowingly incriminated himself. He admitted: 'discarding etiquette, I have telegraphed direct to the King of Italy'. Lascelles could hardly believe his eyes, and thought to himself, 'What would Queen Victoria have said, had [Prime Minister Palmerston] telegraphed to a crowned head without first consulting her?' But Lascelles managed to sooth the King's temper, arguing that the matter was 'a really urgent one' and the King himself was away in Scotland at the time. The King accepted it as a one-off offense. But it was a close call.[47]

As these disputes show, Lascelles had to be fully alert at all times to ensure that Churchill was not playing fast and loose with the royal prerogative. Just a few weeks after Churchill had contacted the King of Italy, Lascelles noticed that Winston and his Cabinet were exchanging numerous telegrams regarding the preferred venue for the upcoming tripartite Foreign Secretaries' conference. Lascelles discovered that Windsor Castle was up for consideration, except there was just one obstacle: no one had asked the King or his advisers whether they would be willing to play host. Though the matter was resolved, it once again needed Lascelles' good sense to prevent an unnecessary confrontation.[48]

Most intriguing of all these incidents was an occasion in Malta, in November 1943, when Churchill was on his way to Tehran for talks with Roosevelt and Stalin. During his stop on the island he presented, without the King's permission, two specially designed North Africa campaign medals, called Africa Stars, to Winston's favourite British general, Harold Alexander, and – more problematically – to American General

Dwight Eisenhower. As Churchill recalled in his history of the Second World War, 'They were both taken by surprise, and seemed highly gratified when I pinned the ribbons on their coats.'[49]

Not as surprised as the King, who was furious at Winston's behaviour. Lascelles suspected that again, Churchill 'knows he has been naughty'. He went on to explain, 'As it was a fundamental principle of the creation of the [Africa] Star that it should not be worn by any foreigner (a principle strongly insisted on by Winston himself), he is, like Pompey, *suarum legum idem auctor et subversor* [both the creator and transgressor of his own laws].' Churchill had broken an important rule of military honours by bestowing a special medal on Eisenhower, who, though an important military figure, remained a foreigner. As Lascelles noted, 'I only narrowly dissuaded his Sovereign (who feels about the incident almost as strongly as Queen Victoria did about Palmerston's more flagrant peccadilloes) from sending him a very sharp telegram.'[50]

While Churchill might have overstepped the boundaries of propriety from time to time there was never any question of his loyalty, as he demonstrated when he spoke to the House of Representatives in Washington. The Duke of Windsor also came to the Capitol building to hear his friend speak. According to Churchill's doctor Lord Moran, the duke received more applause than Churchill himself. As he watched the unfolding tableaux Moran reflected that while Churchill was wrong about the abdication, he was not a man to dwell for long on his mistakes. He observed, 'He is a very loyal servant of King George and is no longer ... interested in the Duke; when they tell him that the Duke has asked for an appointment, the P.M. sighs and arranges the day and hour.'[51] During a private meeting on this trip, the duke once again asked Churchill about a promotion. It took Winston a month to suggest the island of Bermuda, which the duke promptly turned down.[52]

Loyalty aside, there was a sense of comradeship about the King and Churchill's burgeoning relationship. During his meetings with Roosevelt and Harry Hopkins, Churchill was always aware that George VI missed out on the innocent and casual banter that attended these get-togethers. Over this visit, the trio formed a 'Short Snorter Dollar Club', essentially a drinking club, modelled after those established by Allied air force servicemen. Each member possessed a dollar bill signed by themselves and the other initiates. They were a sign of worldly experience, difficult travel, drinking or comradeship. Churchill felt that the King, isolated in his castle, might enjoy being a member of this exclusive club. The Prime Minister wrote to FDR requesting an additional bill for the King. He assured the President that 'Repayment and subscriptions will be made in due course apart from lend-lease'. Several days later Winston updated his fellows that the 'new member' had been instructed as to his duties and properly initiated. The friendship between the four of them was appropriately notarized.[53]

That summer Churchill was at the heart of a ticklish matter roiling the royal family. As Princess Elizabeth's eighteenth birthday approached, senior officials began to ponder the heir presumptive's title and position. The first question related to whether the Princess would be able to serve as a 'regent' in the event of her father's absence or incapacitation, as described by the Regency Act of 1937. For example, when the King travelled to Malta that summer to see the damage caused by Axis air strikes, the Queen acted as a Counsellor of State, signing documents, hosting receptions and even entertaining the Prime Minister to lunch for the regular Tuesday meeting. The issue at stake now was that for someone to qualify as regent, they had to be 'of age', meaning twenty-one years old. But since the King's eldest child was eligible to occupy the throne once she turned eighteen, this ruling, as far as the King was concerned, seemed backward. Surely his daughter should be able to deputize for him in his absence if, at the same age, she would become Queen in the event of his death. Churchill agreed and told the King that it would be presented to the War Cabinet immediately, with the goal of passing a Bill as soon as possible.[54]

This issue provoked another question: should Elizabeth be titled Princess of Wales, like her controversial uncle David, who had been

Prince of Wales before acceding to the throne? The council of the Welsh town of Pwllheli petitioned Churchill for an investiture, a move that attracted support from the *Carmarthen Journal* and the Welsh Parliamentary Party among other organizations. When the Cabinet formally submitted a proposal for the King's consideration, word came back that he did not favour the idea. Elizabeth was heir presumptive, not the heir apparent, meaning that in the unlikely but theoretically possible event that the King and Queen gave birth to a son, the princess would cease to be heir, and her Princess of Wales title would have to be revoked. The fact that it would, in principle, be a contingent designation made the King uncomfortable. He told Churchill as much at their next lunchtime audience, and Churchill promised to ask the Minister of Information to 'damp down all discussion of this question in the Press'. He kept his word, and within a month, the Palace was able to announce, without backlash, that there would be no change to the princess' title when she came of age in the following spring.[55]

In August of 1943, while the successful amphibious invasion of Sicily was underway, Churchill again crossed the Atlantic to meet Roosevelt in Quebec to discuss their joint strategy for winning the war. During the conference, plans were hatched for the invasion of northern France, code-named Operation Overlord, which was tentatively set to take place on 1 May 1944. From the beginning of these discussions, Churchill felt the soft southern European underbelly was a much safer approach. When speaking to Eisenhower and Roosevelt, he tended to take a baleful view of Overlord. 'He seemed always to see great and decisive possibilities in the Mediterranean,' Eisenhower recalled, 'while the project of invasion across the English Channel left him cold. How often I heard him say, in speaking of Overlord prospects: "We must take care that the tides do not run red with the blood of American and British youth, or the beaches be choked with their bodies."'[56]

The King agreed and even went so far as to try to persuade Churchill to change the minds of Allied commanders. He also discussed the possibility of changing tack with Jan Smuts, who visited London that October. The King's misgivings were confirmed when he received a telegram from the King of Italy, urging the Allies to occupy Rome as quickly as possible so that they could launch operations into the country's northern industrial region, thereby preventing the Nazis from using these factories to produce weapons of war. The invasion of Sicily had only taken six weeks but hopes of an easy victory on the mainland had quickly evaporated with Allied troops slogging their way through hostile countryside.

The British monarch took his time in approaching Churchill on the subject, knowing that his Prime Minister could be intransigent even at the calmest of times. At 11 p.m. on 13 October, Tommy Lascelles 'found him wrestling with the draft of a letter to Winston'. In the letter, the King leaned on Jan Smuts' expertise for military authority. 'I have thought about this matter a lot,' he wrote, '& am wondering whether we three could not discuss it together.' He went on to lay out the arguments for a new front in southern Europe. At the same time he sympathized with Churchill's tenuous position as the junior partner of the Big Three. He noted: 'I know there are many difficulties for a change of plan at this late hour, but you, F.D.R. & Stalin are to meet in the near future.' He finally ended by asking Churchill to dine with him and Smuts that evening, so they could discuss it all in person.

Though Churchill never refused an invitation to dine at the palace he did not want to lead the King down a blind alley. In his acceptance note he wrote: 'There is no possibility of our going back on what is agreed. Both the US Staff and Stalin would violently disagree with us.' The King later wrote in his diary that over the meal they 'discussed the whole strategy of the war at length'. While Winston was unwilling, or at least unable, to take Overlord off the table, he reaffirmed his argument that 'there are resources for both theatres'. If the time proved ripe for an operation in Italy or the Balkans, the King had Winston's assurance that it would be done.[57]

The following month, Winston travelled to Tehran in Iran for a conference of the Big Three, that is, Churchill, Stalin and Roosevelt. This mission, in addition to the strategy negotiations relating to Operation Overlord, involved an important symbolic gesture on behalf of the King. It was Winston's solemn duty to deliver the Sword of Stalingrad to Marshal Stalin in recognition of the valiant resistance the Russians had put up against the Nazis. It would be the first communication with the Russians by a member of the English royal family since the murder of the Romanovs in 1918.

At the conferral ceremony, Churchill stood ramrod-straight – 'most dignified and impressive', according to his bodyguard – as he delivered the speech and the sword: 'Marshal Stalin, I have a command from His Majesty King George VI to present you, for transmission to the city of Stalingrad, this sword of honour, the design of which His Majesty himself approved. This blade bears the inscription, 'To the steel-hearted citizens of Stalingrad,' a gift from George VI in token of homage of the British peoples.' With tears in his eyes, Stalin took the sword, brought it to his lips, and kissed it; he then turned to hand it off to Marshal Voroshilov.[58] As Voroshilov received it, the sword slipped from its scabbard and clattered onto the floor, falling directly onto his toe. Churchill left this mishap out of his report to the King.[59]

Unlike Voroshilov's handling of this diplomatic offering, Churchill's trip – to Cairo, then Tehran, then back to Cairo – was a great success. However, its pressures and demands proved too much for his immune system. He found himself once again stricken with pneumonia and what his doctor euphemistically called a 'heart-disturbance'.[60] In reality, it was likely another heart attack. He would have to remain in Egypt until he was well enough to travel back to London. On behalf of the King, Lascelles wrote to Clementine, 'It is cruel that the PM's triumphant journey should end in this way.' He expressed the King and Queen's 'hope that good may come out of evil, and that, in the long run, this spell of comparative rest may be a blessing in disguise to him'.[61]

It was 17 January before Winston was able to make the return journey. One of his first ports of call was Buckingham Palace for luncheon with the King, who was delighted to have him back and looking in robust health.

On closer inspection, though, it was clear that Winston was putting on a show. He seemed noticeably weaker, the fire behind his eyes gone. Various senior politicians reported their concerns to Lascelles, telling him that at Cabinet meetings Churchill rambled 'incessantly' and that he now 'thought (and spoke) of himself as an old man'. He had become 'impossibly prolix and obstructive' and risked losing the backing of his colleagues at a crucial point in the war.[62]

It was easy to understand why, after almost four years of leading Britain through the war, Winston was exhausted and distracted. His loyal staff began to think that winning this war just might be the death of the great man.

There was little time for rest, as each day Operation Overlord crept nearer. By mid-May 1944, most of the important details had been ironed out. The King, Churchill, and Jan Smuts attended a briefing at St Paul's School in London, which then served as General Montgomery's army group headquarters. As the top military brass from America and Great Britain detailed the attack, scheduled to take place on 4 June, the King felt compelled to deliver an impromptu address. He surprised everyone, especially Tommy Lascelles, when he stood up and spoke, without notes, to the august gathering. The King told the top brass: 'This is the biggest Combined Operation ever thought out in the world. But it is so much more than this. It is a Combined Operation of two countries, the United States & the British Empire. As I look around this audience of British & Americans I can see that you have equally taken a part in its preparation. I wish you all success & with God's help you will succeed.' Lascelles knew that with these simple words, the King had 'said exactly the right things and said them very well'.[63]

The King's unplanned speech was not the only surprise in store. At a Tuesday luncheon near the end of the month, Churchill let the King in on a secret. When the Allied battleships crossed the English Channel on D-Day, he would be on board one of them, among the troops, watching the bombardment first-hand.

CHAPTER THIRTEEN

D-Day Dodgers

A T FIRST BLUSH, it seemed like a once-in-a-lifetime adventure, the type of real-life Hollywood action movie that Winston enjoyed so much. The King, who had seen action in the battle of Jutland in the First World War, was intrigued by the thought of watching the D-Day landings from the vantage point of a Royal Navy destroyer. In spite of the potential dangers, he wanted to go, too. While he knew that Churchill would be wary of his Sovereign taking unnecessary risks, he also saw that 'W. cannot say no if he goes himself, & I don't want to have to tell him he cannot.' The King then turned to his wife, to gauge her thoughts: 'She was wonderful as always & encouraged me to do it.'[1]

But when the scheme inevitably crossed the desk of the King's redoubtable private secretary, Tommy Lascelles, who had risen to the rank of captain during the First World War, he was appalled. So, too, when they learned of the potentially ruinous plan, were the top brass, including Supreme Allied Commander Dwight Eisenhower, Admiral Ramsay, overall commander of the D-Day naval operations, and Churchill's chief military adviser, General Sir Hastings 'Pug' Ismay. Lascelles was quick to turn the big guns on the King. With limpet-like logic he asked the King, a family man to his fingertips, if it would be fair to the Queen, and 'whether he was prepared to face the possibility of having to advise Princess Elizabeth on the choice of her first Prime Minister, in the event of her father and Winston being sent to the bottom of the English Channel'. Furthermore, he argued, the responsibility of keeping the King and his first minister out of harm's way would have a 'paralysing' effect on the captain and crew of HMS *Belfast*, whose primary task was to shell the French coast, a role that would invite direct Luftwaffe counterattack.[2]

These arguments convinced the King that the plan, though gallantly romantic, was too fraught with danger to be workable. He agreed to write a letter to Churchill, urging him to join him in withdrawing. 'I have come to the conclusion that it would not be right for either you or I to be where we planned to be on D-Day ... We should both I know love to be there, but in all seriousness I would ask you to reconsider your plan.' He ended his letter on a sentimental, rather than an authoritative, note: 'The anxiety of these coming days would be very greatly increased for me if I thought that, in addition to everything else, there was a risk, however remote, of my losing your help & guidance.'[3]

The following day, the King and Lascelles visited the map room at the Downing Street Annexe, where Admiral Ramsay demonstrated a model of the attack positions and strategy for the June invasion. During the meeting, Ramsay discussed the details of Winston's proposed journey aboard the HMS *Belfast*. It soon became clear that, in spite of running the gauntlet of mines, torpedoes, and bombardment from both land and air, those on board would see almost none of the action, as the ship would be miles from the French coast.[4] Winston, for all the risks he was prepared to take, would have far less information than the military planners who remained in London. Despite the discouraging picture painted by Ramsay, and the King's plaintive letter, Winston remained set on going. The six-year bromance between King and first minister seemed to be heading for the rocks. As the King confided in his diary, 'I am very worried over the PM's seemingly selfish way of looking at the matter. He doesn't seem to care about the future, or how much depends on him.'[5]

After the King's appeal to the heart, Lascelles went for the head, challenging Winston to a game of constitutional chess. Churchill argued that there were no constitutional constraints on his attendance as either first minister or minister of defence, whereas the King would need Cabinet approval, which would not be forthcoming. Lascelles countered by arguing that no Minister of the Crown could leave the country without the Sovereign's consent. After a moment's pause, Winston cleverly retorted that since he would remain on a British warcraft for the duration, he would not technically be leaving British territory. Nothing would work, with Churchill informing the group that if he was to die during the operation, the naming of his successor had already been taken care of. This presumably was the letter he had written during his earlier trips to the Mediterranean theatre of operations, in which he had named Anthony Eden as his successor. Finally, as the group took their leave of the annexe, Lascelles whispered to Admiral Ramsay, 'For God's sake, stop him going.'[6]

The Prime Minister was deaf to all entreaties, his main argument being that a commander should share the risks of those he sends into battle. 'A man who has to play an effective part in taking, with the highest responsibility, grave and terrible decisions of war,' he later wrote, 'may need the refreshment of adventure. He may need also the comfort that when sending so many others to their death he may share in a small way their risks.'[7]

Lascelles thought differently, accusing the Prime Minister of vanity and selfishness. Winston was, he argued, 'just like a naughty child when he starts planning an escapade'.[8] Now fully aware of the military opposition to Churchill's plans after being briefed by Lascelles, the King resolved to write one more letter. It was after all his constitutional duty to consult, to encourage, and also to warn his Prime Minister. 'I want to make one more appeal to you not to go to sea on D day,' the King wrote. 'Please consider my own position. I am a younger man than you, I am a sailor, & as King I am the head of all three Services. There is nothing I would like better than to go to sea but I have agreed to stay at home; is it fair that you should then do exactly what I should have liked to do myself?' The King then focused on the possible military and personal consequences of his attendance: 'You will see very little, you will run a considerable risk, you will be inaccessible at a critical time when vital decisions might have to be taken, & however unobtrusive you may be, your mere presence on board is bound to be a very heavy additional responsibility to the Admiral & Captain.' Although the King wrote, 'Your being there would add immeasurably to my anxieties,' he stopped short of commanding Winston to remain on home soil. Instead, he appealed to his Prime Minister's better judgment: 'I ask you most earnestly to consider the whole question again, & not let your personal wishes, which I very well understand, lead you to depart from your own high standard of duty to the State.'[9] Of all the King's arguments, however, it was the element of fairness and historical propriety that held the most sway for Winston. In centuries past, it was the British monarch who led his forces into battle; now that the age-old custom had been abandoned in modern warfare, would it be constitutionally or symbolically proper for the Prime Minister to replace him? Would it not paint a cowardly picture of the head of the British forces? 'That is certainly a strong argument,' Winston told his private secretary, John Martin.[10]

Churchill did not have a chance to respond to the King's letter before he left for Portsmouth in his private train. As he waited to hear back, George VI was so disturbed by the whole episode that he threatened to drive to Churchill's rendezvous with HMS *Belfast* and personally prevent him going to sea. A few late-night phone calls settled the matter. Lascelles called the Prime Minister on his train where, on a crackling telephone line, Winston conceded, saying that in deference to the King's wishes, he would abandon his plan of going to sea. With the clock showing nearly midnight, Lascelles phoned the King, knowing that he would sleep better after hearing the good news.[11]

Winston's official, written response arrived at Windsor Castle before breakfast. The Prime Minister laid out his complaints in constitutional terms. 'As Prime Minister and Minister of the Defence, I ought to be allowed to go where I consider it necessary to the discharge of my duty ... I rely on my own judgment, invoked in many serious matters, as to what are the proper limits of risk which a person who discharges my duties is entitled to run. I must most earnestly ask Your Majesty that no principle shall be laid down which inhibits my freedom of movement when I judge it necessary to acquaint myself with conditions in the various theatres of war.' Finally, he admitted defeat, writing bitterly, 'I must defer to Your Majesty's wishes and indeed commands.'[12] Despite Churchill's tone of resentful compliance, Tommy and the King were at ease: 'Anyhow, we have bested him, which not many people have succeeded in doing in the last four years!'[13] As Churchill's personal motto, which he lived by, was 'never, ever, ever give in', this was quite the triumph. His biographer, Andrew Roberts, commented on the episode, 'Churchill had set his heart on attending the D-Day operations, and was angry enough after being stymied to write a letter to the King that verged, despite his fervent monarchism, on *lèse-majesté*.'[14]

At a time when military victory was within reach, when the war was about to enter its most compelling and controlled phase, these two men, who had worked in lockstep through the trials and misfortunes of the past six years, found themselves at loggerheads. Churchill's obdurate behaviour did little to help the crucial last-minute preparations for D-Day. It could be argued that the episode was a time-wasting distraction that drove an unnecessary wedge between the King and his first minister. What did unite both men – and their wives – was a sickening sense of tension as they waited for a signal that the invasion had begun. As the Queen reflected, the thought of all the men who would soon lose their lives lay 'heavy on the heart & mind'.[15] Churchill laboured under the same emotional burden. The night before D-Day, he asked Clementine, 'Do you realise that by the time you wake up in the morning twenty thousand men may have been killed?'[16]

Thankfully, the casualty rate was much lower at around 4,400 killed, as 156,000 troops made landfall at five sites – code-named Utah, Omaha, Gold, Sword and Juno – using more than 5,000 vessels. After the first hours of the invasion, Churchill and the King met at the palace to enjoy their now traditional Tuesday luncheon, where the one topic off the conversational menu was their recent disagreement. After the meal, the King drove with Churchill to Allied Air Headquarters and then to the command centre of the Supreme Headquarters Allied Expeditionary Force (SHAEF) at Bushey, on the outskirts of London, to follow the latest developments of the historic attack.[17]

Afterwards the King worked with his speech coach, Lionel Logue, on the radio broadcast he was due to make that evening, since the monumental landing called for an international address. Churchill and the King had been vying for the prime-time slot, but pressure from the King's family was a force to be reckoned with. Queen Elizabeth wrote to Queen Mary to say that she wanted Bertie, rather than Winston, to deliver the message. Queen Mary agreed, arguing, 'Bertie's message will be far more popular. Do persuade him to do it.' The King, too, felt it should fall to him, but as ever, he needed assistance. Instead of consulting Churchill, as usual, he recruited the help of the Bishop of Lichfield. After going through many drafts, and several hours of practice with Logue, the King delivered a seven-minute address to a worldwide audience. Far from being a rousing talk which described the heroic events of the momentous day, it was a spiritual meditation on the power of prayer with only an oblique reference to 'the great crusade' going forth.[18] Given the fact that German high command was still unsure as to whether this was the real invasion or an elaborate feint, the King's focus on Christian principles may have been born out of miliary necessity as much as stylistic preference.

During what the King described as 'very anxious days', he and the Queen kept continually abreast of developments at the front.[19] On 8 June, they visited Churchill's secret map room, where they studied model-size reproductions of the Mulberry harbours, the purpose-built ports constructed to land troops, tanks, and trucks on the beaches of Normandy.

Of course, both the King and Churchill were eager to see the real thing. On 10 June, Churchill phoned the King to ask whether he might finally cross the Channel and 'see how the Mulberries were getting on, returning the same evening'. The King approved, on the condition that Churchill also get Admiral Ramsay's go-ahead. This he did, crossing the English Channel two days later.[20]

The King was keen to follow suit, but, in the constitutional merry-go-round of that week, he had to secure permission from the Prime Minister and the Cabinet to leave the country. It was duly given on 16 June. The King, Lascelles and top military leaders crossed the choppy Channel in an amphibious landing craft before waddling up the beach to meet with General Montgomery, who had organized a picnic for his VIP guests. It was the first time they had tasted Camembert cheese in four years.[21]

The King returned to Buckingham Palace to contend with a new and terrifying German weapon – the self-directing V-1 flying bomb, known colloquially as the 'doodlebug'. The bombs were unpredictable and deadly, falling out of the sky wherever they reached their predetermined target area and the engine cut out. Just a few days after the King arrived back from Normandy, one landed in the palace grounds, the royal couple feeling the concussion blast inside their air raid shelter. In some ways the onslaught of V-1 flying bombs was even worse than the Blitz had been, because the deadly devices were inhuman in their complete randomness.[22] Once again, the air raid siren became the background music to life in London.

In response, the King moved all of his formal ceremonies, including investitures, official audiences and, significantly, his Tuesday lunch with the Prime Minister, into the bomb shelter. When Winston arrived for lunch, he found it 'all wrong'. Though Churchill had finally, and reluctantly, admitted that attending the D-Day operations involved too much risk, he nonetheless felt that some amount of risk must be accepted and borne valiantly. Both for himself as Prime Minister and the King as Commander-in-Chief of all British forces, to be seen as playing it safe would erode morale at a time when a generation of young men and women were fighting to maintain freedom.[23]

After leaving the palace, Churchill phoned Lascelles and described the King's practice as 'a bad example, when the Government were urging people to go about their business as usual during working hours, no matter how many sirens sounded'. Lascelles passed the message along to the King, who 'at once agreed to hold the next of these functions above ground'.[24] It was a rare instance of a Prime Minister upbraiding his Sovereign, and a further example of Winston instinctively protecting the image of the monarchy.

Indeed, Churchill's role in the King's life and that of other members of the royal family transcended strict constitutional boundaries. He was at once an adviser, a brother-in-arms, a boon companion and a father figure. It was a complex relationship that needed tact and diplomacy if it was to endure. Nowhere was this more apparent than the King's awkward relationship with his elder brother, the Duke of Windsor. Several days before D-Day, Churchill sent a letter to Lascelles regarding the duke's next move now that his time as Governor of the Bahamas was coming to an end. Consideration of this matter gave the King, according to Lascelles, 'deeper and more painful concern' than even the impending historic events that were due to be played out on the beaches of Normandy. Eventually, the advice that emerged from Buckingham Palace was to keep the duke away from Britain at any price. Winston's initial response, on 28 June, was a human rights defence of the duke, who was, he argued, still a peer of the realm, and a British citizen, with a legal right to return to his homeland. 'Nothing that I am aware of,' he wrote, 'can stop him returning to this country.'[25] At lunch with the King a couple of days later, however, Churchill changed his tune and agreed that it would be best for all concerned if the ex-King did not return. Rather than give him the bad news in a telegram or letter, Churchill would talk to him after the second Quebec conference in September.[26]

In preparation for this delicate meeting, Churchill asked the King whether he 'should pass along any fraternal greeting'. In response, the King sent Winston what Jock Colville called 'a most cold message'.[27] It was as much of a rebuke of Winston as an indication of where the King wanted his brother to relocate: 'In any discussion as to his future perhaps you would put forward my conviction, which you already know, namely that his happiness will be best promoted by his making his home in the USA. Repeat USA.'[28] Colville then recorded that Churchill 'dictated to me a rather crushing answer, but, as often, he subsequently had it destroyed and replaced by one more conciliatory'.[29] That response included the line, 'With humble duty, Mr. Churchill feels that if he delivered himself of such a message, it might well have the effect of leading HRH to establish himself in England.' He told the King that he 'had never abandoned the idea of the Duke discharging Ambassadorial or Governor functions if suitable openings can be found'.[30]

When Churchill and the Duke of Windsor finally broke bread at Hyde Park, Roosevelt's summer home in upstate New York, the duke described their conversation as 'a long and satisfactory talk – in so far as it went, which was not very far'. Churchill discouraged the duke and duchess from returning to Britain and emphasized that they would be welcome to return to their rented villa in the south of France, which had recently been liberated from German control. Privately the duke found it absurd that the royal family still felt threatened by him some eight years after the abdication. When it came to substantive conversations about the duke's future career, Winston was cagey and evasive. In his report to the King he stated that there was no discussion about a future role as a governor or ambassador.[31]

On 3 October, the duke wrote to Churchill from the Bahamas to follow up on their meeting. If he was to quietly accept his permanent exile from England, he had one condition in mind: that his family agree to a meeting, just once, just briefly, with him and his wife. 'It could never be a very happy meeting,' the duke acknowledged, but it would be 'quite painless' and would show the 'malicious circles' who gossiped about his banishment and his wife's sullied reputation that they remained in good standing with the royal family. 'I will be very surprised if you do not think my remedy the best cure for this evil situation, and decide to advise the King and Queen to swallow the "Windsor Pill" just once, however bitter they may think it is going to taste!'[32]

Any advice Winston may have considered very quickly became redundant. The King, the Queen and Queen Mary were all in resolute agreement that they would not hear of any conditions on the duke's compliance. To emphasize the point, Queens Elizabeth and Mary signed a joint statement to the effect that they would not be willing to receive 'that woman' for tea, or any other social gathering, either then or at any point in the future.

Lascelles advised the King that if Winston tried to intercede, he ought to take a bifurcated approach: 'On personal and family grounds, we are all averse from meeting the Duchess of Windsor; but if you and your colleagues advise me that it is to the interests of the Monarchy and the Empire at large that we should do so, that is, of course, another matter.' Drawing on his long experience, Lascelles felt that the Prime Minister had no right to advise the King on what was a purely private matter, nor would the Cabinet stand with Winston against the wishes of the royal family.[33] And he was right. The case was closed.

As a dewy-eyed monarchist, Winston had hoped against hope that the brothers could let bygones be bygones so that the duke could take up a noble, if socially excluded, position in British society. He felt deeply that the glory and grace of the monarchy should come above petty personal disputes and grudges. As far as Lascelles, who had worked closely with the duke when he was Prince of Wales, was concerned, Churchill's 'sentimental loyalty' was completely misplaced and rested on a tragic misreading of the duke's personality.[34]

Eventually, it became clear to the duke and duchess that no member of the royal family was going to swallow the 'Windsor Pill'. It was just too bitter. They were simply not wanted. In February 1945, the duke wrote to Winston to announce that he was abandoning all hope of returning to England, even to pass through on his way to continental Europe. 'The persistence of my mother's attitude towards my wife, which you infer represents the great mass of the British nation ... makes it preferable not to go to Great Britain for the present. We most certainly do not wish to expose ourselves unnecessarily to insults that can be so simply avoided, by travelling some other way to the Continent of Europe.'[35]

Churchill had done his best, but it had to be acknowledged that he was dedicated to the King and all his works. Such was the closeness between Churchill and George VI that they considered travelling to Italy together to meet the Pope, to visit the battlefields of Operation Dragoon, and to stand hand-in-hand on Mussolini's famous balcony, in Rome's Palazzo Venezia. In Churchill's mind, it would showcase the triumph of British constitutional monarchy over Fascism. The double act never came off, the two men agreeing that it would be better to visit Italy separately.[36]

While the King was there, Princess Elizabeth, who had just turned eighteen, acted as a Counsellor of State for the first time.[37] Winston, during his turn, watched the military progress and informed the King that Italy could now be considered 'a friendly co-belligerent and no longer as an enemy state'. Churchill also enjoyed an audience with Pope Pius XII, writing to the King, 'At the outset of a friendly conversation His Holiness asked me to convey to Your Majesty and to the Queen his respectful greetings and his assurance of the revered esteem in which he holds Your Majesties.'[38] It was, perhaps, the friendliest exchange of words between the two heads of the Roman Catholic and Anglican churches since the schism of the sixteenth century.

When Churchill returned to London in late August, he was once again hit with a bout of illness that forced him to bed. As the King was travelling from Balmoral to see his Prime Minister, he had to change his plans, visiting him in his sickbed where he lay wrapped in a luxurious blue silk robe. During their unconventional audience Churchill sought the King's permission to travel to Quebec for the conference in two weeks' time, as well as his consent to promote General Montgomery to Field Marshal. As Tommy Lascelles entered the room, he saw the paperwork, bearing the King's signature, lying on Churchill's bed. 'I don't think a general has ever before been thus promoted,' Tommy reflected later. 'Certainly none has ever had his appointment signed by his Sovereign on the Prime Minister's pillow.'[39]

Naturally, the King worried about his Prime Minister's health. He had been ill with pneumonia on three occasions in the last four years, and even when healthy, kept a remorseless schedule; in January 1944, he had only been in Britain for five weeks out of the previous five months.[40] After the Quebec Conference, Churchill travelled to Moscow in November, Athens in December and Yalta in February 1945, to decide on the shape of Europe after the end of the war as well as the formation of the United Nations. Though he suffered from bouts of chronic fatigue, his energy level was astonishing for a man who had just turned seventy and drank with such gusto.[41]

The King signalled his admiration for Churchill's work ethic and central contribution to the war effort in another, more significant way. At one audience, Winston brought up the end-of-year honours list and suggested that his Foreign Secretary, Anthony Eden, should be invited to join the Order of the Garter, the most ancient honour the King could confer. The King, somewhat unexpectedly, refused. As Lascelles noted, 'It seemed to him all wrong to give it to the PM's lieutenant when the PM himself would not take it.' The King later told his private secretary that at this comment, Winston 'became all blubby'. He and his Sovereign then embraced each other 'in an ecstasy of fraternal emotion'.[42]

That mutual devotion quickly evaporated when Winston thwarted the King from fulfilling a long-held ambition. As King and emperor, he wanted to visit his troops and subjects based on the Indian sub-continent, which he had never yet seen during his short reign. With the war in Europe coming to a close and independence movements in India gaining popular support, he worried that time was running out for him to make an official visit.

When Churchill told him that it would not be possible, the King was furious. Winston was sensitive to the views of the Americans, especially the Roosevelts, who had always been suspicious of British imperialism. Despite his great respect for the King and Prime Minister, FDR considered Great Britain a bastion of regressive, anti-democratic, mid-Victorian ideals. For Britain to flaunt its colonial rule over India with a royal visit would risk alienating Roosevelt at a time when the Allies needed to be united in the face of Stalin's growing ambitions in Eastern Europe. It wasn't worth the risk, so Churchill vetoed the idea without even informing the Cabinet. A month later, the King told Leo Amery, the Secretary of State for India, 'how cross he was with Winston for not allowing him to go ... on the ground that this would at once give rise to the idea that he had some big political declaration about India's future. Amery sympathized with the King's irritation: 'I must say that it is a little typical of Winston to have done this without consulting me ... Personally I should have seen no great objection.'[43] Amery, though, did not have to deal with Roosevelt. Churchill did.

Though there were many bumps in the road, with every passing week the King and his Prime Minister enjoyed the fruits of impending victory.[44] In early April 1945, the pair spent most of an afternoon together at the Palace of Westminster, finalizing their plans for a State Opening of Parliament. They agreed that it would need to be appropriately ceremonial and spectacular, since Winston expected a full German surrender by the end of the month.[45] This was, of course, a thrilling prospect, though it was attended by a sense of sadness as Churchill realized that his long and intimate relationship with the King would inevitably change. The bomb shelter dinners and visits to Churchill's sickbed would become the stuff of amused anecdote, the two men reverting to their traditional peacetime roles. He said as much in a letter to Clementine, writing, 'Next Wednesday the King comes, and this will I expect be the last of the dinners of our war-time Cabinet, famous I think I may call it.'[46] It was the end of an era, an exhausting but exhilarating era.

At their final War Cabinet dinner, Lascelles noticed that everyone in attendance was 'very tired, yet we sat there till 1.45 a.m.' He called it a 'dullish, but good dinner'. It might not have been so dull if any of the guests had known what the following day had in store. President Roosevelt, on a retreat in Georgia, died of a cerebral haemorrhage at sixty-three years old. Though he had looked ill at Yalta, there were few statesmen towards the end of the conflict who had not been visibly the worse for wear, and his death came, in the King's words, 'as a great shock'.[47] The man who had so steadfastly stood with Britain during the war in the Atlantic and Pacific would never savour the fruits of victory.

The King wrote Churchill a long letter of sympathy. Though at times he had felt a twinge of envy over the closeness of Churchill's relationship with the American President, he appreciated that his Prime Minister had lost much more than a friend. He wrote, 'To you who have known him for so long & so intimately during this war, the sudden loss to yourself personally of a colleague & helpmate in the framing of far-reaching decisions both for the prosecution of the war & for the future peace of the world must be overwhelming.' Winston, in his response, glossed over the differences in their individual relationships with FDR and opted, almost exclusively, for the first-person plural. He wrote, 'The sudden loss of this great friend and comrade in all our affairs is very hard for me. Ties have been shorn asunder which years had woven. We have to begin again in many ways.'[48]

Churchill spoke in the House of Commons and proposed an adjournment of the House in tribute to their fallen ally, 'whose friendship for the cause of freedom and for the causes of the weak and poor have won his immortal renown'. He had already begun making preparations to travel to Washington to attend Roosevelt's funeral, but he soon realized that the pace of events on the battlefront was such that it was not in the country's best interests for him to leave. 'It would have been a solace to me to be present at Franklin's funeral,' Winston wrote to Harry Hopkins, the fourth bereaved member of the Short Snorter Dollar Club, 'but everyone here thought my duty next week lay at home, at a time when so many Ministers are out of the country.'[49]

Instead, on 17 April, he attended a memorial service at St Paul's Cathedral along with King George VI and four other sovereigns: the King's godson King Peter of Yugoslavia, King George of Greece, King Olaf of Norway and Queen Wilhelmina of Holland. Diarist Chips Channon recalled that as he was leaving the service, he turned back towards the cathedral and saw 'Winston standing bare-headed, framed between two columns of the portico, and he was sobbing as the shaft of sunlight fell on his face and the cameras clicked.'[50] Even in the depths of grief, Churchill made sure the paparazzi got their shot.

Winston was wise not to fly to Washington, since in the early hours of Monday 7 May, at Supreme headquarters in Reims, in northern France, General Alfred Jodl signed Germany's unconditional surrender. Churchill was informed by Field Marshal Montgomery and immediately called a meeting of his chiefs of staff. When they arrived, he was found recounting the details of the surrender to the King on the telephone. As Sir Alan Brooke wrote in his diary, 'He was evidently seriously affected by the fact that the war was to all intents and purposes over as far as Germany was concerned. He thanked us all very nicely and with tears in his eyes for all we had done in the war and all the endless work we had put in.'[51]

London hummed with preparations for Victory in Europe day on 8 May, the city decked with red, white and blue Union flags, loudspeakers installed to carry speeches by the King and Prime Minister while floodlights illuminated the historic, but frequently bomb-battered buildings. Heavy thunderstorms hovered over the city the night before the celebration, but by the morning everything was set for a warm spring day.[52]

By happy coincidence, VE Day fell on a Tuesday. Just as he had done every Tuesday for the previous five years, Churchill went to Buckingham

Palace for lunch – only this time, he drove through much heavier crowds en route. Riding in an open car, he arrived at the palace gates and delivered a few words before going inside for luncheon. The King later wrote in his diary, 'We congratulated each other on the end of the European War. The day we have been longing for has arrived at last and we can look back with thankfulness to God that our tribulation is over.' After the meal, Churchill took his leave to return to 10 Downing Street to finish writing the broadcast he would deliver that afternoon.[53]

In addition to perfecting his own speech, Churchill took the time to add a final paragraph to the King's broadcast. It read, 'All organized resistance by Germany is at an end. The German High Command has ordered that firing shall cease on all fronts at midnight tonight; and even though some fanatical groups should seek to prolong for a time the struggle in the South and East of Europe, they will soon be overcome. The power and might of Germany is finally broken.'[54]

After Churchill's 3 p.m. broadcast, he went to the House of Commons to repeat his statement more formally. Then, as he prepared to head back to the palace to meet the King, the War Cabinet and chiefs of staff, he turned to his private protection officer, Walter Thompson, and asked for his trademark cigar. Thompson was mortified: for the first time in the whole course of the war, he had forgotten his boss' cigar case. Churchill, buoyed by the crowds, simply suggested they return to the Downing Street Annexe so he could get one. 'I must put on a cigar. They expect it!' Winston said. Ever the showman, he couldn't take to the stage without his props.[55]

Once he arrived at Buckingham Palace, he joined the chiefs of staff and the Cabinet in a congratulatory audience with King George VI. After this gathering, Churchill was invited to join the King, Queen and princesses on the Buckingham Palace balcony, waving to the adoring multitudes below. He stood in the middle of them all, surveying the exuberant masses from exactly the position where, seven years before, Prime Minister Neville Chamberlain had waved to the crowds after he had returned to London from a meeting with Hitler in Munich where the two leaders agreed that their countries would never go to war again. He promised the nation 'peace in our time'. He was proved wrong. How dramatically his fortunes, and the nation's, had changed. The boarded-up windows behind them could attest to that. So, too, could the 'V' for victory that Churchill held up to the millions of cheering subjects below.

CHAPTER FOURTEEN

Changing of the Guard

THE CELEBRATIONS FOR VE Day lasted for more than a week, the capital and the country alive with street parties, sing-songs and casual encounters. For a few days, all care was forgotten. On 17 May, the King gave a fifteen-minute speech in the Great Hall of Westminster to the joint Houses of Parliament. His voice carried with purpose and resolution, with only one stammer and a tearful moment when he mentioned the death of his youngest brother, the Duke of Kent. Watching from the wings was Tommy Lascelles, who fulsomely described the assembly as 'a perfect example of British ceremonial at its best, ordered and impressive'. As the King reached the end of his speech, his audience looked around uneasily: were they supposed to clap, stand, shout or sit in silence as if it were the end of a funeral oration? They had not long to ponder, as Churchill, holding his silk top hat, took to the dais where the King stood and called for three cheers. Diarist Harold Nicolson said of the moment, 'All our pent up energies responded with three yells such as I should have thought impossible to emanate from so many elderly throats.'[1]

Though VE day was a time for celebration, both the King and Winston were soberly looking east. They knew that there would still be long months of fighting in the Pacific arena ahead, since the Japanese were far from surrendering. In spite of the battles that lay in the future, at home the spirit of unity that followed victory in Europe would not last long. Churchill felt the pressure, not from the remaining Axis Powers but from within his own government. After serving loyally in the National Government during the war, Clement Attlee, the leader of the Labour Party and Deputy Prime Minister, now called for a general election. The current government, he argued, had been formed under exceptional circumstances; now that Germany was defeated, the will of the people ought to have the chance to decide which party would take the country forward.

On 22 May, Churchill accepted the inevitable and kick-started the electoral process. He spent the morning working from bed, meticulously crafting a letter to the King. It was to be a letter for posterity, he told Jock Colville with a smirk, 'for the archives'. The letter celebrated the fact that the King's 'affairs are now in a much better posture than they were when the National Government was formed', but it also acknowledged that new and equally difficult perils lay ahead: 'All that has been gained at such sacrifice and hazard may all be thrown away and new dangers of a serious character appear in view.' In order for the 'conditions of amity and singlemindedness' necessary for such an endeavour to prevail, he wrote, the government would have to return to single-party leadership.[2]

Churchill planned to go to Buckingham Palace to seek the King's permission to resign and dissolve the government. Then, he would return to 10 Downing Street to give the King an interval of a few hours to think, only to return to Buckingham Palace at 4 p.m. Winston 'was anxious to emphasise to the public that the King has the right to decide' who would be his interim Prime Minister until the election. At the palace, Churchill's sense of constitutional propriety was met with a wink and a nudge – when Lascelles told the King that the plan 'involved his being without a Prime Minister between twelve and four', the King wryly remarked that during the interval, he would 'send for Winston and give him the Garter – he won't be able to refuse!'[3]

He was, in the King's name, invited at four in the afternoon to form a Conservative caretaker government. Afterwards, the King wrote in his diary, 'Thus has ended the Coalition Government which during the War has done admirable work. Country before Party has been its watchword. But now what?'[4]

As the election season began, the general consensus was that the Conservative Party would win an easy victory. After all, at the head of the party was the man who had won the war and inspired a generation to follow his leadership. Those in Churchill's close circle were not so sure. The war had taken a terrible toll on the old bulldog, Winston electing to spend much of June in bed or in the gardens at Chartwell, catching up on his reading. When he gave his first campaign speech on 4 June, it left Lascelles with 'the impression of a tired man unwillingly reading something that had been written for him and that he didn't much like'.[5] By 20 June, when he and the King talked over the possible electoral outcomes, Churchill was convinced that 'all the young men and women in the Services will vote against him'. After fighting against the Germans so steadfastly for so many years, it was the fight against the Labour Party which threatened to undermine Churchill's legacy.[6] During one radio interview, his suggestion that the Labour Party would need 'some form of a Gestapo' to implement their policies badly backfired.[7]

In the meantime, however, there was a war to conclude. Churchill went to Potsdam, Germany, for a final meeting with Stalin and the new American President, Harry S. Truman, to determine the borders of Europe following the collapse of the German Reich. It was good for Churchill's spirits to be back in the saddle, and when he returned to London on 25 July to await the election results, his outlook was much sunnier than when he had left. Again, he met with the King, this time telling him that he believed that he and his Conservative Party would be returned to power, estimating a majority of somewhere between thirty and eighty seats. The next day showed his optimism was misplaced: Attlee's Labour Party won in a landslide. Once again, Churchill travelled to Buckingham Palace to tender his resignation, but this time, he advised the King to send for Clement Attlee.[8]

The King was devastated. He called their audience 'a very sad meeting', and told Churchill that he found the British electorate very ungrateful 'after the way they had been led in the War'. He was too upset to say more, but five days later, he wrote Winston not one, but two separate letters in an attempt to express himself more fully. 'My heart was too full to say much at our last meeting,' he began, writing that he was 'shocked at the result'. In the second missive he wrote of his sadness that Winston was no longer his Prime Minister and reflected on the hundreds of occasions they had spent together during the war. He wrote, 'I shall always remember our talks with pleasure & only wish they could have continued longer.' The King was effusive in his praise of the great man, telling him, 'Your breadth of vision & your grasp of the essential things were a great comfort to me in the darkest days of the War ... I feel that your conduct as Prime Minister & Minister of Defence has never been surpassed.' He was eager, however, to assure Winston that although their relationship as Sovereign and first minister had come to an abrupt close, their friendship would remain: 'I shall miss your counsel to me more than I can say. But please remember that as a friend I hope we shall be able to meet at intervals.'

In this second letter, the King showed that he had learned from the master; like Churchill, he crafted a version of history with blurred contours and softened edges, one that he hoped would be recorded for posterity: 'I like to think,' he wrote, 'that we have never disagreed on any really important matter.' This has in fact become, more or less, the official line on their wartime relationship: two men who, despite differences in temperament, background and loyalties, overcame their initial mutual scepticism in pursuit of a joint goal and along the way established a durable and trusting partnership. As romantic as this account is, it elides the many 'important matters' on which they did, in fact, disagree, sometimes vehemently, notably the Duke of Windsor, Prince Paul of Yugoslavia, the King's trip to India, and most pointedly, the question of whether Winston would participate in the Normandy landings. In retrospect, however, even these vital questions appeared to the King to be mere quibbles, dwarfing in comparison to his lasting affection and reverence for the great man.[9]

Churchill, in his response to these two heartfelt letters, wrote, 'It was always a relief to me to lay before my Sovereign all the dread secrets and perils wh[ich] oppressed my mind, & the plans wh[ich] I was forming, & to receive on crucial occasions much encouragement.' He could not let the King's reference to the personal side of their relationship go unremarked: 'Yr. Majesty has mentioned our friendship & this is indeed a v[er]y. Strong sentiment with me, & an honour which I cherish.'[10]

The King took the opportunity during his last audience with Churchill to officially invite his wartime premier into the Order of the Garter, the monarch's most senior order of chivalry conferred on only twenty-four members, reserved for those who have rendered outstanding service to the Crown and the nation. The King had offered him the Garter three times – on 15 December 1944, 23 May 1945 and now 26 July 1945 – and Churchill refused it each time. Though Winston was deeply touched by the signal honour, he begged His Majesty's permission to refuse, feeling it would be inappropriate to accept it when the country had rejected him so resoundingly at the polls. 'I felt that the times were too sad for honours or rewards,' he wrote a few days later to Lascelles. 'After all, my great reward is the kindness and intimacy with which the King has treated me during these hard and perilous years which we have endured and enjoyed in common.'[11] This was yet another disappointment for the King. 'I feel that the country will expect me to give you a high honour which it will acclaim as a fitting tribute for all your arduous work in this war,' he told Churchill.[12]

Nor was Churchill's 'arduous work' quite over. Two weeks later, when the Americans dropped the first nuclear bomb on the Japanese city of Hiroshima, it was Churchill's voice that broke the news to the nation, as well as Churchill's pen that wrote Attlee's published statement on the historic event. Though the bomb continues to inspire doleful images of the Armageddon, Churchill told the House of Commons that the alternative to the bomb would have meant an invasion of Japan and the sacrifice of 'a million American, and a quarter of a million British, lives'.[13]

When the nation celebrated Victory in Japan Day ten days later – only after the US had dropped a second nuclear bomb on Nagasaki – it was Attlee, not Churchill, who received the accolades. The King thought this was an injustice, feeling that Winston should have been given a proper reception by the people. As Clementine observed, 'The crowds shout "Churchill for ever" & "We want Churchill". But all the King's horses and all the King's men can't put Humpty Dumpty together again.'[14] That afternoon, Attlee and his government came to the Buckingham Palace terrace to congratulate the King on the end of the war. Winston had been invited, but he nobly responded that he could not be present at such a ceremony without the other leaders who had so faithfully served in his War Cabinet, and who were now relegated to the opposition benches. Instead, he appeared by himself, half an hour after the Labour ministers had gone, for a private one-on-one with the King.[15]

Perhaps the only person not in mourning over the election was Churchill himself. On election day, Clementine had tried to comfort him by saying that 'it may well be a blessing in disguise'. Churchill responded, 'At the moment, it seems quite effectively disguised.'[16] But she turned out to be right, and before long, Churchill recovered the ebullient mischievousness that had come so naturally to him before the many stresses of the war had dampened his spirits. On VJ Day, Lascelles noticed that Winston was 'gleefully anticipating the speech which he was going to make in the House of Commons the following day, and evidently looking forward to the delights of front-bench opposition warfare'.[17]

As for Clement Attlee, the man who replaced Churchill, the King had his reservations. Since their first wartime meeting in 1940, when Attlee was a member of the National Government, the King had found him 'shy & reserved and difficult to talk to'.[18] Their first meeting as King and Prime Minister became the stuff of legend. For what seemed like an eternity, the King and his new premier stood in silence; Attlee finally broke the impasse by offering a groundbreaking revelation: 'I've won the election.' The King replied, 'I know. I heard it on the Six o'clock News.'[19]

It was hardly the scintillating repartee the King had grown so accustomed to. He complained that Attlee was 'completely mute', especially after he had grown so used to Winston's loquacious ways.[20] He found himself dreading these Tuesday audiences with Attlee, which were burdened by long periods of discomfiting silence. He nicknamed his new premier 'Clem the Clam'.[21] When Winston and Clementine came to Buckingham Palace for a dinner later in the year, the King wrote in his diary, 'How refreshing to have a friend to talk to for a change.'[22]

In addition to his complaints about Attlee's personality, the King was concerned that the change in government would add to his already heavy workload. Not to mention his almost inevitable suspicion, for a man at the apex of a hierarchical society, towards the ideals and values of the Labour Party which extolled the virtues of Socialism and quickly set about taking vast tracts of British industry into public ownership. During the Attlee premiership, the notion of the Sovereign as an impartial observer of the political scene was exposed for what it was: a chimera.

One man was able to unite the King, his new Prime Minister, and the old political guard in common purpose: the Duke of Windsor. Shortly after the end of the war in Europe, tons of vital German files were discovered and translated. The most sensational cache of what the Foreign Office called 'pirate gold' were files relating to the behaviour of the Duke and Duchess of Windsor during the war, especially the summer of 1940. The files, which comprised his unguarded utterances to German diplomats, Spanish aristocrats and others, were collated by German high command at a time when they had hoped to groom the duke as a potential puppet King. Not only had the duke expressed himself strongly against Churchill and the war, but he was evidently convinced that if he had stayed on the throne rather than abdicating, the whole European conflict could have been avoided. He also let the Germans know his view that continued heavy bombing of British cities would force Britain to the negotiating table.

The publication of this material would be enormously damaging to the duke's reputation and, as the King recognized immediately, harmful to the reputation of the monarchy itself. After all, the German lineage of the royal house had motivated George V to change the family name to Windsor during the First World War. As George VI's biographer Sarah Bradford observed, 'The king was very concerned about the image of the monarchy. He took several steps to ensure that the crown would not encounter hostility or be unnecessarily damaged.'[23]

Within days of the file crossing the Prime Minister's desk, by 25 August 1945, it was in the hands of Winston Churchill for his take on the contents. 'I honestly trust it may be possible to destroy all traces of these German intrigues,' he minuted promptly.[24] He took the view, echoed by Attlee, that the contents of the files were exaggerated propaganda that had 'little or no credence' and 'might do the greatest possible harm'.[25] After further consultations with his Cabinet colleagues, the consensus was for destruction.

Unfortunately for them, it would not prove so easy. All of the important German government documents, including the Windsor file, had been copied upon discovery, as per routine protocol. One copy was sent to the Foreign Office, while the other was forwarded to the American Embassy in London and later shipped to the US State Department in Washington. This second copy would prove troublesome, since the American policy was to publish German communications to explain to the public why so much blood and treasure had been expended on defeating the Nazis. Both the Foreign Office in London and the British Embassy in DC pressured the Americans to destroy or return their copy of the file. As historian Astrid Eckert observed, 'The British argued that the Windsor File was historically irrelevant, but the Americans disagreed.'[26] Ultimately, they bowed to pressure, agreeing not to publish or circulate the documents or make any further copies. Crucially, they promised not to use files, particularly the Windsor file, at the upcoming Nuremberg trials of Nazi war criminals.[27]

It would be some time before the Duke of Windsor would hear anything of these behind-the-scenes dealings on his behalf. At the end of the war, his biggest concern was to find a diplomatic or ambassadorial position. After leaving the Bahamas in May 1945, he and the duchess stayed at the Waldorf Towers Hotel in New York City for an extended holiday. It was here where he learned the news of Churchill's election loss. He wrote to Duff Cooper:

> The outcome of the British elections certainly was a surprise to me as it must have been to you and Winston and all your colleagues. The reaction in America is, in the main, one of disappointment ... American opinion is profoundly disturbed over Attlee's pledge of closer co-operation with the Soviets, and the disappearance of Winston from power as the last bulwark against the spread of Communism in Europe.[28]

It was no coincidence that the duke paid such close attention to political opinion in America. When he returned to London in October for a meeting with the King, he suggested that he might be able to continue living there, under the auspices of the British Embassy, with the goal of helping to maintain and improve Anglo-American relations. Churchill himself had suggested the move. For once, the King was supportive of his older brother's plans, even offering to write a letter of recommendation to

President Truman. However, he drew the line at the idea of allowing the Windsors to serve as official representatives of the Crown abroad.[29] In this he was supported by Attlee. When he visited the royal family at Balmoral for the traditional 'Prime Minister's weekend' he agreed with the King that the duke and duchess could not live permanently in Britain and that he was not prepared to offer him a government job of the ambassadorial calibre he required in either Britain or the wider world.

This would not fly for the duke. Money was the key issue. Without a role that fell, in Winston's words, 'within the ambit' of the British Embassy in Washington, he and the duchess would be subject to United States taxes, considerably reducing their budget for luxury living. Over the next months, the duke enlisted Churchill's help in convincing the King to create a special job for him, one that would connect him to the British Embassy via some sort of 'silken thread'.[30] As the Duke of Windsor's biographer Michael Bloch observed, the duke 'believed that all would still be well thanks to Churchill's intervention'.[31]

Indeed, Churchill began to see a lot more of the Windsors, who moved back to France after the war. As Leader of the Opposition, Winston had ample opportunity to take rest-cures to the continent. In November, he met with the duke and duchess in Paris, where he continued to encourage the duke in his ambition to work for the government in America. In advance of the visit, the King had asked Churchill to emphasize the difficulty of an official position in America for the duke. But the duke's biographer Philip Ziegler has noted, 'If the King had wanted to settle the matter once and for all, he could hardly have found a more dangerous emissary.'[32] Instead of letting the duke down gently, Winston continued to encourage his belief that an imaginative solution might still be found. The duke wrote enthusiastically to his brother, 'If you will see Winston on his return to London, he will explain how I could be appointed to work in America.'[33] He made sure to remind the King, though, that 'it was essential that no hint or suggestion ever be made in America of the question of my taxation'.[34] Nor, during this lengthy episode, was any mention made of the ex-King lending his name or energy to a prestigious charity or NGO, such as the Red Cross. They would presumably attract taxation – and this, clearly, was the first consideration.

If the duke's primary concern was money, Winston's was control. When he returned to London to debrief with the King, he framed the question of finding a job for the Windsors as one of mitigating risk, stressing the importance of keeping the duke's wayward behaviour in check. He told the King, 'There might be serious disadvantages in utterly casting off the Duke of Windsor and his wife from all official contact with Great Britain, and leaving him in a disturbed and distressed state of mind to make his own life in the United States.' The King listened sympathetically to Winston's argument and asked Tommy Lascelles to talk up the option. Lascelles was sceptical. He believed the plan to be a vain daydream 'which raised false hopes but had no real meaning'.[35]

To hedge his bets, the duke visited the new Foreign Secretary, Ernest Bevin, and proposed that a role of ambassador-at-large to the United States be created for him. Bevin sent a minute of the meeting to Attlee without comment.[36] What the duke was not aware of at that time was the existence of the Windsor file. Others most certainly were – including Bevin, who referred to it in his strong West Country accent as 'an 'ot potato'.[37]

It was left to Attlee to deliver the *coup de grace* on 27 January, when he rose in the House of Commons to declare that there would be no diplomatic position offered to the Duke of Windsor. The duke's faith in Churchill's powers of persuasion had all come to naught: his life inside 'Official England' was effectively over.[38] He could, though, try to follow in Winston's literary footsteps. Just as Churchill began his war memoirs, the duke started work on his own autobiography. As his ghost writer, Charles J. V. Murphy, recalled, 'In 1947 the Duke of Windsor was feeling forgotten. To arrest this process, to restore the lustre of his reputation, to assure that his side of the story was presented fairly, and to regain some measure of his self-respect, he decided to write an apologia, although it would be disguised as his autobiography.'[39]

The royal family were horrified. But what did they expect? They had consistently rejected overtures from the ex-King and his wife and cast them into the outer darkness. Churchill's warning had been ignored, and the duke had gone his own, ornery way after it was made clear he would never be offered an official post. The result, published in 1951, was *A King's Story*, which explored his early life and the abdication crisis from his perspective.

As the duke's light in the public eye dimmed, life for Churchill out of office overflowed with invitations to honorary award ceremonies, international speaking engagements and social requests. He hardly had time to work on his war memoirs, for which he had secured a publishing contract that allowed him, for the first time in his life, to put concerns about finances altogether out of his mind.[40] No wonder he was in high spirits when in November he hosted Lascelles for dinner at his new home, 28 Hyde Park Gate.

During the meal, Churchill asked Lascelles whether the King would approve of his accepting military decorations from the Czech and Belgian governments. Lascelles had anticipated the question and had already spoken to the King about it. He noted, 'Though the rule is that British statesmen do not ordinarily accept these foreign dingle-berries, HM agreed with me that no rule is worth anything if it can't be broken, and that Winston's case was certainly exceptional and non-recurring.' However, based on the King's earlier instructions, Lascelles played it cool. The reason soon became clear. As far as the King was concerned, if Winston would 'accept awards from foreign Heads of State then his own Sovereign expected him to accept the OM at the New Year.'

The OM, or Order of Merit, is one of the most prestigious honours on earth: only twenty-four living people are allowed to hold the title at any given time, and it is reserved for signal services to Britain, the Commonwealth and the wider world. At the suggestion that he would be invited to join this most exclusive club, Churchill 'wept a little, as he so easily does when deeply moved, and paced the room in silence for a while. Then he said, with obvious sincerity, that this was only one more instance of the many kindnesses which the King had consistently shown him, and he would of course be honoured to take it.'[41] He was duly initiated into the Order the following January.

A few weeks later, Churchill received a less formal, but no less touching gift from the King and his family. On the occasion of his seventy-first birthday, the King sent him a photograph depicting 'our famous balcony scene', as Winston liked to call it, as he was centre stage among the royal family on VE Day. It was signed by the King, the Queen and Princesses Elizabeth and Margaret. 'This is indeed a magnificent Christmas Card for me,' Churchill replied in thanks, the card eventually hanging in his sparsely decorated bedroom.[42]

It wasn't just one-way traffic with the gifts. Churchill had struck a special bronze medallion for those who worked with him in Cabinet, the chiefs of staff and other important positions during his leadership of the wartime coalition. Only one of these 150 or so medals was plated in silver. It was addressed: 'To the King, From his Faithful and Devoted Servant Winston Churchill.' When he sent it to Buckingham Palace in late July, he wrote to Lascelles to explain why the King would receive a medallion. He explained, 'After all, His Majesty saw a great deal of his principal Ministers in those days.' If nothing else, he quipped, 'It would make an excellent paperweight.' The King went one better, donating his medallion to the British museum.[43]

The months after the Second World War were not just a time for back-slapping. As with German resurgence during the 1930s, Churchill was alert to the threat posed by an aggressively ambitious Soviet Union.

This time, the world listened to his warnings. He may have toasted Stalin in vodka during their various conferences, but he remained deeply suspicious of the ideology and influence of the Soviets. He said as much in a speech he made in Fulton, Missouri in March 1946, where he spoke of an 'Iron Curtain' descending between the West and Communist Russia and its allies.

For once, his trenchant speech reunited the royal brothers. The duke commended his 'frankness' and noted that the speech 'impressed me profoundly.' 'No one but you,' he wrote, 'has the experience to tell the world the true implications of Soviet foreign policy ... I can see no hope of avoiding a third global war in our time unless our two countries can think and act in closer harmony than they used to.'[44]

The King, too, praised Churchill's 'statesmanlike' appeal for an even stronger 'special relationship' between America and Great Britain. The King told Churchill that 'the whole world has been waiting' for such a cogent analysis.[45] The following month, when Winston and Clementine were overnight guests of the King and Queen at Windsor Castle, the King continued to praise Churchill's wisdom in foreign affairs. He laid it on thick, telling him 'how much good it had done in the world'.[46]

When he was finally invested as Lord Warden of the Cinque Ports in August, Churchill used the occasion to warn of the dangers of the new world order, in which an atomic bomb could, at any moment, destroy entire civilizations:

> We have moved into a new age. Secrets have been wrested from Nature which ought to awe us and prevent the quarrels of mankind even if they cannot assuage their rivalries and suspicions. One thing at least we can promise to all: In our own place and in our own way, this glorious and pure foreshore of England, the shrine of its Christianity, the cradle of its institutions, the bulwark of its defence, will still do its best for all. We will strive forward – wearied it may be – toward that

fair future for all the men in all the lands which we thought we had won but of which we shall never despair.[47]

In spite of his election defeat, Churchill's personal star had never shone brighter. His fame was truly international. On holiday in Venice, Churchill happened to be staying at the same hotel as the actor and director Orson Welles, with whom Churchill had worked on a film project during the war. As Welles later recalled on the Dick Cavett Show, he spotted Churchill and Clemmie sitting at a table in the hotel's restaurant as he entered with a Russian financier he was courting for funding for a film venture. When Welles and the Russian money man walked past Winston's table, Churchill briefly nodded to Welles in greeting. The Russian was so impressed by Welles' apparent intimacy with the war leader that he had no trouble forking out the money. The following morning, Welles met Churchill while they were both paddling in the waters of the lido and explained what had happened, thanking him for his help, albeit inadvertent. Lunch that day was a repeat of the previous. This time, though, as Welles and the Russian financier walked past Churchill's table, the great man stood and formally, ostentatiously bowed. In spite of his advancing years and creaky limbs, he still had eyes that twinkled with a childlike sense of mischief.

Within the UK, Churchill had become an almost totemic force in British society, reminding his compatriots of the nation's historical significance and stirring in their breasts the semi-religious sense that it was good, right and noble to be British. That is to say, Churchill did for his fellow Brits exactly what a monarch did for their subjects. This was true even for the King himself. When the royal family were preparing to set off for a three-month tour of South Africa in late January 1947, the King summoned Winston to the palace. 'His Majesty,' wrote Lascelles, 'would just like to shake you by the hand before he goes.'[48]

In the event, the King wanted to do more than shake Winston's hand, keeping his former first minister at the palace for an hour-long discussion of the nation's political climate. The King was uncharacteristically indiscreet about the resentment he felt towards his Labour government, telling Churchill that 'they were going too fast in their legislation & were offending every class of people who were ready to help them if they were asked to'.[49] The King, evidently, found it hard to break his habit of confiding all his deepest feelings to the man he had come to know, to love, and to trust so fully.

If Winston had come into his own as a great British statesman, the King's firstborn was well on the road to winning her wings as a royal princess and heir presumptive to the British throne. In April 1947, while the family was in South Africa, Elizabeth celebrated her twenty-first birthday, meaning that she had fully 'come of age'. To mark the occasion, she gave her first major broadcast to Britain and the Commonwealth, uttering the words that would come to define her eventual reign: 'I declare before you all that my whole life, whether it be long or short, shall be devoted to your service and the service of our great imperial family to which we all belong. But I shall not have the strength to carry out this resolution alone unless you join in it with me, as I now invite you to do.' Two very different personalities, Queen Mary and Winston Churchill, both admitted to weeping as they listened to the princess make this vow to the realm that would later be hers.[50]

Now that she had officially come of age, Elizabeth had her own lady-in-waiting, private secretary and suite of rooms at Buckingham Palace. Most important, in her eyes, was that she had a sweetheart. During the war, Prince Philip of Greece and Denmark had watched as the gangly, socially awkward teenage girl, who wore the same clothes as her younger sister, metamorphosized into a striking beauty. The two had their first significant meeting in 1939 aboard the royal yacht HMY *Victoria and*

Albert during a visit to Dartmouth naval college in Devon, where he was a cadet. Elizabeth was immediately smitten by the blonde-haired, blue-eyed young man with the looks of a handsome Viking. She and Philip kept up a platonic but heartfelt correspondence throughout the war, Philip laconically describing the navy action he had seen in several battles in the Mediterranean. Well before her eighteenth birthday, highborn circles were whispering that Philip, a *bona fide* war hero, was the chosen one. Diarist Chips Channon observed, 'He is to be our Prince Consort and that is why he is serving in our Navy.'[51] Throughout the war, Philip visited the royal family whenever he was on leave, but when the war in Europe was over, he was moved to the Pacific theatre of conflict. By the time full peace came, the cadet had turned lieutenant and the girl had become a young woman. Upon his return to Britain, his courtship of the princess, aided and abetted by Philip's uncle, Lord Louis Mountbatten, and the princess' aunt Marina, Duchess of Kent, became much more serious.

It was by no means a smooth courtship. Philip's background was questionable: his sisters were married to Nazi aristocrats while his father lived a louche life in the south of France, having abandoned his wife when she suffered a breakdown. His brusque manner earned the disapproval of a circle of aristocrats, including the Queen's brother and courtiers, particularly Lascelles. In spite of the opposition, the match went ahead.

On 7 July 1947, Tommy Lascelles wrote to Churchill to inform him of a 'profound secret', that the King had 'given his consent to the betrothal of Princess Elizabeth to Philip Mountbatten'. The old romantic felt his heart quivering, writing to the King that the match 'has certainly given the keenest pleasure to all classes and the marriage will be an occasion of national rejoicing, standing out all the more against the sombre background of our lives'.[52]

'The young people have known each other for some years now,' the King responded, '& it is their happiness which we hope for in their married life.'[53]

The princess, too, had a congratulatory message from Winston that needed replying to: 'Dear Mr Churchill,' she began, with her usual upright formality:

> I write to send you my sincere thanks for your kind letter of congratulations on my engagement, which has touched me deeply. We are both extremely happy, and Philip and I are quite overwhelmed by the kindness of people who have written sending us their good wishes. It is so nice to know that friends are thinking of one at this important moment in one's life, and I would like to thank you once again for being one of the first who have sent their good wishes.[54]

From his perspective, Winston Churchill had no difficulty in seeing this young beauty's fitness for the throne. It was Prince Philip – the grandson of Winston's colleague during the First World War, Prince Louis Battenberg, and the nephew of the ambitious Lord Louis Mountbatten – that he worried about. Nor was he alone in his concerns. Two months later, in September, the King asked his former Prime Minister to run the rule over the future royal consort during a lunch at his home at 28 Hyde Park Gate.[55] As Churchill's secretary, Lettice Marston, recalled, Churchill wanted Philip 'to realize how serious it was, marrying the heir to the throne'.[56] It was only a short car journey from the Admiralty where Philip worked – 2.6 miles to be precise – but for Prince Philip, it was a car ride that anticipated the many dramatic changes in his life. Over meat and veg, followed presumably by the obligatory cigars and cigarettes, Churchill outlined the rights (few) and responsibilities (many) that would attend Philip's position as consort to the future Queen. In short, though he stood to become one of the wealthiest and most famous men in the world, he would gain such riches only at the cost of all power, independence of action and hope of career success. He was expected to accept one singular purpose in life: to support the Queen, in any way he possibly could.

Under normal social circumstances, it would be the bride's father who would read the marital equivalent to the Riot Act to the prospective son-in-law. But the royal family operate by different rules. It is left to others to do the dirty work for them, a tradition that is deeply embedded in royal life. In recent times when Prince Harry decided to step down as a senior royal, it was the then Prime Minister Boris Johnson who was asked by palace officials to try to convince him to stay and continue working for the 'Firm'. He was singularly unsuccessful, with Harry and his American actress wife, Meghan Markle, soon opting to fly the coop and make a new life for themselves in Montecito, California.

While Prime Minister Attlee delivered the speech of congratulations to the royal family on behalf of His Majesty's Government, it was the great phrasemaker himself who stole the show with a memorable spark of oratory to describe the occasion. 'One touch of nature makes the whole world kin, and millions will welcome this joyous event as a flash of colour on the hard road we have to travel.'[57] Nor could Churchill's augury have proven more accurate. The days leading up to the wedding were, as the Countess of Airlie noted, 'a week of gaiety such as the Court had not seen for years.'[58] Though the guests were 'sadly shabby' and the jewellery had not been cleaned since 1939, everyone wanted to enjoy themselves in the festivities. There were parades and parties, banquets and balls as the entire Commonwealth rejoiced to see the next generation of the House of Windsor taking centre stage in the royal drama. In the eyes of George V's biographer John Wheeler-Bennett, the mood of togetherness was 'an object lesson, doubly expressive in the existing distressed state of Europe, of the stability of Britain's political institutions, and of the unity of the nation in its respect for tradition and its loyalty to the throne.'[59]

While the wedding ceremony at Westminster Abbey was an international who's who of British and European royalty and aristocracy, there were several notable absentees, namely Prince Philip's Nazi sisters and the Duke and Duchess of Windsor. But as the abbey filled with esteemed guests and the clock ticked down to the arrival of the bride, there were two reserved seats, at a prime location in the sacrarium, that stood uncomfortably vacant. Finally, a black car pulled up to the kerb, and out stepped Winston and Clementine Spencer-Churchill. As they strode into the abbey, Winston donned his usual top hat, extended his familiar V for Victory salute and cracked his trademark smirk. As *The Times* recorded, the whole congregation 'by a spontaneous gesture … rose in their places to honour the entry of Mr. Churchill as he walked alone to his stall in the choir.'[60] Having paved the way for the bridal procession – both literally as the last guest to enter, and symbolically as the leader who had made the event possible by securing victory in Europe – Winston took his seat. At last, the ceremony could begin.[61]

CHAPTER FIFTEEN

The Long Goodbye

WHILE ELIZABETH AND Philip were away on their honeymoon, the King invited politicians from Britain, the United States and the Soviet Union to a reception at Buckingham Palace. It was part of the continued diplomatic effort to bring Britain's two former allies into closer harmony, in the hope of staving off another global conflict in the age of the nuclear bomb. Though Churchill was still out of government, the King loyally extended an invitation to him, the British politician with by far the widest international profile. While his former private secretary Jock Colville recorded that 'Winston and Molotov (Russia's foreign minister) talked like old friends', what surprised the gathering most was the presence of a headstrong and articulate Princess Margaret, who, at just seventeen years old, engaged Stalin's state prosecutor and Deputy Foreign Minister, Andrey Vyshinsky, in 'a twenty minutes' argument which much impressed him. He said to me that if only she had not been a Princess she would assuredly have made a most formidable advocate.'[1]

For much of 1948, Churchill focused on his memoirs of the Second World War while leading the Opposition in the House of Commons. The King had no stouter advocate than Winston when it came to the Civil List, the monies voted by Parliament for the upkeep of the monarchy and subsistence of the royal family. With her marriage and added royal workload now that she had come of age, it was proposed that Princess Elizabeth's allowance be increased and that the newly titled Duke of Edinburgh also receive a separate allowance. The Civil List debate was like a verbal coconut shy, with a handful of left-wing MPs trying, unfruitfully, to knock down a stationary if ripe target. In this latest debate, held in December 1947, some MPs supported a motion to cut Princess Elizabeth's allowance by £5,000 in the hope, as voiced by Labour MP Emrys Hughes, of taking them 'out of the gilded cage'.[2]

In Churchill's eyes, the Civil List debate was a mixture of pantomime and unnecessary rudeness to a revered institution and admired family. Once the motion was defeated and the family's funds secured, Winston wrote to tell the King how gratified he was by the debate. Not only had the desired outcome, from Winston's perspective, been achieved, but 'Yr Majesty's Ministers ... behaved in a most becoming manner & all is now settled in accordance with the dignity of the Crown & in its lasting interests.' The only lamentable part of the episode, to his mind, was the 'number of venomous people in a free country who write spiteful letters & say poisonous things'. But, of course, 'these never represented the British Nation wh[ich] is devoted to our Ancient Constitutional Monarchy the form of which has been enhanced by the ten years glorious reign of Yr Majesty, & wh[ich] finds its sure foundation in the people's heart'.[3]

However, at the end of the year there was another, far less cheerful topic on Churchill's mind: 'In signing my Christmas Card I observed that Yr Majesty wrote R instead of RI.' The initial for 'Imperator', signalling the King's dominion over the British Empire, had been pointedly omitted. Churchill closed his letter by calling the shortened signature 'v[er]y painful', but added, 'I still hope that much will one day return.'[4]

Wearing his historian's hat, Churchill was in reflective mood, pondering his own place in the great events that he had been a witness to and a participant in. In late November, when he dined with his children at Chartwell, his daughter Sarah pointed at an empty chair and asked who Winston would seat there if he were able to pick anyone. He immediately responded, 'Oh, my father, of course.' He then told them of a recent dream he had had, in which his father's ghost appeared to him. Churchill's children encouraged him to write about the dreamed encounter and publish it. Though he followed the first part of their advice and wrote it right away, it would not be

Prime Minister Neville Chamberlain and his wife Anne join King George VI and Queen Elizabeth on the balcony at Buckingham Palace to celebrate the Munich Agreement, which allowed Hitler to annex part of Czechoslovakia in return for 'peace in our time'. The royal family enthusiastically welcomed Chamberlain's negotiation and could not understand Churchill's thunderous opposition to the deal. Within a year Britain was at war with the Nazi regime.

The new Prime Minister Winston Churchill joins George VI at a military parade in August 1940 to celebrate the sinking of the German cruiser *Admiral Graf Spee*. It marked a welcome slice of good news, as well as improving relations between the King and Churchill.

George VI, Queen Elizabeth and Churchill inspect bomb damage at Buckingham Palace in 1940, after the royal couple luckily escaped being hit themselves. Churchill shrewdly used the episode to make the public aware that everyone was in this war together.

Though Churchill had corresponded frequently with President Roosevelt, it wasn't until August 1941 that the two men met face to face on board the presidential flagship USS *Augusta* off the coast of Newfoundland. He hand-delivered a letter from the King to the president, formally introducing his Prime Minister. The meeting cemented friendly personal relations between the two men and led to the release of the Atlantic Charter, which articulated the values of freedom that people were fighting for.

George VI and Prime Minister Churchill in the grounds of Buckingham Palace. They met for luncheon every Tuesday, where Winston would brief the King on the state of the war. The King's initial wariness of Churchill, especially after his role during the abdication crisis, eventually warmed to mutual respect and admiration.

During 1943, Churchill presents the Sword of Stalingrad, a gift from the King, to Russian leader Joseph Stalin in acknowledgement of the heroic defeat of the Nazis who had besieged the Soviet city. It was also the first acknowledgment by the House of Windsor of the Soviet regime since the murder of the Romanov royal family in July 1918.

For the most part, the King and Churchill worked in harmony, though they disagreed fiercely when Churchill announced he was going to watch the D-Day landings on 6 June 1944 from the battleship HMS *Belfast* stationed offshore. It took a pleading letter from the King to get him to delay his planned front-line visit. The King, who was equally eager to set foot on French soil, sailed across a few days after his Prime Minister.

On 8 May 1945, Churchill formally announced the end of hostilities with the unconditional surrender of all German forces. VE Day was the starting gun for days of raucous celebration, much of the jubilation focused on Buckingham Palace. The King invited Churchill to join him, the Queen and Princesses Elizabeth and Margaret on the balcony, where they acknowledged the cheers of the crowds.

Churchill's long-suffering wife Clemmie once observed that he was the last believer in the divine right of kings. Here he is bowing low to the youthful Princess Elizabeth at a reception at the Guildhall in March 1950. Clement and Violet Attlee look on.

Princess Elizabeth opens the International Youth Centre in Chigwell, north London, in July 1951, as Winston Churchill looks on. He saw himself as her teacher in the niceties of constitutional monarchy.

Churchill holds back tears as he leaves the Accession Council after the death of King George VI.

The Queen arrives back in London from Kenya, following the death of her father, George VI, on 6 February 1952. She was greeted by Prime Minister Churchill, the Leader of the Opposition Clement Attlee and Foreign Secretary Anthony Eden. It was the beginning of what Churchill called a 'new Elizabethan age'.

Churchill and Clemmie relaxing in his Woodford constituency in 1953, shortly before a coronation procession. Later, they attended the coronation itself at Westminster Abbey.

Sir Winston Churchill acknowledges the crowds outside Windsor Castle in June 1954, after being installed as a Knight of the Order of the Garter, the nation's oldest chivalric honour. He was first offered the honour by King George V in 1945, after he lost the election by a landslide. The chastened war leader said: 'How can I accept the Order of the Garter when the British people have given me the Order of the Boot.' It was left to Queen Elizabeth to convince him to change his mind.

Top: The Queen Mother is greeted by her grandson and granddaughter, Prince Charles and Princess Anne, after arriving home following a successful trip to Canada and the United States in September 1954. Churchill, who was part of the welcome party, convinced her to come out of retirement following the death of her husband.

Bottom: When Prime Minister Churchill finally decided to retire on 5 April 1955, he was given a suitable send off, the Queen and Prince Philip attending a dinner in his honour at 10 Downing Street.

Top: A sign of the Queen's respect for and appreciation of Churchill's contribution to the nation was signified by commending him for a state funeral and, in a personal touch, arriving at St Paul's Cathedral before the Churchill family. Traditionally, the Sovereign does not attend funerals. She led the royal family, European crowned heads, politicians, diplomats and military personnel in remembrance. The participation of the Duke of Windsor, who was undergoing an eye operation, would have completed the tableaux.

Bottom: The Queen's wreath read simply: 'From the Nation and the Commonwealth in grateful remembrance, Elizabeth R'.

published, under the title *The Dream*, until after his death nearly two decades later.[5]

As Churchill recalled, he was in his painting studio, attempting to reproduce an old, torn portrait of Lord Randolph Churchill, when he turned around to find his father – a man he both feared and revered – sitting in his red upright armchair. The two men began a conversation; one of Randolph's first questions to his son pertained not to his own life, but to that of the monarchy: 'Does the Monarchy go on?' To this, the seventy-three-year-old son responded, 'Yes, stronger than in the days of Queen Victoria.' The two Churchills briefly discussed the reigns of the intervening monarchs and problems that assailed them – notably republicanism, socialism, the Anglican Church, women's suffrage, Irish Home Rule, both world wars and the military competition between the United States and Russia. At no point did Winston reveal his personal role in these dramatic events. He did not even tell his father that he had been elected a Member of Parliament, let alone that he had been Prime Minister during the most dramatic military conflict in British history. The most that Winston said for himself was in response to Randolph asking him how he made a living and Churchill replied, 'I write books and articles for the Press.' His father was just as disapproving of him in death as he had ever been in life:

'What party is in power now? Liberals or Tories?'

'Neither, Papa. We have a Socialist Government ...'

'Socialist!' he exclaimed. "But I thought you said we still have a Monarchy.'

'The Socialists are quite in favour of the Monarchy, and make generous provisions for it.'

'You mean in regard to Royal grants, the Civil List, and so forth? How can they get those through the Commons?'

'Of course they have a few rebels, but the old Republicanism of [Charles] Dilke and Labby [Henry Labouchere] is dead as mutton. The Labour men and the trade unions look upon the Monarchy not only as a national but a nationalised institution. They even go to the parties at Buckingham Palace. Those who have very extreme principles wear sweaters.'[6]

In these days, Winston often visited his fellow scribe, the Duke of Windsor, dining at the duke's memorable table, swimming and sunning himself under the Mediterranean skies at their rented villa. Though he spent many hours with the ducal couple – he and Clementine even celebrated their 40th wedding anniversary with them – his first loyalty was to the King, and eventually the duke came to recognize that immutable reality. As the duke himself wrote, 'Winston flitted in and out of my life,' and was 'drawn to me by old affection'.[7]

Winston was, however, careful about how his friendship with the duke would be framed for posterity. As he basked in the lingering glory of his wartime victory, he was keen to ensure that his very public folly in supporting the former King against the current incumbent was downplayed. But the duke's memoirs were primed to produce exactly the opposite effect, threatening to re-open a dozen-year-old wound. Before the duke hosted Winston in August 1948, he wrote to his editor, 'I am hoping to get him alone and clear up some points that are confused in my mind.' As he would soon find, though, Winston was elusive. At almost every opportunity, Winston dissembled instead of answering direct questions about his involvement in the abdication crisis.[8]

In private, the duke was irritated by the evasions of both Winston and Lord Beaverbrook, expressing his frustration to his editor. 'Today even they have difficulty in remembering much about it.' That summer, he and his two erstwhile bulldogs and supporters were taking the air at Beaverbrook's villa La Capponcina on the French Riviera. As Churchill, wearing his ten-gallon hat, attended to his canvas and tried to capture the scene, the duke felt the time was right, as he put it euphemistically, 'to reminisce'. He asked Beaverbrook if there had ever been a true 'King's Party'. When Beaverbrook answered in the affirmative, Churchill interjected – keeping his eyes on his canvas – 'There never was a "King's Party".'[9] The duke, it seemed, would have to look elsewhere to confirm the pivotal moments of this unique royal drama. Churchill would not be singing for his five-star supper.

Though Churchill carefully guarded his own legacy, acutely aware that history is made by the victors, he was prepared to help the duke with matters other than himself. He even added the final, florid line of the duke's memoir: 'Though it has proved my fate to sacrifice my cherished British heritage along with all the years in its service, I today draw comfort from the knowledge that time has long since sanctified a true and faithful union.'[10]

While the duke was eager to relive the history of the abdication, another domestic event impelled Churchill towards the future of the monarchy. On 14 November 1948, Princess Elizabeth gave birth to a son and future King, Charles Philip Arthur George, now King Charles III. While newspaper sellers went breathless shouting the monosyllable, 'Boy!', Winston summoned his most resounding rhetoric for his address to the House of Commons: 'The British monarchy presides ancient, calm and supreme within its functions, over all the treasures that have been saved from the past and all the glories that we write in the annals of our country. Our thoughts go out to the mother and father and, in a special way, to the little prince, now born into this world of strife and storm.'[11]

Amid the rejoicing of new birth came a sober reminder of the transitory nature of life. A message from the King's private secretary to Churchill informed him that the King's forthcoming tour of Australia and New Zealand was to be postponed because of the King's ill health. His left leg had been bothering him, and upon examination, his doctors told him that he would have to be carefully observed and treated in order to avoid gangrene or thrombosis, which could result in an amputation. Churchill took up his pen to write sympathetically, albeit with nostalgic cheer, to the King:

> Sir,
>
> It is with sorrow that I learn that Yr Majesty has had to abandon Your visit to Australia and New Zealand. I am sure that the decision is a wise one. I had been concerned to think of the intense and prolonged exertions the tour w[oul]d have demanded from both Yr Majesty and the Queen. They w[oul]d have killed you by kindness! The distances are enormous and everywhere there w[oul]d have been delighted and loyal crowds. One must not underrate the strain of such enjoyable contacts with enthusiastic friends.
>
> Sir, I trust that the rest and relief will restore yr health, and enable you to add long years to your reign. It has been a time of intense stress and trial. It may well be that history will regard it as 'our finest hour'. I am proud to have been Yr First Minister in all these great adventures. I ever hope in spite of my age to stand at Yr Majesty's side once again. However this may befall, I remain,
>
> Yr Majesty's devoted and grateful servant,
> Winston S. Churchill [12]

When Churchill wrote to Lascelles, his tone was more cautionary, admitting that he had 'always dreaded this Australian visit ... Few human beings could undergo such an ordeal without an immense loss of vitality. Now I trust the King will take things easy ... All will come right.'[13]

In responding to Churchill, the King wrote not to a minister but to a dear friend. He said that he was 'very sorry' that his tour had to be delayed, but he knew it was for the better. 'I do genuinely feel relief that this malady of mine, which has been aggravated by constant worry &

anxiety over the World situation, will keep me at home & will give me a period of rest for a time.' It was more likely his lifelong chain-smoking that was to blame, rather than the state of global affairs, but in any case, the King was glad for the opportunity to relax.[14]

While the King recuperated, Winston enjoyed a new lease of life. Just three days before his seventy-fourth birthday, he astonished his friends and worried his family by joining the Old Surrey and Burstow hunt. He recounted the adventure to his Sovereign a few days later. 'I was glad to be able to have a gallop,' he wrote, 'and not to be tired at all ... I trust and pray Yr Majesty's progress is good.'[15] While it was his final time on a horse, it sparked a new hobby that brought him into closer social contact with the royal family. Much to Clementine's consternation, he became the proud owner of a racehorse, choosing for his riding colours the same ones as his father, a dusty-pink jacket with chocolate sleeves and a chocolate cap. His first horse, the French-born thoroughbred Colonist II, proved to be a winner, the lithe grey dashing to victory three times in his debut year. After Churchill's horse won the third time, a racing reporter at *The Times* wrote, 'Racegoers are delighted that his eminent owner has entered the turf with the same ready success that he has achieved in all of his many pursuits.' Whenever Churchill's horse sailed across the finish line, uproarious supporters would wave their V signs in the air and cry, 'Winnie Wins!'[16]

In May 1951, Colonist II was entered in the opening race of the season, which was suitably named after Churchill himself, the Winston Churchill Stakes, held at Hurst Park. Princess Elizabeth, who had come to watch her father's horse Above Board, invited Churchill for lunch and to watch the event together. As the field pelted around the mile-long course, Colonist II led at the turn. Charging hard was the King's Above Board, with W.H. Carr in the saddle, wearing the royal colours of purple with scarlet sleeves and a black cap with gold tassel. Heading for the winning post, Churchill's grey came in first, two lengths ahead of His Majesty's filly, with a black colt, Star-Spangled Banner, placing third.

That evening, the King proved himself a good sport, sending a telegram to Churchill from Balmoral Castle to congratulate him on his win. Churchill replied, 'I am deeply grateful for your Majesty's most kind and gracious telegram.' Six days later, Winston wrote to Princess Elizabeth at greater length: 'Madam, I must thank Your Royal Highness for so kindly asking me to luncheon with you ... and for the gracious congratulations with which you honoured me. I wish indeed that we could both have been victorious – but that would be no foundation for the excitements and liveliness of the Turf.'[17] This was only the beginning of what would become a years-long shared interest between Elizabeth and Winston.

In this season, Churchill proved a winner away from the turf, too. In spite of suffering a minor stroke in September 1949, he was able to lead the Conservative Party in the February 1950 general election, slashing the Labour government's majority to just five. His health issues, though, continued to plague him – in March 1951 he had a nasty staph infection – and concerned his colleagues who felt privately that it was time for him to step down. But success was success, and Churchill went on to lead his party to parliamentary victory in October 1951 after Attlee called a snap election.

The election had taken place in the shadow of the King's declining health. On the day Attlee announced the election, an official palace bulletin declared, vaguely but ominously, that the King's doctors had found 'structural changes' in his left lung, which would require treatment. Churchill asked his own doctor, Lord Moran, to decode the ambiguous message, and finally heard the word that the doctors had been afraid to say aloud: cancer. In the early 1950s, patients were rarely told directly when they were suspected to have the disease, as treatment options were crude and unsuccessful. Few survived. Moran told Churchill that the King had not been told, because the only treatment plan available was an invasive form of 'modern surgery', which would remove the lung entirely. 'Poor fellow,' Churchill told Moran. 'He does not know what it means.'[18]

Tommy Lascelles wrote to Attlee and Churchill to inform them that the King's doctor had scheduled an operation on his lung for Monday, 24 September. Jointly with Clement Davies, the Liberal Party leader, Attlee and Churchill sent the King a message at once: 'It is our earnest prayer that His Majesty may soon be fully restored to health.'[19] Aside from such formalities, there were pressing logistical difficulties that needed to be addressed. Chief among them was the trip to United States and Canada due to be undertaken by Princess Elizabeth and the Duke of Edinburgh in October. While it would undoubtedly need to be postponed, some courtiers suggested flying, rather than taking a ship, to make up for lost time.

Churchill would not hear of it. When, on the morning of the King's surgery, he was told of the suggestion, he immediately wrote to Attlee: 'In the present circumstances it would be, in my opinion, wrong for the Princess Elizabeth to fly the Atlantic. This seems to me more important than any of the inconveniences which may be caused by changing plans and programmes in Canada.' It was of course 'more important' because, considering that the King was at that very minute recovering from an extremely risky procedure, the continuous occupation of the throne was a matter of critical importance. To jeopardize the safety of the next-in-line at a time when the reigning King's own life was at stake struck Churchill as an altogether unjustifiable risk. If the King expired on the operating room table, and Elizabeth's plane crashed into the Atlantic, who then could possibly take up the throne?[20] The day before the surgery, Winston confessed to Lascelles, 'I did a thing ... that I haven't done for many years – I went down on my knees by my bedside and prayed.' Tommy promptly conveyed his confession to the Queen.[21]

Whether it was Churchill's prayers or the surgeon's skill, the operation was successful, insofar as it went. Still unsuspecting that it was cancer, the King believed himself cured and tried to get back to 'business as usual' through a combination of willpower and modern pharmaceuticals.[22] He was well enough to celebrate the election results as they streamed in on

25 October, joining in the chorus of racing fans across the country who cried, 'Winnie wins!' The next day, an aged Winston Churchill hobbled into Buckingham Palace for an audience. It had been almost six years since his last official encounter with the King as First Minister. Though weary, the King was delighted to see his friend back at the helm of his government. They discussed the road ahead, as the post-war economic recovery trudged along and the threat of war between Russia and the United States loomed ever larger.

With the conclusion of the general election, the starter's pistol had also been fired on the publication of the Duke of Windsor's memoirs, *A King's Story*. Though the book had been launched at the Windsors' hotel suite in New York in April 1951, Churchill had prevailed on him not to release the memoir in Britain until after the election. The King's illness had added another layer of difficulty for the duke. He planned an exclusive dinner in London to launch the book but found even his former supporters, including his one-time Lord Chamberlain, Lord Cromer, against the idea. Cromer wrote to advise him to cancel the dinner because it 'savoured too much of the boosting of a commercial enterprise' at a time when the monarch was critically ill. The duke remained intransigent until he received a letter from Churchill. The premier knew from long experience which button he would have to push to win him over: self-interest. He wrote, 'It is so important that the first time you address the British public [you] sh[ou]ld have the most cordial welcome and be an unqualified success.' With his ego sufficiently stroked, the duke somewhat grudgingly abandoned his plans. Later, he complained that on the very day he was to have hosted his dinner, Princesses Elizabeth and Margaret had been seen riding at the Ascot races. He moaned, 'Pretty blatant discrimination, isn't it?'[23] What he saw as a clear double standard didn't stop him from trying, for the umpteenth time, to secure his wife an HRH handle. As Winston returned to power, so the duke returned to the subject that, as his ghost writer Charles J.V. Murphy described, 'was a fox to [Wallis'] vitals, gnawing at her pride'.[24] When the duke raised the subject, the Prime Minister affected not to hear the request. While he was indeed growing increasingly deaf, this was most likely an instance of diplomatic selective deafness. In any case, the duke finally took the hint, and this would be the last time he ever brought up the subject of his wife's rightful status with Winston Churchill.[25]

When it was clear that the King's operation was truly a success, planning for Elizabeth and Philip's visit to North America resumed. The couple did, in fact, cross the Atlantic by plane, despite Churchill's protestations. Philip later recalled that he had had to remind the inveterate politician 'of his flights across the Atlantic during the war while he was in the rather more responsible position of Prime Minister'.[26] It was during their overseas trip that Winston was returned to that 'responsible position', the Conservative Party winning a majority of seventeen seats in the general election. When the couple arrived in Washington, President Truman introduced Elizabeth and Philip to his mother, who made it clear that she knew little of Britain's constitution. 'Mother!' President Truman shouted into the elderly woman's ear, 'I've brought Princess Elizabeth to see you!' Truman's mother gave the princess a warm smile of recognition and said, 'I'm so glad your father has been re-elected.'[27]

A few days later, Churchill welcomed the royal couple home after a successful trip, praising the princess especially for the way she had carried off the visit. Her personality, he told her, would go a long way in 'mellowing the forward march of society the world over'.[28] In his own show of gratitude, the King invited the pair to join the ranks of Privy Counsellors and then to begin planning for the upcoming tour of Australia and New Zealand – youthful replacements for the convalescing King.[29]

If the King and Churchill had hoped, in Churchill's second term, to resuscitate the spirit that had so invigorated them during his first, they were both in for disappointment. Even when Churchill arrived at Buckingham Palace to take up his office in the evening of 26 October, it was obvious that the spirit of their younger days had tapered into the dull, exhausted torpor of old age. Winston was now approaching seventy-seven years old; he was partially deaf and his trademark bullish hunch had faded into a sagging stoop. What was once a distinctive lisp had degenerated into, at times, a difficult-to-decode stream of consciousness, not helped by his most recent stroke. Once he held the reins of responsibility and power, some of his old vitality began to course through his veins and the trademark smirk and quick wit made a more frequent appearance in his daily life. As his doctor, Lord Moran, noticed, this was not Winston as he had been during the war. Instead of struggling against the Axis forces, he was now 'struggling only with the humiliations of old age and with economic problems that are quite beyond his ken'.[30]

United by the ailments of old age – and chain-smoking – there was, though, genuine friendship between the two men. There were also constitutional proprieties to be acknowledged. When Churchill submitted his suggestions for ministerial appointments, the King went through them with the same red pen as always. He noticed that Anthony Eden, who was predictably suggested as Foreign Secretary, bore another title: Deputy Prime Minister. In Churchill's mind, this was a continuation of the practice he had adopted during his coalition government, where Attlee held the title in case of Winston's incapacitation or death. In the King's eyes, Churchill was usurping the King's prerogative to decide for whom to send. The position of Deputy Prime Minister suggested that that decision was no longer the King's to make.[31]

At the same time, the King was eager to make contact with the leaders of the United States to formally reintroduce his returned Prime Minister to the stage of global governance. Before Winston sailed to Washington for a summit meeting with American leaders, he wrote to both President Truman and General Eisenhower singing his praises. 'I am glad that you are going to renew your relations with Mr Churchill shortly,' he wrote to President Truman. 'He is a wise man and understands the problems of this troubled world. I have always felt that our two countries cannot progress one without the other, & I feel that this meeting will unite us even more closely.'[32]

Once the conference was over, Churchill hastened back to London. A telegram from the King's private secretary warning of the King's deteriorating health made his return all the more urgent. As it was, the haste was unnecessary. The King and his family were relaxing at Sandringham and only planned to travel to London for the King to briefly see Churchill and to give Princess Elizabeth and the Duke of Edinburgh a personal send-off from London airport (now Heathrow) as they flew to Nairobi in Kenya on the first leg of their flight to Australia and New Zealand where they were to undertake a six-month official tour.

The take-off, scheduled for the morning of 31 January, attracted thousands of well-wishers who surrounded the nearby roads and airport perimeter. In spite of the bitterly cold winter weather, they were to see both the King after his operation and the newlyweds as they left the grey skies of England for the sunshine of Kenya.

The cheers for the royal party, who included the King, Queen, Princesses Elizabeth and Margaret as well as Prince Philip, the Gloucesters and the Mountbattens, was matched only by the uproarious welcome for Churchill, wearing his trademark bowler hat, who arrived a few minutes later with assorted ministers and high commissioners in tow. They joined the royal party on board the four-engine airliner for a welcome glass of champagne before wishing the couple 'Bon voyage'.

Ten minutes later, the entire party – except for Elizabeth, Philip and their private secretaries – descended the stairs and took their positions on the tarmac, where they waved goodbye to the departing entourage. The King was acutely aware that he was under the microscope and, as Churchill remarked to Lord Moran, initially seemed 'gay and even jaunty' as he took what turned out to be his final leave from his eldest daughter.[33]

As the plane readied for take-off, the King and Queen mounted a stand that had been erected on the roof of the airport. From this vantage point, they watched as Elizabeth and Philip's plane lifted off. *The Times* recorded that: 'The King, bareheaded, stood watching until the Atalanta was no more than a speck against the clouds.'[34]

In spite of the King's efforts at feigning health, it was obvious that he was struggling. His face was drawn, his walk laboured, and he could barely manage a goodbye wave to the departing Atalanta aircraft. Churchill, standing at his side, got the distinct impression that 'he knew he had not long to live'.[35] The Colonial Secretary, Lord Chandos, had the same hunch. 'I felt with foreboding,' he later recalled, 'that this would be the last time he was to see his daughter, and that he thought so himself.'[36]

With Elizabeth gone, the King, Queen and Princess Margaret returned to Sandringham to resume their holiday. On his final day, the King, using a light gun, went shooting and then enjoyed a dinner with friends as Margaret serenaded the party on the piano. On the morning of 6 February, when an attendant came to wake the King for his breakfast, he found in the bedchamber not a King, but a body, peacefully at rest. The Queen, Princess Margaret and the wider household were duly informed.[37]

From Sandringham, Lascelles phoned Buckingham Palace to tell the King's assistant private secretary, Edward Ford, that he needed to go to 10 Downing Street to break the news to the Prime Minister. When Ford walked into Churchill's bedroom, he found the old man in his typical morning position: sitting upright in bed, wearing one of his Oriental silk robes, a blanket of state papers covering his lap and pillows and the usual cigar balanced between his fingertips. He had much on his plate politically that day. He faced a personal censure motion over what the Opposition believed was Churchill's secret agreement with America to use a nuclear bomb against China should the Korean war flare up again. Winston had a knockout attack lined up and was enjoying writing a speech in his self-defence. So, he looked up impatiently from his papers as the junior courtier entered the room.

'Prime Minister, I've got bad news for you,' Ford told him before conveying Lascelles' message.

'Bad news?' Churchill responded – still in speech-writing mode, thinking first and foremost of the appropriate phrasing – 'Bad news? The worst.' He dismissed Ford and looked down at all his scattered documents. 'How trivial this all seems now.'[38]

A few moments later, his private secretary, Jock Colville, oblivious to the news, arrived at 10 Downing Street to collect the final version of the speech on nuclear weapons that Winston would have delivered in the House of Commons later that day. The attendant on duty told him simply, 'There is no need to think of it further.' Jock rushed into Churchill's room to find him still in bed – just enough time had passed for tears to well up in the old man's eyes. The papers were still scattered around him, but Churchill was looking at none of them, nor at his daily diet of newspapers. Jock, as he recalled, did his best to console him, telling him 'how well he would get on with the new Queen'.

The only thing Churchill could say was that he did not know her – and that 'she was only a child'.[39]

CHAPTER SIXTEEN

Disconsolate Consort and the Shining Crown

A S QUEEN ELIZABETH II descended the stairs to the runway at London airport late in the steel-grey afternoon of 7 February 1952, Churchill – flanked by Foreign Secretary Anthony Eden and opposition leader Clement Attlee – dropped into a deep bow to greet his new Sovereign for the first time. The premier was devastated not only by the loss of a man who had become a close friend, but by the enormity of the transition from one reign to the next. Churchill knew that the country would want to hear his thoughts on the death of the King, and while he rode to the airport in his black official limousine to meet the young Queen, he began to craft the broadcast he would give that night, dictating to his secretary as tears ran down his cheeks. On the journey back to 10 Downing Street, he was too overcome to continue working, and merely sat silently, weeping in the backseat.[1] Not for nothing did the Duke of Windsor call him 'Cry Baby'.

In his broadcast that night, Winston spoke movingly about the King as 'a devoted and tireless servant of his country' and listed his many virtues. It was only appropriate that the demise of such a noble King should strike 'a deep and solemn note in our lives which, as it resounded far and wide, stilled the clatter and traffic of twentieth century life in many lands and made countless millions of human beings pause and look around them.' Churchill described the King's bravery and patience as he awaited the closing curtain: 'The King walked with death, as if death were a companion he did not fear.' He comforted his many millions of listeners with the assurance that the King's final hours had been spent peacefully: 'In the end death came as a friend; and after a happy day of sunshine and sport, and after "good night" to those who loved him best, he fell asleep as every man or woman who strives to fear God and nothing else in the world may hope to do.'

Churchill had lost not only a King but also a close companion. The reign of George VI, in his memory, was inextricably tied to the crest of his own political career. In his broadcast to his fellow mourners, Churchill signalled the closeness that had grown between the two men: 'I who saw him often, knew how keenly, with all his full knowledge and understanding of what was happening, he felt personally the ups and down of this terrific struggle and how he longed to fight it, arms in hand, himself.'[2]

No speech in the genre of royal eulogy would be complete without the formal signal of the crown's transition to a new head: 'The King is dead; Long live the Queen!' Churchill ended his historic message with a gesture of fealty towards his new Sovereign, one which reached back into the annals of British history and his own long life: 'I whose youth was passed in the august, unchallenged and tranquil glories of the Victorian era, may well feel a thrill in invoking, once more, the prayer and the anthem, "God Save the Queen".'[3]

Behind closed doors, though, and despite his protestation of loyalty, Churchill maintained some reservations about the Queen's ability to fill her father's shoes. Elizabeth II was only twenty-five years old, after all, and had not been tutored thoroughly in the many responsibilities of the Crown. This task, Churchill felt, was one that would rightly fall to him, as the young Queen's first Prime Minister. The burden of this responsibility would have felt especially heavy during the Accession Council, which met at St James' Palace the day after Elizabeth's return from Kenya. As the former Chancellor of the Exchequer Hugh Dalton noted, the Queen's youth presented a striking contrast to the tired, wrinkled faces of the Privy Counsellors in attendance – 'people one didn't remember were still alive'. Meanwhile, the Queen looked 'very small' and had a 'high-pitched, rather reedy voice'. But Dalton and the assorted aristocrats and politicians felt that, for all her inexperience, she 'does her part well'. As the Queen stepped in front of the window in Friary Court to proclaim the beginning of her reign, the then Housing Minister Harold Macmillan respected 'her firm yet charming voice'. There was promise and potential in this young Sovereign, but it needed cultivation, nurturing, and a boost of confidence – and it fell to Churchill to see that these would be provided.[4]

It was only one of the many tasks that faced Churchill at the start of Queen Elizabeth's reign. There were formal ceremonies and rites to undertake, namely delivering a speech in the House of Commons, which Churchill did on 11 February. In his address, Churchill reminded his audience of his longevity in the chamber, noting that he had been present at all three of the previous addresses of the twentieth century: when Balfour spoke after the death of Victoria in 1901, when Asquith grieved the loss of Edward VII in 1910 and when Baldwin mourned George V in 1936. In his own address, Churchill aimed to uphold the legacy of 'those eminent men', and briefly surveyed the many changes that had taken place in the British nation and empire since his first days in office, as well as the achievements and legacies of the sovereigns he had personally mourned in the same period. Of them all, Churchill argued, it had been under George VI that Britain had endured the 'greatest shocks'. 'The late King lived through every minute of this struggle with a heart that never quavered and a spirit undaunted ... he never lost his courage or faith that Great Britain, her Commonwealth and Empire, would in the end come through.'[5]

As in his broadcast, Churchill ended his House of Commons address by directing his audience's attention to the 'fair and youthful figure' of the new Queen, whose accession must make them 'all feel our contact with the future'. Churchill did not yet know Elizabeth well enough to dwell on any particular features of her personality, so he kept to the historical and political context of her accession, and to the collective aspirations of the British Commonwealth – 'That it should be a golden age of art and letters, we can only hope,' he commented vaguely.[6]

On a more practical note, the Cabinet needed to decide when the Queen's coronation should take place. Some ministers argued for a swift ceremony so that the Queen and Duke of Edinburgh could fulfil the much-delayed visit to Australia and New Zealand as soon as possible. On the other side, Churchill argued for a later date, feeling that there must be plenty of time for excitement to build, so that the ceremonies around the Queen's anointing would be celebrated with full-throated enthusiasm. It would not be – in his classic phrase of 1937 – in line with 'the honour and dignity of the Crown' to rush such a significant event.[7] Plus, the country's post-war economic recovery in 1952 remained torpid, such that any unnecessary additional holiday prompted by the coronation would have a significant impact on productivity. Not a single working day could be lost to the festivities: 'Can't have coronations with bailiffs in the house,' he quipped.[8]

Some of those sitting round the Cabinet table also suspected that Churchill's campaign for a later date was motivated by a desire to use a delayed coronation to postpone his own retirement, playing Melbourne to Elizabeth's Victoria. Certainly, that was the conclusion of Churchill's doctor, Lord Moran, who noted that the premier 'had set his mind on seeing the Queen crowned before he gave up office'.[9] Those hoping for an early coronation ceded the field, and the date was set for 2 June 1953, a full sixteen months after Queen Elizabeth's accession to the throne.[10]

The day after this Cabinet meeting, at 6.30 p.m., Churchill drove to Buckingham Palace for his first audience with Queen Elizabeth II. Although he had lived under five, now six, different British sovereigns, this was the first and only time that he was able to officially usher the monarch into their reign in the official capacity of Prime Minister. He recognized the gravity of the transition and felt it as a great burden of responsibility. 'Terrific things are happening,' Winston murmured to his doctor as he prepared for the meeting.[11]

The Queen, too, must have felt some trepidation as she took her seat ahead of their audience; her hand may have trembled when she rang the bell to signal to her equerry to admit the legendary Prime Minister – now *her* Prime Minister. But the man who entered was no stranger to the twenty-five-year-old monarch; Winston Churchill had been a figure in the Queen's world since before she could remember, and had featured in many of the most important moments of her life – during the abdication crisis with Uncle David in 1936; when he opposed sending her to Canada at the beginning of the Second World War; seeing her at Windsor Castle during hostilities; standing with her on the balcony of Buckingham Palace to wave to the exuberant multitudes below; and of course, standing with her father as she caught her final glimpses of him as she departed for Kenya. And yet, as much as she had grown up in Churchill's personal presence, the stooped figure who entered the audience room was also a politician of staggering historical importance, myth as much as man – the most senior statesman in Parliament, a decorated veteran, a world-renowned writer and speaker, a British national hero, the saviour of the free world. And although he was owed respect and obedience as her constitutional adviser, she was the one to receive obeisance as his Sovereign.

Any worries Churchill may have harboured about the Queen's capacity to reign dissolved as he observed the naturalness with which the Queen stepped into the role during their first audience. Immediately afterwards, Churchill's language about the new reign became far more personal and assured. He no longer saw the Queen as merely 'fair and youthful,' a blank slate on which to paint the nation's vaguely defined aspirations, but as a competent, prudent and steadfast woman. The morning after his first audience, he replied to a letter from his American friend and host Bernard Baruch, who had written to Churchill praising his broadcasted eulogy of the King. 'We have sustained a terrible loss,'

Churchill admitted. 'But I am sure that in his daughter we have one who is in every way able to bear the heavy burden she must now carry.'[12]

The change in Elizabeth's manner upon becoming Queen was not only noticed by Churchill, but also by the Queen herself. 'I no longer feel anxious or worried,' she told a friend in the first days of her reign. She was as baffled as anyone by her transformation, but she suggested that her audience with Churchill was fundamental: 'I don't know what it is – but I have lost all my timidity somehow becoming the Sovereign and having to receive the Prime Minister.'[13]

Queen Elizabeth would need all of this new-found fortitude in the coming months. The death of her father resulted in a dramatic shift in the family hierarchy. As they mourned the premature death of the King, family members tried to cope with the reversal of roles, bruising displacement and shifting expectations. Foremost among them was the King's widow, now Queen Elizabeth the Queen Mother. Ever since late 1936, following Edward VIII's abdication, she had been accustomed to taking the senior position at all formal events. If the monarchy is about anything, it is about hierarchy, and the Queen Mother found it difficult to cope with the notion that she had gone down in the pecking order and now owed deference to her daughter. Apprehensive observers noticed that, in the weeks following the new Queen's accession, there was an 'awkwardness about precedence' – the young Queen felt it would be ungracious to walk in front of her mother during formal ceremonies, and so, for instance, allowed the grieving Queen Mother to take the monarch's seat at Sunday church services.[14]

Princess Margaret was even more of a wreck. She had spent much of her time during her father's final months in his company, playing jaunty show tunes on the piano to lighten his spirits. To make matters worse, Margaret had lost with his death not only a father, but also a sister. While Elizabeth's marriage and subsequent motherhood had changed the family dynamic, her ascendence to the throne brought down another, much more rigid and formal barrier between them.

Margaret was expected to greet her sister with a curtsey and the deferential salutation, 'Ma'am.'[15] None of these changes could have been easy for the new Queen, either – but she showed herself to possess all the composure and poise necessary to manage the familial tension and its attendant isolation. Margaret, less so.

However much these abrupt reversals strained relations within the royal family, the grieving women came together for the lying-in-state and funeral for the late King. On 11 February, the royal coffin was taken by train and foot procession from Sandringham to Westminster Hall in central London, where the King lay in state for three days. During this time, over 300,000 mourners filed past the bier to pay their respects before the funeral at St George's Chapel at Windsor. When the Archbishop of Canterbury had finished his funerary liturgy, the kingly trappings were removed from the coffin: the Royal Standard, his crown and other regalia taken off, and in their place heaps of flowers to accompany his coffin into the ground. Prominent among them was a white wreath, adorned with a hand-written note, in Winston Churchill's script: 'For Valour.' It was the rubric of the Victoria Cross, Britain's highest military medal for bravery and extreme devotion to duty. The royal family 'loved the words' and found it altogether fitting that Winston's final tribute to the King he had served so well should accompany his coffin to its final resting place.[16] At the funeral itself, Churchill sat next to General Eisenhower and wept. More privately, and much more unusually, Churchill refused a whiskey and soda at the reception at the Deanery later that day, feeling it would be improper to indulge in his favourite alcoholic beverage under the solemn shadow cast by the demise of his good friend and most noble King.[17]

Not everyone was so tactful during the official mourning period, which was scheduled to last sixteen weeks. Just two days after the King's funeral, the grieving Queen Mary was told about a celebratory dinner party held at Broadlands, the country estate in Hampshire which was home to Dickie and Edwina Mountbatten. During dinner

Dickie Mountbatten, Prince Philip's uncle, proudly announced that 'the House of Mountbatten now reigned.'[18] The claim was not altogether far-fetched: before he married Princess Elizabeth, Philip had renounced his foreign titles and assumed the surname of his maternal line, Mountbatten. As it was customary in common law that a woman take her husband's surname on marriage, it was reasonable to expect the new Queen and her family to adopt Philip's surname and be known as Elizabeth Mountbatten, and that their children, too, would one day reign as Mountbattens rather than Windsors.

One of the guests at Broadlands, Prince Ernst of Hanover, reported the incident to Queen Mary. Suitably outraged, she contacted Churchill's private secretary Jock Colville and asked him to brief the old man. Churchill was equally perturbed. Not only was he hostile to Dickie politically, blaming him for the 'loss' of India, but personally he found him pompous, overly concerned with titles, medals and rank, and boastful of his own intelligence. So the notion of applying Mountbatten to the royal house struck him as downright absurd.[19] After all, the original surname was Battenberg, its Germanic origins anglicized during the First World War to counter anti-German sentiment. Moreover, the late King George V had deliberately proclaimed Windsor to be the royal family's surname in 1917, again to mask the royal family's German origins and to choose a surname that projected Englishness. For the sterling new reign to be tarnished by a return to the Germanic lineage, so soon after the German threat had been defeated a second time, struck Churchill as nothing less than an affront to the English national character. His Cabinet agreed that it could not stand.

On the other hand, past precedent seemed to be on Dickie's side. Even Queen Victoria, that bastion of social propriety and tradition, had allowed the surname of her husband, Prince Albert of Saxe-Coburg and Gotha, to be passed on to their issue, ending the rule of the House of Hanover. There was, too, ambiguity in the verbiage of King George V's Royal Proclamation of 1917, announcing the name of Windsor, since it only explicitly applied to the King's male issue. Eager to maintain his surname, Philip seized on these inconsistencies. Opposition was formidable, in the shape of Queen Mary, Churchill and the Cabinet.[20]

In the following weeks, Churchill and the Privy Council drafted a proclamation that related not only to Queen Elizabeth, but – adding to Philip's grievances – to all their children, whether directly in the line of succession or not. Philip's fury during this process was no secret. His friend and equerry Mike Parker described him as 'spitting' mad, while the junior courtier Martin Charteris was more understated: 'Philip was not happy.' Inevitably, it caused a rift between husband and wife, however tactfully the Queen discussed the issue. As politician Rab Butler observed, it was the only occasion where he saw the Queen close to tears.[21]

The prince wrote, according to Colville, 'a strongly, but ably, worded memorandum protesting against' the draft proclamation. He resented the idea that he, a royal prince and a decorated naval veteran, should be the only man in the country unable to pass his surname on to his children. But his memo served no purpose other than to further irritate Churchill, who instructed 'a firm, negative answer' to be sent.[22] It was the first conflict between Churchill and the coming man. There would be many more. As Philip was to find, there were three of them in the marriage, and at times it got rather crowded. Finally, on 6 April, Queen Elizabeth formally declared her 'Will and Pleasure' that both she and all her children would maintain the title of the House of Windsor.[23]

Even before the spat over the royal surname, Philip was already mistrusted by the establishment. He was a man with great energy, drive and creativity, qualities that boded ill for a life of a consort who was meant to remain, quiet and passive, in the shadow of his wife. His questionable family background had already meant that his behaviour was looked upon with a degree of suspicion. It was felt too that living in the thrall of his uncle, Dickie Mountbatten, may create further tensions at court.

Philip had never expected to be king or even king consort. When he first dined with Churchill at Hyde Park Gate in 1947 shortly before his marriage, he explained that his driving ambition was to make a career in the navy. He had had a good war and was seen as a future Sea Lord. Like the majority at Court, he expected the King to live much longer, giving him the chance, sadly snatched away, to build a life for himself and his family as he had done when the couple lived for a time in Malta. He blamed the restrictions and limitations on his marriage, his family life and even where he lived on the Prime Minister and senior palace courtiers. Others also witnessed his difficulties. Philip's cousin, Pamela Mountbatten, recalled that he felt 'unwelcome at Buckingham Palace. Courtiers closed ranks. Churchill made him feel apart from the whole thing.' Philip himself famously complained, 'I am nothing but a bloody amoeba.'[24]

Nor was Philip's insistence on passing his surname on to his children the only source of tension between him and Churchill, the Cabinet, and the court. The other domestic matter that needed to be settled was where the Queen and her husband were going to live. Ever since July 1949, when they moved into Clarence House just off the Mall, Philip had devoted himself to making it feel like home. Up to then, he had spent much of his life on the move – or on the run from persecution – and here was the opportunity to put down roots, at least for a few years. He chose the paint colours, the curtains and the carpets, even installing the latest gadgets such as a motorized wardrobe. Nothing escaped Philip's nesting efforts.[25]

It was only natural, then, that he hoped to remain in Clarence House when his wife acceded to the throne. The Queen herself was inclined to agree – especially since her mother and sister were in no rush to vacate Buckingham Palace, where they had lived since before the war. For the Queen Mother, the idea of being evicted from the home she had shared with her late husband, where they had endured the darkest days of the Battle of Britain side by side, was enough to bring her to tears. While

Churchill recognized the royal family's domestic difficulties, he argued strongly that the constitution took precedence. He declared firmly that the flagpole at Buckingham Palace 'flies the Queen's Standard and that's where she must be.' He recruited the Queen's veteran private secretary, Tommy Lascelles, to convince her that she and her family must move 'across the road'.[26]

Again, Prince Philip was dragged kicking and screaming into this revised arrangement. 'It was bloody difficult for him,' explained Mike Parker; 'In the Navy, he was in command of his own ship – literally. At Clarence House, it was very much his show. When we got to Buckingham Palace, all that changed.'[27] And everyone knew that the change was at Churchill's behest. As Parker later recalled, Philip's patience with the aged Prime Minister was running thin: 'We thought: you old bastard! We loved him dearly, but he did things like that.'[28]

Even when he attempted to integrate himself into the body politic that spring, by attending a debate in the House of Commons, he could not escape censure. Seated in the peers' gallery, he was observed making overly expressive faces at the policy positions articulated by various speakers. Some members were scandalized, complaining that it was constitutionally inappropriate as well as unbecoming for a royal consort to display any personal judgment on any political matter under consideration. Churchill received a formal letter of complaint from Enoch Powell, a Conservative MP. The Chief Whip endorsed the complaint, and Churchill was forced to convey it to the monarch. 'It kept happening,' recalled Lord Brabourne, Patricia Mountbatten's filmmaker husband. 'Philip was constantly being squashed, snubbed, ticked off, rapped over the knuckles. It was intolerable.'[29]

Although Churchill was the first to chastise Prince Philip when he stepped out of line, he recognized that the current state of affairs could not possibly continue forever. He knew that Philip was 'insupportable when idle,' and needed a job of some kind, something to keep him busy and give him an outlet for his energy.[30] He was granted a leading advisory role in the Royal Mint's project to manufacture new coins and medals bearing Elizabeth's likeness, and was appointed Chair of the Coronation Commission, on which Churchill and various other bulwarks of the old guard – the Duke of Norfolk, the Archbishop of Canterbury and Clement Attlee – also served. The commission's first meeting took place on 5 May, the same day that Elizabeth and Philip finally moved into Buckingham Palace. Philip began the first session with a brusqueness that betrayed both his eagerness to get on with the task at hand, and his resentment at having been so roughly handled in the past several months. 'Welcome to the first meeting of the coronation commission. There is a tremendous amount of work to be done, so the sooner we get on with it the better.'[31]

The following month, Churchill was among the VIPs on Horse Guards Parade who stood to watch Queen Elizabeth II's first Trooping of the Colour. The ceremony, which marks the Sovereign's official birthday and has run annually since 1748, is much more than a colourful tourist attraction. Not only is it a focal point of monarchical adulation, but a reminder that the serried ranks of the military owe their allegiance to a head of state who is not a politician but an embodied representative of the nation as a whole. As Churchill pithily observed, it was a physical manifestation of the 'separation of pomp from power'.[32] The seventy-seven-year-old Prime Minister, standing to attention as his Queen saluted her troops, reflected upon how much had changed in such a short time – for himself, for his country, and for the monarchy. 'I thought of the history of the past and the hopes of the future,' he said of the ceremony a few days later. 'Not only of the distant past – it is barely ten years since we upheld on our strong, unyielding shoulders the symbols, the honour and even perhaps the life of the free world.' Though the shoulders were now dainty, feminine and youthful, the burdens were just as heavy, though different in nature. 'In war we were united, now in peace we find ourselves torn apart by quarrels which bear no relation to our dangers, and while we brawl along, our thought and action are distracted by a vast superficial process of reciprocal calumniation.'[33]

As Churchill lectured the nation, he may have reflected that he, too, bore some of the responsibility for the widespread, overblown and superficial bickering, particularly with regard to the Coronation Commission where clashes between the venerable war veteran and the youthful progressive became a familiar sight. Most tense of all was the question of whether the new technology of broadcast television would have its part to play in the ancient rites. Philip, fascinated by the scientific and technological advances of the day, felt it was essential that the monarchy showed itself up-to-date. It was the surest way, he felt, to ensure that the common man would feel connected to such a rarefied institution, and specifically to their Queen at the moment of her crowning.

On the other side, Churchill and the Archbishop of Canterbury worried that to broadcast the sacred ceremony over the airwaves would be to desecrate it. They were concerned that some irreverent viewers might casually watch the coronation slouched in their pyjamas, 'over the coffee cups'. Or in the pub over a pint. There was also the issue of numbers. If the public stayed at home to watch the ceremony on a new-fangled TV, the crowds on the processional route might be embarrassingly thin. Finally, and much closer to home, a live broadcast would inevitably place additional pressure on the Queen to perform every step perfectly. She was already terrified of making some misstep or another in front of the congregation. Throngs of viewers watching the ceremony remotely would, she felt, merely add to the nervous tension. The committee were sympathetic, worrying that 'any mistakes, unintentional incidents or undignified behaviour by spectators would be seen by millions of people.' On this issue the Queen was in complete agreement, relieved that the coronation would only be broadcast over the much more familiar medium of radio. Philip was once again in the disgruntled minority.[34]

Though Churchill had never been known for his discretion, he did what he could to keep his distaste for Philip under wraps. He could scarcely prevent it from becoming known amongst the 10 Downing Street secretariat that, 'Although he wished the Duke of Edinburgh no ill, he neither liked nor trusted him and only hoped that he would not do the country harm.'[35] And yet, when he travelled to New York in January 1953 to meet with General Eisenhower, he sang the duke's praises. He spoke about 'the charm of the Queen' in one breath and 'the intelligence of the Duke of Edinburgh' in another, in between some discussion of 'a few war-time indiscretions'.[36] Whatever animosity there might be between the young pup and the old bulldog was considered the kind of dirty laundry never aired in public, especially in front of friends from the other side of the Atlantic.

There was, though, a wide-bodied streak of hypocrisy in Churchill's behaviour when he attempted to ban Philip from learning to fly jet aircraft. After all, this was the man who had nearly met his maker on numerous occasions when, during the First World War and beyond, he made frequent flights in primitive aircraft, at least two of which ended in crash landings.[37] When Philp began training as a pilot in November 1952, Churchill put his foot down. 'In view of his public position and responsibilities,' Winston argued, 'His Royal Highness should not expose himself to unnecessary risks.'[38] He did not have precedent on his side – his friend the Duke of Windsor had flown his airplane frequently when he was King.

Although Churchill had travelled by air many times during the war, he felt it was inappropriate to do so for anything other than essential purposes. Spurred by Churchill's anxiety, the Cabinet discussed Prince Philip's new hobby no fewer than eight times. But on this front, Churchill's antagonism was overcome – the Queen sided with her husband and allowed him to pursue his hobby. Indeed, he was photographed flying solo over Windsor Castle in May 1953 and later took a ride in a helicopter from the Buckingham Palace gardens and flew around the country to inspect various regiments. When he got to hear about the jaunt Churchill was furious, writing to Philip's now private secretary Mike Parker: 'Is it your intention to destroy the entire Royal Family in the shortest possible time?'[39]

Far safer, Churchill felt, was his own hobby of racing and, more recently, breeding horses. It was a passion he shared with the Queen, with whom he discussed the news of the turf at many of their private audiences. Over the summer, these meetings grew increasingly long – the standard was half an hour, but their free-wheeling discussions often dragged on for up to ninety minutes. Tommy Lascelles, who ushered Churchill into the Bow Room and waited for him outside the door, noticed that Churchill would often take leave of the Queen with tears in his eyes. He could not hear what they discussed, but noticed that their audiences were, 'more often than not, punctuated by peals of laughter'. One evening, Churchill was especially enamoured: 'She's *en grande beauté ce soir*,' he told Tommy Lascelles, in his 'schoolboy French'.[40]

The Prime Minister's unusually long meetings with the Queen caused a great deal of curiosity. 'What do you talk about?' Jock Colville asked him one day. 'Oh, mostly racing,' Churchill responded vaguely.[41] Though she had loved horses since she was a little girl, the Queen's passion for breeding and racing truly developed after the death of her father. Then she inherited his stud at Sandringham and with that the King's champion racer, Aureole. The horse was a superstar, winning eleven out of the fourteen races in which he competed during his short career from 1952 to 1954, when he was retired. So great was Churchill's and the Queen's bond over their love of racing that the Queen consented to allow Aureole to breed with Churchill's brood mare, Turkish Blood, to create another champion, Vienna.[42]

But of course, the Sovereign and first minister also had other, more sober topics to discuss during their weekly meetings, particularly Britain's place in the world, parliamentary gossip and public personalities. In their first months of audiences, Churchill was impressed by how quickly the new Queen had taken up her role. 'Her immediate grasp of the routine business of kingship was remarkable,' he wrote.

> She never seemed to need an explanation on any point. Time after time I would submit to her papers on which several decisions were possible. She would look out of the window for half a minute and then say: "The second or third suggestion is the right decision" – and she was invariably right. She had an intuitive grasp of the problems of government and indeed of life generally, that I suppose had descended to her from Queen Victoria.[43]

So great was Churchill's respect for Queen Elizabeth's preternatural ability to rule that some worried he might be too quick to bow to her will. The Queen's assistant private secretary, Edward Ford, noticed how Churchill 'acted upon her lightest word'. For instance, one of their meetings took place the day after the Queen had attended a screening of *Beau Brummell*, which had been selected especially for her with the expectation that she would enjoy seeing the historical film about Kings George III and IV. To the contrary, she found the film unsettling and distasteful. When Churchill learned that she had not enjoyed it, he was horrified, and he left the audience muttering, 'The Queen has had an awful evening. This must not recur.' By the next day, Churchill had told the Home Secretary to arrange a formal review to scrutinize the choice of films to be screened for the Sovereign.[44] He had Hollywood on his mind when he picked up a photograph of the Queen and muttered, as he studied it, 'Lovely, inspiring.' Now in the mood for hyperbole he continued: 'All the film people in the world, if they had scoured the globe, could not have found anyone so suited to the part.'[45]

For all his eagerness to please the Queen, though, Churchill, as Philip had discovered, was no pushover. When Sir Richard Molyneux, a former courtier, asked Elizabeth if Winston played the part of the 'over-indulgent' Lord Melbourne to her Queen Victoria, Elizabeth could only laugh at the comparison. 'On the contrary,' she replied, 'I sometimes find him very obstinate.'[46]

A slice of this obstinacy was on display when Churchill invited himself to visit the Queen and her family at Balmoral in early October 1952. Though he hadn't held a gun in years and found walking difficult, let alone crawling, he was most disconcerted when the young guns made up a stalking party and left him out of their calculations. Obstinate to the last, he felt that he should have been included.[47]

He had, though, a more delicate mission in mind: to gently encourage the Queen Mother to return to a life of public service rather than hiding away in the shadows at Birkhall, her Scottish home. Before he saw her, he tested the water with her lady in waiting, who advised that he should arrive unannounced. He duly drove over on 2 October for a heart-to-heart conversation with the Queen Mother. After he arrived he found a woman who, only in her early fifties, continued to struggle terribly under the burden of her grief, feeling that the significance of her life as Queen had been abruptly and cruelly snatched away with the death of her husband. Her swift demotion in the court hierarchy had been difficult to come to terms with. Though Churchill was sensitive to her needs, he was also aware that she was a great asset for the monarchy and the nation. Earlier that year, Churchill had discussed her possible appointment as Governor General of Australia in the hope of giving her a substantive position in the Commonwealth as befitting her age and experience. In the end, though, nothing came of it.[48] During their conversation at Birkhall, Churchill snuffed out any discussion of her retirement. 'Absolutely not!' he told her, according to the Queen's lady-in-waiting. 'This young Queen is going to need you by her side an awful lot. And this is no time for you to sit in Scotland.'[49]

The Queen Mother knew that in Churchill, with whom she and her husband had spent so many anxious hours during the war, she had a true and faithful companion. After the two had met at a cocktail party in August, she wrote to her friend Betty Salisbury, 'Winston was so angelic about the King – he has such tender understanding, & I was so touched & helped.'[50] During their conversation at Birkhall, he made her realize how valued she was not just by her immediate family and friends, but by the nation at large. She needed to be inside the loop of Society, rather than cutting herself off. He clearly worked his magic. As William Shawcross, her official biographer, observed, 'This may have been the conversation during which he persuaded her that she still had a vital national role.'[51]

Indeed, another of the Queen Mother's ladies-in-waiting, Jean Rankin, noticed an immediate change in her demeanour, speculating that Churchill 'must have said things which made her realize how important it was for her to carry on, how much people wanted her to do things as she had before'. Of the many services Churchill performed for the royal family during his lifetime, the way he wrangled the Queen Mother back into the royal fold was one of the more significant. Her links to the war generation, her military associations, and her innate charm and smiling personality added an extra dimension to her daughter's reign. Not for nothing was she hailed as a National Treasure, her rededication to royal service due in large measure to the intervention of Winston.

He was much less successful in trying to convince fellow MPs and the wider public to listen to the coronation on the radio rather than watch it on television. Though the decision had been reached by a majority in the coronation committee and accepted by the government, the public greeted the news of the television ban with fury. MPs, watching their postbags fill with letters of complaint, voiced their opposition, excoriating the decision as outmoded, elitist and backwards. They blamed the greybeards like Churchill and the clergy for the decision, assuming, wrongly, that the Queen would be disappointed that her big moment on the world stage would not be televised. In the end, on 8 December, the government climbed down and reversed their decision 'in the light of serious public disappointment'. The Queen too had a change of heart, agreeing to cameras only if they were kept away from the sacred aspects of the ceremony. As a result Philip enjoyed some much-delayed gratification while television retailers rubbed their hands in glee.[52]

While sales of TV sets soared, the British economy was in the doldrums. Virtually every Cabinet meeting during this time referred to the country's precarious economic state. No one was more conscious of that than the Prime Minister. Even so, he refused to countenance a threadbare coronation, broadly agreeing with the strictures of the Victorian constitutionalist Walter Bagehot who stated, 'There are arguments for not having a Court and there are arguments for having a splendid Court but there are no arguments for having a mean Court.'[53] Churchill was in the 'no mean Court' corner, objecting, for instance, to suggestions that members of the congregation should have to pay for sandwiches. In December 1952, as he prepared to head to New York City for a summit, he rehearsed facing hostile questions from the press. It was anticipated that journalists would want to know how the country could justify such public expenditure on the Queen's coronation when it was in such dire financial straits. Winston's response, given with a sly grin, set the tone: 'Everybody likes to wear a flower when he goes to see his girl.'[54] However, it wasn't flowers, but rather sugar that he decided to give to the public. Though food rationing was still in effect, Churchill gave the nation a sweet deal, allowing consumers an extra pound of sugar for making plum jam (due to an excess of plums), sweets, cakes, pastries and other items for domestic consumption and street parties.[55]

While a teaspoon of sugar helped the dreadful economic medicine go down for the man and woman in the street, Churchill was not minded to help when the Duke of Windsor came round with the begging bowl. He and the duchess hoped to be included in the new Civil List. They were out of luck. The new reign would not let bygones be bygone. If anything, the hostility to the royal couple intensified after George VI's death, the Queen Mother blaming her husband's early death on the strain he endured as an unwilling recipient of the throne. 'It's hell,' the duke wrote to his wife, 'to be even this much dependent on these ice-veined bitches.'[56]

He would be dependent no longer: in October 1952, he was told that there would be no allowance in the Civil List given the monies he received from the rent at Sandringham and Balmoral. Not to mention the small matter of the million and change he had earned from sales and serialization of his 1951 memoir, *A King's Story*. The duke's first port of call after he received the news was the Prime Minister. Winston, though, was in no position to help them out, either financially or in terms of the royal family recognizing the duchess. As Wallis wrote to her aunt Bessie: 'Winston though very friendly won't interfere in what he calls a family matter.'[57] However, Churchill was prepared to uphold the dignity of the duke and duchess when it came to explaining why they would not be invited to the Coronation. He formally endorsed the duke's statement saying that it would be against precedent for any Sovereign or former Sovereign to attend the ceremony. As when Churchill first became Prime Minister in 1940, the duke was forced to the conclusion that Winston's loyalty, first and foremost, was to the institution of constitutional monarchy and the Sovereign at its head.

Queen Mary's death on 24 March, just weeks before the coronation, once more brought attention to the family rift. Though the duke raced to be by his ailing mother's side, he arrived too late. All his bitterness towards his family welled up in a letter he sent Wallis, who was in New York City, alone and uninvited, during her husband's hour of need: 'What a smug stinking lot my relations are and you've never seen such a seedy worn-out bunch of old hags most of them have become.'[58]

The duke's anger was a long way from the gracious tribute Churchill paid to Queen Mary in a radio broadcast. Churchill recalled how, 'During six reigns ... she has moved among us with the poise and the dignity which, as age drew on, made her a figure of almost legendary distinction.'[59] This was Churchill in his now-familiar role as father figure to both the nation and the royal family itself. His unique standing vis-a-vis the House of Windsor had been further validated in 1952 when the Queen commissioned a bust of him to be made by the eminent sculptor

Oscar Nemon and displayed at Windsor Castle. Though Nemon found him 'bellicose, challenging and deliberately provocative'[60] – a verdict with which several members of the royal family, notably Prince Philip, would have agreed – Churchill was 'deeply moved' by the Queen's gift, 'proud to be immortalized in company with his great ancestor the first Duke of Marlborough.'[61]

The Queen had another family housekeeping matter to deal with before her Coronation: making sure Winston would be able to wear the most highly coveted regalia on the big day. When Churchill had been offered the Order of the Garter by the late King in 1945, the elderly politician refused, arguing that it would be wrong to accept such a distinguished honour just after losing the election by a landslide. The King had been so disappointed by Winston's refusal that in 1946 he changed the rules surrounding the appointment of Knights of the Garter, so that it rested upon the Sovereign's sole discretion, rather than needing the premier's sign-off. But the late King had not found another opportunity to offer it, and so it fell to his daughter to finish the job.[62] During their audience on 24 April, the Queen conferred upon Churchill the title of Knight Companion of the Most Noble Order of the Garter, investing him with the proper insignia. He was now Sir Winston Churchill. In the end, King George VI had triumphed.

Sir Winston had the modern making of the monarchy in mind when he laid out his thoughts in a speech to the Commonwealth Parliamentary Association in May 1953, with the Queen looking on. Churchill referred to the long history of conflict between Parliament and Crown, personified above all by Oliver Cromwell, whose statue stood a few hundred feet away – 'But those days,' Churchill told his audience, 'are done.' Since Cromwell's time, the British constitution had evolved in such a way that it was, he argued, 'no longer a case of Crown versus Parliament, but of Crown and Parliament … It is natural for Parliaments to talk and for the Crown to shine.' Churchill had been developing this theory of constitutional monarchy since his earliest days of government, when King

Edward VII had chastised him for suggesting that ministers might create peers to resolve the budget crisis. 'All round,' he concluded his speech, 'we see the proofs of the unifying sentiment which makes the Crown the central link in all our modern changing life, and the one which above all others claims our allegiance to the death. We feel that Her Gracious Majesty here with us to-day has consecrated her life to all her peoples in all her realms. We are resolved to prove on the pages of history that this sacrifice shall not be made in vain.'[63]

This was Winston speaking with one voice on behalf of the nation and the monarchy. 'Oh, the Queen liked my speech,' he later boasted to his doctor, Lord Moran. 'I was bold, too, about the conflict between the Crown and Parliament – a hundred yards from Cromwell's statue; the dirty dog, I never liked him.'[64] Churchill had obviously forgotten his headstrong insistence during the reign of George V on naming one of the newly built dreadnought battleships after the English revolutionary.

But speaking in abstracts was one thing; the practical day-to-day matters of monarchical stewardship were another, and the working relationship between the British monarch and her parliament would have a chance to be tested in the lead-up to the Coronation. In late May, the Queen herself asked her ministers to change the 1937 Regency Act. Its current state specified that Princess Margaret would serve as a regent in the event of Elizabeth's absence or incapacitation. She wanted that to change so that Prince Philip would instead fill the position until Charles, then just four years old, came of age. When the Queen petitioned Churchill on the matter, he and others were unconvinced, feeling that the change would make for awkward publicity, especially so close to the Coronation. The public very well might think that the Queen had come to the decision out of mistrust of her sister. At a Cabinet meeting on 27 May 1953, Churchill revealed that both he and 'MPs from all sides' had serious doubts as to whether Philip was the appropriate choice. James Stuart, then Scottish Secretary, agreed that Philip should be Prince Charles' guardian, but thought it went too far to strip Margaret of her rights to the Regency, instead favouring a Regency Council. But the problem was, as Lord Salisbury, the minister for economic affairs, put it clearly, 'there is no reason on which we could oppose the Queen's wishes. The Duke of Edinburgh would regard it as an affront, and that would be a very serious matter.'[65] With the Coronation only days away, it was decided to postpone the regency deliberations until later in the year, after the Queen was crowned.[66]

The acid test for the nation's goodwill towards the new Queen lay, not in the arcane propositions comprising the Regency Act, but in the public taking to the streets to watch this ancient ceremony of Coronation. Churchill's gamble to delay the Coronation paid off as the streets of the capital and other towns, cities and villages across the nation exploded in the red, white, and blue of the Union flag. The threatening grey skies on the morning of 2 June failed to deter the crowds who crammed the Mall and other streets chosen for the stately procession in the hope of catching a glimpse of the Queen and her attendants.

As Churchill was aware, the Queen had been terribly nervous before the big day and had painstakingly rehearsed every aspect of the ceremony inside Buckingham Palace. She went about her day-to-day routines while wearing the five-pound coronation crown atop her head – or, when it was unavailable, a sack of flour – so that she could don it gracefully when the real moment came. All the practice paid off, the young Queen approaching her big day with a steady serenity. Asked on the morning of her coronation whether she was feeling nervous, she famously responded, 'Of course I am, but I really do think Aureole will win.' The star racehorse she had inherited from her father was due to compete in the Epsom Derby the following Saturday – and it was this, more than her own performance that day, which occupied her thoughts. With confident resolve, Elizabeth went through each step of the ritualistic ceremony with textbook precision, as twenty-seven million people in Britain alone watched the broadcast on TV and millions more braved the late-morning downpour to throng the streets of London.[67]

At the centre of the ritual inside Westminster Abbey was the juxtaposition between past and future, continuity and change. The former was represented by Churchill himself, the still cherubic-looking politician who had begun his career under Queen Victoria. Or, as photographer Cecil Beaton somewhat unkindly described, 'That great old relic, [who] lurches forward on unsteady feet.' The future, on the other hand, was embodied by the fresh-faced monarch in satin, silver and gold. Beaton again: 'Then the most dramatic and spectacular, at the head of her retinue of white lily-like ladies, the Queen.'[68]

In careworn, hard-up, ration-book Britain, still pockmarked by bomb sites and collapsed buildings, the nation gathered round its TV sets and whispered to itself that a new Elizabethan age had dawned. At the centre of it all, the chief cheerleader for this magical, even mythic monarchy was Sir Winston S. Churchill.

CHAPTER SEVENTEEN

A Tainted Love

CELEBRATIONS FOR THE Queen's coronation did not end with the ceremony in Westminster Abbey. That was just the starting gun for a parade of parties, dances, and dinners. There was even the performance of an opera by Benjamin Britten, titled *Gloriana*, to recognize this historic occasion. For Churchill, this was a time of undiluted bliss. Two days after the Coronation, the Prime Minister, in his full dress as Lord Warden of the Cinque Ports, hosted the Queen at a sumptuous banquet inside the newly renovated Lancaster House. After years of rationing, make-do and mend, this was the opportunity for the nation to unbutton its stays and let its hair down – however briefly. The following day, Churchill was invited to join the Queen and the Queen Mother at the Epsom Derby, where the Queen's Aureole, though highly favoured, took second to Victor Sassoon's Pinza.[1]

All too soon the Queen and Prime Minister were yanked back to sober reality. For several months the Queen and her sharp-eyed secretary, Tommy Lascelles, had been aware of a potential storm brewing within Buckingham Palace. Princess Margaret had begun an affair with a married member of the royal household, the King's former equerry Group Captain Peter Townsend. Sixteen years her senior and a father of two boys, Townsend was in the throes of a painful divorce. In the aftermath of her father's death, Margaret had drawn close to Townsend, the two expressing their love in snatched moments of togetherness. In the hothouse atmosphere of Buckingham Palace where every look, gesture and glance is watched, it didn't take long for the rumour mill to grind into action. Lascelles, horrified at the very thought of a member of the household crossing the romantic line with the royal family, summoned Townsend and, according to his memoir, warned him that his behaviour was encouraging gossip. 'You must be either bad or mad' to be involved with the princess, he told him.[2] In an age when divorce was severely frowned upon – the BBC forbade any divorced members of its staff from reading the news – and with the abdication drama still relatively fresh, the idea of the princess falling for a divorcee induced a collective attack of the vapours.

Weeks before the Coronation, Margaret had informed her sister about her feelings for Townsend and that he had, in December 1952, quietly been granted a decree nisi by the divorce court, clearing the way for their eventual marriage. In turn, the Queen asked her to do nothing until after the big day. The signals from the royal family were decidedly mixed, variously disapproving and accepting. While Lascelles had articulated the traditional, negative response, the Queen Mother buoyed the lovers when she asked Townsend to join her senior staff. Even the Queen's response was ambivalent: she invited her sister and Townsend for dinner with her and Prince Philip, where the prince disconcerted the Second World War flying ace by making off-colour jokes about their predicament.[3]

For months the palace kept a lid on the affair. It was an unconscious gesture on Princess Margaret's part at the end of the coronation ceremony that caused the dam to burst. An eagle-eyed reporter noticed Margaret idly brush a piece of fluff off Townsend's sky-blue RAF uniform, a gesture that suggested a level of casual intimacy not typically shown to palace staff, no matter how senior. While the British press focused on the Coronation, the American papers ran breathless rumours of the possible royal romance. The storm was about to break. Within days Lascelles was informed that the British Sunday newspaper, *The People*, was set to release a story about the alleged dalliance.

This was not just personal, it was constitutional. As Margaret was in the direct line of succession to the throne, her romantic life was subject to the Royal Marriages Act, passed under George III in 1772. The Act stipulated that before the age of twenty-five, she would need to secure permission to marry from the Sovereign, in this case, her sister. Once she was twenty-five, in three years' time, she was free to choose any partner she pleased. This placed the Queen in an unhappy quandary, with her sense of loyalty to and love for her sister coming into direct conflict with her position as titular head of the Church of England. Her freedom of action was, however, constrained by whatever formal advice her Prime Minister might give. The Queen accordingly gave Lascelles permission to sound out Churchill. On 13 June, only eleven days after the excitement of the coronation, Lascelles arranged to see Churchill at Chartwell, his beloved country home in Kent.

Lascelles was welcomed to the drawing room, with its floor-to-ceiling windows that overlooked the lakes and walled gardens of the manicured estate. Winston, Clementine, Jock Colville and Lascelles took their seats on the plush sofas, and Lascelles informed the Prime Minister of the impending publicity crisis. Lascelles had barely spoken two sentences when Churchill interjected: 'This is most important. One motor accident, and this young lady might be our queen.'[4]

Though Winston appreciated the constitutional issue at stake, especially the possible impact on the Commonwealth, he did not initially share Lascelles' attitude of doom and gloom. 'What a delightful match!' he gushed. 'A lovely young royal lady married to a gallant young airman, safe from the perils and horrors of war!' As usual, his response anticipated that of the man and woman in the street when they learned of the romance. Once the story broke, a poll in the *Daily Mirror* showed an overwhelming majority in favour of the match.

The rest of the party was less enthused, Clementine in particular. 'Winston,' she scolded, 'if you are going to begin the Abdication all over again, I'm going to leave! I shall take a flat and go and live in Brighton.'[5] Of course this was nothing like the abdication crisis; however, after due consideration, Churchill came around to the view that, at the very least, Margaret must renounce her rights to the throne if she chose to pursue the relationship. Moreover, Churchill fretted over the reaction of the Commonwealth towards Margaret and Townsend, should something happen to the Queen. If the elder sister were to become incapacitated, it was Margaret who would serve as regent until Prince Charles came of age. It was this variable in the equation that captured Churchill's imagination, though there were other, no less difficult hurdles – chiefly, the opposition of the Church of England, which refused to remarry people who had been divorced.

It is a sign of the acceptance of Winston as an ersatz member of the royal family that when he suggested that he consult the chief members of his Cabinet, the Queen said that she would prefer Winston keep it to himself, feeling 'that the matter was still in the stage of being a family affair'.[6]

Within days, though, it was front-page news, the Queen now agreeing with Lascelles and Churchill that Townsend should go abroad forthwith. Churchill was concerned that all the goodwill towards the monarch and monarchy inspired by the successful coronation would be dissipated by a long-running scandal. He reported to the Queen that even though several members of the Cabinet were divorced, opposition to the marriage was unanimous. This view was also reflected among Commonwealth leaders. Matters now moved at speed, and Townsend was offered the choice of three postings: Singapore, Johannesburg, or Brussels. He chose the Belgian capital and was sent there within days, both Churchill and Lascelles hoping that a year-long separation would be long enough for their ill-advised love affair to fizzle out. The star-crossed lovers promised each other that the distance would be no obstacle, and that they would find a way to hang on until the princess' twenty-fifth birthday, when they could finally marry.[7] This issue was the first telling example of the Queen's characteristic reaction to a tricky situation: to kick the problem into the long grass and play for time.

Margaret's love affair with Peter Townsend had one positive result for Churchill, in that it clarified the vexed issue of the new Regency Act. Before the coronation, Churchill's Cabinet were unconvinced about the

Queen's request to make Prince Philip regent should anything untoward happen to her. At that time, there was some sensitivity about seeming to publicly humiliate Princess Margaret by demoting her so ruthlessly and without any evident cause. Following the scandal around Margaret so soon after the coronation, though, senior politicians could hardly make the change fast enough. Churchill and the Queen, together with the rest of the Privy Council, set about drafting the Regency Act of 1953, in compliance with her initial request. Through the Act, she declared her Will and Pleasure that 'in the event of a Regent becoming necessary in my lifetime, my husband should be Regent and should be charged with the guardianship of the Sovereign'. In addition, the Queen Mother was made a Counsellor of State, able to step in for the Queen when she was out of the country.

As a result, within weeks of being crowned Queen, her position had compelled her sister into making two life-defining sacrifices: a painful parting from the love of her life, and the relinquishing of her most significant constitutional role. She was devastated and furious.[8]

For once, Churchill had to think about his own health, rather than that of the royal family and wider nation. On 23 June, Churchill and Clemmie were hosting a dinner party at 10 Downing Street when he suffered a stroke, leaving him unsteady on his feet and slurring his words. Most of his guests did not recognize the symptoms, thinking only that he was a little worse for wear after a night's drinking.[9]

Churchill's initial recovery from his stroke was remarkably swift, so much so that he was able to preside over a Cabinet meeting the following day. While he looked pale and kept his interjections brief, most of those present did not suspect anything was wrong with the leader affectionately known as 'the old man.'[10]

The air of normality was quickly exposed for the illusion that it was, as the Prime Minister began to show increasing signs of impairment over the next few days. He had difficulty moving and speaking, and he lost the use of his left arm. When he went to Chartwell to convalesce, his doctor Lord Moran feared the worst. He told Jock Colville that he 'did not think the Prime Minister could possibly live over the weekend'. It was a dire prognosis, one which caused Colville to disobey Churchill's direct order – to keep his infirmity under wraps – by informing the Queen. He spoke to Tommy Lascelles and told him that the Queen should be prepared to deal with the burden of appointing a replacement premier as early as Monday morning. The situation was further complicated by the fact that the man chosen as his successor, Foreign Secretary Anthony Eden, was also medically indisposed as he awaited a gall bladder operation. Several other senior ministers were informed. Loyally, they all kept these worrying developments secret. The policy of secrecy did mean, however, that the country was without a fully competent Prime Minister for a time.[11]

Churchill only found out that Jock had disobeyed him when he received a letter from the Queen, written in her own hand, on 26 June. She was characteristically understated in her appraisal of the calamity: 'I am so sorry to hear from Tommy Lascelles that you have not been feeling too well these last few days. I do hope it is not serious and that you will be quite recovered in a very short time.' She went on to describe the visit she and Prince Philip had made to Edinburgh, where the weather was fine and the locals had been 'thrilled by all the pageantry'. Although seriously impaired, Winston responded immediately, relaying details of his stroke but ending on a note of optimism, suggesting that he would soon be out and about and able to discharge his duties until the autumn, at which point Eden would be well enough to take over.[12]

It was the first time, at least in writing, that Winston had broached the topic of his own retirement with the Queen. Inside and outside the Conservative Party, the chorus of voices calling for his resignation and his replacement by a younger man, in this case Anthony Eden, had grown progressively louder and more numerous since the Coronation. But there was no established precedent for getting rid of an ageing Prime Minister – he was then seventy-eight – especially one who was so highly regarded by his Sovereign and his country. At this stage only the Queen, speaking to him in strict privacy in the weekly briefing meeting, could have nudged him towards resignation, but she was too young and inexperienced, and if she did indeed say anything, it was deftly brushed aside by the old warrior.

In any case, his recovery was indeed remarkable. Every passing day gave him more strength to continue. Just four days after his stroke, on 27 June, he felt well enough to write a three-page letter to American President General Eisenhower, asking him to use his authority to prevent the imminent publication of the infernal Windsor file.[13] It is a measure of the importance Churchill placed on the suppression of these documents, which related in part to the Duke of Windsor's intemperate comments about the Nazi bombing campaign over Britain, that it was one of his first orders of business as he recovered from his life-threatening stroke.

In his letter to Eisenhower, Churchill argued that the 'historical importance' of the material contained in the Windsor file was 'negligible,' and that the legitimacy of its claims rested 'only on the assertions of German and pro-German officials in making the most of anything they could pick up.' But wholly apart from the file's inherent lack of legitimacy, Churchill made a personal appeal to his old Second World War comrade: 'I feel sure your sense of justice and chivalry will make you wish to prevent the United States, by an official publication, from inflicting distress and injury upon one who has so long enjoyed their kindness and hospitality.'[14] Eisenhower replied right away, describing himself as 'completely astonished' that such a microfilm even existed, and expressing the hope that the matter could be settled with 'decency, justice and finality.'[15] However, he pointed out, as the material was already duplicated, he was powerless to stop its eventual publication.

In fact, the American editors of the *Documents on German Foreign*

Policy, as the compendium was entitled, were up in arms over the idea that anyone, government or otherwise, should dictate what they were allowed to publish. The French, whose Prime Minister Churchill had also contacted, were equally recalcitrant. When Walter Monckton met with their Foreign Minister Georges Bidault, he was discouraged to hear that the 'historians were not to be commanded'. The volume's editors would likely resign in the face of any attempt to suppress the documents.[16]

When Churchill returned to London from Chartwell on 25 August, he brought up the Windsor file at the first Cabinet meeting he presided over.[17] By then, he had abandoned the idea of destroying the documents. Instead, he advocated delaying publication for ten or twenty years, or ideally, after the duke's death. To that end, he took it upon himself to invite the British editor-in-chief, the Honourable Margaret Lambert, to Downing Street on 6 September to take the temperature. The meeting, which also involved his old friend Lord Beaverbrook as well as Lord Salisbury, lord president of the council, and Minister of Labour Sir Walter Monckton, agreed upon a change in emphasis. Instead of focusing on the fall of France in 1940, the publication spotlight would instead be trained on documents relating to the 1925 Locarno Treaty. Work on the Windsor file would accordingly be suspended but not ended, thus avoiding the appearance of government censorship. Like a dog with a bone, Winston kept himself fully apprised of progress and took to phoning Miss Lambert late in the evening for updates.[18]

The autumn of 1953 seemed like Winston's swansong, with his work on the Windsor file coming as a sort of capstone on a life of devoted service to the royal family, his last major intervention on their behalf. His first thoughts were to resign after he had made the leader's speech at the Conservative Party conference at the seaside resort town of Margate in October. In early August, as his recovery continued, he met with the Queen at Royal Lodge, Windsor, where he told her of his plans. She, perhaps relieved that the old man was finally readying himself to step aside, made no gesture of dissent. But her preparedness to see him leave office was not based on any personal animus. Quite to the contrary, she demonstrated her desire to keep Winston in her social circle past the point of his departure from politics. In September 1953, she invited him to accompany her to the St Leger races at Doncaster, followed by a trip to Balmoral. Both his doctor and his wife, knowing what a frail condition he was in, were staunchly opposed. Clementine phoned her husband at Chequers and when these calls failed, sent him a plaintive letter. But all her words, both spoken and written, fell on deaf ears.[19]

This was the Queen. It was a mark both of Churchill's great affection for her personally, and also of his reverence for the monarchy itself, that he was so unwilling to decline the invitation, even in the face of such vigorous disapproval from his wife. In the end, the trip was a sparkling tonic, Churchill fortified by the shows of public adulation that he received. When, for example, the Queen went to the banister of the royal enclosure at Doncaster to wave to the cheering crowds, Winston stayed politely in the background. But when the Queen returned, she approached him and said, 'They want you.' The great man took his turn in the window, positively basking in the fact that – as he wrote to Clementine – 'I got as much cheering as she did.'[20]

From the races, Churchill took the royal train to Balmoral where he accompanied the Queen to Sunday service at Crathie Kirk. The last time he had sat in those pews, it had been as the guest of Edward VII, forty-five years before. Times had certainly changed – back then, he was a politically ascendant young man, freshly appointed president of the Board of Trade. Now, 'long avenues of people' crowded to catch a glimpse of him as he strode out of the church, 'and they raised their hands, waving and cheering, which I was told had never happened before.'[21] The obvious veneration he received lifted his spirits and gave him confidence that he would have the energy and stamina to make his speech at the upcoming Margate conference. 'I have important things to say that concern the country,' he said on his return to London.[22]

In his letter of thanks to the Queen, he consoled her on her horse's defeat at the races, reassuring her that 'there will be many Legers in which the Royal colours will claim their due.' Finally, Churchill mentioned the Queen's long delayed Commonwealth tour, during which she was to visit Australia, New Zealand, and several smaller island nations. 'The opportunity is well chosen for the Royal Visit,' he wrote.[23] After the success of his October speech – much to the chagrin of his detractors who prayed for his resignation – Churchill decided to use the Queen's tour Down Under, due to finish in May 1954, as the new marker for his departure.

When the afterglow of the successful Margate speech subsided, however, his energies waned substantially; he was oversleeping, feeling sickly, and generally in the lowest of spirits. Despite his ailments, his obsession with the Queen was as strong as ever. When he came back to 10 Downing Street after an audience with her on 20 October, his doctor noticed that he was 'overflowing with her praises.' Ignoring his doctor's advice, he attended a meeting of Trinity House, the general lighthouse and pilotage authority, in which both he and the Queen ranked as Elder Brethren. Lord Moran complained to his diary, 'It was no use trying to persuade him to give up the [event] when the Queen was going.'[24]

On 23 November, when it was finally time for the Queen and her entourage to set off on her journey, nothing could dissuade Churchill from travelling to London airport to see her off, even though his doctor feared that after a hard day of politicking, he would be unsteady on his feet. He brushed aside these concerns. Queen Elizabeth was to be the first British Sovereign to travel completely around the world, and Churchill would not miss it for, well, the world. He took up his position on the tarmac at around seven o'clock, waiting for over an hour with his fellow ministers for the Queen's limousine, bearing the royal standard, to drive along the crowd-lined airport road. As the Sovereign took her leave from the gathered well-wishers, it was Churchill, her veteran Prime Minister, with whom she had her final parting words.[25]

Exactly one week later, as the Queen and Prince Philip made their way across the Pacific Ocean towards Fiji on board the SS *Gothic*, they did not forget to send Winston a cheerful message of congratulations: he was celebrating his seventy-ninth birthday. Churchill responded immediately. 'I am deeply honoured by the kind telegram I have received from Your Majesty and the Duke of Edinburgh. I do hope the sun shines and the seas are smooth.'[26]

Churchill's intention to retire upon the Queen's return from her tour was only informally declared to his inner circle, and as the year drew to a close, his commitment to it began to waver. On 17 December, he told his son-in-law Christopher Soames, 'I may go in a month's time, or wait till the Queen returns. Probably I shall wait.' Christopher laughed and replied, 'You will wait till the Queen returns and then you will find a reason why you must carry on.' Winston feigned a jolly ignorance, and with a smile said, 'I don't know why you should say that.'[27]

When the Queen wrote to Churchill at Christmas, the *Gothic* was finally approaching Fiji. Churchill took a week to write a thoughtful response, which he sent on New Year's Day. 'My wife and I cherish this token of Yr Majesty's thought,' he told her. 'Today I have the belief that the New Year starts well and good hopes that its end may be better still. If this sh[oul]d prove true it will be largely due to the sparkle, youth and unity which the amazing exertions of Yr Majesty and the Duke are making for the sake of our world-wide but hard-pressed combination.' He ended his letter with a word of concern: 'My only misgiving is lest too much may be drawn from You by the love and admiration of your subjects in so many lands.'[28]

This concern – that those around the Queen were demanding too much of her, or that enthusiastic crowds would push her to exhaustion – became a familiar theme. He should not have worried as the young Queen and her consort undertook all their official duties with grace, elegance, and humour.

While the Queen was away, Churchill met with both Princess Margaret and the Queen Mother in their capacity as counsellors of state for official audiences at Buckingham Palace. After one meeting in March, the Queen Mother wrote to the Queen to express her admiration for the dogged premier: 'What a privilege to have lived in his day – He is a truly great man.'[29] Great he may have been, but for his colleagues, his continual prevarication regarding his retirement was a source of frustration.

Now in his eightieth year, Churchill behaved like an excited schoolboy as the Queen sailed through the Mediterranean on board the new royal yacht, HMY *Britannia*. He planned to meet the boat at the Needles, a small archipelago off the western coast of the Isle of Wight, and sail up the river Thames with the Queen and Prince Philip.

On 14 May, Churchill mounted the gangway – 'Quite a remarkable achievement,' as Jock Colville commented – to board the *Britannia* and be reunited with his Sovereign. Together they sailed past Cowes, where the Queen's great-grandfather Bertie, Prince of Wales, had introduced Churchill's parents, before entering the mouth of the mightiest of British rivers. The Queen, wearied by her travel, was disinclined to notice anything special about the 'dirty commercial river,' as she described the Thames. But Churchill's words had the power evoke the river's beauty and mystique. 'He was describing it as the silver thread which runs through the history of Britain,' Elizabeth later remarked, struck by Churchill's uncanny ability to turn the trivial into the tremendous. He saw things, she realized, 'in a very romantic and glittering way; perhaps one was looking at it in a rather too mundane way'.[30]

It was just the Queen's mundanity, though, which filled Churchill with admiration for the young monarch: he was completely taken in by Elizabeth's casual, approachable demeanour. 'She is so completely natural,' he told Moran upon his return, more enamoured than ever.[31]

Three days later, he delivered a formal address of welcome in the House of Commons. He told the crammed House that, during the couple's arduous tour, 'Even Envy wore a friendly smile.' He praised the Queen's stamina and poise and the limitless 'reinforcement which this Royal journey may have brought to the health, the wisdom, the sanity and hopefulness of mankind.'[32] Then it was down to the serious business: racing. He cut short a Cabinet meeting on 2 June so that he and his ministers could attend the Queen at the Epsom Derby. Though her horse Landau did not win the Derby itself, she was thrilled when Aureole won the Coronation Cup the following day. [33]

Later that month, Churchill took part in what was possibly the most glorious ritual of his long and storied career, the Ceremony of the Garter. His long-time bodyguard Walter Thompson called it 'the crowning honour of Winston's life.' In the wood-panelled Throne Room at Windsor Castle, with summer sunshine flooding through the large bay windows, the Queen buckled the jewelled Garter below Churchill's left knee and bestowed upon him the Riband and the Star, the mantle collar, and the chain – a suitably long list of regalia for Britain's most venerable politician. After a traditional luncheon with the other Knights Companion, the group walked – Winston beaming the whole way as he led the procession – to St George's chapel, where the Queen announced Churchill's installation and Lord Halifax proclaimed his newly minted title: 'The Right Honourable Sir Winston Leonard Spencer Churchill.' As Thompson recalled, 'A moment of absolute silence followed. It was as though the ghosts of the knights of the past were looking down on this most memorable occasion.'[34]

Though it was the Queen's sole prerogative to confer honours, Winston paid back her gifts in full measure. Churchill was much more than a Prime Minister with certain constitutional rights and duties. His was in a unique position. Over the years, he had become a family advisor, friend and confidante who kept a constant watchful eye on the status and integrity of the monarchy. Hence the expenditure of time, energy and political capital on the issue of the Windsor file, or the trouble he took to gently guide the Queen Mother back into public life. This policy paid off handsomely in the autumn of 1954, when the Queen Mother embarked on a three-week solo tour of the United States and Canada. Initially apprehensive, she was confident enough by the end of the trip, having charmed her hosts so thoroughly, that she realized she could be an ambassador for Britain. As her biographer William Shawcross observed, 'Her success stimulated her; now she could see that she could play a useful part in promoting both the monarchy and Britain herself in overseas visits.'[35]

On her return she was praised to the heavens, but none of the kind words mattered as much as the warm approval she received from Winston: 'The maintenance, and continuous improvement, of friendship between the English-speaking peoples, and more especially between these Islands and the great North American Democracies, is the safeguard of the future,' he wrote. 'Your Majesty has made a notable contribution to this end.'[36]

Later that month, Winston celebrated his eightieth birthday, making him the first Prime Minister since that great Victorian, William Gladstone, to reach that milestone while in office. A sign of his universal popularity was demonstrated in the 30,000 birthday cards and 900 presents he received from the general public. Although there was still no immediate plan in place for him to step down, the occasion was marked with all due celebration from the whole royal family. The Queen presented him with a gift of silver wine coasters, engraved with initials from the entire clan: the Queen and Philip, of course, as well as the Queen Mother, Princess Margaret, the Duke and Duchess of Gloucestershire, Princess Mary (the Princess Royal, and Elizabeth's aunt), Duchess Marina of Kent, Princess Alice and the Earl of Athlone.[37] It was a long roster of all the extant royals that Churchill had known and served for so many decades. He responded a few days later, thanking the Queen for the present, which he called 'a source of intense pleasure and pride to me and my wife.'[38]

As much as he cherished the coasters, another gesture from the Queen was likely to have flattered him even more, namely a 'subscription' to Aureole – that is, a chance for Churchill to breed the late King's prize horse with a mare of his own. When Churchill had been asked, three years before, whether he would retire Colonist II and put him out to stud,

Winston had replied, 'To stud? And have it said that the Prime Minister of Great Britain is living off the immoral earnings of a horse?'[39] But hardly anyone could have expected Churchill to turn down the honour of claiming the offspring of the Queen's own champion. He told Elizabeth that he was 'much obliged,' and promised that he would 'buy the most suitable mare I can find in the December sales and hope for the future.[40]

Apart from these touching gifts, Churchill received an alloy bust of the Duke of Windsor from the ex-King himself. He placed it at the head of the main stairway at Chartwell, a daily reminder that Churchill had, for a time, attempted to be the servant of two masters.[41]

At the beginning of February, the Queen hosted a dinner for the Commonwealth Prime Ministers at Buckingham Palace. It was just the kind of occasion that Churchill enjoyed, seeing the leaders of British territories gathered around the Sovereign, united in a common purpose. He was, though, shocked when the former Labour Prime Minister Clement Attlee approached him, quivering, and then fainted in his arms.[42] Eight years Attlee's senior, and in less than perfect health himself, Churchill recognized the episode as an ill omen. It was time to bow out.

He began to make concrete plans for his own retirement, when the torch would be passed to his deputy, Anthony Eden, now fully recovered. The cornerstone event of Winston's departure was a dinner at 10 Downing Street with the Queen as guest of honour. He wrote jokingly to Michael Adeane, who had taken over for Tommy Lascelles as the Queen's private secretary, 'I do not think we shall have to go down to the dug-out in the midst of our proceedings, as we several times had to do in those bygone days.' But in one sense, the dinner kept with the wartime precedent, in that the plans were, as Jock Colville recorded, a 'closely guarded' secret.[43]

Even with these plans in motion, Churchill was tempted to try and stay in power for a little longer. At the end of March, he had an audience with the Queen and told her that he was considering delaying his resignation. He asked if she would mind, and astonishingly – whether out of deference to his age and position or from familial affection – she responded that she would not.[44] After further reflection, though, he stuck to the original course, writing to Adeane on the morning of 31 March to ask him to inform the Queen of his decision to resign on 5 April. Adeane replied the same day with the Queen's carefully worded acknowledgment: 'Her Majesty said at once that she was most grateful to you telling her privately of your intention and that I was to emphasize in replying to you that she fully understood why it was that when she received you last Tuesday there still seemed to be some uncertainty about the future.' The Queen made sure to seal the deal, giving her approval to Winston's announcement in the constitutionally correct manner: 'She added that I must tell you that though she recognized your wisdom in taking the decision which you had, she felt the greatest personal regrets and that she would especially miss the weekly audiences which she has found so instructive and, if one can say so of State matters, so entertaining.'[45]

This piece of housekeeping out of the way, Winston set to writing the toast he would make on 4 April, the eve of his official resignation. In his speech, he reflected on his early years, telling the fifty guests of the toasts 'which I used to enjoy drinking during the years when I was a Cavalry Subaltern in the Reign of Your Majesty's Great-great-Grandmother, Queen Victoria.' Speaking on behalf of the entire Commonwealth, he professed a 'deep and lively sense of gratitude' for all the 'help and inspiration' that the Queen and Prince Philip provided. 'Never,' Churchill concluded, 'have the august duties which fall upon the British Monarchy been discharged with more devotion than in the brilliant opening of Your Majesty's reign. We thank God for the gifts he has bestowed upon us and vow ourselves anew to the sacred causes and wise and kindly way of life of which Your Majesty is the young, gleaming champion.'[46]

After a lively dinner, the Queen stopped outside the threshold of

10 Downing Street, giving the waiting photographers the chance to capture an historic moment, her long-serving Prime Minister bowing to his Queen. When everyone had left, a deflated Churchill went up to his bedroom with Jock, who recorded that the old bulldog 'sat on his bed, still wearing his Garter, Order of Merit and knee-breeches.' When Churchill was silent for several minutes, Jock assumed that it was because he was overcome with emotion on such a significant and final night; until, that is, Churchill blurted out, 'I don't believe Anthony can do it.'[47]

In spite of his last-minute doubts about his successor, Churchill went through with his resignation, donning his frock coat and top hat before making his way to Buckingham Palace to ask his Sovereign's permission to resign. In spite of his resolve, what he encountered in the audience rattled him deeply. During their conversation the Queen offered him a dukedom.

The gesture had been carefully planned. The Queen had wanted to make the offer, as a symbolic gesture of the country's gratitude for his many decades of service. On the other hand, it had been decided by the palace that no more dukedoms, except to royal personages, would ever be created. Nonetheless, Jock Colville felt that it would be appropriate for the Queen to offer and pushed Michael Adeane to ask the Queen to do so. This, though, was only on the explicit guarantee – made by Jock himself – that Churchill would refuse the offer once it was made. Winston had no wish to move to the House of Lords. For one thing, he earnestly wanted to die a commoner, and for another, his elevation would have hindered the political career of his son Randolph. Taking Churchill at his word, Jock advised Adeane that the Queen could offer him dukedom in the full confidence that it would be refused.

Yet, as Colville watched the Prime Minister head to Buckingham Palace, refreshed after a good night's sleep, he had his doubts, 'knowing as I did that he was madly in love with the Queen.' It was possible, after all, that in a moment of rheumy-eyed sentimentality, Churchill might reverse course and accept. When he returned to 10 Downing Street, Colville asked coyly, 'How did it go?'

The great man's eyes brimmed with tears. 'Do you know, the most remarkable thing – she offered to make me a Duke ... I very nearly accepted, I was so moved by her beauty and her charm and the kindness with which she made this offer, that for a moment I thought of accepting. But finally I remembered that I must die as I have always been – Winston Churchill. And so I asked her to forgive my not accepting it. And do you know, it's an odd thing, but she seemed almost relieved.'[48]

CHAPTER EIGHTEEN

'I Have Done My Best'

S HORTLY AFTER CHURCHILL finally retired, he and Clementine boarded a plane bound for Sicily for a much-deserved two-week holiday. Before he settled into his seat, a messenger handed him an eight-page handwritten letter from the Queen. She did not want her first Prime Minister's departure to go unremarked. 'I need not tell you,' she wrote, 'how deeply I felt your resignation last Tuesday, nor how severely I miss, and shall continue to miss, your advice and encouragement.' Although she had the utmost confidence in Eden's preparedness and competence for the role, she admitted that 'it would be useless to pretend that either he or any of those successors who may one day follow him in office will ever, for me, be able to hold the place of my first Prime Minister.' Indeed, many years later, she admitted that Winston was her favourite. He had entered her life at a time of daunting personal trial, family crisis and constitutional stress. During the period of her life where she was most inexperienced, he had guided and advised her, helping to bring her family into safe harbour. And yet none of this was the reason she gave for preferring him above the others: instead, it was because their meetings were 'always such fun,' she recalled.[1] (There were, though, whispers that their relationship could be tricky. As historian Piers Brendon observes: 'There are strong suggestions, too, that the Queen found Churchill stubborn, anachronistic, unwilling to listen and apt to mistake monologue for conversation.'[2]) She reminded him that his services to the nation had earned the deep gratitude of her father, King George VI, who had 'joined his people and the peoples of the whole free world in acknowledging a debt of deep and sincere thankfulness.' As she concluded her affectionate and historic letter, she struck the same tone that her father had done following Churchill's electoral defeat in the summer of 1945: 'I know that in losing my constitutional adviser I gain a wise counsellor to whom I shall not look in vain for help and support in the days which lie ahead. May there be many of them.'[3]

Winston took his time in writing a thoughtful and equally heartfelt response, informing the Queen that he had been 'honoured and cheered' by her letter, which 'will always be one of my most treasured possessions.' He then went into a resume of his time as her Prime Minister and in so doing described the Queen's many virtues:

> Very soon after taking office as First Minister, I realized the comprehension with which Your Majesty entered upon the august duties of a modern Sovereign and the store of knowledge which had already been gathered by an upbringing both wise and lively. This enabled Your Majesty to understand as it seemed by instinct the relationships and the balances of the British constitution so deeply cherished by the mass of the Nation and by the strongest and most stable forces in it. I became conscious of the Royal resolve to serve as well as rule, and indeed to rule by serving ... I regard it as the most direct mark of God's favour we have ever received in my long life that the whole structure of our new formed Commonwealth has been linked and illuminated by a sparkling presence at its summit.

His glowing tribute was a far cry from his initial reaction to her accession, when he dismissed her as 'only a child.' After praising the Duke of Edinburgh and describing his own plans for a peaceful retirement full of painting and writing, he closed his letter in a vein of nostalgia: 'All this is agreeable to the mental and psychological processes of laying down direct responsibility for the guidance of great affairs and falling back upon the comforting reflection 'I have done my best'.[4]

Though he did indeed spend his days painting and reading through the proofs of his book, *A History of the English-Speaking Peoples*, he was constantly kept up to speed on significant events by Prime Minister Anthony Eden, the Queen, and others. He became the backstop's backstop, on occasion advising both the Queen and Prime Minister Eden on tricky issues.

In January 1956, for instance, when Churchill was wintering at La Pausa, the villa of his Hungarian friend Emery Reves, the Queen asked her private secretary Michael Adeane to send Churchill a detailed description of her plans for an upcoming trip to Nigeria – brochures of their travel arrangements, people she expected to meet and ceremonies that she hoped to undertake. 'It is very kind of Your Majesty to think of me at this hour of departure,' he wrote in reply. He admitted that he had been worried about her itinerary 'and all the exertions and sacrifices Your Majesty makes for the public interest.' Throughout his retirement, he continued to worry that the Queen would over-tax herself in her immense effort to do right by her realm. 'I pray she may come home safely,' he wrote to Clementine. 'She works hard!'[5] In response to her briefing, he promised to send her a copy of his latest volume of *A History of the English-Speaking Peoples*, which was due out in April. Churchill was as good as his word, having two copies specially bound and inscribed in his own hand. Of course, the first went to the Queen, who replied promptly from Sandringham that she was 'much touched' and that she looked 'forward keenly to reading it and the subsequent volumes – I have already heard great praise for this first one.' The other copy went to Queen Elizabeth, the Queen Mother, who called it a 'glorious book'.[6] Churchill would later describe the more matter-of-fact response of the Duke of Windsor when he received one of his books. 'Thank you for the book,' the duke wrote, 'I've put it on the shelf with all the others.' His off-hand letter always gave Churchill a chuckle. Although the Windsors came to La Pausa from time to time, there was none of the closeness that might be expected between two men who had undergone so much together. He was dismissive of the man for whom he had done so much, though his pity for the duke's precipitous fall from grace was a constant. On one occasion he wistfully told his private secretary, Anthony Montague Browne, 'He showed such promise. Morning glory.'[7]

During his retirement, Winston wasn't just seen as a national treasure; he graduated to the status of living legend and was treated like an auxiliary member of the royal family. On his birthdays, the postman worked overtime to deliver cards and gifts from well-wishers. Roses, daisies and other flowers were named after him,[8] he was applauded when he visited the roulette tables at Monte Carlo[9] and found himself mobbed during a visit to New York in 1959.[10] His increasingly infrequent appearances in the House of Commons – he became Father of the House in 1959 – were greeted with wild cheering and the waving of order papers.

But despite all this public adulation, Churchill's health rapidly declined. He missed the thrust of politics to keep his mind and body engaged. In early 1953, he had confessed to his doctor, 'I feel that if I retired now it might do me a lot of harm.'[11] His downhearted projection proved right. By the summer of 1956, when he attended a Garter ceremony, he found that he was unable to stand up, even when 'God Save the Queen' was sung out. 'My legs felt wobbly,' he reported.[12] Nor was he able to attend the races as much as he wanted. In October, he wrote to Clementine to proudly announce that his horse had triumphed over the royal colours – 'I hope the Queen is not too vexed at being beaten,' he wrote. 'It was just as well I wasn't there as there w[oul]d have been embarrassing cheers and counter-cheers.'[13]

Although Winston was increasingly unable to take part in these events the way he had, for so long, revelled in doing, there was still one signal service that he was called upon to perform. Anthony Eden, in the aftermath of the Suez Canal Crisis, was forced to resign from the premiership. It was far from clear who his successor ought to be, the two most viable candidates being the time-tested Rab Butler or the younger, more energetic Harold Macmillan. Party sentiments were divided, and

Churchill's private secretary, Anthony Montague Browne, felt that it would only be appropriate for the great man to be consulted: 'It is by no means abnormal for the Sovereign to consult senior figures, and WSC was something very much more than that. If his views had not been taken, the omission might have been interpreted as indicating his disapproval of the Queen's choice.'[14]

Montague Browne badgered the Palace to secure the meeting. Michael Adeane, under considerable pressure during the first parliamentary crisis of his tenure, tried to slough off the request, suggesting instead that he himself should travel to Chartwell, in the Queen's place, to make a public gesture of consulting Churchill for his views. Montague Browne persisted. 'I did not feel that this would adequately indicate the thoroughness of consultation and satisfy public opinion,' he reflected. But there was another motive for his doggedness: 'I knew what a stimulant such a summons would be for WSC. The country, and its Sovereign, owed him full and proper recognition and at the lowest valuation it could do no harm.' Finally, Adeane relented and invited Winston to Buckingham Palace for the following day.[15]

So it was that on 10 January 1957, Winston, aged eighty-two, drove from his country house in Kent to London, a rug featuring the Union Jack covering his now-knobby knees. He entered Buckingham Palace as he had done so many times before, though this time far less stable on his feet, and he delivered his view that Harold Macmillan would be the best option to take Eden's place. But he was less than confident in his suggestion, having been outside of politics for nearly two years. As he left the audience, a courtier heard him remark, 'I said Macmillan. Is that right?' It was. Within a few hours, Macmillan was summoned to the palace and appointed Prime Minister.[16]

Just as Montague Browne had predicted, Churchill was delighted at being asked for his opinion. When he returned home after the audience, he told his son-in-law, Christopher Soames, all about the experience. What Christopher wanted to know was whether Churchill had remembered, in all the excitement, to bring his trademark top hat. 'Oh yes,' the old man replied. 'But it's getting very shabby; as there may be more than one of these consultations in the future I must get a new one.'[17] If he did in fact get a new hat, it sat in solemn desuetude, for this was to be the final time that Winston Churchill was ever officially consulted on matters of British government. He had played his final innings as the backstop's backstop.

As a lifelong believer in the magic and mystique of the British monarchy, he was affronted in August 1957 by a direct attack on the Queen and those who surrounded her. John Grigg, the 2nd Baron Altrincham, argued in his own paper, the *National and English Review*, that Elizabeth's court was stuffy and elitist, comprised of the 'tweedy sort', and that the Queen herself needed to change once she had aged. What was so offensive to Churchill and others was that it was written by 'one of us', a sprig on the tree of the British aristocracy. But just as much, Churchill was pained that so much of the article dwelt on the inadequacies in the Queen's character. 'When she has lost the bloom of youth,' Grigg had written, 'the Queen's reputation will depend, far more than it does now, upon her personality. It will not then be enough for her to go through the motions; she will have to say things which people can remember, and do things on her own initiative which will make people sit up and take notice. As yet there is little sign that such a personality is emerging.' For Churchill, who was rather in love with the Queen, this was an insult too far. During lunch at 10 Downing Street with Harold Macmillan on 8 August, he was 'splendidly indignant about Lord Altrincham's ... foolish attack on the Queen.'[18] The Queen herself was less offended and quietly invited Altrincham to the palace to flesh out his constructive criticisms. Three decades later, the Queen having aged and the monarchy still resilient and popular, the Queen's private secretary Martin Charteris acknowledged that Grigg had rendered 'a great service to the monarchy'.[19]

Churchill wouldn't live long enough to see it that way. Nor, though he was a highly respected historian, did he agree with the work of fellow historians on the controversial Windsor file. In August 1957, at the same time as the Altrincham criticisms, came the long-awaited publication of Volume X Series D, containing the Duke of Windsor's unguarded comments about the direction of the war. In 1945, when Churchill was first made aware of the German foreign office documents relating to the Duke of Windsor's wartime comments during his sojourn in Spain and Portugal, his first instinct was to destroy the files. The new Prime Minister, Clement Attlee, had agreed, as had the American high command. This policy was shown to be impractical given the number of people who had access to the file, especially American historians, and it was modified to a strategy of delay.

As Churchill had hoped, the files' publication proved to be something of an anticlimax. The Foreign Office worked hard to brief journalists on the angle that the duke was an innocent party caught in a web of Nazi intrigue. To emphasize the point, an official Foreign Office notice was inserted into every copy of Volume X defending the duke. It read in part, 'His Royal Highness never wavered in his loyalty to the British cause or in his determination to take up his official post as Governor of the Bahamas on the date agreed. The German records are necessarily a much-tainted source. The only firm evidence is of what the Germans were trying to do in the matter, and of how completely they failed to do it.' It does beg the question of why, if the files were so inconsequential and demonstrably false, Churchill and others had expended so much political and personal capital trying to expunge them from the record. If anything, Churchill's spats with the duke in 1940 about his personal demands when Britain was in danger of being overrun by the Nazis were just as damning as the Windsor file, if not more so. But Churchill was only being consistent, concerned that criticism of the duke could bleed over into the institution he most revered, the monarchy.

The other institution he supported unreservedly was the military. During a dinner at Buckingham Palace in November, Churchill informed the Queen that he intended to be present at the upcoming Armistice Day ceremony. He had attended the traditional commemorative service at the

Cenotaph almost without fail since 1920, and though increasingly infirm, he could not bear to miss it. The Queen, personally aware of the great man's increasing frailty, was concerned that the drearily cold late-autumn weather would gravely affect his heath. She asked Michael Adeane to write privately to Churchill, excusing him from attending: 'Indeed Her Majesty hopes that you will not take the smallest risk to your health by prolonged exposure to November weather which this ceremony entails.' Churchill was flattered at the Queen's concern, but it did not matter – he bundled up and made his way to Whitehall just the same.[20]

The Queen's instincts proved correct. Within three months, while holidaying in the south of France, Churchill was struck down by a severe case of bronchial pneumonia which left him shivering violently. Even though Lord Moran flew to Nice, the infection spread. Buckingham Palace asked for regular updates to keep the Queen informed, and once Churchill had begun his slow recovery, the Queen was anxious to hear from him directly. He sent a message to London that very day: 'My Wife and I are deeply grateful to your Majesty for your most kind inquiries.'[21]

Under Lord Moran's care, Winston eventually recovered, but the episode disturbed Queen Elizabeth deeply. For the first time, it seems, she fully realized that Winston was not as immortal as he seemed, and that he could in fact die at any moment. She took it upon herself to initiate the plans for his funeral, wanting the commemoration to reflect Churchill's status in British national and, indeed, imperial history. Nothing short of a state funeral, with a lying-in-state at Westminster Hall, would suffice. He would be only the third Prime Minister, after Arthur Wellesley, the 1st Duke of Wellington, and William Gladstone, to be so honoured.[22]

Even with the Queen's imprimatur, however, there was serious push-back to the plan, codenamed 'Operation Hope Not'. At a Garter meeting in the summer of 1959, palace courtiers voiced their concerns that if Churchill's funeral was on the scale suggested by the Queen, it would overshadow the funerals given to royal personages. This could not stand, given that Churchill – decorated and esteemed though he undoubtedly was – was nonetheless a 'commoner'. There was also concern about inviting members of the French and American armed forces, as well as civil defence and Commonwealth officers, to march in the ceremony. Not only would it be difficult to know where to stop, but the procession would end up longer than that of a reigning monarch.[23] When Churchill himself got to hear about the plan for a state funeral, he told his private secretary to ensure that there were lots of marching bands. There were nine on the day.[24]

In the last years of Churchill's life, communication between himself and the Queen grew more infrequent, but also more informal and sentimental. In May of 1960, Winston sent the Queen a painting he had made, a landscape of a town called Wilton, where Winston had attended Whitsuntide so often that the locals referred to the festival as 'Winstontide'. The Queen wrote to him in her own hand to express her thanks: 'Philip and I are so thrilled to have one of your pictures for our gallery,' she wrote. 'What a truly lovely place Wilton is and you have captured the feeling and the pleasure of being there so well that all can feel it too.'[25]

Also in May, the Queen and her first Prime Minister had another chance to exchange pleasantries when they gathered, amongst a full congregation, in Westminster Abbey to celebrate the wedding of Princess Margaret to the fashion photographer Antony Armstrong-Jones. When Margaret had finally turned twenty-five in August of 1955, just four months after Winston's retirement, the question had been re-opened as to whether she would renounce her place in the line of succession in order to marry Group Captain Peter Townsend. The pair were reunited after a year, but their courtship floundered. Margaret decided against staining the name of the monarchy by marrying a divorcee, and instead adhered to the teachings of the Anglican faith. Four and a half years later, she became engaged to Armstrong-Jones. As the Queen filed into the Abbey on 6 May to take her front-row seat for the nuptials, her retinue passed right by Winston Churchill. The two exchanged a friendly smile of recognition, as if they were, together, on the inside of a shared, private joke.[26]

A few months later, Winston was delighted to receive a telegram from the Queen and Prince Philip during their tour of Pakistan. 'We both send you our best wishes from Malakand,' the plain but thoughtful message read.[27] How that one simple line must have taken him back – Malakand, of course, being the place where a young Churchill had fought in the armed forces of the Queen's great-great-grandmother, and the scene for the first book he ever published, *The Story of the Malakand Field Force*, which had received such generous praise from King Edward VII, then Prince Albert of Wales. The wheel had come full circle.

Perhaps it was on account of such friendly exchanges that Churchill felt he maintained, in some small way, a certain sway over the Queen's decisions. He tried to exert that influence the following year by attempting to dissuade her from making a trip to Ghana. The West African country, under the leadership of Prime Minister Kwame Nkrumah, had been granted independence three years before, and though it remained in the Commonwealth, the Soviets were trying to encourage the new nation to abandon it in favour of the Communist sphere of influence. Churchill worried, firstly, for the Queen's physical safety, but also that her visit would appear to endorse Nkrumah's socialist regime and give succour to other fidgety Commonwealth members. After consulting with Anthony Eden, Winston sent a letter to Prime Minister Macmillan, urging him to formally advise the Queen to abandon her plans – advice which she would be constitutionally bound to take. 'Nkrumah's vilification of this country and his increasing association with our enemies does not encourage one to think that his country could ever be more than an opportunist member of the Commonwealth family,' he wrote. Macmillan, though sympathetic to Churchill's feelings, emphasized that the Queen was adamant that she should go: 'This is natural with so courageous a personality,' he wrote admiringly.[28]

Despite the nay-sayers and their security concerns, the Queen's visit was a roaring success: she danced with Nkrumah at a formal ball, she returned several Ashanti furniture pieces which had been on display at Windsor Castle since the nineteenth century, and she reviewed the armed forces at a welcome parade in front of a hundred thousand exuberant Ghanaians. Thanks to her personable manner, her non-judgmental presence, and her courage in being willing to make the journey in the first place, Ghana and its fellow African Commonwealth states could see the value of membership of this voluntary association, one that could restore, recognize and celebrate the cultural diversity of its members. If the visit proved anything, it showed that the Queen was now an old hand at the monarchy game, an ingenue no longer. There came a turning moment in her reign – and this very well might have been it – past which her Prime Ministers needed her, much more than she needed them.

Three months later, to mark the ten-year anniversary of the Queen's accession, in February 1962, Churchill wrote a short congratulatory note: 'I would like to express to Your Majesty my fervent hopes and wishes for many happy years to come. It is with pride that I recall that I was your Prime Minister at the inception of these ten years of devoted service to our country.' The Queen responded the following day, saying she was 'most touched' by his letter. 'I shall always count myself fortunate that you were my Prime Minister at the beginning of my reign,' she wrote, 'and that I was able to receive the wise counsel and also friendship which I know my father valued so very much as well.'[29]

Perhaps appropriately, this exchange of letters was to be their last preserved correspondence. Churchill was no longer able to take part in any official ceremonies, while at the informal gatherings he continued to attend, his friends winced to see his diminished vigour. 'It was tragic to see him,' Lascelles wrote in his diary, 'and to hear the universal comment, "Poor old man – they ought not to let him come out to dinner now."'[30]

Churchill suffered a serious stroke on 10 January 1964. When the news broke a few days later, a tide of sorrow and concern swept the country. The following Sunday, churches across the nation offered prayers for his health – including St Lawrence Church, where the Queen was in attendance, in the Norfolk village of Castle Rising near Sandringham. In Westminster Abbey, the Archbishop of York told his congregants, 'Again and again he has found the right words for the right occasion, and rallied faltering nations in the hour of trial.'[31]

Churchill never fully recovered from the latest stroke, which left him drained and weak. He died just over a year later, on the morning of Sunday, 24 January, seventy years to the day after the death of his father, Lord Randolph Churchill. The Queen, who was again at Sandringham, immediately sent her condolences to Clementine. 'The news of Sir Winston Churchill's death caused inexpressible grief to me and my husband ... The whole world is the poorer by the loss of his many-sided genius while the survival of this country and the sister nations of the Commonwealth in the face of the greatest danger that has ever threatened them will be a perpetual memorial to his leadership, his vision, and his indomitable courage.'[32] The Queen was not only the sender, but also the recipient of condolences. French President de Gaulle wrote, 'In the great drama he was the greatest of all.' Even the newly appointed Prime Minister of the Soviet Union wrote to say that the Russians 'remember the untiring efforts of Sir Winston Churchill in the years of the war against Hitlerite Germany.'[33] In the House of Lords, Lord Attlee, the one-time Labour leader and deputy Prime Minister during the war, said of him: 'He had sympathy, incredibly wide sympathy for ordinary people all over the world. My Lords we have lost the great Englishman of our time – I think the greatest citizen of the world of our time.'[34]

As the tributes poured in, the Queen launched Operation Hope Not, for which she needed approval from both Houses of Parliament. She immediately sent a message to be presented in each chamber: 'Confident in the support of Parliament for the due acknowledgement of our debt of gratitude and in thanksgiving for the life and example of a national hero,' it concluded, 'I have directed that Sir Winston's body shall lie in State in Westminster Hall and that thereafter the funeral service shall be held in the Cathedral Church of St Paul.'[35] But this was mere formality: it was unthinkable that either house would veto the state tribute to the fallen hero.[36]

During Winston's lying-in-state, which took place over three days, more than 320,000 people filed past his body to pay their final respects. One of these was the Queen herself, breaking with precedent and becoming the first-ever reigning British Sovereign to publicly pay such homage to a commoner. She, along with Prince Philip, Princess Margaret, and Margaret's husband, now known by the title of Lord Snowdon, quietly entered the hall through the west door and stood next to the catafalque for five minutes as the other mourners filed past, hardly noticing the gathered royals who stood respectfully off to one side.[37]

At nine forty-five on Saturday morning, as Churchill's coffin was removed from Westminster, Big Ben sounded the quarter hour and fell silent. It would remain silent, as it had been for so many dark days of war, for the duration of the funeral for the man who had seen Britain to victory. Millions watched the unique ceremony on television, with broadcaster Richard Dimbleby guiding viewers through the service. Outside the abbey, the coffin was wrapped in a Union flag with Winston's Garter regalia placed on top, before it was loaded onto the same gun carriage that had been used to transport Queen Victoria's remains sixty-five years before. Much had changed since Churchill and his family were denied access to the abbey to pay their respects to the fallen Edward VII – and now, as his body made its way from Westminster to St Paul's Cathedral, half a million grateful Britons stood in the frigid January morning to pay their final respects.[38]

When the coffin arrived at St Paul's, everything was in its place – including, remarkably, the Queen of England. She had decided, as Mary Soames recorded, to waive 'all custom and precedence', which dictated that she ought to arrive last, preferring to await 'the arrival of her greatest subject'.[39] It was, as his grandson Sir Nicholas Soames recalled, 'a beautiful and very touching gesture'.[40] Once Churchill's coffin was unloaded from the gun carriage, it was carefully carried up the steps by eight Grenadier guards, into the cathedral where 3,000 mourners from 112 nations waited in sombre silence.[41] It was a sign of his global appeal that the congregation included five monarchs, sixteen Prime Ministers, and six heads of state. One notable absentee, to make the tableaux complete, was the Duke of Windsor, who was recovering from an eye operation in a London hospital.

Following the service, Churchill's coffin was transferred to the MV *Havengore* to be motored down the Thames. One of the most memorable moments came when a row of cranes on the bank of the great British river bowed their necks in respect as the watercraft passed. At Festival Pier, on the South Bank, the coffin was dismounted and taken to Waterloo station, where it was then loaded onto a Churchill-class locomotive bound for Bladon in Oxfordshire, his parents' burial place. Among the passengers on board the train was Sir Leslie Rowan, one of Churchill's wartime private secretaries. Rowan was moved by the displays of grief and gratitude from common people along the route: one middle-aged man, wearing his old RAF uniform, stood on his roof, rigidly saluting the train as it passed by his home. When the procession finally reached Winston's gravesite, the coffin was shrouded in hundreds of floral tributes. One wreath, all white, stood out from the rest. In its centre was a simple note, written in the Queen's own hand: 'From the Nation and the Commonwealth. In grateful remembrance. Elizabeth R.'[42]

Churchill's passing was much more than a funeral, it was, in the words of Lady Churchill, 'a triumph,' a national and international waypoint that highlighted how Churchill's Britain, nay world, had changed. When he was born – in a palace, to a storied aristocratic family – the British Empire was at its zenith under the august reign of Queen Victoria. In those days, a silver spoon and a country estate were almost mandatory prerequisites for those aspiring to political success. Now, the Prime Minister was Harold Wilson of the socialist Labour Party, the son of a chemist who was born in a tiny, terraced house in the mill town of Huddersfield. While Winston had taken part in the last British Army cavalry charge, Wilson saluted the 'white heat of technology' to take Britain into the future.

Although the funeral ceremony provoked reflection on the drastic changes in the country from the invention of automobiles, planes, tanks, radio, telephones, television, and – most strikingly of all – nuclear weaponry, the touching ceremonial also highlighted how much had remained the same. The monarchy, thanks in part to Winston's tenacity and advocacy, had avoided or weathered numerous crises, though the abdication crisis had found him on the wrong side of the argument.

His had been by no means a smooth induction into the trusted inner circle of the royal family ranks. In his early days in Parliament he, together with Lloyd George, was a youthful advocate for radical change in the social order, with a focus on reducing the influence of the House of Lords. The royal family treated him with suspicion and, at times, contempt. He could be an irritating thorn in the side of the royal house. Nonetheless, his reverence for constitutional monarchy was unwavering, though his attitude to several of the incumbents was not as respectful as they might have wished. He enjoyed the pomp and paraphernalia of a grand parade, but was aware that power should belong elsewhere. The separation of pomp from power was, to his mind, central to the success of a constitutional monarchy. It was this interpretation of the constitution that caused him, from time to time, to push back against the holders of the office. No czars or kaisers wanted here.

His long association with the House of Windsor, particularly during the war years, assured Churchill of semi-royal status himself. With the passing years, he was treated as almost as much a symbol of constitutional monarchy as the very monarch, his image in the public mind defined by his morale-boosting visits to bomb sites in the company of the King and Queen as well as the famous balcony scene at Buckingham Palace to celebrate VE Day. His high-flown language was, to misquote him, a flash of colour that not only lifted spirits during the war years but also helped define and redefine the House of Windsor. His speeches were so memorable that often King George VI, hearing them on the wireless, was inspired enough to take them down in his diary verbatim. For decades, it was Churchill's soaring language, carried by his trademark booming, slurred voice, which marked the beginnings and ends of reigns, a royal marriage, an abdication, the end of the Second – and hopefully, the last – World War, and so much more. Though there were times, as with the televising of Queen Elizabeth's coronation, where he was more ancient than modern, Churchill was a prime mover in making the House of Windsor relevant to the modern world by reaching back into Britain's collective memory of past glories to sustain the opaque myth and mystery of the monarchy, while looking forward to a glowing future.

It was perhaps appropriate, then, that in July 1965, several months after his death, he became the first contemporary individual to be featured on the cover of a British postage stamp. Winston's glowering face dominated the centre foreground while the Queen's head, minimized and marginalized, sat off to one side. The irony is that the Postmaster General, republican Anthony Wedgewood Benn, hoped to diminish the Crown out of existence, hence the oversized picture of Winston. The stamp did nothing of the kind. It reinforced the wide appeal of the royal house by linking the monarchy to a leader who symbolized the resilience of the British nation, who had become almost as much a symbol of the British constitutional monarchy as the Queen herself.[43]

Theirs was a symbiotic relationship and one that worked. Just as Winston's social milieu shaped his love and loyalty towards the monarchy, so his support and advocacy shaped the royal house. He left an indelible mark on the hearts of the British people and on the Kings and Queens whom he served.

Acknowledgements

T HE LITERARY, SOCIAL and political terrain involving Sir Winston Churchill and the House of Windsor is mountainous and often impenetrable. So I was very grateful to the guides who helped find a path through.

I would particularly like to thank Allen Packwood OBE the director of the Churchill Archive Centre (CAC) at Churchill College, University of Cambridge. He was very generous with his time and expertise, heading me away from various blind alleys. Thanks too to Piers Brendon, historian and Churchill veteran, who took a gimlet eye to the manuscript, and to Sean Smith, an expert on the Turf.

My thanks also to James Drake who gave me access to his copious collection of Churchill letters as well as Antonia Keaney, social historian at Blenheim Palace.

The insights into this world provided by Andrew Lownie, Professor Jonathan Petropoulos and Professor Andrew Stewart added much granular detail to the project while Cambridge scholar Taylor Jipp has headed down endless rabbit holes in the hunt for research treasures.

I would like to thank my editor Louise Dixon for her calm amid the literary storm as well as copy-editor Susan Pegg and picture researcher Steve Behan.

As ever my appreciation to my agent Steve Troha, my long-time London publisher Michael O'Mara and my wife Carolyn for her tolerance and forbearance.

Andrew Morton
London
June 2025

Photo Credits

Section 1

Page 1 Central Press / Getty Images

Page 2 top, author collection; bottom left, Ken Welsh / Design Pics / Universal Images Group via Getty Images; bottom right, Pictorial Press / Alamy Stock Photo

Page 3 top left, Percy Lewis Pocock / W & D Downey / Hulton Archive / Getty Images; top right, Hulton Archive / Getty Images; bottom left, Universal History Archive / Getty Images; bottom right, Bettmann / Getty Images

Page 4 top left, Vintage Space / Alamy Stock Photo; top right, Buyenlarge / Getty Images; bottom, Daily Mirror / Mirrorpix / Mirrorpix via Getty Images

Page 5 top left, Central Press / Getty Images; bottom left, Look and Learn / Valerie Jackson Harris Collection / Bridgeman Images; bottom right, Hulton Archive / Getty Images

Page 6 top left, © Hulton-Deutsch Collection / CORBIS / Corbis via Getty Images; top right, The Print Collector / Alamy Stock Photo; bottom left, Freemantle / Alamy Stock Photo; bottom right, Topical Press Agency / Getty Images

Page 7 top, Freemantle / Alamy Stock Photo; bottom, Freemantle / Alamy Stock Photo

Page 8 top left, Rob Welham / Universal History Archive / Universal Images Group via Getty Images; bottom left, The Print Collector / Alamy Stock Photo; bottom right, Bettmann / Getty Images

Section 2

Page 1 top, piemags / rmn / Alamy Stock Photo; bottom, Gerry Cranham / Fox Photos / Getty Images

Page 2 top, Popperfoto via Getty Images / Getty Images; bottom left, SuperStock / Alamy Stock Photo; bottom right, Fox Photos / Hulton Archive / Getty Images

Page 3 top, Freemantle / Alamy Stock Photo; bottom, Pictorial Press Ltd / Alamy Stock Photo

Page 4 top, © CORBIS / Corbis via Getty Images; bottom, AFP via Getty Images

Page 5 top, Central Press / Hulton Archive / Getty Images; bottom left, Freemantle / Alamy Stock Photo; bottom right, Keystone / Hulton Archive / Getty Images

Page 6 top, Edward Miller / Keystone / Hulton Archive / Getty Images; bottom, Mirrorpix via Getty Images

Page 7 top, Keystone / Getty Images; bottom, Daily Mirror / Daily Mirror / Mirrorpix via Getty Images

Page 8 top, Fox Photos / Getty Images; bottom, McCabe / Express / Hulton Archive / Getty Images

Select Bibliography

Bagehot, Walter. *The English Constitution*, ed. Miles Taylor. Oxford: Oxford University Press, 2001.

Barnes, John and David Nicholson (eds.). *The Empire at Bay: The Leo Amery Diaries 1929–1945*. London: Hutchinson, 1988.

Battiscombe, Georgina. *Queen Alexandra*. London: Constable & Company, 1969.

Bedell Smith, Sally. *George VI & Elizabeth: The Marriage that Shaped the Monarchy*. London: Penguin Random House, 2023.

Bloch, Michael. *The Secret File of the Duke of Windsor*. London: Corgi, 1989.

——. *Duke of Windsor's War*. London: Weidenfeld & Nicolson, 1982.

——. *Operation Willi: The Plot to Kidnap the Duke of Windsor*. London: Weidenfeld & Nicolson, 1984.

Brett, Maurice V. (ed.). *Journals and Letters of Reginald Viscount Esher, vol. II*. London: Ivor Nicholson & Watson Limited, 1934.

Bradford, Sarah. *George VI*. London: Fontana, 1991.

Brandreth, Gyles. *Philip & Elizabeth: Portrait of a Marriage*. London: Century, 2004.

Bryan, J. III and Charles J. V. Murphy. *The Windsor Story: An intimate portrait of the Duke & Duchess of Windsor*. London: Granada, 1979.

Cadbury, Deborah. *Princes at War: The British Royal Family's Private Battle in the Second World War*. London: Bloomsbury, 2016.

Churchill, Randolph. *Winston S. Churchill: The Official Biography*.
Volume I: Youth, 1874–1900. London: William Heinemann, 1966.
Companion Part 1: 1874–1896. London: William Heinemann, 1967.
Companion Part 2: 1896–1900. London: William Heinemann, 1967.
Volume II: Young Statesman, 1901–1914. London: William Heinemann, 1967.
Companion Part 1: 1901–1907. London: William Heinemann, 1969.
Companion Part 2: 1907–1911. London: William Heinemann, 1969.
Companion Part 3: 1911–1914. London: William Heinemann, 1969.

Churchill, Winston S. *A History of the English-Speaking Peoples, vol. II*. London: Cassell and Company, 1956.

——. *A History of the English-Speaking Peoples, vol. III*. London: Cassell and Company, 1957.

——. *Europe Unite: speeches 1947 and 1948*. Edited by Randolph Churchill. London: Cassell and Company, 1950.

——. 'Monarchy versus Autocracy', in *The Collected Essays of Sir Winston Churchill, vol. II*, ed. Michael Wolff. London: Library of Imperial History, 1976.

——. *My Early Life: A Roving Commission*. London: Thornton Butterworth, 1930.

——. *The Dream*. London: International Churchill Societies, 1994.

——. *The Second World War, vol. V: Closing the Ring*. London: Cassell and Company, 1952.

——. *The World Crisis, Part IV: The Aftermath*. New York: Scribner, 1929.

Colville, John. *The Fringes of Power: Downing Street Diaries 1939–1955*. London: Weidenfeld & Nicolson, 2004.

Croft, Rodney J. *Churchill's Final Farewell: The State and Private Funeral of Sir Winston Churchill*. Buckhurst Hill, Essex: Croft Publishing, 2014.

Donaldson, Frances. *Edward VIII*. London: Weidenfeld & Nicolson, 1974.

Drake, James and Allen Packwood (eds.). *Letters for the Ages: The Private and Personal Letters of Sir Winston Churchill*. London: Bloomsbury, 2023.

Eckert, Astrid M. *The Struggle for the Files: The Western Allies and the Return of German Archives after the Second World War*. Cambridge: Cambridge University Press, 2012.

Eisenhower, Dwight D. *Crusade in Europe*. London: William Heinemann, 1948.

Ellis, Jennifer (ed.). *Thatched with Gold: The Memoirs of Mabell, Countess of Airlie*. London: Hutchinson, 1962.

Esher, Oliver, Viscount (ed.). *Journals and Letters of Reginald Viscount Esher, vol. III: 1910–1915*. London: Ivor Nicholson & Watson, 1938.

Field, Ophelia. *The Favourite: Sarah, Duchess of Marlborough*. London: Hodder & Stoughton, 2002.

Gilbert, Martin. *Winston S. Churchill: The Official Biography*.
Volume III: 1914–1916. London: William Heinemann, 1971.
Companion Part 1: July 1914–April 1915. London: William Heinemann, 1972.
Companion Part 2: May 1915–December 1916. London: William Heinemann, 1972.
Volume IV: 1916–1922. London: William Heinemann, 1975.
Companion Part 1: January 1917– June 1919. London: William Heinemann, 1977.
Companion Part 2: July 1919–March 1921. London: William Heinemann, 1977.
Companion Part 3: April 1921–November 1922. London: William Heinemann, 1977.
Volume V: 1922–1939. London: William Heinemann, 1976.
Companion Part 1: The Exchequer Years, 1922–1929. London: William Heinemann, 1979.
Companion Part 2: The Wilderness Years, 1929–1935. London: William Heinemann, 1981.
Companion Part 3: The Coming of War, 1936–1939. London: William Heinemann, 1982.
Volume VI: Finest Hour, 1939–1941. London: William Heinemann, 1983.
Volume VII: Road to Victory, 1941–1945. London: William Heinemann, 1986.

Volume VIII: 'Never Despair', 1945–1965. London: William Heinemann, 1988.

——. *The Churchill War Papers, Volume I: At the Admiralty, September 1939–May 1940.* London: William Heinemann, 1993.

——. *The Churchill War Papers, Volume II: Never Surrender, May 1940–December 1940.* London: William Heinemann, 1994.

Green, David. *The Churchills at Blenheim Palace.* London: Constable and Company, 1984.

Gregory, Adrian. *The Last Great War: British Society and the First World War.* Cambridge: Cambridge University Press, 2008.

Halle, Kay. *The Irrepressible Churchill: Winston's World, Wars & Wit.* London: Conway, 2010.

Hart-Davis, Duff (ed.). *King's Counsellor: Abdication and War, the Diaries of Sir Alan Lascelles.* London: Weidenfeld & Nicolson, 2006.

Heffer, Simon (ed.). *Henry 'Chips' Channon: The Diaries, vol. I: 1918–38.* London: Penguin, 2024.

Helme, Nigel. *Thomas Major Cullinan.* Johannesburg: McGraw-Hill Book Company, 1974.

Hough, Richard. *Mountbatten: Hero of our Time.* London: Weidenfeld & Nicolson, 1980.

James, Robert Rhodes. *Churchill: A Study in Failure.* London: Ebenezer Baylis and Son, 1970.

—— (ed.). *Winston S. Churchill: His Complete Speeches, Volume VI: 1935–1942.* London: Chelsea House, 1974.

Jenkins, Roy. *Churchill.* London: Macmillan, 2001.

Johnson, Boris. *The Churchill Factor: How One Man Made History.* London: Hodder & Stoughton, 2014.

Kynaston, David. *Austerity Britain, 1945–1951.* London: Bloomsbury, 2007.

Lacey, Robert. *Royal: Her Majesty Queen Elizabeth II.* London: Little, Brown, 2002.

Larman, Alexander. *The Windsors at War: The Nazi Threat to the Crown.* Weidenfeld & Nicolson, 2023.

Larson, Erik. *The Splendid and the Vile: Churchill, Family and Defiance During the Bombing of London.* London: William Collins, 2021.

Lee, Celia and John Lee. *The Churchills: A Family Portrait.* New York: Palgrave Macmillan, 2010.

——. *Winston & Jack: The Churchill Brothers.* London: Celia Lee, 2007.

Lee, Sir Sidney. *King Edward VII: A Biography. Vol. II: The Reign.* London: Macmillan, 1927.

Lennox, Doug. *Now You Know Royalty: Kings and Rulers.* Toronto: Dundurn Press, 2009.

Leslie, Anita. *Edwardians in Love*. London: Hutchinson, 1972.

Lovell, Mary. *The Churchills: A Family at the Heart of History*. London: Little, Brown, 2011.

Magnus, Philip. *King Edward the Seventh*. London: John Murray, 1964.

Montague Browne, Anthony. *Long Sunset: Memoirs of Winston Churchill's Last Private Secretary*. London: Indigo, 1996.

Moran, Lord Charles. *Winston Churchill: The Struggle for Survival, 1940–1965*. London: Constable & Company, 1966.

Morton, Andrew. *17 Carnations: The Royals, the Nazis, and the Biggest Cover-Up in History*. London: Michael O'Mara Books, 2015.

——. *Elizabeth & Margaret*. London: Michael O'Mara Books, 2021.

——. *The Queen*. London: Michael O'Mara Books, 2022.

——. *Wallis in Love: The untold true passion of the Duchess of Windsor*. London: Michael O'Mara Books, 2018.

Mylius, E. F. 'The Morganatic Marriage of George V'. New York: Privately Printed by Guido Bruno, 1916.

Nicolson, Harold. *King George the Fifth: His Life and Reign*. London: Constable & Company, 1952.

Olson, Lynne. *Citizens of London: The Americans Who Stood with Britain in its Darkest, Finest Hour*. New York: Random House, 2010.

Pimlott, Ben. *The Queen: Elizabeth II and the Monarchy*. London: HarperCollins, 2002.

Powell, Ted. *King Edward VIII*. Oxford: Oxford University Press, 2018.

Ridley, Jane. *Bertie: A Life of Edward VII*. London: Chatto & Windus, 2012.

——. *George V: Never a Dull Moment*. London: Chatto & Windus, 2021.

Roberts, Andrew. *Churchill: Walking with Destiny*. London: Penguin, 2019.

Rose, Kenneth. *King George V*. London: Macmillan, 1984.

Russell, G. W. E. *Collections and Recollections*. London: Smith, Elder, & Company, 1904.

Sebba, Anne. *Jennie Churchill: Winston's American Mother*. London: Weidenfeld & Nicolson, 2007.

Seward, Ingrid. *Prince Philip Revealed: A Man of His Century*. London: Simon & Schuster, 2020.

Shakespeare, Nicholas. 'What Can Brexit Britain learn from Winston Churchill?', *New Statesman*, 28 January 2018.

Shawcross, William. *Queen Elizabeth, the Queen Mother: The Official Biography*. London: Macmillan, 2010.

Smith, Eleanor. *Life's a Circus*. London: Longmans, Green and Company, 1939.

Soames, Mary (ed.). *Speaking for Themselves: The Personal Letters of Winston and Clementine Churchill*. London: Transworld Publishers, 1998.

Speck, W. A. *Robert Southey: Entire Man of Letters*. London: Yale University Press, 2006.

Stafford, David. *Oblivion or Glory: 1921 and the Making of Winston Churchill*. New Haven: Yale University Press, 2019.

Strober, Deborah Hart and Gerald S. Strober. *The Monarchy: An Oral History of Elizabeth II*. London: Hutchinson, 2002.

Taylor, Miles. *Empress: Queen Victoria and India*. New Haven: Yale University Press, 2018.

The Times and Viking Press, Inc. *The Churchill Years*. London: Heinemann, 1965.

Thompson, Walter. *Assignment: Churchill*. New York: Farrar, Straus and Young, 1955.

Tippett, Jane Marguerite. *Once a King: The Lost Memoir of Edward VIII*. London: Hodder & Stoughton, 2023.

Twining, Sir Edward Francis. *A History of the Crown Jewels of Europe*. London: B. T. Batsford, 1960.

Wells, H.G. 'The Future of Monarchy', *In the Fourth Year: Anticipations of a World Peace*, London: Chatto & Windus, 1918.

Wheeler-Bennett, John W. *King George VI: His Life and Reign*. London: Macmillan, 1958.

Williams, Susan. *The People's King: The True Story of the Abdication*. London: Allen Lane, 2003.

Windsor, Wallis, Duchess of. *The Heart Has Its Reasons*. London: Michael Joseph, 1956.

Windsor, Edward, Duke of. *A King's Story: The Memoirs of H.R.H. The Duke of Windsor*. London: Pan Books Ltd., 1957.

Ziegler, Phillip. *King Edward VIII: The Official Biography*. London: William Collins Sons & Co., 1990.

References

Introduction: A Day to Remember

1 Duff Hart-Davis (ed.), *King's Counsellor: Abdication and War, the Diaries of Sir Alan Lascelles* (London: Weidenfeld & Nicolson, 2006), 321–2.

2 Andrew Roberts, *Churchill: Walking with Destiny* (London: Penguin Random House, 2019), 879.

Chapter One: Invitation to a Duel

1 'The Gale', *The Times*, 27 November 1874.

2 'The Gale', *The Times*, 2 December 1874.

3 CHAR 28/41/30-32.

4 Roberts, *Churchill*, 7.

5 David Green, *The Churchills at Blenheim Palace* (London: Constable & Company Ltd., 1984), 113.

6 Green, *Churchills at Blenheim*, 113.

7 *The Times*, 3 December 1874.

8 Victoria's Diaries, 30 November 1874 (online access provided by the Royal Archives).

9 W. A. Speck, *Robert Southey* (London: Yale University Press, 2006), 180.

10 Simon Pipe, 'Woodstock's lost royal palace', BBC, 24 September 2014.

11 Ophelia Field, *The Favourite: Sarah, Duchess of Marlborough* (London: Hodder & Stoughton, 2002), 42–4.

12 Winston S. Churchill, *A History of the English-Speaking Peoples, vol. III* (London: Cassell and Company Ltd., 1957), 32–3.

13 Mary Lovell, *The Churchills: A Family at the Heart of History* (London: Little, Brown, 2011), 66.

14 Eleanor Smith, *Life's a Circus* (London: Longmans, Green and Co., 1939), 48.

15 Georgina Battiscombe, *Queen Alexandra* (London: Constable & Company Ltd., 1969), 108.

16 Anne Sebba, *Jennie Churchill: Winston's American Mother* (London: Weidenfeld & Nicolson, 2007), 36.

17 Sebba, *Jennie*, 32–3.

18 Anne Sebba, 'Jennie Churchill and Her Attempts to Be an Independent Woman', *Finest Hour* 175, Winter 2017.

19 Jane Ridley, *Bertie: A Life of Edward VII* (London: Chatto & Windus, 2012), 246.

20 CHAR 28/103/7.

21 Sebba, *Jennie*, 38–9.

22 Ridley, *Bertie*, 194.

23 Sebba, *Jennie*, 57.

24 Ridley, *Bertie*, 194.

25 Ridley, *Bertie*, 183.

26 Ridley, *Bertie*, 184.

27 Randolph Churchill, *Winston S. Churchill, vol. I: Youth, 1874–1900* (London: Heinemann, 1966), 29.

28 Ridley, *Bertie*, 188.

29 Ridley, *Bertie*, 189.

30 CHAR 28/97/11-13.
31 Philip Magnus, *King Edward the Seventh* (London: John Murray, 1964), 150.
32 Roberts, *Churchill*, 12; *Celia and John Lee, The Churchills: A Family Portrait* (New York: Palgrave Macmillan, 2010), 14.
33 R. Churchill, *Winston S. Churchill, vol. I*, 41.
34 Lee and Lee, *The Churchills*, 22.
35 Roberts, *Churchill*, 14.
36 Sebba, *Jennie*, 115; *Roy Jenkins, Churchill* (London: Macmillan, 2001), 18.
37 Victoria's Diaries, 10 July 1883 (online access provided by the Royal Archives).
38 R. Churchill, *Winston S. Churchill, vol. I*, 68.
39 Miles Taylor, *Empress: Queen Victoria and India* (New Haven: Yale University Press, 2018), 189; Celia and John Lee, *Winston & Jack: The Churchill Brothers* (London: Celia Lee, 2007), 60. '
40 Sebba, *Jennie*, 138–9; Lee and Lee, *The Churchills*, 40.
41 Lee and Lee, *The Churchills*, 42; CHAR 28/47/9.
42 Ridley, *Bertie*, 245.
43 Lee and Lee, *The Churchills*, 32; Lee and Lee, *Winston & Jack*, 47–8.
44 Lee and Lee, *The Churchills*, 32; Lee and Lee, *Winston & Jack*, 47–8.
45 Jenkins, *Churchill*, 15.
46 R. Churchill, *Winston S. Churchill, vol. I*, 77.
47 Ridley, *Bertie*, 245.
48 Lee and Lee, *The Churchills*, 49.
49 R. Churchill, *Winston S. Churchill, vol. I*, 87–91; Roberts, *Churchill*, 19; Lee and Lee, *Winston & Jack*, 72; Harold Nicolson, *King George the Fifth: His Life and Reign* (London: Constable & Company Ltd., 1952), 39.
50 Magnus, *King Edward the Seventh*, 197–200.
51 Lee and Lee, *The Churchills*, 54.
52 Lee and Lee, *The Churchills*, 54.
53 R. Churchill, *Winston S. Churchill, vol. I*, 176; Lee and Lee, *The Churchills*, 62.
54 Jenkins, *Churchill*, 19.
55 Ridley, *Bertie*, 401.
56 Lee and Lee, *The Churchills*, 252 n.2.

Chapter Two: An Unheeded Warning

1 Antoine Capet, 'The Happy Warrior: Winston Churchill and the representation of war 1895–1901', *Automne* 66 (2007).
2 CHAR 28/21/37-39.
3 CHAR 28/21/40-42.
4 Winston S. Churchill, *My Early Life: A Roving Commission* (London: Thornton Butterworth Ltd., 1930), 107–8.
5 R. Churchill, *Winston S. Churchill, vol. I*, 308.
6 R. Churchill, *Winston S. Churchill, vol. I*, 310.
7 Lee and Lee, *The Churchills*, 89.
8 CHAR 28/23/79-81.
9 Lee and Lee, *The Churchills*, 105.
10 CHAR 28/24/13-16.
11 Lee and Lee, *The Churchills*, 90.
12 CHAR 28/24/13-16.
13 CHAR 28/24/40-41.
14 W. Churchill, *My Early Life*, 170.

15 James Drake and Allen Packwood (eds.), *Letters for the Ages: The Private and Personal Letters of Sir Winston Churchill* (London: Bloomsbury, 2023), 25.

16 W. Churchill, *My Early Life*, 170.

17 R. Churchill, *Winston S. Churchill*, vol. I, 420.

18 R. Churchill, *Winston S. Churchill*, vol. I, 421.

19 Packwood, *Letters for the Ages*, 64.

20 Magnus, *King Edward the Seventh*, 67.

21 CHAR 28/63/9-10.

22 R. Churchill, *Winston S. Churchill*, vol. I, 545.

23 'Winston Churchill made boozy £12,000 bet with British Empire would not fall ... and won', *The Telegraph*, 10 March 2016.

24 Ridley, *Bertie*, 368.

25 Battiscombe, *Queen Alexandra*, 249–50.

26 CHAR 28/27/5.

27 Jenkins, *Churchill*, 83.

28 Randolph Churchill, *Winston S. Churchill, vol. II: Young Statesman, 1901–1914* (London: William Heinemann, 1967), 67.

29 Jenkins, *Churchill*, 91; R. Churchill, *Winston S. Churchill*, vol. II, 90.

30 R. Churchill, *Winston S. Churchill*, vol. II, 94.

31 CHAR 28/27/46-47.

32 Jenkins, *Churchill*, 106.

33 Nicolson, *King George the Fifth*, 93.

34 Jenkins, *Churchill*, 119.

35 Jenkins, *Churchill*, 120.

36 Jenkins, *Churchill*, 106.

37 R. Churchill, *Winston S. Churchill*, vol. II, 194–5.

38 CHAR 28/27/54-56.

39 R. Churchill, *Winston S. Churchill*, vol. II, 159–60.

40 Jenkins, *Churchill*, 91.

41 CHAR 28/152B/202.

Chapter Three: Diamond in the Rough

1 *The Times*, 10 November 1908; Sir Edward F. Twining, *A History of the Crown Jewels of Europe* (London: B. T. Batsford Ltd., 1960), 184.

2 Nigel Helme, *Thomas Major Cullinan* (Johannesburg: McGraw-Hill Book Company, 1974), 81–3; Twining, *Crown Jewels*, 185.

3 Helme, *Cullinan*, 76.

4 Sir Sidney Lee, *King Edward VII: A Biography. vol. II: The Reign* (London: Macmillan, 1927), 481–2.

5 R. Churchill, *Winston S. Churchill*, vol. II, 211.

6 CHAR 28/75/22-23.

7 CHAR 2/30/15.

8 *The Times*, 27 April 1907.

9 S. Lee, *Edward VII*, 487–9; R. Churchill, *Winston S. Churchill*, vol. II, 417; *The Times*, 20 August 1907, p. 3.

10 R. Churchill, *Winston S. Churchill*, vol. II, 218.

11 R. Churchill, *Winston S. Churchill*, vol. II, 218.

12 R. Churchill, *Winston S. Churchill*, vol. II, 219.

13 R. Churchill, *Winston S. Churchill*, vol. II, 220.

14 CHAR 2/30/86.

15 R. Churchill, *Winston S. Churchill, vol. II*, 239–40.
16 Roberts, *Churchill*, 120–21.
17 Sebba, *Jennie*, 277.
18 Randolph Churchill, *Winston S. Churchill, vol. II Companion Part 2* (London: William Heinemann, 1969), 803.
19 Magnus, *King Edward the Seventh*, 413.
20 R. Churchill, *Winston S. Churchill, vol. II*, 274.
21 Jane Ridley, *George V: Never a Dull Moment* (London: Chatto & Windus, 2021), 146–7; Kenneth Rose, *King George V* (London: Macmillan, 1984), 71.
22 Maurice V. Brett (ed.), *Journals and Letters of Reginald Viscount Esher, vol. II* (London: Ivor Nicholson & Watson Limited, 1934), 423–4; CAC, ESHR 10/51.
23 Jenkins, *Churchill*, 161.
24 Roberts, *Churchill*, 131.
25 Boris Johnson, *The Churchill Factor: How One Man Made History* (London: Hodder & Stoughton, 2014), 106.
26 Anita Leslie, *Edwardians in Love* (London: Hutchinson, 1972), 248.
27 *The Times*, 11 September 1909.
28 Ridley, *Bertie*, 439–40; R. Churchill, *Winston S. Churchill*, vol. II Companion Part 2, 908.
29 R. Churchill, *Winston S. Churchill, vol. II*, 326.
30 Magnus, *King Edward the Seventh*, 413.
31 Magnus, *King Edward the Seventh*, 411.
32 Jenkins, *Churchill*, 168.
33 Jenkins, *Churchill*, 168.
34 CHAR 12/2/9.
35 Ridley, *Bertie*, 452–3.
36 Sebba, *Jennie*, 287.
37 Ridley, *Bertie*, 458.
38 Ridley, *Bertie*, 466.
39 Ridley, *Bertie*, 460.

Chapter Four: The King and his 'Concubine'

1 Nicolson, *King George the Fifth*, 124.
2 Ridley, *George V*, 186.
3 Rose, *King George V*, 82.
4 *Reynolds's Newspaper*, 5 February 1911.
5 E. F. Mylius, 'The Morganatic Marriage of George V', New York: Privately Printed [by Guido Bruno], 1916.
6 CHAR 12/8/1.
7 Rose, *King George V*, 83.
8 R. Churchill, *Winston S. Churchill, vol. II*, 418.
9 R. Churchill, *Winston S. Churchill, vol. II*, 344.
10 R. Churchill, *Winston S. Churchill, vol. II*, 342.
11 CHAR 12/8/16.
12 CHAR 28/117/67.
13 'The Libel on the King. A "Marriage at Malta". Emphatic Denial by His Majesty', *Manchester Guardian*, 2 February 1911.
14 'The Libel on the King', *Manchester Guardian*, 2 February 1911.
15 R. Churchill, *Winston S. Churchill, vol. II Companion Part 2*: 1237.
16 CHAR 12/2/52.
17 CHAR 12/2/66.

18 Rose, *King George V, 111*; R. Churchill, *Winston S. Churchill, vol. II*, 434.

19 CHAR 12/9/40.

20 R. Churchill, *Winston S. Churchill, vol. II*, 437.

21 R. Churchill, *Winston S. Churchill, vol. II*, 356.

22 Roberts, *Churchill*, 153.

23 Frances Donaldson, *Edward VIII* (London: Weidenfeld & Nicolson, 1974), 36.

24 Doug Lennox, *Now You Know Royalty: Kings and Rulers* (Toronto: Dundurn Press, 2009), *85*.

25 Mary Soames (ed.), *Speaking for Themselves: The Personal Letters of Winston and Clementine Churchill* (London: Transworld Publishers, 1998), 54.

26 Phillip Ziegler, *King Edward VIII: The Official Biography* (London: William Collins, 1990), 27.

27 Susan Williams, *The People's King: The True Story of the Abdication* (London: Allen Lane, 2003), 2.

28 Ziegler, *King Edward VIII*, 46.

29 Nicolson, *King George the Fifth*, 158.

30 R. Churchill, *Winston S. Churchill, vol. II*, 382.

31 R. Churchill, *Winston S. Churchill, vol. II*, 385.

32 Ridley, *George V, 180*; Soames (ed.), *Speaking for Themselves, 55–6*.

33 Oliver Esher (ed.), *Journals and Letters of Reginald, Viscount Esher, vol. III: 1910–1915* (London: Ivor Nicholson & Watson Ltd, 1938), 74.

34 Roberts, *Churchill*, 160.

35 R. Churchill, *Winston S. Churchill, vol. II*, 647.

36 R. Churchill, *Winston S. Churchill, vol. II*, 647.

37 R. Churchill, *Winston S. Churchill, vol. II*, 648.

38 W. Churchill, *A History of English-Speaking Peoples, vol. II* (London: Cassell and Company Ltd., 1956), 251.

39 R. Churchill, *Winston S. Churchill, vol. II*, 652.

40 R. Churchill, *Winston S. Churchill, vol. II*, 653–4.

41 Martin Gilbert, *Winston S. Churchill, vol. III: 1914–1916* (London: William Heinemann, 1971), 87.

42 Churchill Archives, ESHR 6/5, 30 June 1912.

43 Soames (ed.), *Speaking for Themselves, 65–6*.

44 Soames (ed.), *Speaking for Themselves*, 76.

45 Williams, *The People's King*, 30.

46 R. Churchill, *Winston S. Churchill, vol. II*, 706.

47 Max E. Hertwig, 'Guns of August 1914–2014 – The "Kingly Conference", 1914: Churchill's Last Try for Peace', *Finest Hour 163* (Summer 2014).

48 R. Churchill, *Winston S. Churchill, vol. II*, 709.

49 Roberts, *Churchill*, 180.

50 R. Churchill, *Winston S. Churchill, vol. II*, 710.

Chapter Five: Act Fast, Dread Nought

1 Roberts, *Churchill, 186*; Gilbert, *Winston S. Churchill, vol. III*, 383–4.

2 'The German Navy: Mr. Churchill on its choice', *The Times*, 23 September 1914.

3 Gilbert, *Winston S. Churchill, vol. III*, 86–7.

4 Nicolson, *King George the Fifth*, 251.

5 Gilbert, *Winston S. Churchill, vol. III, 149*; Richard Hough, *Mountbatten: Hero of Our Time* (London: Weidenfeld & Nicolson, 1980), 32.

6 Nicolson, *King George the Fifth*, 251.

7   Gilbert, *Winston S. Churchill, vol. III*, 150.
8   Gilbert, *Winston S. Churchill, vol. III*, 151.
9   Nicolson, *King George the Fifth*, 251.
10 Gilbert, *Winston S. Churchill, vol. III*, 151.
11 Rose, *King George V*, 187.
12 Jenkins, *Churchill*, 253.
13 Roberts, *Churchill*, 196.
14 CHAR 13/47/26.
15 Gilbert, *Winston S. Churchill, vol. III*, 456.
16 Gilbert, *Winston S. Churchill, vol. III*, 453.
17 Gilbert, *Winston S. Churchill, vol. III*, 454.
18 Roberts, *Churchill*, 216.
19 Gilbert, *Winston S. Churchill, vol. III*, 454; Ziegler, *King Edward VIII*, 59.
20 Gilbert, *Winston S. Churchill vol. III*, 440.
21 Roberts, *Churchill*, 223.
22 Roberts, *Churchill*, 214.
23 Gilbert, *Winston S. Churchill vol. III*, 473; Roberts, *Churchill*, 219.
24 Gilbert, *Winston S. Churchill, vol. III*, 512.
25 CHAR 21/43A-B.
26 CAC, ESHR 6/9.
27 Roberts, *Churchill*, 227.
28 Roberts, *Churchill*, 230.
29 Roberts, *Churchill*, 233.
30 Roberts, *Churchill*, 238.
31 Roberts, *Churchill*, 239.
32 Roberts, *Churchill*, 244.
33 Ridley, *George V*, 246.
34 Roberts, *Churchill*, 248.
35 Roberts, *Churchill*, 246n.
36 Gilbert, *Winston S. Churchill vol. III*, 822.
37 Roberts, *Churchill*, 249.
38 H. G. Wells, 'The Future of Monarchy' in *In the Fourth Year: Anticipations of a World Peace* (London: Chatto & Windus, 1918), 93.
39 Adrian Gregory, *The Last Great War: British Society and the First World War* (Cambridge: Cambridge University Press, 2008), 153.
40 CHAR 8/518A-B, fol. 207.
41 Nicolson, *King George the Fifth*, 309–10.
42 Nicolson, *King George the Fifth*, 309–10.
43 Martin Gilbert, *Winston S. Churchill, vol. IV: World in Torment, 1916–1922* (London: William Heinemann, 1975), 29.
44 CAC, ESHR 5/52.
45 'Ministerial Changes', *The Times*, 26 July 1917.
46 Roberts, *Churchill*, 252.
47 Roberts, *Churchill*, 252.
48 Ziegler, *King Edward VIII*, 78.
49 Roberts, *Churchill*, 257.
50 Rose, *King George V*, 232.
51 Nicolson, *King George the Fifth*, 339.
52 Jean Chrétien, 'Order-worthy?', *National Post*, 15 July 2009.
53 Gilbert, *Winston S. Churchill, vol. IV*, 907–8.

54 Martin Gilbert, *Winston S. Churchill, vol. IV Companion Part 2* (London: William Heinemann, 1977), 1091.

55 Ziegler, *King Edward VIII*, 165.

56 Ridley, *George V*, 285.

57 Gilbert, *Winston S. Churchill, vol. III*, 665.

58 Gilbert, *Winston S. Churchill, vol. IV*, 665.

59 David Stafford, *Oblivion or Glory: 1921 and the Making of Winston Churchill* (New Haven: Yale University Press, 2019), 258.

60 Gilbert, *Winston S. Churchill, vol. IV*, 696–9.

61 Gilbert, *Winston S. Churchill, vol. IV*, 702.

62 W. Churchill, *The World Crisis, Part IV: The Aftermath* (New York: Scribner, 1929), 348.

63 Gilbert, *Winston S. Churchill, vol. IV*, 702.

64 Morton, *17 Carnations: The Royals, the Nazis, and the Biggest Cover-Up in History* (London: Michael O'Mara Books, 2015), 3.

65 David Cannadine, 'Churchill and the Monarchy', *Transactions of the Royal Historical Society* 11 (2001): 257.

66 Stafford, *Oblivion or Glory*, 11.

Chapter Six: Silver and Gold

1 Ted Powell, *King Edward VIII: An American Life* (Oxford: Oxford University Press, 2018), 35.

2 Edward, Duke of Windsor, *A King's Story: The Memoirs of HRH The Duke of Windsor* (London: Pan Books Ltd., 1957), 135.

3 Duke of Windsor, *A King's Story*, 135.

4 Duke of Windsor, *A King's Story*, 136.

5 David Freeman, 'The Uncrowned King', *Finest Hour*, 184, July 2019.

6 Morton, *17 Carnations*, 23.

7 Powell, *King Edward VIII*, 138.

8 Jenkins, *Churchill*, 357.

9 Gilbert, *Winston S. Churchill, vol. IV*, 606.

10 Gilbert, *Winston S. Churchill, vol. IV Companion Part 3* (London: William Heinemann, 1977), 1709–10.

11 Jenkins, *Churchill*, 357.

12 Gilbert, *Winston S. Churchill, vol. IV*, 891.

13 Jenkins, *Churchill*, 376.

14 Martin Gilbert, *Winston S. Churchill, vol. V: 1922–1939* (William Heinemann, 1976), 7.

15 *The Times and Viking Press, Inc., The Churchill Years 1874 to 1965* (New York: Viking Press, 1965), 70.

16 Sally Bedell Smith, *George VI & Elizabeth: The Marriage That Shaped the Monarchy* (London: Penguin Random House, 2003), 172; William Shawcross, *Queen Elizabeth the Queen Mother: The Official Biography*, (London: Macmillan, 2009), 218.

17 Gilbert, *Winston S. Churchill, vol. V*, 58.

18 *The Times* and Viking Press, *The Churchill Years*, 75.

19 Gilbert, *Winston S. Churchill, vol. V*, 110.

20 Gilbert, *Winston S. Churchill, vol. V*, 116.

21 Nicolson, *King George the Fifth*, 418.

22 Duke of Windsor, *A King's Story, 214*; Donaldson, *Edward VIII*, 121.

23 Gilbert, *Winston S. Churchill, vol. V*, 174.

24 Gilbert, *Winston S. Churchill, vol. V*, 233.

25 Gilbert, *Winston S. Churchill, vol. V*, 235.

26 Gilbert, *Winston S. Churchill, vol. V,* 244.
27 Soames (ed.), *Speaking for Themselves,* 328.
28 Soames (ed.), *Speaking for Themselves,* 329.
29 Alastair Stewart, '"A Happy Scene": Churchill and Balmoral Castle', *Finest Hour: Churchill and the Queen* 199 (Special Issue, 2022), 21; Soames (ed.), *Speaking for Themselves,* 328.
30 Gilbert, *Winston S. Churchill, vol. V,* 283.
31 Gilbert, *Winston S. Churchill, vol. V,* 284.
32 *The Times and Viking Press, The Churchill Years,* 87.
33 Rose, *King George V,* 190.
34 Walter Thompson, *Assignment: Churchill* (New York: Farrar, Straus and Young, 1955), 108; Fred Glueckstein, 'Contasino Meets Churchill, 1931', The Churchill Project, Hillsdale College, 13 March 2016.
35 Thompson, *Assignment: Churchill,* 108.
36 CHAR 1/399B/195.
37 Alsop, Joseph, 'Blundering Into War by Being Anti War', *St Petersburg Times,* 11 May 1970.
38 Nicolson, *King George the Fifth,* 521.
39 Morton, *17 Carnations,* 59.
40 Morton, *17 Carnations,* 64.
41 Nicholas Shakespeare, 'What Can Brexit Britain learn from Winston Churchill?', *New Statesman,* 28 January 2018.
42 Wallis, Duchess of Windsor, *The Heart Has Its Reasons* (London: Michael Joseph, 1956), 217–18.
43 John Fleet, 'Alexander Korda: Churchill's Man in Hollywood', *Finest Hour,* 179, 2018.
44 Ridley, George V, 292–3.
45 Fleet, 'Alexander Korda', *Finest Hour,* 179, 2018.
46 CHAR 8/526.
47 John Tyrrell, 'Pride of Place at Chartwell', *Kent & Surrey Bylines,* 11 February 2021.
48 CHAR 8/520.
49 CHAR 8/520.
50 Ben Pimlott, *The Queen: Elizabeth II and the Monarchy* (London: HarperCollins, 2002), 15.
51 CHAR 8/520.
52 Gilbert, *Winston S. Churchill, vol. V,* 700–701.

Chapter Seven: Three Minutes to Oblivion

1 George W.E. Russell, *Collections & Recollections* (London: Smith, Elder & Co., 1904), 253.
2 Gilbert, *Winston S. Churchill, vol. V,* 809.
3 Roberts, *Churchill,* 409.
4 Gilbert, *Winston S. Churchill, vol. V,* 810.
5 Andrew Morton, *Wallis in Love: The Untold True Passion of the Duchess of Windsor* (London: Michael O'Mara Books, 2018), 228.
6 Bedell Smith, *George VI & Elizabeth,* 275.
7 Gilbert, *Winston S. Churchill, vol. V,* 811.
8 Gilbert, *Winston S. Churchill, vol. V,* 811.
9 Sarah Bradford, *George VI* (London: Fontana, 1991), 219.
10 Jane Marguerite Tippett, *Once a King: The Lost Memoir of Edward VIII* (London: Hodder & Stoughton, 2023), 186.
11 Ziegler, *King Edward VIII,* 287.
12 Gilbert, *Winston S. Churchill, vol. V,* 812.
13 Roberts, *Churchill,* 409.
14 Ziegler, *King Edward VIII,* 303.

15 Roberts, *Churchill*, 408.

16 Simon Heffer (ed.), *Henry 'Chips' Channon: The Diaries, vol. I: 1918–38* (London: Hutchinson, 2021), 593.

17 Williams, *The People's King*, 172.

18 Ziegler, *King Edward VIII*, 302.

19 Heffer (ed.), *Henry 'Chips' Channon, The Diaries: 1918–38*, 598.

20 Gilbert, *Winston S. Churchill, vol. V*, 816.

21 Ziegler, *King Edward VIII*, 314.

22 Tippett, *Once a King*, 186.

23 Ziegler, *King Edward VIII*, 314.

24 Heffer (ed.), *Henry 'Chips' Channon, The Diaries: 1918–38*, 600.

25 Williams, *The People's King*, 172.

26 Gilbert, *Winston S. Churchill, vol. V*, 813.

27 Williams, *The People's King*, 173.

28 Tippett, *Once a King*, 185–6.

29 Tippett, *Once a King*, 186.

30 Tippett, *Once a King*, 188.

31 Duke of Windsor, *A King's Story*, 350.

32 Duke of Windsor, *A King's Story*, 350.

33 Williams, *The People's King*, 175.

34 Donaldson, *Edward VIII*, 277–8.

35 Duke of Windsor, *A King's Story*, 364.

36 Gilbert, *Winston S. Churchill, vol. V*, 816.

37 Ziegler, *King Edward VIII*, 317.

38 Williams, *The People's King*, 209.

39 Donaldson, *Edward VIII*, 280.

40 Robert Rhodes James, *Churchill: A Study in Failure* (London: Ebenezer Baylis & Son, 1970), 273.

41 Ziegler, *King Edward VIII*, 317.

42 Gilbert, *Winston S. Churchill, vol. V*, 818.

43 Heffer (ed.), *Henry 'Chips' Channon, The Diaries: 1918–38*, 611.

44 Williams, *The People's King*, 194–5; Heffer (ed.), *Henry 'Chips' Channon, The Diaries: 1918–38*, 610.

45 Williams, *The People's King*, 199.

46 Roberts, *Churchill*, 411.

47 Gilbert, *Winston S. Churchill, vol. V*, 822.

48 Jenkins, *Churchill*, 503.

49 Morton, *Wallis in Love*, 220.

50 Alistair Lexden, 'On This Day in 1936', *Daily Telegraph, 10 December 2016*.

51 Heffer (ed.), *Henry 'Chips' Channon, The Diaries: 1918–38*, 615–16.

52 Gilbert, *Winston S. Churchill, vol. V*, 827.

53 Gilbert, *Winston S. Churchill, vol. V*, 828.

54 Gilbert, *Winston S. Churchill, vol. V*, 828.

55 Bradford, *George VI*, 234.

56 Ziegler, *King Edward VIII*, 326–7.

57 Ziegler, *King Edward VIII*, 327.

58 Roberts, *Churchill*, 411–12.

59 Morton, *Wallis in Love*, 228; Morton, *17 Carnations*, 101.

60 Gilbert, *Winston S. Churchill, vol. V*, 830; Ziegler, *King Edward VIII*, 334.

61 Roberts, *Churchill*, 413.

Chapter Eight: Into the Wilderness

1 Gilbert, *Winston S. Churchill, vol. V*, 828.
2 Gilbert, *Winston S. Churchill, vol. V*, 830.
3 Ziegler, *King Edward VIII*, 349.
4 Ziegler, *King Edward VIII*, 342.
5 Ziegler, *King Edward VIII*, 344.
6 Ziegler, *King Edward VIII*, 344.
7 Ziegler, *King Edward VIII*, 338.
8 Ziegler, *King Edward VIII*, 339–40.
9 Bedell Smith, *George IV and Elizabeth*, 304.
10 Alexander Larman, *The Windsors at War: The Nazi Threat to the Crown* (London: Weidenfeld & Nicolson, 2023), 18.
11 Gilbert, *Winston S. Churchill, vol. V, Companion Part 3* (London: William Heinemann, 1982), 634.
12 Bradford, *George VI*, 320.
13 Bradford, *George VI*, 247.
14 Bradford, *George VI*, 247.
15 Bradford, *George VI*, 322.
16 Gilbert, *Winston S. Churchill, vol. V Companion Part 3*, 651–3.
17 Gilbert, *Winston S. Churchill, vol. V Companion Part 3*, 661.
18 Ziegler, *King Edward VIII*, 376.
19 Morton, *17 Carnations*, 119.
20 Roberts, *Churchill*, 416–17.
21 Gilbert, *Winston S. Churchill, vol. V*, 856.
22 Ziegler, *King Edward VIII*, 357.
23 Ziegler, *King Edward VIII*, 364.
24 Roberts, *Churchill*, 417.
25 Michael Bloch, *The Secret File of the Duke of Windsor* (London: Corgi, 1989), 143.
26 Deborah Cadbury, *Princes at War: The British Royal Family's Private Battle in the Second World War* (London: Bloomsbury, 2016), 64; Ziegler, King Edward VIII, 393.
27 Roberts, *Churchill*, 417.
28 Williams, *The People's King*, 277.
29 Bradford, *George VI*, 360–61; Gilbert, *Winston S. Churchill, vol. V*, 958.
30 Shawcross, *Queen Mother*, 435; Bradford, *George VI*, 360.
31 Bradford, *George VI*, 368.
32 Heffer (ed.), *Henry 'Chips' Channon, The Diaries: 1918–38*, 937.
33 Ziegler, *King Edward VIII*, 398.
34 Shawcross, *Queen Mother*, 444.
35 Gilbert, *Winston S. Churchill, vol. V*, 1035.
36 Gilbert, *Winston S. Churchill, vol. V*, 1037.
37 Gilbert, *Winston S. Churchill, vol. V*, 1037.
38 *The Times, 24 June 1939.*
39 Hitler, First Greater Reichstag speech, 30 January 1939, *German History in Documents and Images.*
40 Roberts, *Churchill*, 453.
41 Roberts, Churchill, 466.
42 Bedell Smith, *George VI & Elizabeth*, 384.
43 J. Bryan III and Charles J. V. Murphy, *The Windsor Story: An Intimate Portrait of the Duke & Duchess of Windsor* (London: Granada, 1979), 401; Martin Gilbert, *Winston S. Churchill, vol. VI: The Finest Hour, 1939–1941* (London: William Heinemann, 1983), 12–13.

44 Bloch, *Secret File*, 177.

45 Donaldson, *Edward VIII*, 348.

46 Michael Bloch, *The Duke of Windsor's War* (London: Weidenfeld & Nicholson, 1982), 21.

47 Morton, *17 Carnations*, 151.

48 Ziegler, *King Edward VIII*, 411.

49 Ziegler, *King Edward VIII*, 413.

50 Gilbert, *The Churchill War Papers*, vol. I, 776.

51 CHAR 19/5/9.

52 Thompson, *Assignment: Churchill*, 144.

53 Gilbert, *The Churchill War Papers*, vol. I (London: W. W. Norton, 1993), 791–2.

54 Gilbert, *Winston S. Churchill*, vol. VI, 235.

55 Gilbert, *The Churchill War Papers*, vol. I, 1070.

56 Roberts, *Churchill*, 495–6.

57 Bedell Smith, *George VI & Elizabeth*, 390–91.

58 Bedell Smith, *George VI & Elizabeth*, 390–91.

59 Gilbert, *The Churchill War Papers*, vol. I, 1283.

Chapter Nine: Brothers at War

1 Shawcross, *Queen Mother*, 507.

2 Gilbert, *The Churchill War Papers*, vol. I, 1283.

3 Cadbury, *Princes at War*, 134.

4 Bradford, *George VI*, 417–18.

5 Bedell Smith, *George VI & Elizabeth*, 397.

6 Bradford, *George VI*, 413.

7 Gilbert, *The Churchill War Papers*, vol. I, 1286–7; Original source at CHAR 20/11/17-18.

8 CHAR 20/7/96-105.

9 John Colville, *The Fringes of Power: Downing Street Diaries 1939–1955* (London: Weidenfeld & Nicholson, 2004), 117; Bedell Smith, *George VI & Elizabeth*, 453–4; Original sources: CHAR 20/7/96-105.

10 Bradford, *George VI*, 418.

11 Bradford, *George VI*, 417–19; Cadbury, *Princes at War*, 146.

12 Roberts, *Churchill*, 555.

13 Cadbury, *Princes at War*, 147; Winston wrote the same lines, verbatim, to President Roosevelt on 20 May 1940 (CHAR 20/14).

14 Morton, *The Queen*, 51.

15 Cadbury, *Princes at War*, 147; Bradford, *George VI*, 419.

16 Cadbury, *Princes at War*, 152–3.

17 Gilbert, *Winston S. Churchill*, vol. VI, 419.

18 Gilbert, *Winston S. Churchill*, vol. VI, 408–13.

19 Cadbury, *Princes at War*, 155.

20 Robert Rhodes James (ed.), *Winston S. Churchill: His Complete Speeches, vol. VI: 1935–1942* (London: Chelsea House, 1974), 6231.

21 Gilbert, *The Churchill War Papers*, vol. II (London: W. W. Norton, 1994), 249; Bedell Smith, *George VI & Elizabeth*, 469.

22 Morton, *17 Carnations*, 160.

23 Bedell Smith, *George VI & Elizabeth*, 428–9.

24 Michael Bloch, *Operation Willi: The Plot to Kidnap the Duke of Windsor* (London: Weidenfeld & Nicolson, 1984), 169.

25 Roberts, *Churchill*, 537; Morton, *17 Carnations*, 160.

26 Ziegler, *King Edward VIII*, 425; PRO FO 954 33/212 A-C. This conversation was not minuted to the Foreign Office until 1943.
27 Bloch, *Secret File*, 195.
28 CHAR 20/9A/3.
29 Tippett, *Once a King*, 306–7.
30 CHAR 20/9A/6; CHAR 20/9A/7.
31 Bedell Smith, *George VI & Elizabeth*, 401.
32 Bloch, *Operation Willi*, 56; CHAR 20/9A/27-29.
33 Gilbert, *The Churchill War Papers, vol. II*, 432.
34 Gilbert, *The Churchill War Papers, vol. II*, 433.
35 Gilbert, *Winston S. Churchill, vol. VI*, 613.
36 Colville, *Fringes of Power*, 146.
37 Ziegler, *King Edward VIII*, 417.
38 Morton, *Wallis in Love*, 269.
39 Donaldson, *Edward VIII*, 366.
40 Ziegler, *King Edward VIII*, 426.
41 Cadbury, *Princes at War*, 171.
42 Gilbert, *The Churchill War Papers, vol. II*, 462.
43 CHAR 20/9A/19.
44 Morton, *17 Carnations*, 175.
45 Gilbert, *The Churchill War Papers, vol. II*, 463.
46 Bloch, *Secret File*, 262.
47 Gilbert, *Winston S. Churchill, vol. VI*, 700.
48 Donaldson, *Edward VIII*, 371.
49 Bedell Smith, *George VI & Elizabeth*, 403.
50 Ziegler, *King Edward VIII*, 425.
51 Morton, *17 Carnations*, 183.
52 Bloch, *Operation Willi*, 173–4.
53 Bloch, *Operation Willi*, 174.
54 Bloch, *Operation Willi*, 175–6.
55 Bradford, *George VI*, 580.
56 Morton, *17 Carnations*, 190.
57 Morton, *17 Carnations*, 191.

Chapter Ten: Their Finest Hour

1 James, *Churchill: Complete Speeches, vol. VI*, 6266.
2 Gilbert, *The Churchill War Papers, vol. II*, 794; Roberts, *Churchill*, 594.
3 Bedell Smith, *George VI & Elizabeth*, 407–8.
4 Bedell Smith, *George VI & Elizabeth*, 408.
5 Shawcross, *Queen Mother*, 514.
6 Gilbert, *The Churchill War Papers, vol. II*, 794.
7 Bradford, *George VI*, 403.
8 Bedell Smith, *George VI & Elizabeth*, 408.
9 Shawcross, *Queen Mother*, 504.
10 Shawcross, *Queen Mother*, 537.
11 Bedell Smith, *George VI & Elizabeth*, 408.
12 Bedell Smith, *George VI & Elizabeth*, 412.
13 Gilbert, *The Churchill War Papers, vol. II*, 806–7.
14 Shawcross, *Queen Mother*, 533.

15 Shawcross, *Queen Mother*, 539.
16 Shawcross, *Queen Mother*, 539.
17 Bedell Smith, *George VI & Elizabeth*, 436.
18 Gareth Russell, 'Hitler dubbed her "the most dangerous woman in Europe"', *Daily Mail*, 21 April 2023.
19 Cadbury, *Princes at War*, 207–8.
20 Bradford, *George VI*, 323.
21 Colville, *Fringes of Power*, 263.
22 Morton, *17 Carnations*, 217.
23 Erik Larson, *The Splendid and the Vile: Churchill, Family and Defiance During the Bombing of London* (London: William Collins, 2021), 317–18.
24 Larson, *The Splendid and the Vile*, 328; Tom Fleming (ed.), *Voices Out of the Air: The Royal Christmas Broadcasts, 1932–1981* (London: William Heinemann, 1981), 32.
25 CHAR 20/20/1-2.
26 Colville, *Fringes of Power*, 281.
27 CHAR 20/9B/196.
28 CHAR 20/9B/196.
29 Morton, *17 Carnations*, 209.
30 Bloch, *Secret File*, 213–17.
31 Morton, *17 Carnations*, 195.
32 Ziegler, *King Edward VIII*, 463.
33 CHAR 20/14.
34 Morton, *17 Carnations*, 210–11.
35 Colville, *Fringes of Power*, 284.
36 Morton, *17 Carnations*, 211.
37 Colville, *Fringes of Power*, 284.

Chapter Eleven: Royal Defeatist at Large

1 'Father and Son', International Churchill Society, 25 March 2017; Francis Phillips, 'Winston Churchill: great as a statesman, disastrous as a father', *Mercator*, 19 May 2021.
2 Lynne Olson, *Citizens of London: The Americans Who Stood with Britain in its Darkest, Finest Hour* (New York: Random House, 2010), 3.
3 Olson, *Citizens of London*, 4.
4 CHAR 20/31A/11-12.
5 Morton, *17 Carnations*, 214.
6 CHAR 20/31A/10.
7 CHAR 20/31A/10.
8 CHAR 20/31A/16-18.
9 CHAR 20/31A/16-18.
10 CHAR 20/31A/49-50.
11 CHAR 20/31A/22.
12 CHAR 20/31A/33-38.
13 CHAR 20/31A/40.
14 CHAR 20/31A/51-52.
15 Cadbury, *Princes at War*, 220–21.
16 Bradford, *George VI*, 419.
17 Bloch, *Duke of Windsor's War*, 191–2.
18 Hugo Vickers, 'Wise Counsel and Also Friendship: Winston Churchill and HM Queen Elizabeth II', *Finest Hour*, 199; Gilbert, *Churchill, vol. VI*, 1068.
19 Cadbury, *Princes at War*, 225.

20 Cadbury, *Princes at War*, 224–5.
21 Cadbury, *Princes at War*, 226.
22 Cadbury, *Princes at War*, 233.
23 Cadbury, *Princes at War*, 233; Bedell Smith, *George VI & Elizabeth*, 434.
24 CHAR 20/20/18-19.
25 Bradford, *George VI*, 447.
26 Bradford, *George VI*, 447.
27 Bradford, *George VI*, 448.
28 CHAR 20/48/17.
29 Bedell Smith, *George VI & Elizabeth*, 437.
30 Colville, *Fringes of Power*, 383.
31 CHAR 20/20/36-37.
32 Bloch, *Duke of Windsor's War*, 203.
33 CHAR 20/31A/90-96.
34 CHAR 20/31B/160.
35 CHAR 20/31B/177.
36 CHAR 20/31B/178.
37 CHAR 20/20/68.
38 CHAR 20/59/107-112.

Chapter Twelve: Affairs of the Heart

1   Roberts, *Churchill*, 702–3.
2   Martin Gilbert, *Winston S. Churchill vol. VII: Road to Victory, 1941–1945* (London: William Heinemann, 1986), 43–4.
3   Bradford, *George VI*, 451.
4   Cadbury, *Princes at War*, 247.
5   Larman, *Windsors at War*, 237.
6   Bradford, *George VI*, 341.
7   Bradford, *George VI*, 452.
8   Bloch, *Duke of Windsor's War*, 236; Morton, *17 Carnations*, 230.
9   CHAR 20/63/49-61.
10 CHAR 20/63/49-61.
11 Larman, *Windsors at War*, 250.
12 CHAR 20/75/107.
13 CHAR 20/75/82.
14 CHAR 20/52/74-75.
15 Jenkins, *Churchill*, 692–3.
16 Jenkins, *Churchill*, 692–3.
17 *The Times*, 27 June 1942.
18 Cadbury, *Princes at War*, 254.
19 Bradford, *George VI*, 455.
20 CHAR 20/59/115-125.
21 CHAR 20/59/115-125.
22 CHAR 20/59/115-125.
23 Gilbert, *Winston S. Churchill vol. VII*, 221; CHAR 20/54A/56.
24 Cadbury, *Princes at War*, 265; Bradford, *George VI*, 456.
25 Morton, *Wallis in Love*, 280.
26 Bedell Smith, *George VI & Elizabeth*, 454–5; Shawcross, *Queen Mother*, 559.
27 Gilbert, *Winston S. Churchill, vol. VII*, 249.
28 Bradford, *George VI*, 463–4.

29 *The Times,* 16 November 1942.
30 *The Times* and Viking Press, *The Churchill Years,* 135.
31 CHAR 20/63/74-92.
32 CHAR 20/52/96-100.
33 CHAR 20/52/96-100.
34 Morton, *17 Carnations,* 232.
35 CHAR 20/63/74-92.
36 CHAR 20/127/44.
37 Larman, *Windsors at War, 282;* Gilbert, *Winston S. Churchill, vol. VII,* 345; Bradford, *George VI,* 465.
38 Bradford, *George VI,* 466–7; Gilbert, *Winston S. Churchill, vol. VII,* 357.
39 Cadbury, *Princes at War,* 279.
40 CHAR 20/111/108; *The Times* 15 May 1943.
41 Cadbury, *Princes at War,* 280.
42 *The Times,* 'King and Minister', 18 May 1943.
43 Cadbury, *Princes at War,* 280; *The Times,* 'King and Minister', 18 May 1943; Gilbert, *Winston S. Churchill, vol. VII,* 404; Larman, *Windsors at War,* 286; Bedell Smith, *George VI & Elizabeth,* 459.
44 Deborah Strober and Gerald Strober, *The Monarchy: An Oral Biography* (London: Hutchinson, 2002), 56–7.
45 Bradford, *George VI,* 449.
46 Duff Hart-Davis (ed.), *King's Counsellor: Abdication and War, the Diaries of Sir Alan Lascelles* (London: Weidenfeld & Nicolson, 2006), 125.
47 Hart-Davis (ed.), *King's Counsellor,* 149.
48 Hart-Davis (ed.), *King's Counsellor,* 158.
49 Winston S. Churchill, *The Second World War, vol. V: Closing the Ring* (London: Cassell & Co., 1952), 288.
50 Hart-Davis (ed.), *King's Counsellor,* 180.
51 Moran, *Winston Churchill: The Struggle for Survival, 1940–1965* (London: Constable & Company, 1966), 97.
52 Bloch, *The Secret File of the Duke of Windsor* (London: Corgi, 1989), 241; Morton, *17 Carnations,* 232.
53 CHAR 20/114/15; CHAR 20/114/25; CHAR 20/98B/143.
54 Pimlott, *The Queen,* 70.
55 Pimlott, *The Queen,* 73.
56 Dwight D. Eisenhower, *Crusade in Europe: A Personal Account of World War II* (London: William Heinemann, 1948), 213.
57 Gilbert, *Winston S. Churchill, vol. VII,* 531; CHAR 20/94B/191.
58 Moran, *Struggle for Survival,* 136.
59 Thompson, *Assignment: Churchill,* 284; Gilbert, *Winston S. Churchill, vol. VII,* 577; Hart-Davis (ed.), *King's Counsellor,* 136n; CHAR 20/130/28.
60 Hart-Davis (ed.), *King's Counsellor,* 185.
61 Gilbert, *Winston S. Churchill, vol. VII,* 608–9.
62 Hart-Davis (ed.), *King's Counsellor,* 210–11.
63 Bedell Smith, *George VI & Elizabeth,* 474–9. Hart-Davis (ed.), *King's Counsellor,* 219.

Chapter Thirteen: D-Day Dodgers

1 Bradford, *George VI,* 475.
2 Hart-Davis (ed.), *King's Counsellor,* 224.
3 CHAR 20/136/10.

4   Hart-Davis (ed.), *King's Counsellor*, 225.
5   Bradford, *George VI*, 475.
6   Hart-Davis (ed.), *King's Counsellor*, 226–7.
7   Drake and Packwood (eds.), *Letters for the Ages*, 186.
8   Hart-Davis (ed.), *King's Counsellor*, 224–5.
9   CHAR 20/136/4.
10 Hart-Davis (ed.), *King's Counsellor*, 227.
11 Hart-Davis (ed.), *King's Counsellor*, 227–9.
12 Drake and Packwood (eds.), *Letters for the Ages*, 189.
13 Hart-Davis (ed.), *King's Counsellor*, 227–9.
14 Roberts, *Churchill*, 820.
15 Shawcross, *Queen Mother*, 581.
16 Roberts, *Churchill*, 822.
17 Hart-Davis (ed.), *King's Counsellor*, 231.
18 Bedell Smith, *George VI & Elizabeth*, 477.
19 Cadbury, *Princes at War*, 477; Gilbert, *Winston S. Churchill, vol. VII*, 800.
20 Hart-Davis (ed.), *King's Counsellor*, 232.
21 Hart-Davis (ed.), *King's Counsellor*, 232. Bedell Smith, *George VI & Elizabeth*, 477.
22 Bedell Smith, *George VI & Elizabeth*, 478.
23 Hart-Davis (ed.), *King's Counsellor*, 240.
24 Hart-Davis (ed.), *King's Counsellor*, 240.
25 Hart-Davis (ed.), *King's Counsellor*, 224.
26 Larman, *Windsors at War*, 321.
27 Colville, *Fringes of Power*, 491.
28 Larman, *Windsors at War*, 321.
29 Colville, *Fringes of Power*, 491.
30 Ziegler, *King Edward VIII*, 492–3.
31 Larman, *Windsors at War*, 323.
32 Larman, *Windsors at War*, 324.
33 Hart-Davis (ed.), *King's Counsellor*, 269–70.
34 Hart-Davis (ed.), *King's Counsellor*, 269–70.
35 Larman, *Windsors at War*, 332.
36 Hart-Davis (ed.), *King's Counsellor*, 242, 244.
37 Vickers, 'Wise Counsel and Also Friendship,' *Finest Hour* 199 (2022): 9; Pimlott, *The Queen*, 71.
38 Gilbert, *Winston S. Churchill, vol. VII*, 911.
39 Gilbert, *Winston S. Churchill, vol. VII*, 931; Hart-Davis (ed.), *King's Counsellor*, 254.
40 Roberts, *Churchill*, 809.
41 Hart-Davis (ed.), *King's Counsellor*, 274.
42 Hart-Davis (ed.), *King's Counsellor*, 276–7.
43 Bradford, *George VI*, 483–4; John Barnes and David Nicholson (eds.), *The Empire at Bay: The Leo Amery Diaries 1929–1945* (London: Hutchinson, 1988), 1033.
44 Bradford, *George VI*, 450.
45 Colville, *Fringes of Power*, 551.
46 Gilbert, *Winston S. Churchill, vol. VII*, 1284.
47 Larman, *Windsors at War*, 334.
48 Larman, *Windsors at War*, 334–5.
49 Gilbert, *Winston S. Churchill, vol. VII*, 1294.
50 Gilbert, *Winston S. Churchill, vol. VII*, 1300.
51 Gilbert, *Winston S. Churchill vol. VII*, 1331.

52 Bedell Smith, *George VI & Elizabeth*, 487; Hart-Davis (ed.), *King's Counsellor*, 321–2.
53 Gilbert, *Winston S. Churchill*, *vol. VII*, 1341; Bradford, *George VI, 485; Pimlott, The Queen*, 78.
54 Gilbert, *Winston S. Churchill*, *vol. VII*, 1341.
55 Thompson, *Assignment: Churchill*, 306.

Chapter Fourteen: Changing of the Guard

1 Bedell Smith, *George VI & Elizabeth*, 489; Hart-Davis (ed.), *King's Counsellor*, 326.
2 Martin Gilbert, *Winston S. Churchill*, *vol. VIII: Never Despair, 1945–1965* (London: William Heinemann, 1988), 20–22.
3 Colville, *Fringes of Power*, 568; Hart-Davis (ed.), *King's Counsellor*, 327.
4 Bedell Smith, *George VI & Elizabeth*, 494.
5 Hart-Davis (ed.), *King's Counsellor*, 331.
6 Gilbert, *Winston S. Churchill vol. VIII*, 46.
7 James Taylor 'How Did Churchill lose the 1945 General Election?' Imperial War Museum.
8 Bradford, *George VI*, 499.
9 Bradford, *George VI*, 499.
10 Bradford, *George VI*, 500.
11 Gilbert, *Winston S. Churchill*, *vol. VIII*, 109.
12 Larman, *Windsors at War*, 331.
13 Bedell Smith, *George VI & Elizabeth*, 497.
14 Gilbert, *Winston S. Churchill*, *vol. VIII*, 129.
15 Bradford, *George VI*, 502–3; Bedell Smith, *George VI & Elizabeth*, 499.
16 Gilbert, *Winston S. Churchill*, *vol. VIII*, 108.
17 Hart-Davis (ed.), *King's Counsellor*, 352.
18 Bedell Smith, *George & Elizabeth*, 495.
19 David Kynaston, *Austerity Britain, 1945–1951* (London: Bloomsbury, 2007), 75.
20 Bradford, *George VI*, 503.
21 Bedell Smith, *George VI & Elizabeth*, 495.
22 Bedell Smith, *George VI & Elizabeth*, 501.
23 Morton, *17 Carnations*, 259.
24 Cadbury, *Princes at War*, 325.
25 Ziegler, *King Edward VIII*, 549.
26 Astrid M. Eckert, *The Struggle for the Files: The Western Allies and the Return of German Archives after the Second World War* (Cambridge: Cambridge University Press, 2012), 71.
27 Eckert, *The Struggle for the Files*, 71–2; Morton, *17 Carnations*, 251.
28 Bloch, *Duke of Windsor's War*, 361.
29 Bradford, *George VI*, 588.
30 Bedell Smith, *George VI & Elizabeth*, 504.
31 Bloch, *Secret File*, 262.
32 Ziegler, *King Edward VIII*, 505.
33 Bloch, *Secret File*, 262.
34 Ziegler, *King Edward VIII*, 505.
35 Ziegler, *King Edward VIII*, 505.
36 Bryan and Murphy, *The Windsor Story*, 456.
37 Morton, *17 Carnations*, 294.
38 Donaldson, *Edward VIII*, 392.
39 Bryan and Murphy, *The Windsor Story*, 462.
40 Roberts, *Churchill*, 888.
41 Hart-Davis (ed.), *King's Counsellor*, 366.

42 Gilbert, *Winston S. Churchill, vol. VIII*, 174.
43 Gilbert, *Winston S. Churchill, vol. VIII*, 245; Roberts, 'Churchilliana: a Medallion Commemorating the Grand Coalition', *The Churchill Project*, 2018.
44 Ziegler, *King Edward VIII*, 499; Gilbert, *Winston S. Churchill, vol. VIII*, 207*n*1.
45 Bedell Smith, *George VI & Elizabeth*, 527.
46 Shawcross, *Queen Mother*, 605.
47 *The Times*, 15 August 1946; Dal Newfield, 'The Story Behind the Investiture', *Finest Hour* 20 (July–August 1971).
48 Gilbert, *Winston S. Churchill, vol. VIII*, 312.
49 Bedell Smith, *George VI & Elizabeth*, 514.
50 Andrew Morton, *The Queen* (London: Michael O'Mara Books, 2022), 87; Andrew Morton, *Elizabeth & Margaret: The Intimate World of the Windsor Sisters* (London: Michael O'Mara Books, 2022), 79.
51 Morton, *The Queen*, 70.
52 Gilbert, *Winston S. Churchill, vol. VIII*, 340.
53 Gilbert, *Winston S. Churchill, vol. VIII*, 340.
54 Gilbert, *Winston S. Churchill, vol. VIII*, 340–41.
55 Bedell Smith, *George VI & Elizabeth*, 534.
56 Gilbert, *Winston S. Churchill, vol. VIII*, 341.
57 Winston S. Churchill, *Europe Unite: speeches 1947 and 1948* (London: Cassell, 1950), 168.
58 Jennifer Ellis (ed.), *Thatched with Gold: The Memoirs of Mabell, Countess of Airlie* (London: Hutchinson & Co., 1962), 229.
59 Pimlott, *The Queen*, 143.
60 'Memorable Scenes at Royal Wedding', *The Times*, 21 November 1947.
61 Morton, *The Queen*, 96–7; Pimlott, *The Queen*, 140.

Chapter Fifteen: The Long Goodbye

1   Colville, *Fringes of Power*, 584.
2   'Royal Allowances Approved by Commons', *The Times*, 18 December 1947.
3   Gilbert, *Winston S. Churchill, vol. VIII*, 390.
4   Gilbert, *Winston S. Churchill, vol. VIII*, 390.
5   Roberts, *Churchill*, 904; Winston S. Churchill, *The Dream* (London: International Churchill Societies, 1994), 5–8.
6   W. Churchill, *The Dream*, 19–20.
7   Tippett, *Once a King*, 186.
8   Bloch, *Secret File*, 290.
9   Tippett, *Once a King*, 200.
10 Bloch, *Secret File, 302n*.
11 Gyles Brandreth, *Philip & Elizabeth: Portrait of a Marriage* (London: Century, 2004), 258.
12 Gilbert, *Winston S. Churchill, vol. VIII*, 446.
13 Gilbert, *Winston S. Churchill, vol. VIII*, 446.
14 Gilbert, *Winston S. Churchill, vol. VIII*, 446.
15 Gilbert, *Winston S. Churchill, vol. VIII*, 448.
16 Fred Glueckstein, 'Winston Churchill and Colonist II', *Finest Hour*, 125 (2004–5).
17 Gilbert, *Winston S. Churchill, vol. VIII*, 613; Roberts, *Churchill*, 911; Glueckstein, 'Churchill and Colonist II'.
18 Bedell Smith, *George VI & Elizabeth*, 551.
19 Gilbert, *Winston S. Churchill, vol. VIII*, 639.
20 Gilbert, *Winston S. Churchill, vol. VIII*, 639.
21 Cadbury, *Princes at War*, 347–8; Bedell Smith, *George VI & Elizabeth*, 551.

22 Brandreth, *Philip & Elizabeth*, 282.
23 Ziegler, *King Edward VIII*, 526.
24 Bryan and Murphy, *The Windsor Story*, 519.
25 Bryan and Murphy, *The Windsor Story*, 458.
26 Gilbert, *Winston S. Churchill, vol. VIII*, 637–8; Ingrid Seward, *Prince Philip Revealed: A Man of His Century* (London: Simon & Schuster, 2020), 111.
27 Brandreth, *Philip & Elizabeth*, 282.
28 Gilbert, *Winston S. Churchill, vol. VIII*, 662–3.
29 Seward, *Philip Revealed*, 112.
30 Bradford, *George VI*, 602.
31 Bradford, *George VI*, 603.
32 Bradford, *George VI*, 606.
33 Moran, *Struggle for Survival*, 372.
34 *The Times*, 1 February 1952; Bedell Smith, *George VI & Elizabeth*, 557.
35 Bradford, *George VI*, 607.
36 Morton, *The Queen*, 116–17.
37 *The Times*, 7 February 1952.
38 Brandreth, *Philip & Elizabeth*, 289; Roberts, *Churchill*, 928–9.
39 Colville, *Fringes of Power*, 601.

Chapter Sixteen: Disconsolate Consort and the Shining Crown

1 Roberts, *Churchill*, 929; Bedell Smith, *George VI & Elizabeth*, 560.
2 Cadbury, *Princes at War*, 351.
3 Shawcross, *Queen Mother*, 655–6.
4 Pimlott, *The Queen*, 180; Vickers, 'Wise Counsel and Also Friendship', 10.
5 Gilbert, *Winston S. Churchill, vol. VIII*, 699–700.
6 Gilbert, *Winston S. Churchill, vol. VIII*, 700.
7 Gilbert, *Winston S. Churchill, vol. V Companion Part 3*, 634.
8 Shawcross, *Queen Mother*, 677.
9 Moran, *Struggle for Survival*, 83.
10 Pimlott, *The Queen*, 188–9.
11 Moran, *Struggle for Survival*, 373.
12 Gilbert, *Winston S. Churchill, vol. VIII*, 701.
13 Brandreth, *Philip & Elizabeth*, 304.
14 Morton, *The Queen*, 132.
15 Morton, *Elizabeth & Margaret*, 139.
16 Moran, *Struggle for Survival*, 373.
17 Roberts, *Churchill*, 929.
18 Brandreth, *Philip & Elizabeth*, 299.
19 Hough, *Mountbatten*, 257.
20 Colville, *Fringes of Power*, 602.
21 Morton, *The Queen*, 131.
22 Colville, *Fringes of Power*, 602.
23 Brandreth, *Philip & Elizabeth*, 300.
24 Morton, *Elizabeth & Margaret*, 133.
25 Morton, *The Queen*, 132.
26 Morton, *The Queen*, 131–2; Seward, *Philip Revealed*, 121–2.
27 Morton, *The Queen*, 133.
28 Strober and Strober, *The Monarchy*, 80.
29 Brandreth, *Philip & Elizabeth*, 296.

30 Pimlott, *The Queen*, 204.
31 Seward, *Philip Revealed*, 125.
32 Winston S. Churchill, 'Monarchy versus Autocracy', in *The Collected Essays of Sir Winston Churchill, vol. II*, edited by Michael Wolff (London: Library of Imperial History, 1976), 65.
33 Gilbert, *Winston S. Churchill, vol. VIII*, 732–3.
34 Pimlott, *The Queen*, 205; Morton, *The Queen*, 134.
35 Pimlott, *The Queen*, 186.
36 Gilbert, *Winston S. Churchill, vol. VIII*, 789.
37 Roberts, *Churchill, 170–71*, 273–4.
38 Seward, *Philip Revealed*, 205.
39 Seward, *Philip Revealed*, 206.
40 Hart-Davis (ed.), *King's Counsellor*, 430.
41 Brandreth, *Philip & Elizabeth*, 304.
42 Fred Glueckstein, 'Queen Elizabeth II, Winston Churchill, and Horse Racing', *Finest Hour* 199 (2022), 16.
43 Vickers, 'Wise Counsel and also Friendship', 11.
44 Pimlott, *The Queen*, 194.
45 Moran, *Struggle for Survival*, 403.
46 Morton, *The Queen*, 128.
47 Colville, *Fringes of Power*, 613–14.
48 Shawcross, *Queen Mother*, 606.
49 Strober and Strober, *The Monarchy*, 83.
50 Shawcross, *Queen Mother*, 673.
51 Shawcross, *Queen Mother*, 673.
52 Pimlott, *The Queen*, 205; Morton, *The Queen*, 134.
53 Walter Bagehot, *The English Constitution*, ed. Miles Taylor (Oxford: Oxford University Press, 2001) 49.
54 Gilbert, *Winston S. Churchill, vol. VIII*, 788.
55 Colville, *Fringes of Power*, 667.
56 Bloch, *Secret File*, 311.
57 Bloch, *Secret File*, 316.
58 Zeigler, *King Edward VIII*, 539.
59 *The Times,* 26 March 1953.
60 James Lancaster, 'Churchill and Oscar Nemon', International Churchill Society, 13 June 2013.
61 Gilbert, *Winston S. Churchill, vol. VIII*, 770–71.
62 Gilbert, *Winston S. Churchill, vol. VIII*, 822.
63 Gilbert, *Winston S. Churchill, vol. VIII*, 809–10.
64 Moran, *Struggle for Survival*, 405.
65 Chris Hastings and Beth Jones, 'Churchill doubted Philip and Margaret could rule country', *Sunday Telegraph,* 5 August 2007.
66 *The Sunday Telegraph,* 5 August 2007, 2–3.
67 Morton, *Elizabeth & Margaret*, 149–50.
68 Seward, *Philip Revealed*, 128.

Chapter Seventeen: A Tainted Love

1 Gilbert, *Winston S. Churchill, vol. VIII*, 841–2.
2 Morton, *Elizabeth & Margaret*, 140.
3 Morton, *Elizabeth & Margaret*, 140.
4 Hart-Davis (ed.), *King's Counsellor*, 399–400.

5 Shawcross, *Queen Mother*, 684.

6 Hart-Davis (ed.), *King's Counsellor*, 399–400.

7 Morton, *The Queen*, 146.

8 Seward, *Philip Revealed*, 134.

9 Roberts, *Churchill*, 938.

10 Roberts, *Churchill*, 938.

11 Gilbert, *Winston S. Churchill, vol. VIII*, 849; Roberts, *Churchill*, 938–9.

12 Gilbert, *Winston S. Churchill, vol. VIII*, 852.

13 Pimlott, *The Queen*, 221.

14 Morton, *17 Carnations*, 301.

15 Morton, *17 Carnations*, 301–2.

16 Paul R. Sweet, 'The Windsor File', *The Historian* 59.2 (Winter 1997): 273.

17 Eckert, *The Struggle for the Files*, 250.

18 Morton, *17 Carnations*, 305–7.

19 Gilbert, *Winston S. Churchill, vol. VIII*, 880–81.

20 Gilbert, *Winston S. Churchill, vol. VIII*, 884.

21 Moran, *Struggle for Survival*, 472.

22 Gilbert, *Winston S. Churchill, vol. VIII*, 884.

23 Gilbert, *Winston S. Churchill, vol. VIII*, 886.

24 Moran, *Struggle for Survival*, 484.

25 *The Times*, 24 November 1953, 8.

26 Gilbert, *Winston S. Churchill, vol. VIII*, 914.

27 Moran, *Struggle for Survival*, 514.

28 Gilbert, *Winston S. Churchill, vol. VIII*, 942.

29 Shawcross, *Queen Mother*, 689; Vickers, 'Wise Counsel and Also Friendship', 12.

30 Gilbert, *Winston S. Churchill, vol. VIII*, 976.

31 Pimlott, *The Queen*, 227.

32 Gilbert, *Winston S. Churchill, vol. VIII*, 976.

33 *The Times*, 3 June 1954; *The Times*, 4 June 1954,

34 Thompson, *Assignment: Churchill*, 308–9.

35 Shawcross, *Queen Mother*, 696.

36 Shawcross, *Queen Mother*, 695–6.

37 Gilbert, *Winston S. Churchill, vol. VIII*, 1072.

38 Gilbert, *Winston S. Churchill, vol. VIII*, 1076.

39 Roberts, *Churchill*, 911; Kay Halle, *The Irrepressible Churchill: Winston's World, Wars & Wit* (London: Conway, 2010), 266.

40 Gilbert VIII, 1076.

41 Gilbert, *Winston S. Churchill, vol. VIII*, 1069, *n*5.

42 Gilbert, *Winston S. Churchill, vol. VIII*, 1093.

43 Gilbert, *Winston S. Churchill, vol. VIII*, 1097; Colville, *Fringes of Power*, 659.

44 Colville, *Fringes of Power*, 661.

45 Gilbert, *Winston S. Churchill, vol. VIII*, 1117.

46 Gilbert, *Winston S. Churchill, vol. VIII*, 1120.

47 Colville, *Fringes of Power*, 662.

48 Gilbert, *Winston S. Churchill, vol. VIII*, 1123–5.

Chapter Eighteen: 'I Have Done My Best'

1 David Sheward, 'Queen Elizabeth II's Prime Ministers', *Biography*, 15 November 2023.

2 Piers Brendon, 'The death of Sir Winston Churchill and the top-secret plans for his funeral', *History Extra*, 24 January 2020.

3 Gilbert, *Winston S. Churchill, vol. VIII*, 1126–7.
4 Gilbert, *Winston S. Churchill, vol. VIII*, 1128.
5 Gilbert, *Winston S. Churchill, vol. VIII*, 1177–8.
6 Gilbert, *Winston S. Churchill, vol. VIII*, 1193.
7 Anthony Montague Browne, *Long Sunset* (London: Indigo, 1996), 242; Jenkins, *Churchill*, 225.
8 Roberts, *Churchill*, 947.
9 Roberts, *Churchill*, 959.
10 Roberts, *Churchill*, 958.
11 Moran, *Struggle for Survival*, 400.
12 Vickers, 'Wise Counsel and Also Friendship', 14.
13 Gilbert, *Winston S. Churchill, vol. VIII*, 1215.
14 Montague Browne, *Long Sunset*, 215.
15 Montague Browne, *Long Sunset*, 215.
16 Pimlott, *The Queen*, 258.
17 Moran, *Struggle for Survival*, 710.
18 Gilbert, *Winston S. Churchill, vol. VIII*, 1249.
19 Robert Lacey, *Royal: Her Majesty Queen Elizabeth II* (London: Little, Brown, 2002), 201.
20 Gilbert, *Winston S. Churchill, vol. VIII*, 1255.
21 Gilbert, *Winston S. Churchill, vol. VIII*, 1261.
22 Moran, *Struggle for Survival*, 739.
23 Chris Hastings, 'Revealed: How Buckingham Palace courtiers tried to downgrade Winston Churchill's State funeral because he was a "commoner"', *Mail on Sunday*, 24 January 2015.
24 Rodney J. Croft, *Churchill's Final Farewell: The State and Private Funeral of Sir Winston Churchill* (Buckhurst Hill, Essex: Croft Publishing), 2014.
25 Gilbert, *Winston S. Churchill, vol. VIII*, 1313.
26 *The Times*, 7 May 1960.
27 Gilbert, *Winston S. Churchill, vol. VIII*, 1319.
28 Gilbert, *Winston S. Churchill, vol. VIII*, 1331.
29 Gilbert, *Winston S. Churchill, vol. VIII*, 1333.
30 Hart-Davis (ed.), *King's Counsellor*, 418.
31 Gilbert, *Winston S. Churchill, vol. VIII*, 1359.
32 *The Times*, 24 January 1965.
33 Gilbert, *Winston S. Churchill, vol. VIII*, 1360–61.
34 Gilbert, *Winston S. Churchill, vol. VIII*, 1361.
35 Gilbert, *Winston S. Churchill, vol. VIII*, 1360–61.
36 *The Times*, 25 January 1965.
37 Pimlott, *The Queen*, 354–5; Seward, *Philip Revealed*, 174.
38 Rodney Croft, 'Churchill's Final Farewell: The State and Private Funeral of Sir Winston Churchill', *Finest Hour* 166 (2015), 9.
39 Gilbert, *Winston S. Churchill, vol. VIII*, 1362.
40 *Elizabeth Our Queen*, Channel 5, 2018.
41 Lucy Wallis, '"We nearly dropped Churchill's coffin"', *BBC*, 28 January 2015.
42 Gilbert, *Winston S. Churchill, vol. VIII*, 1363–4.
43 Pimlott, *The Queen, 362–3; 'Special Stamp History: Churchill Commemoration'*, The Postal Museum, (URL: https://www.postalmuseum.org/wp-content/uploads/2018/12/Stamp-History-1965-Churchill.pdf).

Index